Family Law

Put your knowledge into practice

- **Criminal Litigation**
- **Property Law**
- **Business Law**
- **Lawyers' Skills**
- **Civil Litigation**
- **Foundations for the LPC**
- **Family Law**
- **Employment Law**

- Supported by a wealth of online case studies and resources.

- Designed to develop legal skills and meet the required LPC Outcomes.

- Each manual comes with an accompanying digital version.

For more vocational law titles please visit
www.oxfordtextbooks.co.uk/law

Family Law

JANE SENDALL

OXFORD

UNIVERSITY PRESS

Great Clarendon Street, Oxford, OX2 6DP,
United Kingdom

Oxford University Press is a department of the University of Oxford.
It furthers the University's objective of excellence in research, scholarship,
and education by publishing worldwide. Oxford is a registered trade mark of
Oxford University Press in the UK and in certain other countries

Fifth edition 2014
Sixth edition 2015
Seventh edition 2016

Impression: 1

Published in the United States of America by Oxford University Press
198 Madison Avenue, New York, NY 10016, United States of America

British Library Cataloguing in Publication Data
Data available

ISBN 978–0–19–878318–3

Printed in Great Britain by
Bell & Bain Ltd., Glasgow

SR16279083025419

For my parents

ACKNOWLEDGEMENTS

The author and publisher would like to thank David Hodson for his kind permission for the use of his article on the case of *Charman*, which illuminates an area in which the decisions of the higher court become progressively more difficult to explain to students. Further information by David about English financial provision law on divorce including in the international context is available at www.davidhodson.com and www.iflg.uk.com.

OUTLINE CONTENTS

DETAILED CONTENTS

NEW TO THIS EDITION

- Updates to the domestic violence gateway relating to the changes introduced by the Civil Legal Aid (Procedure) (Amendment) Regulation 2016 No. 516
- Discussion of the proposed 'no fault divorce' bill currently before Parliament
- Preliminary considerations of the potential effects of the United Kingdom's decision to leave the European Union
- Coverage of the Family Justice Council's 'Guidance on Financial Needs on Divorce'
- Coverage of *Gohil v Gohil* [2015] and *Sharland v Sharland* [2015] in relation to financial orders and failure of disclosure
- Discussion of the Court of Appeal's ruling in *Re C (Internal Relocation)* [2015] in relation to child welfare in relocation cases
- Updates to Child Protection Conferences

PREFACE

Working with families, children, parents, spouses, civil partners, and cohabitants in family law is a demanding job. It is also enjoyable, exhausting, stimulating, and full of variety. Learning family law means grasping a great deal of statute, case-law, and skills quite quickly over a range of topics, and this book is written to assist those learning family law. Family law is in a state of flux as sweeping changes are being made to funding, marriage, the structure of the courts, and the law concerning children. There are various pilots to review procedure in financial proceedings and the Law Commission is reporting on financial remedies. One article asks 'Will I retire before I read all of the changes made to the family system?' and this is not a frivolous question. The changes made to family law in 2014 have been immense. The changes will need some time to settle down and for local practice to become clear. Until then, I have stated the law as it has been enacted and without speculation about how is it playing out in practice.

I would like to extend my love and thanks to David and my family for their support, also to my friends for their encouragement and my students, past and present, for inspiration, honesty, and stimulation. Particular thanks go to Katrina Pescott, my friend and dedicated family solicitor, who advises me on matters of practice with patience and good humour. Her advice was essential in the writing of this book.

This text is designed for students on the LPC and BTPC studying family law and I keep in mind that some are studying family law for the first time. This text is not intended to be as complete as a lengthy, complex practitioner's text. I hope that the text is useful to those in the very early stages of a training contract, but it is primarily designed for the law student. As a result, it does not contain all the case-law and commentary one would expect from a practitioner's text, and emphasis has been placed on including useful pedagogical features and ensuring understanding. Practice varies widely across the country, and so when entering practice, differences will be found. I find practice varies from court to court!

I would also like to acknowledge my past and current colleagues involved in the LPC and BTPC and my colleagues at York University for their inspiration and good humour, and judicial colleagues for their insight.

Family law is a big subject and I would like to acknowledge the assistance of Andrew Hayward of Durham University and Emma Duff of Northumbria University for their helpful comments on Chapter 22, the former Deputy Manager of Derwentside Citizen's Advice Bureau (or 'Mum') for her assistance with Chapter 21, David Hodson for his kind permission for the use of his article on the case of *Charman,* which illuminates an area in which the decisions of the higher court become progressively more difficult to explain to students. Further information by David about English financial provision law on divorce, including in the international context, is available at www.davidhodson.com and www.iflg.uk.com. Invaluable information on collaborative law came from Helen Robson of Caris Robson LLP and Norman Taylor of Zermanskys & Partners.

I would like to acknowledge the advice, encouragement, and enthusiasm of Tom Randall in the completion of this edition and Lucy Read throughout the start of this project, and the excellent help from Fiona Tatham, Julie Stone, Moira Greenhalgh, and Nikhil Kumar.

All errors are entirely my own.

Jane Sendall
August 2016

GUIDED TOUR OF THE BOOK

Sendall's *Family Law* contains numerous features that have been specifically designed to facilitate your learning and understanding of family law and practice. To help you get the most from your text, this 'Guided tour of the book' highlights the features used by the author to explain the law and its application in practical situations.

WITHIN EACH CHAPTER

CHAPTER CONTENTS

Use the detailed contents list featured at the beginning of each chapter to identify quickly and clearly the key topics to be covered and to locate where each topic appears in the wider subject area.

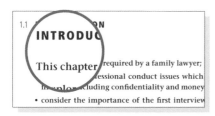

CHAPTER AIMS

Use the brief chapter aims at the start of each chapter to help you focus your reading and learning.

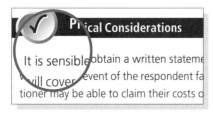

PRACTICAL CONSIDERATIONS

Use these sections to gain a practical understanding of how a solicitor may use the rules and procedures available. This is an opportunity to prepare on a practical level for your training contract.

EXAMPLES

Look for the example icon to find practical scenario-based examples of how the law is applied in a realistic practice situation. These will provide you with a valuable insight into what might happen day to day in a solicitor's practice.

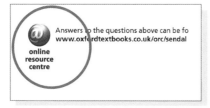

ONLINE RESOURCE CENTRE ICON

Look out for this icon, used to highlight where further information is available on the Online Resource Centre accompanying this manual. Visit **www.oxfordtextbooks.co.uk/orc/sendall17/** to see the full range of supporting resources accompanying this book. Also see page xxvi overleaf for an introduction to these online resources.

SUMMARY POINTS

The key points covered are summarized in a user-friendly list at the end of each chapter. Look at these summaries to help you consolidate your learning or to check your knowledge at revision time.

SELF-TEST QUESTIONS

These questions allow you to test yourself on particular areas of the law in preparation for exams or to assess your learning throughout the duration of the course. Use these questions to uncover areas where you might need to improve your understanding by re-reading the text or asking your lecturer.

CASE STUDIES

Throughout the book, the author refers to two fictional case studies, which provide a practical focus to the law and procedures described in the text. The case studies also show you how the law would be applied in an ongoing scenario, allowing you to see procedures in context from the start of a case through to its conclusion. Example documents available on the Online Resource Centre ensure that these case studies remain realistic. See the 'Guided Tour of the Online Resource Centre' at page xxvi for more information.

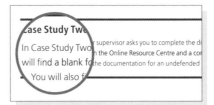

GUIDED TOUR OF THE ONLINE RESOURCE CENTRE

Online Resource Centres have been developed to provide students and lecturers with ready-to-use teaching and learning resources. They are free of charge, designed to complement the text, and offer additional materials that are suited to electronic delivery.

STUDENT RESOURCES

All the resources in this area of the site are freely accessible to all, with no password required. Simply visit the site at **www.oxfordtextbooks.co.uk/orc/sendall17/**

ANSWERS TO SELF-TEST QUESTIONS

This section has now been given student access, following recent lecturer and student feedback. Guidance is given on appropriate answers to the self-test questions which appear in the book. This provides you with feedback on your answers.

PODCASTS

Short podcasts have been created by the author to help consolidate your understanding of key aspects of family law and practice.

UPDATES

Updates will be posted on the website when the law changes or when significant cases pass through the courts, allowing you to keep fully informed of developments. The updates are freely accessible to all and offer an easy way to keep abreast of events in this rapidly changing subject area.

CASE STUDY DOCUMENTATION

Click on the case study section to see the questions from the book and any relevant documentation you may need to answer them. This section of the site features realistic documents that a solicitor may come into contact with at each stage of the case.

LINKS TO USEFUL SITES

This part of the site provides links and useful information which is freely accessible elsewhere on the internet. Use this resource to find relevant guidelines, statutes, codes of practice, and other documentation quickly and easily.

FIGURES

Flowcharts featured in the book are available online, providing you with easily accessible visuals to help you revise.

MULTIPLE-CHOICE QUESTIONS

A suite of multiple-choice questions covering all aspects of the book allows you to test your knowledge of key themes and concepts. Each question is accompanied by feedback which highlights why the selected answer is correct or incorrect, and directs you to the relevant page of the textbook should you need to re-read or clarify a particular point.

GLOSSARY

Ancillary relief	The division of money and property following divorce or dissolution of a civil partnership. Now called financial remedy proceedings
Bailiff	A person employed by the court to serve court papers and to enforce judgments
Bundle	The term given to the collation of documents to be referred to in court. A bundle will contain an index, will be paginated and organized in a useful way
CAFCASS	The Child and Family Court Advisory Support Service. CAFCASS looks after the interests of children in court proceedings and advises the court on what is in the best interests of the children
Charge	A charge is placed on a property and when the property is sold, a certain proportion of the proceeds are given to the person with the charge
Client	The most important person in a family lawyer's job
CPS	The Crown Prosecution Service. The CPS makes decisions on the prosecution of criminal offences and prosecutes criminal cases in court
Decree	A type of court order
Deed	A written document, which must be signed
Disbursements	The name given by solicitors to the various fees which are incurred during a case, e.g. expert fees or court fees
Disclosure	The process by which one party tells the other party certain information about their case or gives information
Duress	Unlawful pressure placed on a person in order to coerce them or overcome their resistance into doing something they do not wish to do
File	To give a document to the court
Free standing	Court proceedings which are made as an application solely based on a cause of action and not within other proceedings
Guardian ad litem	Now called a Children's Guardian; they look after a child's interest in public children proceedings
Inherent jurisdiction	The ability of a superior court to hear a case unless a rule or statute restricts that jurisdiction
Injunction	A court order requiring a person to do or refrain from certain acts
LAA	Legal Aid Agency—it has responsibility for the administration of public funding
Leave	The permission of the court to do a certain act
Litigant in Person	A person who represents themselves at court without a lawyer
LSC	Legal Services Commission who used to run the public funding scheme in England and Wales
Mediation	A process which aims to settle disputes between people over money and property or children
NSPCC	National Society for the Prevention of Cruelty to Children
Nullity	A decree which annuls a marriage

Privilege	A legal device which protects the disclosure (see earlier) of documents to the court or other party in court proceedings
Refuge	A place of safety for those fleeing domestic abuse
Return date	Following a hearing without notice to one party, a return date is the date on which the court will hear the case with all parties present
Serve	When a document is formally given to a person
Spouse	A married person, including same-sex spouses
SRA	The Solicitors Regulation Authority which regulates the solicitors' profession
Undue influence	Where one person takes advantage of a position of power over another person
Usages	A firmly established practice or custom

TABLE OF CASES

TABLE OF STATUTES

TABLE OF SECONDARY LEGISLATION

TABLE OF EUROPEAN SECONDARY LEGISLATION

TABLE OF INTERNATIONAL LEGISLATION

TABLE OF CODES OF PRACTICE

Part 1

INTRODUCTION

1 FAMILY LAW PRACTICE AND THE FIRST INTERVIEW

1.1 **Introduction**

1.2 **Skills**

1.3 **The first interview and client care**

1.4 **Litigants in Person**

1.1 INTRODUCTION

- This chapter will:
- explore the skills required by a family lawyer;
- discuss the professional conduct issues which are crucial to seeing a client for the first time, including confidentiality and money laundering;
- consider the importance of the first interview with the client and the client care letter;
- explore the issue of increasing numbers of Litigants in Person.

The study and practice of family law is a fascinating prospect. The sheer variety of people and problems that you will encounter enlivens an area of law that covers a variety of topics and requires the mastery of problems involving financial and property disputes, resolving where children should live and with whom they have contact, and offering assistance to those facing violence within a relationship.

Family law is in a state of flux for a number of reasons: public funding was withdrawn from a wide variety of cases in April 2013 with an increase in the numbers of Litigants in Person; a Single Family Court has been implemented; and sweeping changes have been made by the Children and Families Act 2014 (see later chapters for more detail). The Online Resource Centre will contain details on each of these changes.

Family law is practised in firms ranging from very small general practices, large commercial firms, and niche practices, although firms have been badly hit by recent changes. It is possible to specialize within family and become an expert in a particular field, e.g. children or finances following divorce. In the early stages of a career in family law, it is common to have a mixed caseload involving divorce, property and finances, problems concerning children, and domestic abuse.

The law on family relationships comes from a wide variety of sources and includes statutes, cases, statutory instruments, European legislation and cases, and international treaties.

 Example

There are many sources of family law and one of the skills of a family lawyer is to be able to find and use law. It is also important to keep up to date. Here are some examples of the sources of family law:

Statute: Matrimonial Causes Act 1973, which governs divorce.

Case-law: *White v White* [2000] 3 WLR 1571, an important case on the distribution of money and property following divorce.

Statutory instrument: The Domestic Violence, Crime and Victims Act 2004 (Commencement No. 9 and Transitional Provisions) Order 2007, S.I. 2007 No. 1845 introducing changes to domestic abuse legislation.

> ***European law:*** Regulation (EC) No. 1347/2000 on jurisdiction and the recognition and enforcement of judgments in matrimonial matters and in matters of parental responsibility for children of both spouses.
> ***European cases:*** *Glaser v UK* [2001] 1 FLR 153, which concerned the enforcement of contact orders by UK courts.
> ***International treaties:*** Hague Convention on the Civil Aspects of Child Abduction governing the return of children removed by a parent to a foreign jurisdiction.

Cases handled by a family lawyer may cover the consequences of relationship breakdown including the division of money and property, disputes about children, the protection of those suffering domestic abuse, and advising clients whose children require local authority intervention.

Additionally, a family lawyer must be able to advise on how a client can fund a case, and also the procedural matters involved in taking proceedings. This chapter briefly examines the issues surrounding family practice and the first interview with a client.

1.2 **SKILLS**

A successful family lawyer must also possess very good client care skills, as family law proceedings often bring out the very worst in your client's behaviour. You may meet a client during a stressful point in their lives where their relationship, home life, and financial situation are changing rapidly. A successful family lawyer can help their client to understand the law and procedures, making this transition less bewildering and keeping costs under control. You should have excellent communication skills, be able to put yourself into the client's position to understand their point of view, but also have the strength of character to tell a client what they may not wish to hear. You will need to ensure your clients are kept up to date and all matters are explained in a clear and accessible way.

A family lawyer will act for the most vulnerable members of society, e.g. children that have been taken into the care of their local authority or a person fleeing domestic abuse. The variety of work is wide, and includes arranging personal protection for a client suffering domestic abuse (often at short notice), advising a parent who wishes to have more contact with their child, negotiating the family finances following separation, and advising on how to end a civil partnership. This challenging aspect of family practice can also be the most rewarding, as you will have a varied and interesting job. Your skills of time management, persuasion, negotiation, and diplomacy will be tested often.

 Practical Considerations

What skills do you think are useful for a family lawyer?

- Advocacy: there will be a variety of hearings to attend in all types of proceedings;
- Interviewing: clients often come to meetings in a state of distress and so the solicitor should be prepared to deal with a client's emotional state. Clients are often reluctant to discuss embarrassing and sensitive issues and this requires a skilled interviewer;
- Negotiation: in family law cases it is preferable to agree a settlement rather than have an acrimonious court hearing, and so a considerable proportion of a family solicitor's time is spent negotiating to reach an agreement;
- Writing: a family law client must be able to understand the advice that they receive and a family law solicitor must be able to communicate clearly;
- Drafting: a family law solicitor will be required to produce divorce petitions, client statements, and many other court documents.

As well as technical skills required by family lawyers, 'soft' skills are equally important. 'Soft' skills are the interpersonal and organizational skills that contribute to a successful practice and include:

- persuasiveness;
- tact;
- negotiation;
- diplomacy;
- time management;
- organization;
- communication.

This is not an exhaustive list!

1.3 THE FIRST INTERVIEW AND CLIENT CARE

When meeting the client for the first time, it is important to be fully prepared. The client may be nervous, apprehensive, angry, or fearful. It is important that the client is reassured and offered an appointment promptly and also that the solicitor is fully prepared for the first interview.

Before the interview, the Law Society, in a practice note, advises that when the client attends the interview the following information must be explained to them and confirmed in writing:

- name and status of the solicitor or other person conducting the interview;
- information on the costs for the interview;
- details of who to contact if they have a complaint.

This information can be prepared in a pro forma document in advance. Keep a copy on file.

 Practical Considerations

What do you need to have in your office when your client comes for their first appointment?

- pens/paper;
- funding/CLS forms;
- court forms in case there is a need to make an urgent application;
- toys to distract small children;
- tissues;
- pro forma forms, e.g. file checklist;
- business card for client to keep.

1.3.1 GETTING THE BASICS RIGHT

In the first interview, you must remember to cover all of the professional conduct issues, money laundering regulations, and legal issues as well as the basic details from the client.

You must efficiently take all the client's basic details, including name, date of birth, address, and details of their family including children. Many firms have a pro forma checklist for initial interviews and there is an example of one in Case Study One.

There are times when some information must be handled with care. For instance, in cases where violence has been a feature of family life, an address must not be given to the violent partner, as this will put your client in danger. You have a professional conduct duty (see **1.3.2**) to keep all client information confidential.

1.3.2 PROFESSIONAL CONDUCT

You have professional conduct rules that govern the relationship between you and your client. There are some core duties to the client found in the Solicitors Regulatory Authority's (SRA) Solicitors' Code of Conduct, which came into force in October 2011. The following principles and outcomes (O) apply to all clients and your practice in family law:

- O(1.1) you treat your clients fairly;
- O(1.2) you provide services to your clients in a manner which protects their interests in their matter, subject to the proper administration of justice;
- O(1.3) when deciding whether to act, or terminate your instructions, you comply with the law and the Code.

According to Outcome 1.4 of the Code, you are free to decide whether to take on a client, but you must have the resources and skills to act in a case. This is extremely important in the early stages of a solicitor's career as it is tempting to take cases that require a very high level of expertise.

During the interview, according to the Code, a solicitor demonstrates they are achieving the principles of good client care through Indicative Behaviours (IB) and these behaviours include: agreeing an appropriate level of service and explaining your responsibilities in the case as well as the client's responsibilities. This may be the duty of full disclosure in ancillary relief. You must also inform the client, in writing, of the name and status of the person dealing with the matter as well as the person who has overall responsibility for supervision of the case.

The client should be given certain information following the first interview, including:

- the basis and terms of the firm's charges and whether they are to be increased;
- any likely payments that the client or the firm may need to make to others;
- whether the client is eligible and should apply for public funding;
- any potential liability for the other party's costs;
- details of the firm's complaints handling scheme;
- the effect of the statutory charge (if the client is a publicly funded client).

online resource centre

Many solicitors keep a selection of leaflets and information on local services and agencies that can help families as well as national organizations that offer advice and information. More information can be found on the Online Resource Centre.

 Practical Considerations

There are some more family law-orientated organizations that have their own codes of conduct or guides to good practice, such as Resolution.

From the Resolution website www.resolution.org.uk:

Resolution, which was formerly known as the Solicitors Family Law Association (SFLA), is an organisation of 6500 lawyers who believe in a constructive, non-confrontational approach to family law matters. Resolution also campaigns for improvements to the family justice system.

Resolution supports the development of family lawyers through its national and regional training programmes, through publications and good practice guides and through its accreditation scheme.

Resolution's codes of conduct are excellent and very helpful for the new practitioner. It is recommended that all those practising family law learn best practice and (harder still) try to keep to best practice at all times.

1.3.2.1 Money laundering

Money laundering is the process by which criminals attempt to hide or obscure the origins of criminal proceeds in order to make it easier to spend the money. The proceeds may arise from activities as diverse as drug trafficking and selling, prostitution, people trafficking, robbery, and all other forms of illegal activity including tax avoidance, benefit fraud, or fraud.

Solicitors' firms are targeted by money launderers as firms keep money within client accounts, move money from client to bank, and in property transactions. The risks to the firm include criminal and disciplinary action against the firm and individual members of staff with the attendant damage to reputation and bad publicity.

 online resource centre

The Law Society has published a practice note which is available on the Online Resource Centre. The principal statute governing money laundering is the Proceeds of Crime Act 2002 (POCA 2002) and the Money Laundering Regulations 2007.

A firm will assess the risks to it from money laundering and must have systems in place to ensure compliance with the Regulations. Customer due diligence (CDD) is the systems and processes the firm employ to verify the client's identity using documentation (e.g. a passport) and this must be done at the time of the first interview, i.e. at the time that the business relationship is established.

Each firm will have a nominated person who will be a point of contact for queries about money laundering.

There are certain warning signs that may indicate money laundering activity, e.g. disputes that settle too easily, as this may indicate 'sham' litigation, or clients wishing to pay in large sums in cash.

Practical Considerations

When the client is new to a firm, their identity needs to be verified. Clients should be asked to bring some form of identification with them, e.g. a passport and verification of their address, e.g. a recent utilities bill.

Following the case of *Bowman v Fels* [2005] EWCA 226, the Law Society issued guidance on money laundering issues. The case concerned an ancillary relief case where a report to the National Criminal Intelligence Service (NCIS) had been made and an adjournment sought until the 'appropriate consent' had been obtained from NCIS to continue the case. The Court of Appeal's judgment excluded certain activities from the scope of offences under POCA 2002. These activities include litigation from issue of proceedings to its disposal by final judgment and the Law Society guidance indicates that this also includes settlements, negotiations, and alternative dispute resolution (ADR).

1.3.2.2 Conflicts of interest

There will be occasions when you find that your firm already acts for another person whose interests conflict with the new client. Chapter 3 of the Code of Conduct 2011 prevents a solicitor acting where a conflict of interest exists.

It is important to carry out a conflict check as soon as possible. Ideally, information should be obtained from the client before the interview:

- name, address, and telephone number;
- area of law on which advice is needed (e.g. matrimonial or crime);
- name and address of any potential opponent or other involved (if applicable).

If this information is not obtained in advance of the interview, a conflict check should be done when the client arrives at the office and then the interview may progress if there is no conflict of interest.

 Example

There are a number of ways in which a conflict can arise. It is not uncommon for a client to seek legal advice if they are thinking about leaving a relationship, even if the other person is unaware of this. The advice sought can be general and a one-off. A conflict would arise if the other person came to the firm for advice if the relationship broke down. Another common conflict situation arises where the criminal department of a firm acts for someone accused of a criminal offence arising out of domestic abuse and then their partner/spouse/civil partner seeks advice on seeking an order preventing further harm.

1.3.3 FUNDING THE CASE

A client may come to you for a free interview, as offered by many firms, or may pay a fixed fee. You also have a duty to advise the client on whether they are eligible for public funding. Funding will be considered in detail in **Chapter 2**. Public funding has been substantially reduced since April 2013 and the Online Resource Centre will contain full details.

As a matter of professional conduct, you must also give your client the best overall information about the possible cost both at the outset of the case but also as the case progresses. Outcome 1.13 of the Code of Conduct 2011 states clients should receive the best possible information, both at the time of engagement and when appropriate as their matter progresses, about the likely overall cost of their matter. The behaviour required by the Code in relation to fees includes discussing whether the potential outcomes of the client's matter are likely to justify the expense or risk involved, including any risk of having to pay someone else's legal fees, clearly explaining your fees and if and when they are likely to change, warning about any other payments for which the client may be responsible, discussing how the client will pay, including whether public funding may be available, whether the client has insurance that might cover the fees; where you are acting for a publicly-funded client, explaining how their publicly funded status affects the costs and providing the information in a clear and accessible form which is appropriate to the needs and circumstances of the client.

Any information about the cost must be clear and confirmed in writing. You must discuss with your client whether the potential outcomes of any legal case will justify the expense or risk involved including, if relevant, the risk of having to pay an opponent's costs.

1.3.4 ATTENDANCE NOTES AND FILES

A client will give you a great deal of information and it is important that you keep good records, as others in your firm may assist in the case; keep a record of the time spent on the matter, and a permanent record of client instructions. Attendance notes are very important as they are a permanent record of instructions, action taken, and time recorded. Attendance notes should be sufficiently full to allow other members of the firm to use the file with ease. In case of complaint, attendance notes are a good record of the work done for a client.

It is also very important to maintain your files in an orderly and organized manner. A file should be logically organized with all documents securely stored in a way to make access to important information easy for someone not familiar with the file. The file should be reviewed regularly to avoid missing dates or allowing the case to 'drift'. As a trainee solicitor, the author was taught that files should be so well organized that if a file were dropped, it could be picked up without a single document being misplaced. Files often become very large in a complex case and so the file must be sufficiently well organized to cope with this.

Copies of documents, particularly court forms, should be kept on the file in order to keep track of the case documents. The file will be audited if it is a publicly funded case and all firms will probably have some form of file check as part of a quality control, and so it is important to maintain a tidy, up-to-date, and well-organized file.

1.3.5 CLIENT CARE POST INTERVIEW

The Code of Conduct requires that certain client care and funding issues must be discussed with a client and includes:

- costs/funding;
- complaints;
- supervision of the case;
- timescales.

These are often detailed in a client care letter sent to the client following the first interview and an example can be found in Case Study One.

1.4 LITIGANTS IN PERSON

The numbers of Litigants in Person (LiP) have increased exponentially in family proceedings. Many simply cannot afford to pay legal fees and the withdrawal of public funding in divorce, financial remedy, and private children cases (see **Chapter 2**) have led to many people being unable to access legal advice. This has been compounded by cuts in advice services which may have previously provided help.

As a family lawyer, you will come across LiP as either a person seeking some advice or in court. It is important to realise that some LiP will be extremely court-literate and be able to negotiate proceedings with some confidence but many will find the process extremely daunting. As a family lawyer, your duty is to the court and to your client but there are also other issues to bear in mind.

 Example

> The Law Society practice note on Litigants in Person reminds solicitors that they must not take 'unfair advantage' of a Litigant in Person. An example of this would be to use your professional status to demand something which could not properly be demanded. For instance, you should not tell a LiP that they have to agree to their new partner handing over their bank statements. This is not within the scope of the law and a solicitor would be subject to sanction by a judge or the SRA if such conduct were identified.

It is commonly a difficult balance with your own client, as it is often necessary to discuss matters at length with a LiP and a client may perceive that they are funding assistance to their opponent. Behave helpfully and courteously to a LiP but do remember your duty is to the court and your client. A good example is to remind your opponent of a deadline for court orders as this assists the court, your client, and the LiP to avoid undue delay. Keep good attendance notes of any discussions.

On the Online Resource Centre, there are a selection of useful publications for LiP which are helpful for both family lawyers to direct LiP to, and for lawyers to learn good practice.

online resource centre

SUMMARY POINTS

- Family law is a fascinating and varied area in which to practice.

- The successful family lawyer will require not only an excellent grasp of the law, but also good legal skills in terms of advocacy, interviewing, drafting, negotiation, and legal research.

- Family clients come to see a solicitor in often difficult circumstances and a family lawyer needs excellent interpersonal skills.

- As in all legal practice, solicitors and advisers are bound by rules of professional conduct, including rules on confidentiality, conflicts of interest, and money laundering.

- The first interview is an important meeting for both client and lawyer and it is important to get the basics right, to cover the available law and remedies fully, and to use communication skills fully.

- A conflict check should be done prior to the interview to avoid conflicts of interest between clients.

- A client needs the best possible information on costs and an estimate of the total costs likely to arise in the case.

- A client care letter should be sent to the client containing details of costs, supervision of the case, any relevant time estimates, and details of the firm's complaints procedures.

- Litigants in Person are firmly established in the family law landscape and face particular challenges in the family court system.

SELF-TEST QUESTIONS

1. Name two core outcomes imposed by the Code of Conduct.

2. A client asks you to accept instructions in divorce proceedings. You saw his wife this morning at an earlier appointment. Can you accept his instructions?

3. A client comes in for advice on a divorce and insists on paying 'up front' for the proceedings in cash. The client telephones later in the week to say that he and his wife have been reconciled and he wants his money back. What issues does this raise for the firm?

Case Study One

Case Study One is a stand-alone case study for Part One of the text. Read through the documents featured on the Online Resource Centre and answer the following questions:

1. Has the solicitor complied with all of their professional conduct obligations?

2. Has the client had all of their questions answered?

**online
resource
centre**

Answers to the questions above can be found on the Online Resource Centre:
www.oxfordtextbooks.co.uk/orc/sendall17/.

2 FUNDING

2.1 INTRODUCTION

This chapter will:

- discuss the changes made to public funding in family cases;
- discuss the availability of public funding for family law proceedings;
- examine the levels of funding available to the client;
- consider the tests to decide if a client is eligible for public funding;
- consider the recovery of public funding through the statutory charge;
- consider how a privately paying client can fund proceedings.

Public funding is administered by the Legal Aid Agency (LAA) which is an executive agency of the Ministry of Justice. It came into existence on 1 April 2013 following the abolition of the Legal Services Commission as a result of the Legal Aid, Sentencing and Punishment of Offenders (LASPO) Act 2012 and it delivers two schemes of public funding, the Public Defender Service and Civil Legal Advice (CLA). Family proceedings are civil proceedings and so fall within the CLA. This chapter provides an introduction to the levels of public funding available to family law clients and the eligibility criteria. It deals with each type of funding generally; the specific considerations for each type of work will be covered separately within the relevant chapters. References are made to the documents available on the website of the Ministry of Justice and will be available on the Online Resource Centre.

 online resource centre

2.1.1 LASPO AND CHANGES TO PUBLIC FUNDING

The Legal Aid, Sentencing and Punishment of Offenders Act 2012 (LASPO) enacted very wide changes to public funding of family cases. The changes were made in April 2013.

2.1.1.1 Scope of work

The scope of work which will be covered by public funding in family law has been greatly reduced and now the following are covered by public funding:

- public family law regarding protection of children;
- private family where there is evidence of domestic violence;

- private law children cases where there is evidence of child abuse;
- child abduction matters;
- representation for child parties in private family cases;
- legal advice in support of mediation;
- domestic violence injunction cases;
- forced marriage protection order cases.

This means that clients will generally not receive public funding for divorce proceedings or to resolve financial and property disputes following divorces and cohabitation disputes, with exceptions made for those facing domestic violence (see **2.1.1.2**). Families in dispute about contact and residence of children will not receive public funding unless there is domestic violence present in the relationship.

The effect of these changes has been profound. The Ministry of Justice's own statistics for all public funding show:

- a reduction of 50% in the overall amount of legal help matters started;
- a fall of 60% in the number of family cases, and 40% in the number of family mediations;
- the number of civil legal aid providers has halved since 2008, and the number of crime providers has fallen by 16% over the same period;
- in 2012–13 there were 870 Not for Profit legal aid providers. In 2013–14 there were just 95—a fall of 90%.

This chapter will cover the types of public funding available to those who qualify for family law but for many clients the choice is to be a Litigant in Person (LiP) (see **Chapter 1**) or to fund a solicitor privately. The numbers eligible for public funding will be very small.

The case of *Q v Q* [2014] EWFC 31 (actually three conjoined cases before the President) concerned private children proceedings. All involved serious issues including the need for translators, expert evidence and all had unrepresented parties, mainly fathers. The President was concerned that the experts, translators, and representation for unrepresented parties were required for a fair trial and that, in the absence of public funding, Her Majesty's Courts and Tribunal Service (HMCTS) may have to foot the bill. As HMCTS is part of the Ministry of Justice (MoJ), then it would be the MoJ who is effectively paying. This creates an interesting situation, as the MoJ were invited to intervene in the case but did not. Any developments arising from this judgment will be updated on the Online Resource Centre.

online
resource
centre

2.1.1.2 Domestic violence gateway

Legal aid for divorce, financial proceedings following divorce and private children cases may, however, still be available in cases where there has been, or is a risk of, domestic violence and where women can provide one of the following pieces of evidence:

- that their perpetrator has been convicted of a domestic violence offence against them and that conviction is unspent;
- that their perpetrator has accepted a caution for a domestic violence offence against them within the past 60 months;
- that there are ongoing criminal proceedings in respect of a domestic violence offence against them;
- that they have a protective injunction (such as a non-molestation or forced marriage protection order) in force or one had been made within the past 60 months;
- that their perpetrator had given an undertaking in respect of domestic violence and the undertaking is still in force or had been made within the past 60 months and where no cross-undertaking has been given;
- that they have been referred to a Multi Agency Risk Assessment Conference as a high-risk victim of domestic violence and a plan put in place within the past 60 months;

- that they have a report from a doctor, nurse, or midwife confirming they were examined in respect of an injury or condition consistent with domestic violence within the past 60 months;

- that they have been assessed by Social Services as experiencing or being at risk of domestic violence within the past 60 months;

- that they have a letter from a refuge confirming that they stayed there for a period of more than 24 hours within the past 60 months.

This means that clients should be screened for cases of domestic violence as this will assist an application for public funding. There has been some early research suggesting that many struggle to produce evidence of domestic abuse and so are not able to use the gateway to access public funding. This system of evidence before funding is given was initially restricted to two years, but after a challenge succeeded in the Court of Appeal the period has been extended to 60 months by the Civil Legal Aid (Procedure) (Amendment) Regulations 2016 No. 516. As a result of the concerns expressed by the Court of Appeal, evidence of financial abuse can now be submitted as evidence of domestic abuse, and it is suggested that bank statements and communications by the perpetrator (texts/emails) and as much detail as possible should be supplied.

2.1.1.3 Residence test

A proposed amendment under the Legal Aid, Sentencing and Punishment of Offenders Act 2012 (Amendment of Schedule 1) Order 2014 sought to introduce a residence requirement to public funding eligibility. The proposed requirement was a residence of at least 12 months (with some exceptions) before funding would be granted. This was found to be unlawful by the Supreme Court in *R (on the application of the Public Law Project) v Secretary of State* [2016] UKSC 39.

 Practical Considerations

You will often hear about the 'means' and 'merits' tests in public funding. 'Means' refers to whether or not the client will qualify financially for assistance and 'merits' refers to whether or not the client's case has sufficient strength to receive funding.

2.2 DEFINITION OF FAMILY PROCEEDINGS

The Funding Code used by the LAA defines 'family proceedings' at section 2.2 as 'proceedings which arise out of family relationships, including proceedings in which the welfare of the children is determined (other than judicial review proceedings)'. Family proceedings include all proceedings under any one or more of the following:

- the Matrimonial Causes Act 1973;

- the Inheritance (Provision for Family and Dependants) Act 1975;

- the Adoption Act 1976 and Adoption and Children Act 2002;

- the Domestic Proceedings and Magistrates' Courts Act 1978;

- Part III of the Matrimonial and Family Proceedings Act 1984;

- Parts I, II, and IV of the Children Act 1989;

- Part IV of the Family Law Act 1996;

- the inherent jurisdiction of the High Court in relation to children;

- the Civil Partnership Act 2004.

The concept of 'family relationships' in the Code is very widely drawn and includes:

- marriage;

- heterosexual or same-sex relationships between partners whether cohabiting or not;

- blood relations;
- step relations;
- adoption or long-term care of children such that they can reasonably be regarded as part of the family.

Proceedings will only come within the Code if the basis of the dispute or the jurisdiction arises out of a family relationship rather than whether the parties are family members.

 Example

Martin and Hannah are married. Martin drives very quickly and this is a source of dispute between them. Martin is driving them to a party one evening and drives recklessly, causing a crash, which is his fault. Hannah is injured and sues Martin for damages for personal injury. She also decides this is the final straw and that she can't bear to be married to Martin any more.

The subsequent personal injury proceedings are not family proceedings, as the dispute has not arisen in any of the statutes listed earlier and is not a result of the relationship between the pair. The divorce proceedings are family proceedings, as they are conducted under the Matrimonial Causes Act 1973 and a result of their married status.

2.3 LEVELS OF ASSISTANCE

There are a number of levels of assistance available for family law clients. They are:

- legal help;
- family mediation;
- family help (lower);
- family help (higher);
- legal representation.

Legal help and family help (lower) are described as 'controlled work' and can only be carried out by solicitors' firms who have a specialist quality mark (SQM).

Family help (higher) and legal representation are described as 'licensed work' and an application has to be made to the LAA for a certificate to conduct the work under public funding.

Each level is suitable for different types of work or cases at different stages of proceedings. Each level is discussed separately.

2.4 LEGAL HELP

Legal help (also called level one advice) allows a client to gain advice and assistance from a solicitor on family law. Legal help does not cover the issue or conduct of court proceedings or any advocacy on behalf of the client. The main exception to this is undefended divorce proceedings.

The following types of work can be covered by legal help at level one:

- initial meeting with the solicitor;
- legal advice;
- letter writing;
- telephone calls;
- referrals to other organizations.

The solicitor is paid a single fee for the issue dealt with under legal help.

Legal help can also be used to complete applications for family help and legal representation.

Some work is only remunerated at legal help level, including a change of name or advice about the Child Support Agency.

2.4.1 ELIGIBILITY FOR LEGAL HELP

If the client is eligible for a form of work covered by public funding or is eligible under the domestic violence gateway, they must also be eligible on financial grounds as well as on the merits of their case. There are 'means' (financial eligibility) and 'merits' (whether the client's case merits the advice being given) tests in order to decide if the client is eligible for public funding. The client must provide evidence of their income.

2.4.1.1 Prospects of Success test

The LAA will only fund a case when there will be a good prospect of succeeding having regard to the circumstances of the matter, including the personal circumstances of the client, to justify the work being carried out. This means that cases involving no legal advice at all, e.g. simple form filling, are not eligible for legal help. The sufficient benefit test also rules out frivolous or vexatious cases.

2.4.1.2 Financial eligibility

Additionally, funding may only be provided if it is reasonable for the matter to be funded out of the CLA fund, having regard to other possible sources of funding.

Some welfare benefits will mean that the client is automatically eligible.

These benefits are:

- income support;
- income-based jobseeker's allowance;
- income-based Employment and Support Allowance;
- Guarantee Credit;
- Universal Credit;
- NASS support (for asylum seekers).

For those who are not on the above benefits, the gross income of the client is then worked out.

2.4.1.3 Aggregation of income

The first step is to determine whether the client has a partner whose means should be aggregated for the purposes of financial eligibility assessment. 'Partner' is defined as anyone (including a person of the same sex) with whom the applicant lives as a couple, and includes people who are in a relationship but do not cohabit.

 Practical Considerations

LAA Guidance gives the following further guidance:

This means that there must be a breakdown in the relationship that is likely to be permanent (i.e. at least one of the parties considers the relationship to be at an end) rather than mere physical separation if the partners' means are not to be aggregated. Therefore a couple who is physically separated owing to financial or practical reasons, e.g. job location or the fact that one of the parties is in prison, hospital, residential care etc. must be aggregated.

If the partner's income is to be aggregated, then the joint income should be calculated.

2.4.1.4 Income

The current income limit is £2,657 per month (this increases if the client has more than four children). If the gross income of the client, including that of any partner, is more than this, the client will be ineligible for funding for all levels and the process would stop there. Some forms of income are disregarded, e.g. disability living allowance and housing benefit.

If the client's income is less than £2,657, fixed allowances are made for dependants and employment expenses. Other allowances are made for tax, NI, maintenance paid, housing costs, and child minding. **Table 2.1** gives the allowances:

TABLE 2.1 DEPENDANTS' ALLOWANCES

Work related expenses for those receiving a wage or salary	£45
Partner	£181.91
Child aged 15 or under	£291.49
Child aged 16 or over	£291.49
Housing cap (for those without dependants)	£545.00

If the client's gross income less allowances is less than £733 per month, the client will be financially eligible on income.

 Example

Mary is a single parent with a total gross income of £1,800 per month. She pays £750 in tax, NI, and housing costs. Mary has two children aged less than 15 years old and so will have 2 × £291.49 dependants allowances.

$$£1800–750–(2 × £291.49) = £467.02 \text{ disposable income.}$$

Mary has less than £733 disposable income per month and so will be financially eligible for legal help. A higher gross income gap applies with more than four child dependants.

online
resource
centre

Information on the income limits and a guide to assessing whether a client is eligible can be found on the CLS Keycard which is issued every April and can be accessed via the gov.uk website. The Online Resource Centre contains more information.

2.4.1.5 Capital

The client's capital should be calculated. The upper limit for capital is £8,000 in family proceedings. LAA Guidance gives more detail on disregarded categories and jointly owned capital. The only items of capital that are not taken into account include the following:

• household furniture and effects (unless of exceptional value);

• clothes;

• tools and implements of trade;

• some welfare benefits or community care payments;

• capital value of the client's business in the case of the self-employed;

• cars or other vehicles in regular use (unless of exceptional value).

Under the regulations the value of the subject matter of any claim in respect of which a person is seeking funding is required to be left out of account in computing the capital of that person. This situation only applies to capital assets. It is a very important rule in the context of family/matrimonial cases, as often disputed assets are the only assets that the client owns. It means that assets that are being fought over in relation to the dispute for which funding is required, where the client's interest in those assets does not exceed £100,000, must not be taken into account when assessing capital.

Where a client's main or only dwelling in which he resides is the subject matter of dispute:

1. the property should be valued at the amount for which it could be sold on the open market;

2. the amount of any mortgage or charge registered on the property must be deducted but the maximum amount that can be deducted for such a mortgage or charge is £100,000; and

3. the first £100,000 of the value of the client's interest after making the above mortgage deduction must be disregarded (known as the 'equity disregard').

 Example

The applicant has a home worth £205,000 and the mortgage is £200,000.

Value of home:	£205,000
Deduct mortgage up to maximum allowable:	£100,000
Deduct equity disregard:	£100,000
Amount to be taken into account in assessing financial eligibility:	£5,000

In this example the client is eligible.

(Example based on the Funding Code)

The subject matter of dispute exemption (i.e. £100,000 disregard) should be applied to the main dwelling property first; the remainder (if any) should then be applied to the other assets that are in dispute. The total amount disregarded as subject matter of dispute is not to exceed £100,000.

Sometimes it will be obvious that a particular asset is in dispute between the parties, but in the family/matrimonial context the point is more difficult to determine if parties seek funding at an early stage and there are a range of assets that may or may not be at issue. The general approach should be that an asset should not be treated as the subject matter of the dispute if the other party has made no specific claim against it and if in practice it is available to the applicant to use as his or her own and could be used to fund legal costs. However, the amount disregarded under the 'subject matter of dispute' rule must not exceed £100,000.

2.4.1.6 Specified family proceedings

Under reg 44 of the Civil Legal Aid (Financial Resources and Payment for Services) Regulations 2013, where a client applies for Legal Representation, Family Help (higher) or assistance under s10 LASPO and their disposable income exceeds £135, then a client must pay a contribution to their legal aid.

These contributions must be paid by the client throughout the life of the case. Clients frequently resent these contributions, but it is worth reminding them that they represent a fraction of a solicitor's hourly rate.

Table 2.2 shows the levels of contributions that clients can expect to pay:

TABLE 2.2 CONTRIBUTIONS

Band	Monthly disposable income	Monthly contribution
A	£311 to £465	35% of income
B	£466 to £616	45% of income
C	£617 and above	70% of income

For all applications, evidence of means is required, e.g. bank statements or payslips, and a copy of this evidence must be kept on file.

If the client's income and capital are below the limit, the client can be awarded funding.

2.4.1.7 Fees

The fee paid to the solicitor for legal help is a single fee irrespective of the number of issues presented by the client. Legal help can be used to apply for higher levels of funding. Where the work done under the legal help scheme is three times the standard fee (due to the complexity of the case) a higher fee may be paid.

2.5 FAMILY MEDIATION

This level of funding authorizes mediation of a family dispute and an assessment of whether mediation appears to be suitable for the resolution of the dispute between the parties. **Chapter 3** discusses the process of mediation in more detail. Mediation may be suitable for cases where there are issues of money and property to be divided or where parents need to agree where children are to live and with whom they shall have contact. It is not widely known by the public that public funding is still available for a much wider range of issues than other forms of legal aid. As a result of this, and a lack of public funding leading to fewer solicitors seeing clients to refer them to mediation, has led to mediation funding being underused. The Ministry of Justice has recently announced a collapse in attendance at mediation and a large underspend on mediation.

All family mediation requires that an assessment of whether mediation will be suitable is carried out, and this is called an 'assessment meeting'. This is done by a recognized mediator and the funding will only continue where the mediator is satisfied that mediation is suitable for the dispute and the parties.

If one party fails to attend the assessment meeting, a second appointment will only be given if it is reasonable under the circumstances, especially if they fail to give a good reason for non-attendance. The mediator will also screen the parties for any domestic abuse.

The criteria for financial eligibility are as for legal help (see **2.4.1**).

2.6 FAMILY HELP

2.6.1 FAMILY HELP (LOWER)

Family help (lower) is also, like legal help, a fixed fee.

It is available in both public and private law cases. Family help (lower) does not include the issue of proceedings or representation in proceedings other than help in obtaining a consent order following settlement of a family dispute. Family help (lower) allows advice, and assistance in pre-proceedings work unless and until it becomes clear that the matter cannot be resolved through negotiation without the issue of proceedings.

In order to be eligible, the prospects of success test (see **2.4.1.1**) must be met and also the financial eligibility must be met. The client's case must also be a 'significant family dispute'. A significant family dispute is one which, if not resolved, may lead to family proceedings and for which legal advice and assistance is necessary to enable the client to resolve the issues.

There is also a cost–benefit criterion. This is a further test where family help will be refused unless the likely benefits gained from the proceedings for the client justify the likely costs, such that a reasonable private-paying client would be prepared to pay to take or defend the proceedings in all the circumstances.

 Example

Melissa has recently separated from Chris. Melissa wishes to seek a divorce. There are three children in the family, and they are currently not having contact with Chris as Melissa claims that he cannot be trusted to look after them properly as the children come back with unexplained bruises. She has no evidence to support this claim and eventually agrees to allow contact. Chris wishes to have all three children live with him in his one-bedroom flat. Melissa offers contact every Tuesday and Saturday. Chris wishes to have contact on Wednesday and Sunday.

Melissa will not be granted public funding as all the dispute concerns private children work and there is no evidence to use the domestic violence gateway.

No application to the LAA is required and the solicitor should complete Legal Help Controlled Work 1 form with confirmation that the case meets the criteria to move to family help (lower) when the criteria are met.

In private cases, family help (lower) has separate fees for both children and finance issues and the solicitor can claim a separate fee for both.

A solicitor may claim a settlement fee if a case settles under family help (lower).

These fees are built up as the case progresses.

 Example

Melissa has received advice and assistance on her divorce under legal help after Chris assaulted her during an argument. The dispute regarding the children required negotiation between parties under family help (lower) and settled before going to court, and this will attract a settlement fee. The fees given in **Table 2.3** are those that are paid to solicitors by the LAA for the work done under public funding schemes. A diagram of the fee structure for public funding is shown in **Figure 2.1**.

FIGURE 2.1 FEE STRUCTURE FOR PUBLIC FUNDING

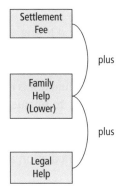

The total claimed by the solicitor depends upon the location of the client and the type of work undertaken. In certain circumstances, an hourly fee can be claimed.

TABLE 2.3 FEES FOR PUBLIC FUNDING

Family Help (Lower) – Children

	Fee	Settlement Fee
London	£230	£138
Non-London	£199	£119

Family Help (Lower) – Finance

	Fee	Settlement Fee
London	£241	£145
Non-London	£208	£125

2.6.2 **FAMILY HELP (HIGHER)**

This is covered by a certificate rather than being administered by the solicitor and will be paid at an hourly rate. A fee is paid for work under the Family Help (higher) scheme but, in certain cases, an hourly rate is paid, e.g. in child abduction proceedings. Family help (higher) is justified only where it is necessary to issue proceedings having exhausted all other reasonable avenues to resolve the dispute or where proceedings already exist.

Family help (higher) will be refused if the case is one that must be referred to a recognized mediator for a determination as to whether mediation is suitable for the resolution of the dispute, for the parties, and in all the circumstances.

The client must meet the cost–benefit criteria (see **2.6.1**), i.e. the reasonable private client approach. An element of reasonableness to the proportionality of the dispute and the benefits and costs involved is also required.

 Example

Further to the earlier example, contact between Chris and the children has been progressing well.

He sees them every Wednesday between 4 and 7pm and Saturday between 11am and 6pm. Chris wishes to change the contact on Saturday to 10am–6pm. Melissa does not wish to change the times as it is difficult to get the children ready in time for 10am, and offers 10.30am as a compromise.

A privately paying client would probably not pay a great deal of money to argue over 30 minutes of contact, nor is it proportionate to spend public money on this dispute. The costs would outweigh the benefits gained by the client and purely private children matters are no longer publicly funded.

A certificate for family help (higher) will not cover representation at a final contested hearing but it will cover the issue of proceedings where it is necessary to gain disclosure of information. In children cases, family help (higher) covers all steps short of a contested hearing.

2.6.2.1 Prospects of success

While family law is not about winning and losing, if public money is going to be used the case should have some prospect of success. The Civil Legal Aid (Merits Criteria) Regulations 2013 states that an individual may qualify for family help only if the Director is satisfied that the reasonable private-paying individual test is met. This test is one which asks whether a reasonable private individual would pay to pursue their case. Additionally, an individual may qualify for family help (higher) only if the LAA is satisfied that the individual has exhausted all reasonable alternatives to bringing proceedings. Alternatives to bringing proceedings include, but are not limited to, mediation and negotiation.

2.7 **LEGAL REPRESENTATION**

Legal representation covers preparation for, and representation at, a final hearing in contested proceedings.

While it is to be hoped that a case will settle either by negotiation or in the early stages, some cases do progress as far as a final hearing. A case may have very complex legal or evidential issues. At a final hearing the court may wish to hear from witnesses and for these witnesses to be cross-examined. The court may also wish to hear legal argument and proceedings may require a solicitor or barrister who has very good advocacy skills. Legal representation allows the client to be fully represented at a final hearing and can be used to instruct a barrister, should this be necessary.

There are a range of different criteria applied to the granting of legal representation in different types of case and these will be covered within the requisite chapter. There generally is a requirement for the client's case to meet cost–benefit criteria and also have good prospects of success. Also, there should have been reasonable attempts to settle the dispute without recourse to contested proceedings. However, if the matter is urgent or there is a risk of a significant miscarriage of justice, legal representation can be granted on an emergency basis.

2.7.1 FAMILY ADVOCACY SCHEME

The Family Advocacy Scheme is a graduated fee scheme where specific fees are paid for appearing at specific court hearings. The Family Advocacy Scheme applies to the following work:

- advocacy at court hearings;
- advocate's meetings (public law only);
- conferences (counsel only);
- counsel's opinions (counsel only).

Some areas of law are excluded, e.g. defended divorces. The fee paid depends upon the type of hearing and 'bolt on' fees are paid in a number of different circumstances, e.g. when a client has difficulty in understanding proceedings or giving instructions. The Online Resource Centre contains more information.

 online resource centre

2.8 EMERGENCY FUNDING

There are occasions where the nature of a client's case means that public funding is required urgently, e.g. in domestic abuse or in child abduction cases. The funding can be authorized by the LAA and an application can be made by post, fax, email, or telephone if the urgency of the case dictates.

Emergency funding will only be granted if it is in the interests of justice to do so and the client must pass all of the tests required for the level of service applied for.

The client must be financially eligible and if it is found that he is subsequently financially ineligible, the certificate will be revoked. The client may then be liable to repay the LAA. If an emergency certificate is granted, an application must be made as soon as possible for a substantive certificate.

If the solicitor's firm has an SQM (Specialist Quality Mark) in family law, then they will have 'devolved powers' to grant emergency funding. The LAA devolves decision-making powers to the solicitor to make decisions on emergency funding.

The solicitor can use their devolved powers for either family help (higher) or legal representation depending on the stage of proceedings.

2.9 STATUTORY CHARGE

'Costs' is the term commonly used to describe a party's legal expenses, including solicitors' fees, barristers' fees, court fees, payments to experts, and other expenses.

Many clients assume that when they are granted a public funding certificate the LAA will pay for their case fully and do not consider that their funding comes from public money. The statutory charge is generally explained to clients in terms of a loan. The money is 'loaned' to the client by the LAA to pursue their case.

The LAA has a statutory duty to recoup money wherever possible and this can come from an order by the court for the publicly funded person's costs to be paid by the other party. If that is not sufficient, or a costs order is not made by the court, then the LAA will look to any money or property recovered or preserved by the client during the proceedings, in order to make up the shortfall. This is known as the statutory charge. The LAA will use the money recovered to fund other cases.

Section 25 LASPO 2012 allows the LAA a first charge on any property recovered or preserved by the client (whether for himself or any other person) in any proceedings or in any compliance or settlement of any dispute in connection with which the services were provided. Property includes money, e.g. a lump sum.

2.9.1 RECOVERED OR PRESERVED

Whether property has been recovered or preserved is a complex issue. The House of Lords considered the issue in *Hanlon v Law Society* [1981] AC 124 where their Lordships held that property is recovered or preserved if it was 'in issue' in proceedings and the funded party either made a successful claim in relation to it or successfully defended a claim in respect of it.

 Example

Melissa and Chris have begun divorce proceedings after Melissa obtains funding through the domestic violence gateway. Through mediation they agree a settlement for all their assets apart from a holiday home in the Cotswolds valued at £250,000.

Proceedings are issued for financial orders and the court awards 50% of the value to each party. Melissa was publicly funded. Chris is ordered to pay £5,000 towards Melissa's legal costs but there is a shortfall of £1,500. Melissa will pay this £1,500 out of the proceeds of the court award as the property was recovered as a result of the proceedings.

In *Curling v Law Society* [1985] 1 All ER 707, the family home was in joint names. The publicly funded wife sought an order that the house be sold. Her husband did not dispute that one half of the house belonged to the wife and eventually an agreement was reached whereby the husband bought out the wife's interest in the house. The wife argued that as the title of the property was not in dispute, the sum she had received for her share was not recovered or preserved in the proceedings. The Court of Appeal held that the ownership of the property could not be looked at in isolation and the fact that a party had recovered something to which she was already entitled did not of itself prevent the statutory charge.

Exemptions from the statutory charge include:

- periodical payments of maintenance for a spouse, former spouse, civil partner, or former civil partner;
- pension-sharing orders;
- where the family home is recovered or preserved and the only funding received by the client has been legal help;
- a lump sum received by way of a petition attachment order or attachment of death-in-service benefits under ss25B and 25C of the Matrimonial Causes Act 1973.

2.9.2 MEDIATION AND THE STATUTORY CHARGE

If a settlement has been reached by mediation and funded by a certificate for family mediation, the costs are exempt from the statutory charge.

2.9.3 MINIMIZING THE STATUTORY CHARGE

In **2.9.2**, settling through mediation is one way to avoid the charge completely. If the issues are narrowed down as far as possible at the beginning of the case this will reduce the property 'at issue' in the proceedings.

 Example

In the earlier example, Melissa and Chris agreed all issues surrounding money, property, and maintenance at mediation. No statutory charge will be recovered.

2.9.4 RECOVERY OF THE STATUTORY CHARGE

The relevant legislation that governs the enforcement of the statutory charge is the Civil Legal Aid (Statutory Charge) Regulations 2013. If both cash and a dwelling house are preserved, the charge will be enforced against the cash first and then the dwelling house. The LAA has the discretion to postpone the charge, particularly if the charge relates to the family home. The LAA will register a charge over the property, payable when the property is sold unless the LAA agrees to transfer the charge to another property. Interest will accrue at a simple rate until the charge is redeemed, currently 8%. The client can pay off the statutory charge at any time.

2.9.5 IMPORTANCE OF MAKING THE CLIENT AWARE OF THE POTENTIAL IMPACT OF THE STATUTORY CHARGE

Clients will often claim that they did not know about the effect of the statutory charge. This selective memory is often despite several letters containing the advice and explanations from their solicitor. This demonstrates the importance of giving full advice at initial meetings, in client care letters, and regular updates, as well as keeping detailed attendance notes.

2.10 PRIVATELY PAYING CLIENTS

Many clients will be ineligible for public funding, even clients of fairly moderate means. Conditional fees are not permitted in family law, but there are other methods of funding a case:

- the client pays for the case privately and takes a loan from a bank or credit card;
- the client may be loaned money by family or friends;
- the client may be able to gain some limited assistance from voluntary agencies, e.g. a Citizens' Advice Bureau. This may be general advice only and will not cover advocacy at court;
- a 'Sears Tooth' agreement (see **Chapter 14**);
- an application for maintenance pending suit in proceedings for a financial order (see **Chapter 12**).

Many people will simply be litigants in person (see **Chapter 1**) and will receive assistance from the remaining voluntary sector bodies which still remain, e.g. Citizen's Advice Bureaux or Personal Support Unit (PSU). There has been a move towards the 'unbundling' of solicitors' fees. This refers to a move away from a traditional solicitor's retainer where the solicitor provides a full service from the inception of instructions. Solicitors will unbundle services to undertake discrete advice and tasks within a case.

 Example

In a family case where a party cannot receive public funding, a solicitor may be asked to provide some initial advice. A client may then issue their own divorce and then return to their solicitor later for assistance with drafting documents in financial remedy proceedings and for advocacy at a final hearing. All other tasks are undertaken by the client.

The solicitor can offer a 'pay as you go' fee structure or a fixed fee for a specific task rather than charge an hourly rate. There are some risks to the solicitor as they may not know enough about their client's case or may not be clear about the limits of the retainer. As the withdrawal of public funding has created a new landscape for most family lawyers, this is one way that solicitors are able to retain clients.

SUMMARY POINTS

- Public funding has undergone radical reform in April 2013 and the scope of public funding in family law cases has been greatly reduced.

- Legal proceedings can be funded privately or through public funding. Public funding is administered by the Legal Aid Agency of the Ministry of Justice.

- There are a number of levels of assistance available according to the type of advice or representation required including legal help, family mediation, family help, and legal representation. Funding can be applied for in an emergency.

- In order to receive public funding, a client must be eligible financially and there must be merit in funding the case through public money.

- Public funding is recouped by the Legal Aid Agency through the statutory charge. This can be mitigated by the parties agreeing as many issues as possible.

- Solicitors are providing different fee structures and services in order to assist clients no longer eligible for public funding.

SELF-TEST QUESTIONS

1. Which categories of cases attract public funding?

2. Which welfare benefits make a client automatically financially eligible for public funding?

3. Explain the statutory charge in a way that a client will understand it.

online
resource
centre

Answers to the questions above can be found on the Online Resource Centre:
www.oxfordtextbooks.co.uk/orc/sendall17/

3 ALTERNATIVE DISPUTE RESOLUTION IN FAMILY LAW

3.1 INTRODUCTION

This chapter will:

- discuss the methods by which a family lawyer may resolve family law disputes, including Alternative Dispute Resolution (ADR);
- review the various forms of negotiation which a family lawyer may undertake;
- discuss mediation and collaborative law as different forms of ADR used in family law.

Family law is often complex and daunting for clients, and the very nature of the substance of the dispute means that often parties bring their emotional disputes into the case. Most clients wish to resolve disputes cheaply, quickly, and without involving lawyers. Unfortunately, this is not possible in some cases for a number of reasons. Many people do not have the confidence to negotiate with their ex-partners or some will have difficulty in obtaining all the information they need in order to decide whether an offer is fair and should be accepted. Clients often have unrealistic expectations about the settlement or outcome to be achieved by the courts. As the ability to gain public funding diminishes, dissatisfaction with paying for legal advice increases. Family lawyers must also be good value for money.

However unfairly, family lawyers rarely get a good press from the general public. Family lawyers are perceived to have an interest in making the dispute last as long as possible with a view to making as much money as possible. Disputes are often very polarized and campaign groups have grown up surrounding issues of arrangements for children following separation, e.g. Fathers 4 Justice. One of the most important considerations for a new family lawyer is to ensure that a case is conducted as professionally and as calmly as possible. Family lawyers are bound by their professional codes of conduct. Family lawyers may also join organizations that promote good practice in family law, such as Resolution.

Cuts to public funding have had unforeseen consequences for ADR. As fewer people have access to public funding and so do not visit a lawyer, the link between lawyers and mediation has been weakened and the numbers being referred to mediation have fallen sharply. This is ironic, as there is still public funding available for mediation (see **Chapter 2**).

There are a number of ways in which a dispute can be resolved without resort to litigation. This chapter will look at a number of ADR techniques. Some, possibly all, will be relevant to your clients and some will not. It is part of the skill of a family lawyer to know which type of ADR is appropriate and available and which is not. Your firm may also wish to offer ADR services as part of the firm's services, e.g. collaborative law or mediation.

3.2 RELATIONSHIP AND MARRIAGE COUNSELLING

When a client attends your firm for advice, there should not be an automatic assumption that the client has decided that the relationship is at an end, nor that they wish to move straight into divorce or dissolution proceedings. If a client is having difficulties in their relationship and they wish to try to resolve these difficulties, then there are organizations that can assist the client.

 Practical Considerations

Two national organizations that provide support are:

- *Relate.* Relate offers advice, relationship counselling, sex therapy, workshops, mediation, consultations, and support face-to-face, by phone and through its website: www.relate.org.uk.

- *Marriage Care.* Marriage Care offers counselling nationwide to those wishing to become married or enter a long-term relationship or for those requiring help to sustain these relationships and can be found at www.marriagecare.org.uk.

Many practitioners keep leaflets and contact details of local services to provide to clients. It is important to be aware of local services and also to provide support where possible.

3.3 RESOLVING FAMILY LAW DISPUTES

Disputes are resolved in family law either through litigation or through some form of ADR or a combination of both. When litigation is used, not all cases end up being taken to a final hearing; the parties often agree with the assistance of the court.

Although ADR is available in family law, it is important to remember that if ADR fails, litigation will be the method by which disputes are resolved.

3.3.1 COMPARING ADR AND LITIGATION

There are many advantages and disadvantages of choosing ADR over litigation. See **Table 3.1**. Each type of ADR is different and so this is a general comparison.

TABLE 3.1 ADR AND LITIGATION

	ADR	Litigation
Speed	May be quicker than litigation and the parties have greater control over the timetable.	Courts' timetables try to ensure that proceedings are not too lengthy. There can be difficulties in finding court time that leads to delay.
Cost	Will often be cheaper than litigation but can be costly if counsel and other professionals become involved. Mediation may be covered by LAA Funding.	Can be funded by LAA funding if the client is eligible. Can be very costly if proceedings are lengthy and especially if the proceedings go to a final hearing. Can also be more expensive if counsel and other professionals are required.
	If collaborative law fails (see **3.7**), there may be duplication of legal costs.	
Emotional issues involved in separation	Some forms of ADR attempt to deal with the emotional fallout of separation as well as the legal issues.	Litigation is not designed to resolve emotional difficulties. Aggressive litigation will often heighten emotions.
Preservation of relationships between the parties	One of the aims of ADR is to preserve the good relations between the parties, especially those families with children.	Litigation will attempt to preserve good relationships but the 'court experience' may promote hostility between the parties.

Formality	Less formal than litigation but some forms of ADR are slightly more structured, e.g. collaborative law or arbitration.	Court proceedings do have a greater element of formality which is sometimes necessary to protect a client's interests.
Finality	Most ADR will attempt to produce a final settlement that can be recorded in a final court order.	Court will give a final order.
Proportionality	ADR costs can be more proportionate to the assets or dispute between the parties.	Litigation costs are often disproportionate to the assets in dispute between the parties.
Flexibility	ADR can meet a number of needs and can choose the method of ADR to suit the party's situation.	Court proceedings are designed to allow negotiation between the parties.

3.4 NEGOTIATION

Most lawyers will start negotiation of some kind well before litigation is commenced. Most lawyers find that client satisfaction is higher if a settlement is reached although sometimes it is difficult to persuade the client of this!

Courts will also expect the parties to have undertaken some form of negotiation prior to issuing court proceedings. Judges are often concerned that legal costs are disproportionate to the value of the assets involved and courts are hard pressed to accommodate parties' wishes for a final hearing.

3.4.1 FORMS OF NEGOTIATION

3.4.1.1 Settlement between clients

Clients may negotiate directly between themselves. An advantage is that the client retains complete control over the dispute resolution.

Problems may occur if a spouse in a weaker position has agreed without full disclosure or has been pressurized into agreement. One party may be too afraid of the other party to disagree or negotiate properly and there is always a risk that one party may be psychologically or financially in a stronger position and may be able to dictate an agreement. Some clients feel guilty about ending a relationship and may agree an unadvisedly generous settlement. Independent advice from a family lawyer is essential before the settlement has been finalized.

3.4.1.2 Negotiation through correspondence

Negotiating through correspondence is very commonly done and works well if the correspondence is drafted well, is clear, complete, and comprehensive. Correspondence is a permanent record of the negotiation and is often the opening point for negotiations. Clients retain an element of control as correspondence can be read before sending. Some lawyers do not enjoy a round-table meeting or face-to-face negotiations and some may find correspondence easier when they are a less experienced practitioner.

However, correspondence is slow as lawyers will have to wait for post or DX and then seek instructions from the client. It can be less efficient than face-to-face contact. If correspondence is poorly drafted or contains material that is likely to offend parties, problems can arise as misunderstandings may follow as well as raising the 'temperature' of the dispute.

 Practical Considerations

Be careful with emails and faxes. Many solicitors use faxes to put pressure on their opponents. Faxes or emails have a legitimate place in urgent matters. When you receive a fax, you should consider whether an immediate response is required or whether it would be better to deal with the issue in ordinary correspondence, especially if the fax supersedes a letter already awaiting a response. Do not be rushed into an ill-advised course of action.

Emails are very useful but care should be taken to ensure that they are used in a constructive way. Consider your draft carefully; don't simply type and send. Once an email has been sent, it cannot be recovered, unlike a letter that has been typed and must be considered again on signing. Emails should be drafted with the same formality as letters and one should not be tempted to treat emails as a more casual form of communication.

Resolution Guide to Good Practice is an excellent guide to avoiding common pitfalls in drafting correspondence. The Guide considers issues about the reason for writing a letter, timing of letters, and ensuring correspondence is constructive, informative, and effective.

3.4.1.3 Negotiation via telephone or in person

Many lawyers will pick up the telephone to negotiate a settlement. The advantages are that it is a quick, cheap, and relatively informal way of resolving disputes and has the advantage of human contact. Using the telephone can deal with one or more issues of the ongoing case, e.g. a contact dispute over a holiday, while negotiations in the case continue.

Using the telephone has some disadvantages. A telephone negotiation should ideally be diarized between parties or your colleague may be unavailable or unprepared. Always confirm the outcome of a negotiation in writing to ensure that no misunderstandings arise.

With careful preparation, negotiations can be conducted between lawyers in person. Lawyers may need to meet more than once to resolve the dispute but it will be an efficient way of resolving a dispute. Lawyers can discuss one or more issues at a meeting and areas of dispute can be resolved. A comprehensive note of the meeting must be kept. Clients may be present but equally, the lawyers involved in the dispute can meet separately.

3.4.1.4 Meeting between Counsel

Involving Counsel (barristers) is sometimes necessary in complex cases and can assist less experienced lawyers. Sometimes a fresh pair of eyes is needed to clarify the issues and also Counsel can provide an objective opinion for a client as it can provide a 'reality check'. Negotiations can proceed between Counsel engaged in a dispute and prove to be a good way to resolve proceedings quickly. However, involving Counsel can be costly and Counsel can feel remote for the client who is used to more frequent contact with their solicitor.

3.4.1.5 At-court negotiation

Negotiations can continue all the way to the door of the court and frequently produce settlement even during the course of court hearings. There is no extra cost as the lawyers are present anyway and negotiations can involve Counsel. In financial relief proceedings (see **Chapter 14**), the parties will get an indication from the judge about what they can reasonably expect to gain in proceedings. The client may feel under slightly more pressure to settle if they have been unwilling to do so before then.

This form of negotiation can be problematic as a client may buckle under pressure or rush to accept and settle on less favourable terms. The court experience is rarely helpful to a client if negotiations fail.

3.5 MEDIATION

The Family Mediators Association sets out the four principles of mediation:

- it is voluntary;
- the mediator is impartial;
- it is confidential;
- it is flexible.

Mediation is a voluntary process and parties attend in person with a mediator to discuss problems. It is a safe environment, which promotes long-term agreement and hopefully reduces hostility between the parties. Parties can communicate directly with each other and any issue can be raised between the parties including more formal issues of financial and property matters or children's residence or contact.

The mediator will identify and clarify issues between the parties and discuss the choices available. The children's welfare will be at the forefront of the discussions. The mediator is an impartial third party who manages the process of exchanging information, ideas, and feelings constructively, although they have no power to impose a settlement and the responsibility of settling remains with the parties participating in the mediation.

The mediator will not advise on the best option for either party, nor is it their role to protect an individual, and the parties will probably seek independent legal advice during or after mediation.

As the parties have been completely involved in reaching agreements, it is hoped that this will make it acceptable to the parties, as an imposed order is often resented.

Once an agreement has been reached, the agreement will be recorded as a summary and this summary can be taken by the parties to their own legal advisers for advice. Any agreement reached will not be binding on the parties unless put in the form of a consent order.

A consent order is agreed by the courts and ends the parties' claims against each other. One significant advantage of mediation is that the statutory charge will not apply to property recovered or preserved (see **Chapter 2**). If the client is publicly funded, this is a major consideration. Mediation is also now a part of the procedure of court applications. Chapters concerning procedural matters will contain further details.

3.6 **MIAMS**

Practice Direction 3A Family Procedure Rules 2010 (FPR 2010) introduces a scheme of compulsory mediation for clients issuing proceedings after 6 April 2011. The rules introduce a MIAM (Mediation Information Assessment Meeting). The MIAM is a meeting between the proposed litigant(s) to find out what options exist and whether the case will be suitable for mediation. The meeting will also explain what mediation is and the potential benefits of using mediation rather than the courts. A MIAM can be attended by one party on their own or both parties can attend. Numbers attending MIAMs have fallen to levels of around 60% of pre-LASPO levels.

 Practical Considerations

In a MIAM, the mediator will explain how mediation works, and will work with the client (and possibly the other party too) to find out if mediation will be suitable. If mediation might be suitable, the mediator will discuss how much it will cost, how many sessions might be needed to resolve the dispute(s), and if public funding might be available. The mediator can also advise on other organizations or resources which may be useful to assist the parties, e.g. debt advice or counselling.

After the MIAM, the parties may choose to commence mediation. The mediator should complete Form C100 if the parties decide that mediation will not be the route they wish to take.

Attendance at a MIAM is compulsory for certain forms of cases including private children disputes and applications for a financial remedy. Paragraphs 12 and 13 PD 3A FPR 2010 list the types of proceedings where a MIAM is compulsory:

PARAGRAPH 12 PD 3A FPR 2010:

(1) (a) a child arrangements order and other orders with respect to a child or children under section 8 of the Children Act 1989;

(b) a parental responsibility order (under sections 4(1)(c), 4ZA(1)(c) or 4A(1)(b) of the Children Act 1989) or an order terminating parental responsibility (under sections 4(2A), 4ZA(5) or 4A(3) of that Act);

(c) an order appointing a child's guardian (under section 5(1) of the Children Act 1989) or an order terminating the appointment (under section 6(7) of that Act);

(d) an order giving permission to change a child's surname or remove a child from the United Kingdom (under sections 13(1) or 14C of the Children Act 1989);

(e) a special guardianship order; and

(f) an order varying or discharging such an order (under section 14D of the Children Act 1989).

(2) The circumstances referred to in sub-paragraph (1) are that the proceedings—

(a) are for a consent order;

(b) are for an order relating to a child or children in respect of whom there are ongoing emergency proceedings, care proceedings or supervision proceedings; or

(c) are for an order relating to a child or children who are the subject of an an emergency protection order, a care order or a supervision order.

PARAGRAPH 13 PD 3A FPR 2010:

(1) The proceedings for a financial remedy referred to in paragraph 11 are proceedings for the following orders, unless one of the circumstances specified in sub-paragraph (2) applies—

(a) the following financial orders—

(i) an order for maintenance pending suit;

(ii) an order for maintenance pending outcome of proceedings;

(iii) an order for periodical payments or lump sum provision as mentioned in section 21(1) of the Matrimonial Causes Act 1973, except an order under section 27(6) of that Act;

(iv) an order for periodical payments or lump sum provision as mentioned in paragraph 2(1) of Schedule 5 to the Civil Partnership Act 2004, made under Part 1 of Schedule 5 to that Act;

(v) a property adjustment order;

(vi) a variation order;

(vii) a pension sharing order; or

(viii) a pension compensation sharing order;

(b) an order for financial provision for children (under Schedule 1 to the Children Act 1989);

(c) an order for financial provision in a case of neglect to maintain (under section 27 of the Matrimonial Causes Act 1973 or under Part 9 of Schedule 5 to the Civil Partnership Act 2004);

(d) an order for alteration of a maintenance agreement (under section 35 of the Matrimonial Causes Act 1973 or under paragraph 69 of Schedule 5 to the 2004 Act);

(e) an order for financial provision for failure to maintain for parties to a marriage and children of the family (under Part 1 of the Domestic Proceedings and Magistrates' Courts Act 1978 or an order under Schedule 6 to the Civil Partnership Act 2004); and

(f) an order for special protection for respondent in certain separation cases (under section 10(2) of the Matrimonial Causes Act 1973 or under section 48(2) of the Civil Partnership Act 2004).

(2) The circumstances referred to in sub-paragraph (1) are that the proceedings—

    (a) are for a consent order; or

    (b) are for enforcement of any order made in proceedings for a financial remedy or of any agreement made in or in contemplation of proceedings for a financial remedy.

3.6.1 EXEMPTIONS TO MIAMS

Rule 3.8 FPR 2010 contains exemptions to attendance to a MIAM. The exemptions are where:

- there has been domestic violence but this must be subject to evidence (as detailed in para 20 PD 3A FPR 2010);
- there are child protection concerns;
- the application is urgent;
- there has been a prior attendance at a MIAM within the last four months;
- in financial remedy proceedings, the respondent is bankrupt;
- there is an unwillingness to attend on the part of the respondent;
- there are various difficulties in finding a suitable mediator.

These exemptions are detailed on application forms (e.g. C100) and some forms require the mediator to sign the form indicating whether the case is an exemption and also confirming attendance at a MIAM. In other cases a Form FM1 should be submitted. The various chapters on procedure will provide more details.

3.7 COLLABORATIVE LAW

3.7.1 INTRODUCTION

Collaborative law is a process in which lawyers and clients work together to resolve disputes respectfully without going to court, and hopes to provide the parties with a 'good divorce'. This may seem like an impossible ideal. But collaborative law aims to be a forum in which the legal, financial, and practical aspects of separation or divorce are addressed as well as considering the person's future relationships with children and wider family members. It allows the client to start to deal with their emotions too. Collaborative law is currently used most commonly in proceedings for financial orders (see **Chapter 14**).

 Practical Considerations

Collaborative law may be suitable if the client:

- wishes a dignified, non-aggressive resolution of the issues;
- has children and wishes to reach a resolution by agreements with their needs and interests being the foremost consideration;
- wishes to keep open, good relations with their partner in the future;
- does not wish to 'hand over' decision making to the litigation process;
- does not want to 'seek revenge'.

Clearly, not every client will be able to meet these requirements and may not wish to pursue collaborative law. Many clients simply cannot detach their emotional reaction from their divorce or separation and will not be suitable for collaborative law.

3.7.2 **WHAT IS THE DIFFERENCE BETWEEN COLLABORATIVE LAW AND MEDIATION?**

In mediation, the mediator will not give legal advice and is neutral. In the collaborative law process, lawyers are present at the meetings to advise the client and negotiate. Lawyers are not generally present at mediation.

3.7.3 **HOW DOES COLLABORATIVE LAW WORK?**

3.7.3.1 Initial meeting with the client

The first meeting aims to establish rapport and explain the process to the client and the options available to them, to identify what the client wants, their main priorities, and consider their suitability for collaborative practice. The lawyer should discuss with the client what they would like to achieve and any issues that would make them walk away from the negotiations.

The client should be screened for suitability. A client must be able to participate in good faith, have an ability to see perspectives beyond their own, have a belief in the future, and a determination to resolve issues via collaborative law, and to acknowledge the views and needs of others. Not all clients will exhibit all of these virtues but will still be able to make the collaborative process work. One of the skills of a collaborative lawyer is to listen carefully to a client to understand their fears, concerns, and ability to participate.

3.7.3.2 Agreements between client and lawyer in collaborative law

Collaborative law is different to a situation where a lawyer is acting in litigation, where the lawyer represents the client until a final written agreement is reached.

If the collaborative process ends (either by client or the other spouse ending the process) the lawyer will no longer be able to act and the client will have to get a new lawyer. The lawyer cannot guarantee that the other side will make full disclosure nor that the other side will act in good faith, but should advise the client if they have any suspicion of bad faith on the other side. Nor can a lawyer guarantee that collaborative law will definitely work!

3.7.3.3 Preparation meeting with the client

The lawyer and client will discuss goals and objectives of the client in their choice of collaborative law and lay the foundations for good faith, interest-based bargaining. There may be a number of issues to be discussed, including children or finances. The process of collaborative law should be explained and the client will try to identify any anxieties or vulnerabilities before the first meeting. The lawyer should prepare the client for the meeting ahead.

3.7.3.4 Four-way meetings

Four-way meetings occur when both clients and their lawyers meet to discuss settlement.

Before the first four-way meeting, the lawyers will meet without clients to build rapport with each other and will consider the agenda, the ground rules, and work out practicalities for the first four-way meeting.

For the first four-way meeting, both clients and their lawyers will attend. The parties will reiterate the foundation and understanding of the collaborative process especially:

- constructive and respectful approach;
- pacing and timing;
- full disclosure;
- team support.

The clients will be invited to share their objectives and ensure their voices are heard.

The parties will review and sign a four-way participation agreement.

The lawyers agree:

- not to go to court to resolve the clients' differences;
- to think creatively and constructively to find a fair solution to all issues;

- that the priority is the well-being of the children and, after that, the clients;
- to be courteous and cooperative, truthful, open, and honest;
- to jointly instruct all professionals.

The clients agree:

- not to discuss past events;
- to avoid threats and inflammatory language;
- not to denigrate or criticize the other in front of the children and not to involve the children in disputes;
- to promote and support a loving and caring and involved relationship between the children and the other parent;
- to supply promptly all documentation and disclosure required;
- only to discuss the settlement at face-to-face meetings;
- to pay their lawyer.

If the collaborative process breaks down, the clients can withdraw at any time, but a 'cooling off' period of 21 days is agreed to before court proceedings can start to allow the lawyers to attempt to rescue the negotiations. If there is an emergency or either client has broken the agreement, this will not apply.

If a court is involved in the family break-up, then the client's instruction of the lawyers will immediately lapse and the clients must place themselves on the court record. The lawyers involved in the collaborative process *will not* then be involved in the court proceedings. The clients cannot use as evidence any of the lawyer's notes to the extent that financial information is recorded, nor any evidence given by the joint expert's reports, nor refer a judge to the negotiations conducted under collaborative law.

3.7.3.5 Intermediate four-way meetings

There may be a number of four-way meetings before all issues are resolved.

Each four-way meeting will have an agenda and will discuss the parties' priorities and concerns and deal with any pressing or short-term issues. Each meeting will review progress and revise key issues.

Part of the function of these meetings will be for information-gathering and exchange and clients are encouraged to take the lead in sharing documentation.

There may be involvement from other professionals. A separation can produce a number of issues that need to be resolved. For instance, advice may be required on inheritance tax planning, financial planning, and parenting plans. Clients and lawyers may call upon a number of professionals to assist with the collaborative process, including independent financial advisers, child specialists, accountants, and pension experts. Any professional involved in the collaborative process must share a commitment to the principles of collaborative law.

The lawyers will assist the clients in brainstorming options, identifying preferred solutions, and preparing final documents.

The collaborative lawyer's role within these meetings involves:

- conflict management and resolution;
- dealing with full disclosure and organizing assets and preparing schedules of agreed assets and liabilities;
- using and instructing 'joint' experts or professionals;
- advising the client;
- keeping track of progress and moving the process forward;
- preparing court documentation to record agreement;
- planning ahead.

3.7.3.6 Final four-way meeting

Once agreement is reached, the final meeting will deal with the formalities of signing documentation and discuss how the parties will handle possible future difficulties. The lawyers will explain legal processes of divorce and consent orders (proceedings will have to be issued in order to obtain divorce and also to make a final order).

3.8 ARBITRATION

A recent development in family ADR is Arbitration. This is a form of dispute resolution. The parties enter into an agreement under which they appoint a suitably qualified person (an 'arbitrator') to adjudicate a dispute and make an award. An arbitration is more akin to court proceedings than mediation, as an arbitrator will produce a decision, an award, after hearing the evidence and each party's case. Arbitration also covers disputes concerning children.

The courts considered arbitral awards in *S v S* [2014] EWHC 7 (Fam). The judgment helpfully identifies the progression of the law in terms of agreements reached in family law proceedings. In his judgment, the President described the choice of parties to sign an arbitration agreement was a magnetic factor of determinative importance. He stated at para 21 that:

> The judge will not need to play the detective unless something leaps off the page to indicate that something has gone so seriously wrong in the arbitral process as fundamentally to vitiate the arbitral award. Although recognising that the judge is not a rubber stamp, the combination of (a) the fact that the parties have agreed to be bound by the arbitral award, (b) the fact of the arbitral award and (c) the fact that the parties are putting the matter before the court by consent, means that it can only be in the rarest of cases that it will be appropriate for the judge to do other than approve the order.

online resource centre

More information can be found on the Online Resource Centre.

SUMMARY POINTS

- There are a number of ways in which a lawyer can negotiate a settlement in family law proceedings.
- Each form of negotiation has advantages and disadvantages and these must be carefully weighed when choosing how to negotiate.
- Negotiation can take the form of client settlement, by telephone, correspondence, meetings, through counsel, and at court.
- Mediation is a form of ADR.
- A MIAM is required for some court proceedings.
- A mediator is a neutral third party who assists clients to come to a fair settlement.
- Mediation is unsuitable for some clients. Some parties may not be cooperative or there may be a power imbalance.
- Collaborative law is a process in which clients choose not to involve the court in settling family law cases.
- Collaborative law involves a negotiation in a four-way meeting with lawyers and clients present.
- Agreements between the parties and lawyers include that if collaborative law fails the lawyers will no longer be able to act for the clients.
- Arbitration is a form of ADR producing binding agreements.

SELF-TEST QUESTIONS

1. List and explain three advantages of ADR over a litigated settlement.

2. Explain the difference between mediation and collaborative law.

3. A client chooses collaborative law as a way of resolving their case. Explain to the client how the collaborative process works. If collaborative law doesn't work, can the client keep their lawyer?

online resource centre

Answers to the questions above can be found on the Online Resource Centre: **www.oxfordtextbooks.co.uk/orc/sendall17/.**

4 THE SINGLE FAMILY COURT

4.1 Introduction

4.2 An overview of the Single Family Court

4.1 INTRODUCTION

This chapter will:

• provide an overview of the Single Family Court created in April 2014.

4.2 AN OVERVIEW OF THE SINGLE FAMILY COURT

There has been a great deal of change in a relatively short period in family law. One of the changes made has been the creation of a Single Family Court (SFC), established on 22 April 2014. This was brought about by the Crime and Courts Act 2013 which inserted s31A into the Matrimonial and Family Proceedings Act 1984. In particular, the Family Proceedings Court (this described the magistrates' court when hearing family matters) has disappeared.

The effect of the SFC will be that an application can be made to any court (magistrates' or county court) and the days of working out which court to apply to are over. The Family Court is a national court which sits in a wide range of geographical locations in magistrates' and county courts and the Principal Registry of the Family Court is now the Central Family Court. There will be a degree of geographical centralization as designated family judges will preside over a cluster of courts and provide leadership to judges of all levels in that area.

The Judiciary of the SFC will include High Court judges, Circuit judges, Recorders, District Judges of the county and magistrates' court, magistrates, and legal advisers. There is a unified system of administration and a single point of entry into the SFC.

The allocation of cases within the SFC is done by 'gatekeepers' and the rules for this are found in the Family Court (Composition and Distribution of Business) Rules 2014, which has a Schedule. This Schedule has a very useful table which shows the level of judge the case is to be allocated and which judges have the jurisdiction to make orders in certain proceedings. The High Court still has exclusive jurisdiction in cases involving the inherent jurisdiction and international proceedings in child abduction.

There is a blizzard of procedural and legislative changes which have occurred in 2014. One of the early changes made is to centralize the administration of divorce petitions to a single centre in each circuit. More details on this are available in **Chapter 9**.

SUMMARY POINTS

• There is now one Single Family Court.

• There will be one point of entry in family law cases.

• Cases are allocated by gatekeepers.

Part 2

RELATIONSHIP BREAKDOWN

5 SEPARATION AND NULLITY

5.1 INTRODUCTION

In Part 2 of this text we will be considering the law and procedure following the breakdown of a relationship. We will consider divorce and civil partnerships, as all are likely to form part of a solicitor's caseload. The financial consequences of relationship breakdown for spouses and civil partners are considered in Part 3. This chapter focuses on alternatives to divorce, whilst subsequent chapters will cover divorce, defences to divorce, jurisdiction, and divorce procedure fully. Part 4 will consider cohabitants.

This chapter will:

- discuss the remedy of separation as an alternative to divorce proceedings;
- discuss nullity as a remedy including void and voidable marriages and civil partnerships;
- discuss nullity as a remedy for those escaping a forced marriage.

The number of marriages that end in separation or nullity is relatively small. In 2011 (the last set of statistics to be published), there were just over 277 applications for separation. The term 'separation' here includes judicial separation for marriages and separation orders for civil partners. Most clients will seek divorce at the end of the marriage rather than the expensive step of judicial separation that does not dissolve the marriage. Nullity is an unusual remedy in modern family law practice but remains important to a small number of clients. In 2011, there were 112 applications for nullity. Nullity remains a relevant remedy for clients escaping a forced marriage or for those whose religious views preclude or discourage divorce.

5.2 SEPARATION

As stated earlier, the term 'separation' includes judicial separation for divorce and separation orders for civil partnerships. For marriages, the principal statute concerned with judicial separation is the Matrimonial Causes Act 1973 (MCA 1973). For civil partners, the principal statute is the Civil Partnership Act 2004 (CPA 2004).

For separation, the petition is based upon one of the facts listed at s1(2) MCA 1973 or s44 CPA 2004 (see **Chapter 6**), but the court does not enquire whether the marriage has irretrievably broken down (s17(2) MCA 1973 and s55 CPA 2004). The marriage is not dissolved by a judicial separation, but the parties do not have to live with one another and the parties can apply to the court to resolve disputes about finances (see **Chapter 11** onwards).

The family lawyer will see few applications for judicial separation and so the procedural aspects of the application are not detailed here. Most clients seeking a judicial separation do so for religious or ethical reasons.

5.2.1 CIVIL PARTNERSHIP

A court can make a separation order under s56 CPA 2004 based on the facts of s44(5) CPA 2004. As with judicial separation in marriage, there is no requirement to prove that the civil partnership has broken down irretrievably.

5.3 NULLITY

A petition for nullity is based on there being a problem with marriage or civil partnership formalities or capacity. The marriage or civil partnership will be treated as if it never existed. A void marriage or civil partnership (see **5.4**) has never existed, whereas a voidable marriage or civil partnership (see **5.5**) will be treated as being in existence until it is annulled.

The effect of a decree of nullity for void marriages or civil partnerships will mean that although the marriage has never existed, financial, pension, and property orders are available under MCA 1973 or CPA 2004, children will be legitimate, and parties can still claim under the Inheritance (Provision for Family and Dependants) Act 1975. A voidable marriage or civil partnership will be held to exist until the date of the decree of nullity and parties can claim as above.

5.4 VOID MARRIAGES

Section 11 MCA 1973 lists the grounds for finding a marriage to be void, namely:

(a) that it is not a valid marriage under the provisions of the Marriage Acts 1949 to 1986 (that is to say where—

  (i) the parties are within the prohibited degree of relationship;

  (ii) either party is under the age of sixteen; or

  (iii) the parties have intermarried in disregard of certain requirements as to the formation of marriage);

(b) that at the time of the marriage either party was already lawfully married or a civil partner;

(c) repealed;

(d) in the case of a polygamous marriage entered into outside England and Wales, that either party was at the time of the marriage domiciled in England and Wales.

Section 49 CPA 2004 gives the grounds for a civil partnership to be void:

Where two people register as civil partners of each other in England and Wales, the civil partnership is void if—

(a) at the time when they do so, they are not eligible to register as civil partners of each other under Chapter 1 (see section 3 as parties are ineligible to register if they are not of the same sex, either of them is already in a civil partnership or marriage, either of them is under the age of 16 or they are within the prohibited degrees of relationship),

(b) at the time when they do so they both know—

  (i) that due notice of proposed civil partnership has not been given,

  (ii) that the civil partnership document has not been duly issued,

  (iii) that the civil partnership document is void under section 17(3) or 27(2) (registration after end of time allowed for registering),

(iv) that the place of registration is a place other than that specified in the notices (or notice) of proposed civil partnership and the civil partnership document,

(v) that a civil partnership registrar is not present, or

(vi) that the place of registration is on premises that are not approved premises although the registration is purportedly in accordance with section 6(3A)(a), or

(c) the civil partnership document is void under paragraph 6(5) of Schedule 2 (civil partnership between a child and another person is forbidden).

5.4.1 PROHIBITED DEGREES OF RELATIONSHIP

The Marriage (Prohibited Degrees of Relationship) Act 1986 lists family relationships that are too close for marriage, e.g. mother and son. The prohibited degrees are consanguinity (e.g. mother/son, father/daughter, sister/brother, aunt/nephew etc.) and affinity. There are two classes of affinity. The first class prevents stepfather/stepdaughter, stepmother/stepson and stepgrandparent/stepgrandchild from marrying unless both parties are over 21 and the child was not at any time a child of the family in relation to the other whilst under 18 years.

The second class of affinity was changed on 1 March 2007 by the Marriage Act 1949 (Remedial) Order 2007 following a judgment in the European Court of Human Rights (ECtHR). Formerly, a person could not marry his child's former spouse or his parent's former spouse unless certain conditions were met. This was held to be incompatible with Art. 12 of the European Convention on Human Rights (ECHR).

Consanguinity prohibitions arose from genetic consideration to prevent marriage between people related by blood where the shared proportion of genes is one-quarter or more. The rules on affinity are based on social policy considerations. Prohibited degrees of relationship for civil partnerships can be found in Sch 1 CPA 2004 and are divided into absolute and qualified provisions. The ideas and prohibitions are along very similar lines to those for marriage with the same logic behind the provisions.

5.4.2 AGE

Both parties to the marriage or civil partnership must be aged over 16 at the time of the ceremony.

5.4.3 ALREADY MARRIED OR IN A CIVIL PARTNERSHIP

Parties must not be already married or in a civil partnership when they marry or enter a civil partnership. A criminal charge of bigamy may ensue. Clients must be advised firmly that they must have a decree absolute or dissolution order (see **Chapter 9**) before they are free to marry or enter a new civil partnership.

5.4.4 POLYGAMOUS MARRIAGE

A marriage in which one party is domiciled (see **Chapter 8**) in England and Wales must not be polygamous. No such provision exists for civil partners.

5.5 VOIDABLE MARRIAGES OR CIVIL PARTNERSHIPS

Section 12 MCA 1973 lists the grounds for finding a marriage voidable:

(1)

(a) that the marriage has not been consummated owing to the incapacity of either party to consummate it;

(b) that the marriage has not been consummated owing to the wilful refusal of the respondent to consummate it;

(c) that either party to the marriage did not validly consent to it, whether in consequence of duress, mistake, unsoundness of mind, or otherwise;

(d) that at the time of the marriage either party, though capable of giving a valid consent, was suffering (whether continuously or intermittently) from mental disorder within the meaning of the Mental Health Act 1983 of such a kind or to such an extent to be unfitted for marriage;

(e) that at the time of the marriage the respondent was suffering from venereal disease in a communicable form;

(f) that at the time of the marriage the respondent was pregnant by some person other than the petitioner;

(g) that an interim gender recognition certificate under the Gender Recognition Act 2004 has, after the time of the marriage, been issued to either party to the marriage;

(h) that the respondent is a person whose gender at the time of the marriage had become the acquired gender under the Gender Recognition Act 2004.

(2) Paragraphs (a) and (b) of subsection (1) do not apply to the marriage of a same-sex couple.

As mentioned earlier, nullity is not a common remedy. As such, some limited comments on some of the grounds are included below.

The grounds for a voidable civil partnership in s50 CPA 2004 are as follows:

Where two people register as civil partners of each other in England and Wales, the civil partnership is voidable if:

(a) either of them did not validly consent to its formation (whether as a result of duress, mistake, unsoundness of mind or otherwise);

(b) at the time of its formation either of them, though capable of giving a valid consent, was suffering (whether continuously or intermittently) from mental disorder of such a kind or to such an extent as to be unfitted for civil partnership;

(c) at the time of its formation, the respondent was pregnant by some person other than the applicant;

(d) an interim gender recognition certificate under the Gender Recognition Act 2004 (c. 7) has, after the time of its formation, been issued to either civil partner;

(e) the respondent is a person whose gender at the time of its formation had become the acquired gender under the 2004 Act.

5.5.1 NON-CONSUMMATION OF A MARRIAGE

Consummation takes place as soon as the parties have sexual intercourse after the marriage has been solemnized. For a marriage to be voidable, the failure to consummate must result from incapacity of either party or the wilful refusal of the respondent. This does not apply to civil partnerships or same-sex marriages.

5.5.2 INCAPACITY

Incapacity can be based on a physical abnormality or psychological causes. An 'invincible repugnance' may suffice (*G v G* [1924] AC 348, HL) but a rational decision not to permit intercourse will not (*Singh v Singh* [1971] P 226). The incapacity must be permanent and incurable and the petitioner must prove that the incapacity exists.

5.5.3 WILFUL REFUSAL

Wilful refusal must be a settled and definite decision come to without just excuse (*Horton v Horton* [1947] 2 All ER 871). The court will look at the history of the marriage and a petition will fail if the respondent can show a just cause or reason for his/her behaviour, e.g. in

Jodla v Jodla [1960] 1 WLR 236 where the parties had married on the understanding that they would not live together until a religious ceremony was complete. One party's refusal to go through with or organize the second ceremony would amount to a wilful refusal.

5.5.4 LACK OF CONSENT

A lack of consent can result from duress, mistake, or as a result of being of unsound mind. Duress has been refined by the courts through a series of decisions that have not always been entirely consistent. There must be fear sufficient to vitiate consent (*Singh v Singh* [1971] P 226) and this fear must be sufficiently grave. In *Szechter v Szechter* [1971] P 286 this was defined as a 'threat of immediate danger' and in *Hirani v Hirani* [1982] 4 FLR 232, CA as undue pressure overbearing the will.

5.6 FORCED MARRIAGES

In 2013, the Forced Marriage Unit at the Foreign Office advised in 1,302 cases of forced marriage, although research suggests the actual number of such cases may be higher. In these circumstances, divorce can be upsetting as it carries cultural stigma and is distressing for the survivor as it indicates that the marriage was in existence. Nullity is therefore a very useful alternative to those forced into marriage.

The cases of *P v R (Forced Marriage: Annulment: Procedure)* [2003] 1 FLR 661 and *NS v MI* [2007] 1 FLR 444 established that nullity can be used with the ground being lack of consent due to duress.

In *P v R*, the petitioner was a 21-year-old woman who was persuaded to attend her sister's funeral in Pakistan. The petitioner did not live at home and was in a relationship with a man of whom her parents did not approve. At the end of mourning, the petitioner was informed that marriage arrangements had been made for her. The petitioner's movements were restricted and she was followed and threatened with violence. On the day of the wedding, she was forced to put on a wedding dress; her mother held the back of her head and by pushing it made her nod to indicate consent to marriage.

Coleridge J held that the petitioner had not validly consented to the marriage and her 'consent' had been vitiated by force, both because of the threats of violence and emotional pressures brought to bear in Pakistan.

Forced marriage is further considered in **Chapter 33**.

5.7 BARS TO PETITION

Section 13 MCA 1973 and s51 CPA 2004 set out some bars to petitions based on voidable marriages and civil partnerships, although the provisions do differ in their terms. These include approbation, where a petitioner behaved in a way that indicated acceptance of the marriage or civil partnership. A decree cannot be granted on the grounds of lack of consent, mental unfitness, venereal disease, pregnancy by another, or acquired gender if three years have passed from the date of the marriage. Having knowledge of the respondent's venereal disease, pregnancy by another, or acquired gender will bar a petition on these grounds. For civil partnerships, the three-year bar applies to the grounds for nullity under the CPA 2004 in a similar manner to marriage.

5.8 NULLITY AND CIVIL PARTNERSHIPS

A civil partnership may be void or voidable. Section 37 CPA 2004 allows the court the power to issue a nullity order, annulling the civil partnership.

Section 49 CPA 2004 gives the grounds for a void civil partnership and mainly concerns the formalities of the civil partnership itself:

(a) the parties are ineligible to register as civil partners;

(b) the correct formalities had not been followed (e.g. lack of notice, invalid civil partnership document, registrar not present).

A civil partnership may be voidable under s50 CPA 2004 and the grounds for this are similar to those of marriage but not identical. The grounds include:

(a) lack of valid consent;

(b) either party suffers from a mental disorder of a kind or to such an extent to be unfit for civil partnership;

(c) at the time of the marriage the respondent was pregnant by some person other than the applicant.

There are bars to relief under s51 CPA 2004 that are the same as found in MCA 1973.

SUMMARY POINTS

- Separation is based on the same facts as divorce and civil partnership dissolution but the marriage or civil partnership is not dissolved.

- Nullity covers void and voidable marriages and civil partnerships.

- A void marriage/civil partnership is a marriage/civil partnership that has never validly existed due to a fault.

- A marriage/civil partnership can be void due to marriage within prohibited decrees of relationship, parties being under 16, certain defects within the formalities of marriage, and that the parties are not respectively male and female.

- A voidable marriage exists until a decree is granted.

- A marriage can be voidable due to non-consummation, lack of consent, mental disorder, venereal disease, pregnancy by another, or an acquired gender.

- Nullity is an alternative to divorce in cases of forced marriages.

- There are bars to petitions based on voidable marriages.

- Following a decree of nullity, orders can be obtained for property, pensions, and to declare children are legitimate.

SELF-TEST QUESTIONS

1. Explain the difference between void and voidable marriages.

2. A client was put under pressure by her family to enter into a marriage. She tells you that she was locked in her bedroom and threatened with violence if she did not go through with the ceremony. Finally, your client's family told her that if she did not go through with the marriage, she would be ostracized from the family. Advise your client.

online
resource
centre

Answers to the questions above can be found on the Online Resource Centre: **www.oxfordtextbooks.co.uk/orc/sendall17/.**

6 DIVORCE

6.1 INTRODUCTION

This chapter will:

- discuss the ground for divorce under the Matrimonial Causes Act 1973 (MCA 1973);
- explore each of the five possible facts which prove the ground for divorce;
- discuss the relevance of continued cohabitation between the parties.

Divorce is synonymous with family law. Whilst not every client is married, divorce will form a major part of a family lawyer's caseload. Many clients may make contact with a family lawyer to discuss divorce, but (as in **Chapter 3**) it is not the only option for a failing marriage. It is important to remember that the parties may wish to consider relationship counselling to preserve their marriage. As a result of changes to public funding, many clients cannot access public funding for their divorce.

In England and Wales, divorce is partly based upon fault; while the sole ground for divorce is irretrievable breakdown of the marriage, one party must blame the other for the failure of the marriage unless the parties wish to wait for two or five years. A bill trying to introduce no fault divorce has been introduced into Parliament by Richard Bacon MP but has already suffered postponement and it is unclear how much support there is from the current Government.

In 2014, the right to marry was extended to same-sex couples. This chapter discusses divorce for both heterosexual and same-sex couples. There are a few differences in law but not many. The law of civil partnership is discussed separately in **Chapter 10**. In this chapter, the parties will be referred to as 's/he'. No disrespect is intended to anyone but this text makes no assumptions about the parties to a marriage.

Most divorces are not defended, and this chapter will deal only with the law and procedure for undefended divorces. For those cases with a defended divorce, please refer to specialist family law practitioner texts. This chapter will cover the ground and facts of divorce.

FIGURE 6.1 AVAILABLILITY OF DIVORCE

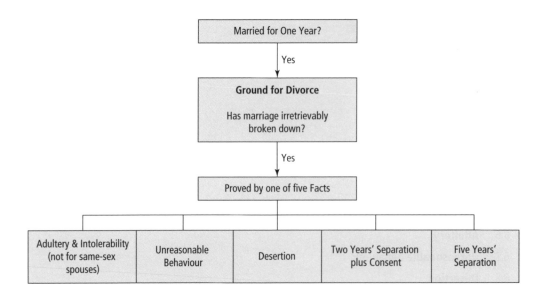

6.2 **DIVORCE AND THE MATRIMONIAL CAUSES ACT 1973**

The statute covering divorce proceedings is the Matrimonial Causes Act 1973 (MCA 1973) and has been amended by the Marriage (Same Sex Couples) Act 2013 (MSSCA 2013). This describes the only ground for divorce and the five facts that prove the ground. The procedure for obtaining a divorce is found in the Family Procedure Rules 2010.

Figure 6.1 is a diagram showing the steps in considering the availability of divorce. Each element is covered within the chapter.

6.3 **FIRST-YEAR BAR**

Section 3 MCA 1973 places a bar on divorce within the first year of marriage. Section 3(1) MCA 1973 states:

> No petition for divorce shall be presented to the court before the expiration of the period of one year from the date of marriage.

Readers may not think that this is a controversial or common point raised in practice; in fact, many newly married people consult a solicitor within the first year of marriage and are often surprised at being told of this rule.

 Practical Considerations

There are other options for a client within the first year of marriage:

- judicial separation (see **Chapter 5**): this does not dissolve the marriage but it does allow the courts to resolve issues of money and property;
- nullity: this applies only if the marriage is void or voidable (see **Chapter 5**) due to some fault with the parties' capacity or the formalities of marriage;
- Child Support Agency/child maintenance options (see **Chapter 18**) for maintenance for children;
- Children Act 1989 can be used to resolve disputes about children (see **Chapters 24–26**). This includes where a child lives or whom they have contact with, and issues involved in raising a child, e.g. the change of a child's name and also orders concerning money and property for the benefit of the child;

- Domestic Proceedings and Magistrates' Courts Act 1978 for maintenance payments or lump sum payments between spouses or for the benefit of a child during the marriage;
- Family Law Act 1996 provides orders for personal protection and occupation of the family home in respect of domestic abuse (see **Chapters 33–36**).

The parties can enter into mediation, negotiation, or another form of alternative dispute resolution (see **Chapter 3**). This may lead to an agreement concerning finances or children (or both) before the petition is issued. This is clearly a cheaper option which is often less fraught than legal proceedings.

The client will simply have to wait if they wish to divorce but it does not prevent the clients entering into negotiation on all issues (see **Chapter 3**). Section 3(2) MCA 1973 also states that this bar does not prevent the client relying on issues that occurred during the first year of marriage when a petition is presented.

6.4 **GROUND FOR DIVORCE**

Section 1(1) MCA 1973 states that '… a petition for divorce may be presented to the court by either party to a marriage on the ground that the marriage has broken down irretrievably'.

 Practical Considerations

Clients (and some lawyers!) are often confused by the terminology of divorce.

Clients commonly refer to a divorce on the grounds of adultery. There is only one ground for divorce—irretrievable breakdown proved by one of the five facts. Without wishing to be terrifyingly pedantic about such matters, the proper way of expressing this would be to say:

I am divorcing on the ground of irretrievable breakdown, evidenced by the fact of adultery.

However, very few clients ever will!

The court must be satisfied that the marriage has irretrievably broken down. This is evidenced by proving one or more of the five facts.

6.5 **THE FIVE FACTS**

In order to satisfy the ground of irretrievable breakdown, the petitioner must satisfy the court under s1(2) MCA 1973 of one or more of the following facts:

(a) the respondent has committed adultery and the petitioner finds it intolerable to live with the respondent;

(b) the respondent has behaved in such a way that the petitioner cannot reasonably be expected to live with the respondent;

(c) the respondent has deserted the petitioner for a continuous period of at least two years immediately preceding the presentation of the petition;

(d) the parties to the marriage have lived apart for a continuous period of at least two years immediately preceding the presentation of the petition and the respondent consents to the decree being granted;

(e) the parties to the marriage have lived apart for a continuous period of at least five years immediately preceding the presentation of the petition.

Each fact must be proved on the balance of probabilities and each fact has different considerations, which will be discussed individually.

6.6 ADULTERY

There are two limbs to the fact of adultery:

- adultery has been committed;
- the petitioner finds it intolerable to live with the respondent.

While adultery is available as a fact for same-sex spouses, it is defined as follows: 'Only conduct between the respondent and a person of the opposite sex may constitute adultery' (s1(6) MCA 1973). Sexual conduct with a person of the same sex is not, therefore adultery.

6.6.1 WHAT IS ADULTERY?

Adultery is defined as voluntary sexual intercourse between a man and a woman who are not married to each other but one of whom is a married person (*Clarkson v Clarkson* [1930] 143 LT 775).

Adultery must be proved by the petitioner. There is no requirement for lurid photographs or witness statements about adultery and proof is normally based on indirect evidence.

The respondent may admit the adultery. This can be done on the acknowledgement of service (see **Chapter 9**) used in adultery cases that asks the question 'Do you admit the adultery alleged in the petition?' Alternatively, the respondent may sign a statement admitting the adultery or write or sign a confession statement of their own.

 Practical Considerations

It is sensible to obtain a written statement admitting the adultery before the petition is issued as this will cover the event of the respondent failing to admit the adultery in the acknowledgement. The petitioner may be able to claim their costs of issuing the petition in reliance on that confession. Proof can also come from the respondent's solicitor, e.g. an admission in previous correspondence.

If there is no admission, then indirect evidence will have to be presented to the court and adultery will be inferred:

- the respondent and another man/woman are living together. The evidence of adultery would be from the petitioner's own observations or from neighbours or friends of the couple, although the court may prefer stronger evidence. In practice it may be easier to proceed under the fact of unreasonable behaviour;
- where the respondent contracts a venereal disease from a person other than the petitioner;
- inclination and opportunity to commit adultery. This means that the respondent and the other party had the opportunity to commit adultery, e.g. they have been seen in public kissing, holding hands, or behaving as an intimate couple, emails, texts, or letters between the couple have been found, and they have spent the night together in a hotel or alone in a house, although the court may prefer stronger evidence. In practice it may be easier to proceed under the fact of unreasonable behaviour;

- the woman has given birth to a child that is not her husband's. Usually, children born during a marriage are presumed to be legitimate, but there may be circumstances which give rise to suspicions, e.g. a husband absent around the time of conception (see *Preston-Jones v Preston-Jones* [1951] AC 891);
- findings in other proceedings, e.g. a Child Support Agency maintenance assessment.

This would be unusual as most practitioners would not issue without an admission. For the courts, Litigants in Person (LiP) often do not understand the necessity to prove this to the civil standard of proof. Please note that a person cannot rely on their own adultery for this fact.

6.6.2 INTOLERABILITY

Normally, a petitioner will simply state in the petition that they find it intolerable to live with the respondent and the court will accept this as sufficient evidence of intolerability. The test is subjective: does this petitioner find it intolerable to live with this respondent? There does not have to be a link between the adultery and intolerability (*Cleary v Cleary* [1974] 1 All ER 498).

6.6.3 THE CO-RESPONDENT

The person with whom the respondent commits adultery can be named in the petition as a co-respondent and made a party to the suit (r7.10 FPR 2010). However, in practice this can complicate matters both procedurally, as the petition has to be served on the third party, but it can also raise the 'temperature' of the dispute.

Clients are discouraged from naming co-respondents and should be advised that there is no need to do so in law (see PD 7 FPR 2010).

6.7 UNREASONABLE BEHAVIOUR

'Unreasonable behaviour' is the shorthand term used to describe the fact that the respondent has behaved in such a way that the petitioner cannot reasonably be expected to live with the respondent: s1(2)(b) MCA 1973. It is important to realize, however, that it is not the behaviour itself which must be established to be unreasonable, it is the expectation that the petitioner continue to live with the respondent.

6.7.1 WHAT IS BEHAVIOUR THAT ONE CANNOT REASONABLY BE EXPECTED TO LIVE WITH?

It is important to realize that there are no set precedents or list of 'usual' issues found in an unreasonable behaviour petition. Each marriage is different and so the behaviour cited in support of this fact will be different. If a client is disenchanted or bored with their marriage, this may not be sufficient to succeed on this fact. Many clients will instruct you that they simply do not love their spouse and this, again, will not be sufficient to base a petition on this fact. The court will use both a subjective and objective test—would any right-thinking person conclude that *this petitioner* cannot reasonably be expected to live with *this respondent,* taking into account all the circumstances of the case and the characters and personalities of the parties?

The court will look at both parties' behaviour and will expect some disparity in conduct and what sort of people the parties are. The whole history of the marriage will be considered. Once all of this evidence has been considered, the court will objectively consider whether it is reasonable for the petitioner to continue to live with the respondent.

Dunn J in *Livingstone-Stallard v Livingstone-Stallard* [1974] Fam 47 asked:

> Would any right-thinking person come to the conclusion that this husband has behaved in such a way that this wife cannot be reasonably expected to live with him, taking into account the whole of the circumstances and the character and personalities of the parties?

Practical Considerations

There is no list of behaviour to include in divorce petitions and there can be one or two very serious incidents, or more examples of continuing behaviour. From the author's practice, the following are common examples:

• domestic abuse;

• unreasonable sexual demands;

• 'improper' association with another person, e.g. spending hours in an internet chatroom and exchanging inappropriate messages with another person or people;

• debt/financial recklessness;

• verbal abuse, shouting, belittling;

• social isolation;

• excessive/lack of socializing;

• excessive/lack of sex;

• drunkenness.

The court will look at the marriage as a whole to see if there is sufficient 'unreasonable behaviour' to grant a divorce. The petitioner's own behaviour will be examined as well as what sort of people the parties are and whether one party is unusually sensitive or vulnerable and the history of the marriage. The court then decides if it is reasonable for the petitioner to go on living with the respondent.

For example in *Livingstone-Stallard*, the wife complained that the husband constantly criticized her dress, friends, cooking, and many other petty aspects of her life and she left after he had thrown her out of the house and locked the door. The evening was very cold and the husband threw cold water over the wife. The wife suffered bruising and required medication for nervous shock. The petition succeeded.

6.7.2 WHETHER BEHAVIOUR IS INTENTIONAL

If the respondent's behaviour is as a result of mental illness, the petitioner may still obtain a divorce. The mental illness will be a factor taken into account as part of the consideration of the facts of the case: *Katz v Katz* [1972] 3 All ER 219. In *Katz*, after 13 years of marriage, the husband began to display signs of mental illness and was admitted to a mental hospital. The husband blamed the wife for sending him there and drove her to attempt suicide. When the husband received the divorce petition he read it to the children and treated it as a joke. The court granted a divorce to the wife as the husband's behaviour (for whatever reason) was such that the wife could not reasonably be expected to live with him.

In *Thurlow v Thurlow* [1976] Fam 32, as a result of severe epilepsy, the wife became progressively less able to function and threw things at her mother-in-law, burnt possessions on an electric heater, and wandered into the street. The husband was granted a decree and the court found that full account should be taken of all the obligations of marriage, including the normal burdens imposed by the wife's illness. However, the court considered the length of time the husband had to bear the stresses of the wife's illness, the effect on his health, and the husband's capacity to bear the stresses involved and decided whether he could fairly be required to live with the wife.

6.8 DESERTION

This fact is rarely used in practice. The fact of two years' separation and consent (s1(2)(d) MCA 1973) is more straightforward as, if the respondent has deserted the petitioner, it is likely that s/he is sufficiently disenchanted with the marriage to consent to a divorce. The facts discussed later (see **6.9**) allowing divorce following separation are easier to establish.

For the fact of desertion under s1(2)(c) MCA 1973, the respondent must have deserted the petitioner for a continuous period of at least two years before the presentation of the petition.

There are a number of elements to be proved:

6.8.1 SEPARATION

This can arise because of one spouse leaving the family home but there can be a separation even if the parties still remain under the same roof (see **6.11**).

6.8.2 INTENTION TO DESERT

Even if separation is established, the deserting party must intend to remain permanently separated. This intention can be inferred from words and actions and must be communicated to the other party (*Beeken v Beeken* [1948] P 302).

6.8.3 ABSENCE OF CONSENT

The petitioner cannot consent to the desertion and this precludes any kind of formal and informal agreement. A separation agreement will be evidence of consent (*Crabtree v Crabtree* [1953] 1 WLR 708) but a maintenance agreement will not (*Holroyd v Holroyd* [1920] 36 TLR 479).

6.8.4 ABSENCE OF GOOD CAUSE

If the petitioner behaves in such a way that the respondent would be justified in leaving them or s/he may have a reasonable belief that s/he is justified in leaving her, there will be no desertion.

The wear and tear of ordinary family life will not suffice but an example of such justification can be found in *Quoraishi v Quoraishi* [1985] FLR 780 where a husband took a second wife, even though he was legally entitled to do so.

The desertion must be for a continuous period of two years. Attempts at reconciliation may interrupt this. This is further discussed at **6.12**.

6.9 TWO YEARS' SEPARATION AND CONSENT

To rely on this fact, two matters must be proved:

- the petitioner and respondent have lived apart for a continuous period of at least two years immediately preceding the presentation of the petition; and
- the respondent consents to the petition being granted.

Consent must be given by the respondent and this consent must be proved by the petitioner. Generally this consent is proved by the respondent signing the acknowledgement of service in divorce proceedings (see **Chapter 9**) and s2(7) MCA 1973 requires that the respondent is given such information as is necessary for him to understand the consequences of consenting to a decree being granted and the steps s/he must take to indicate that he consents. Consent can be withdrawn any time up to the granting of a decree nisi and a respondent may withdraw his/her consent if s/he has been misled by the petitioner (see **Chapter 9**). Consent can be conditional, e.g. on the petitioner paying the costs of the divorce. Should s1(2)(d) MCA 1973 be the only fact relied upon, the divorce will have to be stayed (r7.12 FPR 2010).

The parties must have lived apart for a continuous period of two years. See **6.11** and **6.12** for a discussion of 'living apart' and 'continuous separation'.

6.10 FIVE YEARS' SEPARATION

The only requirement for this fact is that the parties have lived apart for five years. No consent is required from the respondent. There is a defence to divorce based on this fact and this is discussed in **Chapter 7**.

6.11 LIVING APART AND SEPARATE HOUSEHOLDS

Living apart has a physical and mental aspect and is often far from clear. Section 2(6) MCA 1973 states that spouses shall be treated as living apart unless they are living with each other in the *same household*.

There will be few problems when the parties live in different houses but problems can arise (as with desertion) when the parties remain under the same roof. The Online Resource Centre contains articles about the difficulties people face when separating parties cannot afford to run two households. There may also be a dispute about the occupation of the family home and this may fail to be resolved by negotiation or by the provisions of the Family Law Act 1996.

In order to prove that there is a separate household, the parties must show they live completely separate lives. In *Mouncer v Mouncer* [1972] 1 All ER 289 the parties failed to show a separate household as the parties still ate together and the wife continued to do housework for both despite the fact that the parties maintained separate bedrooms.

The parties must also demonstrate a mental separation and if the parties have a reason for living apart, e.g. working away or looking after a relative, they will not be living apart. One party must decide the marriage is over, e.g. they write a letter telling their spouse not to come home (*Santos v Santos* [1972] 2 All ER 246).

6.12 EFFECT OF CONTINUED COHABITATION

It is hoped that parties will try to reconcile and to save their marriages and relationships. The MCA 1973 does allow parties to do this and s2 MCA 1973 contains provision to assist the parties.

6.12.1 ADULTERY

Section 2(1) MCA 1973 allows a petitioner to live with the respondent for six months following the discovery of the adultery. If the parties continue to cohabit for more than six months, there will be an absolute bar to the petition based on the fact of adultery. Section 2(2) MCA 1973 allows the first six months of cohabitation following the discovery of adultery to be disregarded when determining if the petitioner finds it intolerable to live with the respondent.

 Example

Jill is married to Eddie. The marriage has been under strain for a few years. When Jill starts a new job in January 2015, she meets Peter and starts a sexual relationship with him. Eddie finds out about the adultery on 1 March 2016. He and Jill agree to give the marriage another try and they start seeing a relationship counsellor. On 31 December 2016, Eddie decides the marriage is over.

Eddie cannot rely on Jill's adultery as they have cohabited for over six months since he discovered the adultery in March 2016. He will have to rely on a different fact.

6.12.2 UNREASONABLE BEHAVIOUR

Section 2(3) MCA 1973 allows parties to cohabit for six months from the final incident relied upon and for this to be disregarded when considering whether the petitioner can reasonably be expected to live with the respondent. If the behaviour is ongoing, there is no 'final' incident and so time will not have started to run. This provision facilitates reconciliation. The MCA 1973 gives no guidance to the courts about the approach to be taken if the cohabitation continues for more than six months after the final incident or if the behaviour and cohabitation continue for some time. The court must then consider whether the continuing cohabitation means that it is not unreasonable to expect the petitioner to continue to live with the respondent. There is no absolute bar if the parties cohabit beyond six months, but there should be good reasons why the parties continue to cohabit. An example of good reasons for a person not to move out from their partner can be found in *Bradley v Bradley* [1973] 3 All ER 750: Mrs Bradley had a number of small children, no financial resources of her own, and feared domestic violence if she moved out. The court accepted that these were good reasons and granted a divorce.

 Example

Brenda is married to Fred and they have seven children. Fred often behaves violently to Brenda, constantly criticizes her appearance, cooking, and childcare, and belittles her in front of her friends. Fred leaves Brenda short of money and takes absolutely no notice of the children. Brenda issues a divorce petition based on the unreasonable behaviour fact and lists the behaviour that has occurred during 2015. As Brenda has no money of her own and nowhere else to take the children, Brenda continues to live with Fred until shortly before the decree nisi. Even though Brenda has cohabited with Fred for more than six months since the last specific incidents in 2015, this will be disregarded as the behaviour was continuing up to the date when she left and so time did not start to run.

6.12.3 CONTINUOUS SEPARATION

Section 2(5) MCA 1973 states that the court must disregard any period or periods not exceeding six months during which the parties resumed living together but no period during which the parties lived together shall count as part of the period of desertion or the period for which the parties to the marriage lived apart.

This has two practical effects. Any period of reconciliation exceeding six months will mean that the parties wishing to rely on the separation grounds will have to start the period of separation again. And if the parties attempt reconciliation, any period of resumed cohabitation will have to be added on to the period of living apart.

 Example

Sherie and Ali have been married for eight years. After a sustained period of unhappiness, they separate and Ali moves into his own flat. After six months apart, Sherie asks Ali to move back into the house to attempt reconciliation. Things go well for a couple of weeks, but after a month, Ali moves out as the marriage is clearly over.

Sherie and Ali wish to petition for divorce on the basis of two years' separation and consent. When will they be able to issue the petition?

The parties will have to be living apart for two years. As they lived together during the period of separation for one month, this will have to be added on to the two years.

Sherie and Ali will have to live apart for two years plus one month before a petition can be issued.

SUMMARY POINTS

- The principal statute involved with divorce is the Matrimonial Causes Act 1973.

- A divorce petition is issued by a petitioner and the person receiving the petition is the respondent.

- A divorce petition cannot be issued within the first year of marriage.

- The sole ground for divorce is the irretrievable breakdown of marriage.

- To prove the ground for divorce, a petitioner must prove one of five facts:

  – adultery and intolerability (not available for same-sex couples);

  – unreasonable behaviour;

  – desertion;

  – two years' separation and consent;

  – five years' separation.

- Parties 'living apart' must live separately in terms of both a physical and mental separation.

- Parties may live together to attempt a reconciliation but any period of resumed cohabitation may affect the petition.

- A period of six months of resumed cohabitation after discovery of adultery can be a bar to proceedings.

- In a petition based upon the respondent's unreasonable behaviour, resumed cohabitation will be taken into account when considering whether or not the parties can reasonably be expected to remain together.

- In separation grounds, any period of cohabitation during the period of separation under six months will be added on to the time the couple have to spend apart. Any period of cohabitation over six months will result in the period of separation starting again.

SELF-TEST QUESTIONS

1. What is the ground for divorce? How is this ground proved?

2. If a client is within the first year of their marriage, advise them on their alternatives to issuing divorce proceedings.

3. Which facts require no period of separation?

4. Sunita and Ash marry in 2008. Their marriage was happy at first but the couple separated recently when Ash admitted to an affair with a work colleague. After three months apart, the couple decide to attempt reconciliation. After two weeks of living together, Sunita decides that the marriage is at an end and she moves out. Advise Sunita which fact she should rely upon and the effect of their attempted reconciliation.

Case Study Two

You are a family law solicitor in Hepple, Burrell & Young's family law department. Today's date is 3 January 2016.

You have a new client, Helena Wilson. Read the attendance note available on the Online Resource Centre and answer the following questions:

- Has the marriage irretrievably broken down?

- Which of the five facts would you choose to base a divorce petition on? Why?

- Are there any other steps which Helena could take at this stage?

Answers to the questions above can be found on the Online Resource Centre: **www.oxfordtextbooks.co.uk/orc/sendall17/.**

7 DEFENCES TO DIVORCE AND DISSOLUTION

7.1 INTRODUCTION

This chapter will:

• explore the limited defences available in divorce and dissolution proceedings.

Defended divorces or dissolutions of civil partnerships (see **Chapter 10**) are not common in practice. There are many reasons for this, not least that most people do not separate lightly and divorce or dissolution is a decision taken after a great deal of discussion and careful thought. Some clients are uneasy with separation grounds, as they believe that they will be divorced or their civil partnership dissolved without having a say in proceedings. There are limited 'defences' available for divorces or dissolutions that are not based on the respondent challenging the veracity of the evidence cited by the applicant. These rarely amount to a defence, but often can delay proceedings. This chapter will discuss these defences although, in practice, reference should be made to practitioner texts for procedural details.

7.2 PETITIONS AFTER FIVE YEARS' SEPARATION

Section 5 Matrimonial Causes Act 1973:

(1) The respondent to a petition for divorce in which the applicant alleges five years' separation may oppose the grant of a decree on the ground that the dissolution of the marriage will result in grave financial or other hardship to him and that it would in all the circumstances be wrong to dissolve the marriage.

(2) Where the grant of a decree is opposed by virtue of this section, then—

(a) if the court finds that the applicant is entitled to rely in support of his petition on the fact of five years' separation and makes no such finding as to any other fact mentioned in section 1(2), and

(b) if apart from this section the court would grant a decree on the petition, the court shall consider all the circumstances, including the conduct of the parties to the marriage and the interests of those parties and of any children or other persons concerned, and if of opinion that the dissolution of the marriage will result in grave financial or other hardship to the respondent and that it would in all the circumstances be wrong to dissolve the marriage it shall dismiss the petition.

(3) For the purposes of this section hardship shall include the loss of the chance of acquiring any benefit which the respondent might acquire if the marriage were not dissolved.

Section 51 CPA 2004 has a similar provision for civil partnership dissolutions.

If the applicant relies on the five years' separation in his/her divorce under s1(2)(e) MCA 1973 or s44(5)(c) CPA 2004 (see **Chapter 6**), the respondent can oppose the grant of a divorce on the ground that the dissolution of the marriage or civil partnership will result in grave financial or other hardship to him/her and it would in all the circumstances be wrong to dissolve the marriage or civil partnership. This includes the loss of a chance of acquiring any benefit that the respondent may acquire if the marriage or civil partnership were not dissolved. Note that the hardship must be caused by dissolution, not the breakdown of the marriage or civil partnership.

The court under s5(2) MCA 1973 or s47(3) CPA 2004 must consider all the circumstances of the case, including the children of the family, the interests of the parties, and the conduct of the parties.

Commonly, this section was used to claim loss of a pension, especially a widow's pension. In the event of such a claim being made, proposals will have to be made for either a pension sharing order (see **Chapter 19**), a pension attachment order (see **Chapter 19**), or a lump sum order (see **Chapter 19**). Pound for pound compensation for loss of contingent widow's pension rights is not appropriate (see *Le Marchant v Le Marchant* [1977] 3 All ER 610). In *Banik v Banik* [1973] FLR Rep 65, the wife opposed the petition, claiming divorce would make her a social outcast in the society in which she lived. The court found that this could not amount to a defence and granted a decree nisi, but the wife's appeal of this decision was allowed. The Court of Appeal held that grave hardship was a matter of fact and degree, and ordered a retrial before a new judge. At the retrial, the court found as fact that if the decree was granted, the wife would remain living with her brother's family in Calcutta in an unchanged position, dressing and being regarded as still a married woman. She would not be a social outcast, and the decree should therefore be granted subject to an order for the husband to make modest periodic payments. This decision shows that a case based on this argument may be difficult to establish evidentially.

7.3 **PROTECTION IN TWO-YEAR SEPARATION CASES**

Section 10 Matrimonial Causes Act 1973:

(1) Where in any case the court has granted a decree of divorce on the basis of a finding that the applicant was entitled to rely in support of his petition on the fact of two years' separation coupled with the respondent's consent to a decree being granted and has made no such finding as to any other fact mentioned in section 1(2), the court may, on an application made by the respondent at any time before the decree is made absolute, rescind the decree if it is satisfied that the applicant misled the respondent (whether intentionally or unintentionally) about any matter which the respondent took into account in deciding to give his consent.

(2) The following provisions of this section apply where—

    (a) the respondent to a petition for divorce in which the applicant alleged two years' or five years' separation coupled, in the former case, with the respondent's consent to a decree being granted, has applied to the court for consideration under subsection (3) below of his financial position after the divorce; and

    (b) the court has granted a decree on the petition on the basis of a finding that the applicant was entitled to rely in support of his petition on the fact of two years' or five years' separation (as the case may be) and has made no such finding as to any other fact mentioned in section 1(2) above.

(3) The court hearing an application by the respondent under subsection (2) above shall consider all the circumstances, including the age, health, conduct, earning capacity, financial resources and financial obligations of each of the parties, and the financial position of the respondent, as having regard to the divorce, it is likely to be after the death of the applicant should the applicant die first; and, subject to subsection (4) below, the court shall not make the decree absolute unless it is satisfied—

    (a) that the applicant should not be required to make any financial provision for the respondent, or

    (b) that the financial provision made by the applicant for the respondent is reasonable and fair or the best that can be made in the circumstances.

(4) The court may if it thinks fit make the decree absolute notwithstanding the requirements of sub-section (3) above if—

(a) it appears that there are circumstances making it desirable that the decree should be made absolute without delay, and

(b) the court has obtained a satisfactory undertaking from the applicant that he will make such financial provision for the respondent as the court may approve.

This section contains two distinct provisions. Section 48 CPA 2004 contains similar provisions.

Under s10(1) MCA 1973 and s48(1)(c) CPA 2004 if the petition has been based on two years' separation and consent under s1(2)(d) MCA 1973 or s44(5)(d) CPA 2004 (see **Chapter 6**) and the respondent has consented, an application may be made for rescission of a decree nisi if he can satisfy the court that the applicant misled the respondent (whether intentionally or unintentionally) about any matter that the respondent took into account in deciding to give his consent.

If an applicant relies upon either of the separation facts under s1(2)(d) and (e) MCA 1973 or s44(5)(c) and (d) CPA 2004 (see **Chapter 6**), a respondent can apply to the court for consideration of his financial position under s10(2) MCA 1973. The court considers all the circumstances of the case under s10(3) MCA 1973 or s48(3) CPA 2004 and the court will not grant a decree absolute or dissolution order until it is satisfied that:

- the applicant should not be required to make any financial provision for the respondent;
- the financial provision made by the applicant for the respondent is reasonable and fair or the best that can be made in the circumstances.

As financial orders are available following the issue of a divorce petition, this defence is mainly used as a bargaining tool. Please note that under s10(2) MCA 1973 or s48 CPA 2004, the decree absolute may only be delayed.

7.4 **SECTION 10A MATRIMONIAL CAUSES ACT 1973**

This section was passed in the wake of a number of cases of women being refused a religious divorce by their spouse.

 Example

In Jewish religious law, a divorce is granted in the civil court but a divorce must also be obtained through the Beth Din, the Jewish religious courts. This is called a 'get'. It is possible for the husband or wife to withhold consent to the get. The effect of this is that the woman or man becomes agun or augunah (chained) and this has serious consequences. Remarriage without a get can be problematic and if a woman does not have a get and goes on to have another relationship with a man, she will be committing adultery. Any children born from a relationship with another man will be described as 'mamzer'. A mamzer is unable to marry any Jewish person and this status passes to all their descendants and therefore has severe repercussions for the child.

The Family Law Protocol adds guidance on ensuring that a client's religious beliefs are fully explored to ensure that a religious divorce can be obtained if necessary.

Section 10A will apply where a decree of divorce has been granted but not made absolute and the parties to the marriage:

(a) were married in accordance with

(i) the usages of the Jews, or

(ii) any other prescribed religious usages; and

(b) must cooperate if the marriage is to be dissolved.

Either party can apply to the court for an order that the divorce decree is not to be made absolute until a declaration by both parties that they have taken such steps as are required to dissolve the marriage in accordance with those usages is produced to the court. Such an order will be made if the court believes it is just and reasonable to do so considering all the circumstances of the case. The procedural rules are found in r2.45A Family Proceedings Rules 1991 (FPR).

This will prevent the dissolution of the marriage until the court is satisfied that all steps have been taken to secure a religious divorce. This clearly would be a bargaining point for the party wishing to obtain a religious decree of divorce. Practitioners should be aware of the religious background of their clients to ensure that this point is not missed.

The prescribed religious usages are currently Jewish law. In future, other religious marriages, e.g. under Islamic law, may come within the ambit of this section.

SUMMARY POINTS

- Under s5 MCA 1973 or s47 CPA 2004, a divorce can be defended on the basis of hardship caused by the dissolution of the marriage or civil partnership.

- Under s10(1) MCA 1973 or s48 CPA 2004, the respondent may apply to have a decree nisi rescinded if consent was obtained from the respondent after the applicant misled the respondent.

- A decree absolute may be delayed under s10(2) MCA 1973 or s48 CPA 2004 until financial provision between the parties has been resolved.

- Under s10A MCA 1973, a decree absolute may be delayed until all steps are taken to dissolve the religious marriage.

This is a summary of the defences available to divorce and civil partnerships. For further details and for procedural rules, refer to practitioner texts.

SELF-TEST QUESTIONS

1. Your client claims that since her husband moved out of the house six years ago, she has become very short of money. She wishes to defend the divorce on the basis of exceptional hardship. Advise your client on whether she can do this.

2. Your client is Jewish. He wishes to delay the 'get' as he believes he can use this to force his wife into agreeing to a poorer financial settlement than she is entitled to. Advise your client of the consequences of this course of action.

online
resource
centre

Answers to the questions above can be found on the Online Resource Centre:
www.oxfordtextbooks.co.uk/orc/sendall17/.

8 JURISDICTION

8.1 INTRODUCTION

This chapter will:

- discuss the increasingly important question of jurisdiction in divorce and dissolution of civil partnership proceedings;
- explain the concepts of 'domicile' and 'habitual residence' as they apply to divorce and dissolution proceedings.

In order to commence divorce or civil partnership proceedings, the parties must show a connection between themselves and the jurisdiction of the courts. In this text we refer to the jurisdiction of England and Wales. Whilst jurisdiction is not a common problem in practice, we live in an increasingly globalized world where people are more mobile and so may move from their original home to England and Wales. Complexities of jurisdiction may also arise if parties indulge in 'forum shopping'. This is not some complicated form of internet fraud but is when (usually immensely rich) parties try to find the jurisdiction where the law is more favourable to their case. Examples of this can be found on the Online Resource Centre.

This chapter will discuss the European legislation that governs jurisdiction in relationship breakdown and the international law concepts that are a feature of this area of law. In June 2016, the EU referendum produced a majority vote in favour of leaving the EU. At the time of writing it is not clear what effect this will have on the UK's relationship with the EU, and, by extension, the law on jurisdiction.

8.1.1 WHY IS JURISDICTION IMPORTANT?

In order to dissolve a marriage or civil partnership, the court must have jurisdiction to hear the case and as a result the law requires the parties to show a connection to courts in England and Wales. The law is found in the Council Regulation (EC) 2201/2003, Jurisdiction and the recognition and enforcement of matrimonial matters and in matters of parental responsibility, and is sometimes referred to as 'Brussels II bis' as it replaces Regulation EC/1347/2000 of the same name. The purpose of the regulation is to bring together in one document the provisions on divorce.

The regulation states:

Article 3 General jurisdiction

1. In matters relating to divorce, legal separation or marriage annulment, jurisdiction shall lie with the courts of the Member State

   (a) in whose territory:

       – the spouses are habitually resident, or

- the spouses were last habitually resident, insofar as one of them still resides there, or

- the respondent is habitually resident, or

- in the event of a joint application, either of the spouses is habitually resident, or

- the applicant is habitually resident if he or she resided there for at least a year immediately before the application was made, or

- the applicant is habitually resident if he or she resided there for at least six months immediately before the application was made and is either a national of the Member State in question or, in the case of the United Kingdom and Ireland, has his or her 'domicile' there;

(b) of the nationality of both spouses or, in the case of the United Kingdom and Ireland, of the 'domicile' of both spouses.

This regulation amended s8(2) Domicile and Matrimonial Proceedings Act 1973 and this states that:

2. The court shall have jurisdiction to entertain proceedings for divorce or judicial separation if (and only if)—

(a) the court has jurisdiction under the Council Regulation; or

(b) no court of a Contracting State has jurisdiction under the Council Regulation and either of the parties to the marriage is domiciled in England and Wales on the date when the proceedings are begun.

A 'contracting state' means one of the original parties to the regulation, namely, Belgium, Germany, Greece, Spain, France, Ireland, Italy, Luxembourg, the Netherlands, Austria, Portugal, Sweden, and the UK. Denmark is not a contracting state (see a European law text for further details).

Section 219 CPA 2004 introduces the same provisions from the Regulation for dissolution proceedings for civil partners.

There have been recent developments concerning couples who live in many different jurisdictions. Justice Ministers in the EU have reached agreement allowing couples of different European nationalities to choose which divorce laws will apply to them. Where the spouses are from different countries, living apart in different countries, or are from the same country but living abroad, they will be able to choose which nation's laws should apply to their divorce. The agreement will apply where one of a divorcing couple has a connection with any of the following states: Austria, Belgium, Bulgaria, France, Germany, Hungary, Italy, Latvia, Luxembourg, Malta, Portugal, Romania, Slovenia, and Spain. At the time of printing, the European Parliament has still to legislate upon the arrangement, but it is thought that the momentum behind the scheme makes it likely that it will be passed.

The United Kingdom and the Republic of Ireland have not acceded to the proposed scheme.

There are some concepts contained within these rules that require some further explanation before the scope of the court's jurisdiction becomes clearer.

8.1.2 SAME-SEX MARRIAGE

To reflect changes to marriage by the Marriage (Same Sex Couples) Act 2013, the DMPA 1973 is amended to include a new s1A, which is essentially the same as the jurisdiction provisions for civil partnership. Brussels IIA (the Council Regulation) does not apply to same-sex marriages and so there are now new regulations for same-sex marriages and these are found in the Marriage (Same Sex Couples) (Jurisdiction and Recognition of Judgments) Regulations 2014.

8.2 HABITUAL RESIDENCE

The principal definition of habitual residence is found in the case of *Mark v Mark* [2004] 1 FLR 1069, confirmed by the House of Lords at [2005] UKHL 42.

The petitioner wife had not received indefinite leave to remain in the UK at the time of divorce proceedings and was categorized as an 'overstayer'. The Court of Appeal held (and the House of Lords confirmed) that the petitioner was habitually resident and domiciled in England and Wales despite her immigration status. Thorpe LJ stated that it would be a breach of Art. 6 of the European Convention on Human Rights if the petitioner were to be denied access to the court.

In *Ikimi v Ikimi* [2001] 2 FLR 1288 the Court of Appeal considered that to be 'habitually resident' was meant to be the same as 'ordinarily resident'. In this case, the residence was 161 days in the relevant year. However, in *Armstrong v Armstrong* [2003] 2 FLR 378 the husband spent one-fifth of the year in England and Wales and the court decided this was not sufficient to show 'a sufficient degree of continuity to be properly described as settled' and so he was not habitually resident in England and Wales.

Helpful guidance was provided by the Supreme Court in *Re B (A Child)* [2016] UKSC 4. A child had been removed from England and Wales to Pakistan and the court considered how a child's habitual residence may change. Their Lordships considered that a change of habitual residence involved considering how integrated into his or her old life the child was and whether the central figures in the child's life had moved to the new jurisdiction which would influence how integrated a child would become in their new environment, as would the level of pre-planning undertaken by the child's parent or carer.

8.3 DOMICILE

This book contains only an outline of this extremely complex area of law. Domicile is a matter of private international law and reference should be made to textbooks and practitioner texts. Domicile is not the same as nationality and the two are considered separately. Again, reference should be made to specialist texts.

Domicile describes the link an individual has with a particular legal system and is used to determine which country's law should govern disputes. It is not simply a question of asking where a person lives, as domicile and residence are not synonymous.

Domicile is a link to a legal system and not to a country, e.g. I have a domicile of England and Wales, not the UK. The UK has three separate legal systems: England and Wales, Scotland, and Northern Ireland.

Every person has a domicile; in fact, a person can hold more than one domicile at one time. Domicile can change over the course of an individual's lifetime as their life changes and a person is never without a domicile.

There are three types of domicile:

- domicile of origin;
- domicile of dependence; and
- domicile of choice.

8.3.1 DOMICILE OF ORIGIN

When a baby is born, they are attributed with a domicile: their domicile of origin.

If a child has married parents, the child will take as their domicile the domicile of their father at the time of their birth. A child of unmarried parents will take the domicile of their mother. The place of the child's birth is irrelevant as the child will take the domicile of the parent. A person retains the domicile of origin throughout their life but it may be superseded by a different domicile of dependence or choice; but it will revive in the absence of another type of domicile.

8.3.2 DOMICILE OF DEPENDENCE

As above, a child will acquire their domicile from their parents. If the domicile of a parent changes, so will the child's domicile. This is the domicile of dependence. As before, the child of married parents will take the father's domicile and the child of unmarried parents will take the mother's domicile. A child acquires an independent domicile when they are 16 years old but will retain the domicile of dependence until they acquire a domicile of choice. A wife does not take the domicile of her husband (and vice versa).

8.3.3 DOMICILE OF CHOICE

For a person to acquire a domicile by choice, there are two requirements:

* residence; and

* intention.

A person must live in a country that is not the country of their domicile of origin. They must take up residence; an intention to live there is not sufficient. As well as actually taking up residence the person must also decide to live there permanently, or at least indefinitely. Intention can be inferred from all the circumstances of the person's life, e.g. what they say or do etc.

 Example

Milly, Molly, and Mandy all have a domicile of origin in England and Wales. Their lives are changing and they wonder what their domicile is …

Milly wishes to live in New Zealand. She has looked at some brochures and read some books and intends to live there at some point in the future.

Molly has been seconded by her law firm to Tokyo for six months. Molly likes the city but is homesick and wants to come back to England as soon as possible.

Mandy has moved to Edinburgh with her job. She has fallen in love with the city, bought a flat, and wishes to stay there permanently.

Answers:

Milly has insufficient intention to live in New Zealand (and hasn't actually moved there) and has not changed her domicile.

Molly does not intend to stay in Tokyo and so has not changed her domicile.

Mandy has sufficient intention to remain in Scotland and so has changed her domicile to a domicile of choice.

In *R v R (Divorce: Jurisdiction: Domicile)* [2006] 1 FLR 389, a woman claimed domicile of choice in France. The court required a fixed and settled intention to abandon her domicile of origin and to settle permanently in France, and that this must be proved beyond a mere balance of probabilities. This could not be established simply by making declarations or acquiring a home. The woman's driving licence, passport, nationality, bank accounts, credit cards, and medical insurance were all English and this undermined her claim to have acquired a domicile of choice in France.

Domicile of choice can change. If a person gives up residence in that country and decides that they intend not to live there permanently or indefinitely, domicile of choice can be lost. Both residence and intention must change. Domicile of choice may change immediately if the two elements are present in the new jurisdiction. If a person does not immediately acquire a new domicile of choice, the person's domicile will revert back to the domicile of origin, although it is not a requirement for a domicile of choice to be taken immediately.

8.4 JURISDICTION IN PRACTICE

If a client seeks a divorce or dissolution, jurisdiction must be ascertained. In Case Study Two, the initial interview covers this point and it should be a point on any checklist used in practice. In practice it is usually very easy to establish jurisdiction through habitual residence or domicile. If the domicile of the client is uncertain, habitual residence is usually easier to establish.

If proceedings are issued in another contracting state before England and Wales, the court of the state in which proceedings are issued has exclusive jurisdiction. In this situation, the court has a limited scope for discretion. A practitioner text should be consulted.

The Online Resource Centre offers further reading on this topic.

SUMMARY POINTS

- Brussels II (see **8.1.1**) provides the basis for jurisdiction in divorce and the Domicile and Matrimonial Proceedings Act 1973 reflects the law of jurisdiction in divorce.

- Jurisdiction is based on habitual residence and domicile.

- Habitual residence is a concept that considers where a person lives on a day-to-day basis.

- Domicile can be based on origin, dependence, or choice.

- Domicile of origin is based on where a person is born.

- Domicile of dependence depends on where a person's father or mother lives when a person is below the age of 16 years.

- Domicile of choice is based on the intention of a person to reside somewhere permanently.

SELF-TEST QUESTIONS

1. What is 'jurisdiction'?

2. List the ways in which a court in England and Wales may have jurisdiction in a divorce case.

3. What are the two requirements that must be established for a person to have a domicile of choice?

4. Where are you domiciled?

Case Study Two

David Wilson was born in Scotland and moved to England in 1993. He set up his own business in 1995, married Helena in 1995, and bought a house for his family in Longtown, England in 1999. Since his separation from Helena, he spends a number of weekends in Scotland, with his parents.

Explain where (and if) David has his habitual residence.

Answers to the questions above can be found on the Online Resource Centre:
www.oxfordtextbooks.co.uk/orc/sendall17/.

9 PROCEDURE FOR A MATRIMONIAL ORDER

9.1 INTRODUCTION

This chapter will:

- discuss the steps a solicitor should take before issuing divorce proceedings;

- explore the complete procedure for obtaining an undefended divorce.

This chapter covers the procedure for obtaining a divorce. The procedure for obtaining civil partnership dissolution is procedurally identical to that of obtaining a divorce, although obviously the documentation differs.

The procedure for obtaining a divorce is governed by the Family Procedure Rules 2010 (FPR). These rules came into force in 2011. The rules can be a little confusing. The FPR refer to 'matrimonial orders' and this includes:

- a decree of divorce;

- a decree of nullity;

- a decree of judicial separation.

The correct term for proceedings is 'an application for a matrimonial order' rather than divorce proceedings. Confusingly, the forms for divorce have changed little in content and are still called divorce petitions. This chapter will refer to 'applications for a matrimonial order' when describing a client seeking a divorce.

As a result, the terminology used by the rules could be misleading. For the rest of this book, the person issuing the proceedings for a matrimonial order will be known as the 'petitioner' and the person against whom the application is made is referred to as the 'respondent'. It is a matter of note that the Ministry of Justice chose not to dispense with the outdated divorce petition at the time of implementation of the new rules.

This chapter covers the procedure for an application for a matrimonial order, from drafting a divorce petition through to decree absolute. Other chapters deal with some procedural aspects in more detail, e.g. jurisdiction in **Chapter 8**.

9.2 **FLOWCHART**

FIGURE 9.1 THE MAJOR STEPS TAKEN DURING DIVORCE PROCEEDINGS

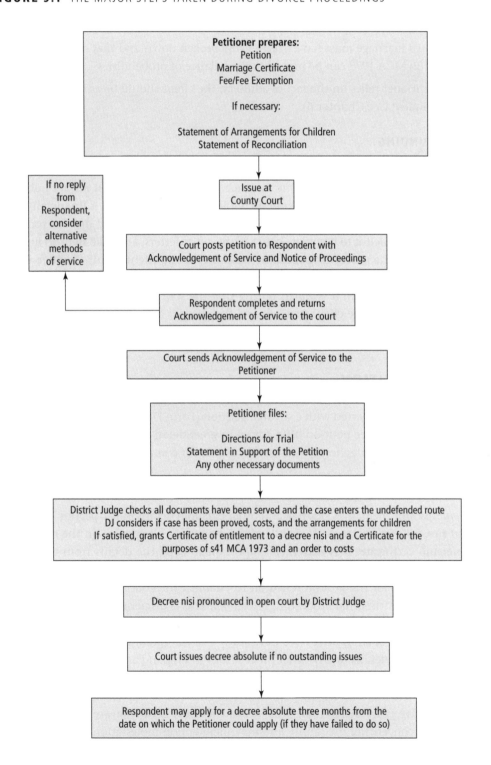

9.3 **PRELIMINARY CONSIDERATIONS**

There are some considerations before the issue of proceedings:

- the client is validly married or validly in a civil partnership (see **Chapter 5**);
- the case must be funded either privately or by public funding (see **Chapter 2**) and this must be sorted out first as the fee alone for divorce is considerable;
- the client should have been advised on the possibility of mediation or relationship counselling services, e.g. Relate, unless it is not appropriate to your client (see **Chapter 3**);
- you must check that your client has been married for one year (see **Chapter 6**) and also that the court has jurisdiction to hear the petition (see **Chapter 8**);
- the client's marriage must have irretrievably broken down and that one of the five facts under s1(2) MCA 1973 can be proved to the balance of probabilities;
- if the petitioner relies on the fact of adultery, the client should be advised about citing a co-respondent (see **Chapter 6**).

9.3.1 **PUBLIC FUNDING**

As considered in **Chapter 2**, public funding for a matrimonial order is restricted to those who have, or are suffering, domestic violence. All other cases do not attract public funding. If the client has evidence of domestic violence (see **2.1.1.2**) and is financially eligible, legal help may be obtained. Legal help is used to fund undefended divorce proceedings and allows the solicitor to complete court forms, write letters, and take steps to finalize the divorce. Should the proceedings become defended or the client require further assistance with financial matters (see **Chapter 14**), the client will have to apply for different forms of funding (see **Chapter 2**). It is worth noting that the solicitor does not go on to the court record as 'acting' for the client (see **9.6**) and the client is acting in person. The client may have to attend a MIAM (see **Chapter 3**).

9.4 **DIVORCE PETITION**

All divorce suits are started with a divorce petition (Form D8) and the supporting notes on completing the divorce petition offer advice in great detail on the completion of the petition. This is a pre-printed form with various blanks for completion.

9.4.1 **DRAFTING THE PETITION**

Part one: asks for the names, address and other personal details of the parties.

Part two: asks for the accurate details of the marriage as it appears on the marriage/civil partnership certificate. It is extremely important to copy the details from the certificate exactly as they appear on the certificate or the court will reject the application.

Part three: asks for the ground relied on to establish the court's jurisdiction under s5(2) Domicile and Matrimonial Proceedings Act 1973. This is discussed in **Chapter 8**. The petition should be drafted to make clear the position of the parties and the notes for guidance suggest a number of alternatives (see Case Study Two for guidance).

Part four: seeks details of any other proceedings in England and Wales with reference to the marriage, civil partnership, or children of the family. The part also seeks details of arrangements made to support the petitioner and children of the family where the petition is based on five years' separation. This means the court is fully aware of past and present proceedings concerning the family and may include non-molestation and occupation orders under the Family Law Act 1996 (see **Chapters 33–37**) or care proceedings under the Children Act 1989 (see **Chapter 29**).

Part five: asks the petitioner to state the ground and fact upon which the petition is based.

Part six: this is the 'Statement of Case' and seeks the facts upon which the petition is based.

Part seven: seeks details of the children of the family including gender and date of birth of all children of the family under s52 MCA 1973. The part also seeks details of children who are not children of the family.

Part eight: seeks details of any special assistance or facilities required by the petitioner should attendance at court be required.

Part nine: seeks details required for the service of the petition.

Part ten is the prayer—see **9.4.3**.

9.4.2 DRAFTING STATEMENT OF CASE

The statement of case gives details to support the fact being used. The following is a brief and very general guide to drafting this part of the petition. Many firms have precedent banks from old cases, practitioners' texts, and precedent texts to assist drafting.

There is no set formula for drafting this part of a petition, but certain guidelines are offered here.

In adultery cases, a statement of when and where the adultery took place is necessary, with specific dates if possible. If not known, a description of how the respondent had the opportunity and the inclination to commit adultery must be stated. The 'co-respondent' (the third party involved in the adultery) need not be named (see **6.6.3**).

 Example

The respondent committed adultery on 13 May 2016 with his work colleague during a staff morale exercise at the Tenbury Hotel in Longtown. The respondent admitted the adultery to the petitioner on 14 May 2016. The respondent started to cohabit with the work colleague on 15 May 2016 and the adultery continues. The petitioner finds it intolerable to continue living with the respondent.

For unreasonable behaviour, the general rule (often repeated) is that the structure of an unreasonable behaviour petition is 'first, worst, last'. The idea is that generally up to five or six individual incidents of behaviour should be cited chronologically with the first incident, with dates, the worst incidents listed, and completed by the last incident (unless the behaviour is continuing). Each new occasion of behaviour should be set out in a separate paragraph. The date should be stated. If the client cannot remember the exact date, then the month should be given. The author has resorted to stating the season on some occasions with a client with a poor memory (e.g. 'in the summer of 1999') although this is less than ideal.

Sufficient detail should be given to allow the court to assess the marriage properly and the effect of the behaviour on the petitioner should be stated, even if it is obvious. Be temperate with your language as the respondent will read the petition and a balance must be struck between obtaining a decree and not unduly fanning the flames of the dispute. See Case Study Two for an example of such drafting. It is vital to state the effect of the behaviour on the petitioner as this will help the court to understand how the statement of case fulfils the subjective test required (see **Chapter 6**).

 Example

Some examples of a draft statement of case for unreasonable behaviour petitions featuring common types of behaviour are the following:

On the 1st day of September 2015 when the respondent was repairing the car the petitioner struck him about the head and back with some force with a spanner causing bruising. The petitioner sought medical treatment and was deeply shocked by the incident.

During 2016 the respondent has incurred large debts as a result of reckless and extravagant spending on clothing and the petitioner is often telephoned by creditors to take proceedings to recover the debt. The petitioner has often felt extremely worried about these debts. The respondent ignores the petitioner's pleas to moderate her spending knowing the distress it causes him.

Since the date of the marriage the respondent has displayed an unwarranted and irrational sense of jealousy where the petitioner is concerned which has persisted despite the assurances of the petitioner. The respondent persists in this jealousy despite knowing that the petitioner feels anxious and afraid.

For desertion, the date and surrounding circumstances of the respondent's desertion should be given with sufficient detail to show the respondent's intention to bring cohabitation to an end.

Separation cases should give the date and circumstances of the separation. If the parties continue to live under the same roof, sufficient information should be given to demonstrate the existence of separate households.

9.4.3 THE PRAYER

The prayer concludes the petition.

The prayer asks the court to dissolve the marriage as well as a request for costs and a consideration of financial remedies.

Costs should be given careful consideration, with a possible agreement reached before the issue of the petition. The general view is that a petitioner receiving legal help should not request costs as the return for the petitioner would be minimal and it may inflame the dispute if the respondent is asked to pay costs. Practice seems to vary around the country. A happy medium may be to draft a claim for costs in the terms that the petitioner does not claim costs unless the petition is defended or the statutory charge (see **Chapter 2**) arises.

The prayer for financial orders should be completed fully and all boxes ticked, as the full range of financial orders should be claimed, even if it is just for the claims to be dismissed.

Where the petitioner is relying on desertion or separation facts the date is important, as specified periods of time, e.g. two or five years, must have elapsed before the petition is presented.

The petition is signed at the bottom by the acting solicitor or the petitioner in person, if being advised under legal help. The names and addresses of the people to be served, i.e. the respondent, the co-respondent, if any, and the petitioner's address for service (which is the name and address of the firm acting or usually 'care of' the firm, if the petitioner is being advised as a petitioner 'in person' under legal help) are inserted.

9.4.4 AMENDMENTS AND ADDITIONS TO A PETITION

A divorce petition may be amended by a party making an application for a matrimonial order if it is done before an answer is filed (r7.13 FPR 2010). When an amendment is made, it must be served correctly on the other parties according to r7.8 FPR 2010. An amendment can be made with the agreement of the parties or with permission of the court (r7.13(4) FPR 2010).

Amendments and substitutions are generally permitted if no injustice will be caused to the respondent.

Despite these provisions, it is important to get the petition right first time. Any amendments will slow down proceedings and increase costs.

9.5 **ISSUING THE DIVORCE PETITION**

Practical Considerations

Civil litigation terms

Issue: to commence proceedings at court. The court will seal the application (stamp it with a court stamp), open a file, and give the proceedings a number. This number will identify the case and should be used on all court documents and correspondence with the court.

Serve: to formally give a document to a party. This can be as simple as posting documents by first class post.

File: to give a document to the court.

'Acting': a solicitor 'acts' in court proceedings when the client pays for them to do so or public funding allows a solicitor to do so.

On the court record: the solicitor is recorded on the court file as acting for the client. All correspondence will be sent to the solicitor and a client will incur the costs of this.

The marriage certificate must be filed with the petition (PD 7 para 3.1 FPR 2010). If the client does not have a copy, many practices encourage the client to obtain their own copy, particularly if publicly funded.

There has been a substantial change to how divorce petitions are issued.

Following the creation of the single county court, there is a single jurisdiction without the previous geographical boundaries of county courts (see **Chapter 4**). Subsequently the Crime and Courts Act 2013 enabled legal advisers to consider decree nisi applications and directions for trial across the family court. In addition, all divorce petitions are now issued in a single court in each circuit (a circuit is a geographical area covering a number of courts). For instance in the North East Circuit, all petitions are now issued in Durham County Court. Legal advisers will therefore deal with the majority of routine decree nisi applications, which will free up judicial time for other work, although judges make decisions when the case is not straightforward. Exceptions are made for urgent cases.

Applications for financial remedies arising from divorce will be transferred to local courts for hearing. The provision for the issue of Children Act cases is unchanged.

What is occurring here is not a change to divorce law and procedure itself but rather a change in how divorce cases are processed. They will now be examined by legal advisers, rather than judges, which will free up the judiciary to undertake more complex cases.

To issue a petition, a number of documents must be taken to the court:

- petition;
- marriage certificate;
- statement of reconciliation (D6) (see **9.6**);
- fee (or fee exemption).

The numbers of each document will depend upon the number of parties. A copy must be supplied to be kept on the court file and one for each party to be served.

Practical Considerations

Mr and Mrs Wilson are to divorce based on the fact of unreasonable behaviour. There is no co-respondent and Mrs Wilson is a Litigant in Person.

To issue proceedings, the documents required are:

- divorce petition and one copy;
- marriage certificate;

    • fee exemption.

    There is no D6 as Mrs Wilson is not legally represented.

Most solicitors also give a copy of the documentation to their client and keep a copy on the client's file.

The petitioner's solicitor will ask the client to approve the issue documentation and sign where necessary. The solicitor should always obtain the client's authority to issue, since circumstances may have changed since the initial instructions. There may, for instance, have been reconciliation between the parties.

The proceedings are issued at the county court office and may be issued in person or by post. The court staff will check the documentation. If there are any obvious errors, they will return it for correction (e.g. if the original marriage certificate has not been enclosed or if the petition is not signed). If all is in order, the staff will issue the divorce proceedings by opening a court file and allocating a case number. The number must be quoted in all subsequent dealings with the court and on all documentation. The court staff will send the petitioner's solicitor notification (on a standard form) of the issue date and case number.

9.6 **D6: STATEMENT OF RECONCILIATION**

Earlier it was said that this document is only filed when a solicitor is fully acting on behalf of the client. Legal help for divorce does not permit a solicitor to 'act' in the court proceedings for the client (the public funding only covers advice and assistance with court documents). The client is considered to be acting 'in person'.

If a person has legal help for divorce proceedings, this document is *not* required.

This statement is a standard form that certifies whether or not the solicitor has discussed with the petitioner the possibility of reconciliation and/or given the petitioner the names and addresses of persons qualified to help effect reconciliation, e.g. Relate. The solicitor does not have to discuss reconciliation or give names of relevant organizations. In some cases, s/he may feel that it is inappropriate, e.g. because of domestic abuse. What s/he does need to do, however, is to state whether s/he has discussed the possibility.

9.7 **FEE**

There is a court fee for issuing a divorce petition which has risen to £550.

Some clients will qualify for a fee exemption or remission. A standard court form, an application for a fee exemption or remission, must be prepared and filed with the issue documents if an exemption or remission is claimed.

Clients who are being advised under legal help may be exempt from payment of the issue fee, but must provide details of their solicitor on the form and include evidence to show that they are receiving such help (e.g. a solicitor's letter). The court staff may contact the solicitor to verify any information given.

Clients who are in receipt of certain benefits such as income support or working families tax credit are also exempt, but they must include up-to-date evidence of receipt of such benefits (e.g. a letter from the Benefits Agency or a payment book).

Other clients may apply for fee exemption/remission (e.g. on grounds of 'hardship'), but must provide full details and evidence of their means. The court staff will then make a decision upon the fee to be paid and notify the client accordingly.

9.8 **SERVICE OF THE PETITION**

The normal method of service is by first class post. The court will send the respondent a sealed copy of the petition and an acknowledgement of service with detachable guidance notes.

If the petition is based on the adultery fact and has chosen to name a co-respondent, the co-respondent will also have to be served with a copy of the petition.

The respondent should complete the acknowledgement of service and return it to the court, showing that he has been properly served. If a respondent does not return the acknowledgement to the court, the petitioner will have to take other steps, as s/he cannot proceed with the divorce until s/he can prove that the petition has been served.

In *Akbar v Rafiq* [2006] 1 FLR 27 the decrees nisi and absolute were held to be void as there had been no proper service of the divorce papers on the respondent wife. The court held that it was not sufficient to state after the event that, although the petition had not been duly served, the respondent wife knew of the proceedings. The FPR 2010 were designed to ensure that the respondent has direct personal knowledge of the divorce proceedings instituted by the petitioner.

The petitioner cannot serve the petition personally (r6.5(3) FPR 2010).

There are several options.

9.8.1 **SERVICE BY COURT BAILIFF**

Under r6.9 FPR 2010, service may be made by a court bailiff. Postal service is expected to have been attempted and an application must be made to the court on a standard form. It is helpful to supply a photograph or description of the respondent. Court bailiffs are very experienced at serving respondents, even in difficult circumstances where they are evading service. A bailiff will attempt to obtain the respondent's signature on an endorsement of service. This will satisfy the court that service has been effected.

9.8.2 **PERSONAL SERVICE**

This can be effected by a process server or enquiry agent (a person employed to serve documents) or by the petitioner's solicitor himself (more unusually). Process servers will charge a fee for their services, but may be more successful in serving difficult respondents. Proof of personal service is provided by an affidavit of service, which must be sworn by the individual effecting service, indicating the date, time, and place of the service. This affidavit is then filed with the county court office as proof of service and, again, will satisfy the court that service has been effected.

9.8.3 **DEEMED SERVICE**

Under r6.15 and r6.16 FPR 2010, where the respondent has not returned an acknowledgement of service but the petitioner can satisfy the court that he has received the petition, the court can grant an order that service be 'deemed'. This means that the court can be satisfied that the respondent has been served or had notice of the proceedings.

Under r6.16 FPR 2010, the evidence that will satisfy the court that service has occurred will differ from case to case: e.g. the respondent may have referred to having received the petition in a letter to the petitioner or some third party. In all cases, however, the evidence will be indirect, e.g. a letter is received from a solicitor instructed by the respondent who is subsequently left without instructions.

 Example

During the author's practice of divorce proceedings, a respondent returned the divorce petition and accompanying documents to the author torn into tiny pieces and with an abusive message written on the envelope. The respondent helpfully signed the abusive message. An application for deemed service was made with the message exhibited to the application. Deemed service was granted.

9.8.4 SERVICE BY ALTERNATIVE METHOD OR AT AN ALTERNATIVE PLACE

Orders from the court for service to be effected by a different method or at a different place are not common. If granted, this means that service is effected in another way (e.g. by placing an advertisement of the proceedings in a place where it is likely to come to the attention of the respondent or by leaving the documents with a relative) (r6.19 FPR 2010). Before granting this type of order the district judge must be satisfied that other service methods have failed, that extensive attempts have been made to serve the respondent, and that there is a reasonable probability that the advertisement or other proposed form of substituted service will come to the respondent's attention.

9.8.5 DISPENSING WITH SERVICE

It should be noted that the court has the power to make an order that service should be dispensed with. Such an order is only granted in exceptional circumstances, where the petitioner cannot trace the respondent, despite strenuous efforts.

 Practical Considerations

A district judge will expect the petitioner to make exhaustive enquiries of the whereabouts of the respondent. Enquiries will have been made with relatives, friends, former employers, and neighbours. Banks, accountants, former solicitors, doctors, and dentists should be asked to forward a stamped envelope to their client, which will avoid them revealing his address. The Department of Work and Pensions, if able to identify the respondent, will forward the petition to him.

Under r6.20 FPR 2010, the district judge must be satisfied that it is 'impracticable' to serve the respondent by any other means available under r6.20 FPR 2010 or it is otherwise 'necessary or expedient' to dispense with service of a copy of a petition on the respondent before an order dispensing with service will be made.

9.9 ACKNOWLEDGEMENT OF SERVICE

The acknowledgement of service contains a series of questions, which include whether the respondent has received the petition, the existence of any proceedings relating to the marriage already continuing outside England and Wales, the respondent's domicile, habitual residence and nationality, and whether the respondent intends to defend the case and details of any solicitor acting for him.

The acknowledgement of service also contains other questions, applicable only to specific divorces. In an adultery divorce, the respondent will be asked whether he admits the adultery alleged in the petition. In a two years' separation plus consent divorce, he will be asked if he consents to a divorce.

The acknowledgement must be signed by either the respondent or his solicitor, if one is acting for him. In divorce based on adultery or two years' separation plus consent, the acknowledgement must be signed by the respondent personally, as it will be used to prove not only procedural matters but also an element of the divorce fact.

The respondent must return the acknowledgement to the court within seven days of receipt. A copy will be sent to the petitioner by the court.

If the respondent does not return the acknowledgement then, as explained at **9.8**, the petitioner will have to take other steps to effect service or to proceed without service. Once the court is satisfied that service has been effected or dispensed with service, the petitioner can proceed with the divorce.

If the respondent does return the acknowledgement, the next step of the petitioner depends upon one of the respondent's responses in the acknowledgement.

If the respondent has answered 'no' to the question 'Do you intend to defend?' the petitioner may proceed to the next stage of the divorce (see **9.10**) after the expiry of seven days from the service of the petition on the respondent.

If the respondent has indicated that he does intend to defend the petition, he has 21 days to file an answer. An answer is broadly equivalent to a defence in civil litigation and it must answer the allegations made in the particulars of the petition. As defended divorces are beyond the scope of this text, reference should be made to a specialist practitioner text.

A co-respondent has the same opportunity as a respondent to give notice of intention to defend and to file an answer (an even more compelling reason to persuade the client not to name a co-respondent).

If an answer is not filed within the 21-day period, the petitioner can proceed with her divorce as an undefended divorce (see **9.10**).

9.10 STATEMENT IN SUPPORT OF THE PETITION

Evidence of the marital breakdown is supplied by the petitioner for the undefended route by a statement supported by a statement of truth. A statement of truth is signed by the client to confirm the contents of the statement are true.

There is a different statement for each of the five facts and the petitioner must complete the correct form. The petitioner will verify that she identifies the respondent's signature on the copy of the acknowledgement of service and formally requests a decree dissolving the marriage.

The statement must be accompanied by a form of application for a decree nisi. This, again, is a pre-printed form and asks the district judge for a decree nisi (or conditional order in civil partnership dissolutions) or for a case management hearing if the matter requires.

This procedure is the normal procedure in undefended cases, and very few cases are defended. The divorce case will proceed without a hearing in court even if there are subsequent court hearings about children or financial matters.

A concern frequently expressed by clients is whether they will have to attend court during the proceedings. The vast majority of clients will not have to attend court and their divorce will not generally be publicized. On rare occasions, the parties may have to attend, for example, to discuss costs, or if the case becomes defended.

Occasionally, the petitioner will file further evidence along with these documents. These might include, for example, medical evidence where the petition was based on the unreasonable behaviour fact and the petitioner received medical treatment for injuries caused by the respondent's behaviour or it might be necessary to file a statement from a relevant person (e.g. an enquiry agent) to substantiate the fact that adultery took place.

If there are children, the statement will also verify the contents of the statement of arrangements for children.

9.11 CONSIDERATION BY LEGAL ADVISER/DISTRICT JUDGE

Once the statement has been filed, the file will be passed for the consideration of the legal adviser (who may also consult a district judge). The legal adviser will review the case to see whether it can be entered in the standard procedure list. She will first check that:

- the respondent (and any co-respondent) has been properly served (or service has been dispensed with);
- no intention to defend has been filed and that the time limit for doing so has expired, or that an intention to defend was filed but no answer has been filed and the time limit for doing so has expired;
- the respondent has provided consent in respect of a petition based on two years' separation and consent;
- the adultery has been admitted or proved.

The respondent's consent/admission is proved by the petitioner identifying the respondent's signature in her statement in support as corroborative evidence of the allegations made in the petition (r7.20(5) FPR 2010).

The legal adviser has to consider the evidence provided to decide whether the ground for divorce (the irretrievable breakdown of marriage) is proved. They must be satisfied that the petitioner has sufficiently proved the contents of the petition. As the wording is 'sufficiently', this is not envisaging a high standard of proof. Once the legal adviser is satisfied the petition has been proved, she will certify that the petitioner is entitled to a decree.

This is a standard court form and not only certifies that the petitioner is entitled to a decree, but also makes any orders for costs and gives notice of the place, time, and date for pronouncement of the decree nisi (see **9.12**).

If the legal adviser is not satisfied that the petition is proved, she may ask the petitioner to file further evidence (r7.20(2)(b) FPR 2010) and would refer the case to a district judge. Alternatively, the district judge can remove the case from the list. The parties would then seek further directions.

9.12 PRONOUNCEMENT OF DECREE NISI OF DIVORCE OR CONDITIONAL ORDER FOR DISSOLUTION OF CIVIL PARTNERSHIP

The petitioner's solicitor will receive a certificate from the court office (i.e. the certificate of entitlement to a decree or conditional order). The petitioner must be advised of the date, time, and place that the decree nisi or conditional order will be pronounced. The pronouncement is generally made in open court by a judge or district judge. The petitioner can be reassured that this is a purely procedural matter. On the appointed date, the judge enters the courtroom and reads out a list of decree nisi and conditional order appointments for the day. If there are no objections or representations, the decree or order is formally pronounced in every case.

The decree nisi does not dissolve the marriage and the conditional order does not dissolve the civil partnership. It is extremely important that the client understands this and does not arrange to be married or to enter into a new civil partnership before the pronouncement of the decree absolute or final order.

The decree nisi and the conditional order are the first decrees in divorce and dissolution proceedings and state that the marriage or civil partnership has broken down irretrievably and that they can be dissolved unless cause be shown within six weeks from the decree why they should not be made absolute or final.

The form of the decree and the order stresses that they are not final and that application for the final decree or order must be made to the court and that the parties are not free to remarry at this stage.

A copy of the decree nisi or conditional order will be sent to both parties.

The petitioner's solicitor will ask the client to confirm their instructions for the final step to dissolve the marriage or civil partnership.

9.13 MAKING DECREE NISI ABSOLUTE OR THE CONDITIONAL ORDER FINAL

Following pronouncement of the decree nisi or conditional order there is a six-week waiting period before a decree absolute or final order is pronounced. The usual practice is that the petitioner will apply for a decree absolute following the lapse of six weeks from the pronouncement of decree nisi.

A decree absolute or final order can be expedited for exceptional reasons, but this is unusual. The usual practice is that the decree absolute may be applied for six weeks and one day after decree nisi is pronounced, but a petitioner is not bound to so apply.

Practical Considerations

A common enquiry from students in the early stages of a family law course concerns the six-week period between decree nisi and decree absolute.

Section 1(5) Matrimonial Causes Act 1973 states:

> every decree of divorce shall be in the first instance a decree nisi and shall not be made absolute before the expiration of six months from its grant unless the High Court by general order from time to time fixes a shorter period . . .

In fact, the Matrimonial Causes (Decree Absolute) Order 1972 shortens the period of waiting from six months to six weeks.

The decree absolute is applied for on a standard application form (Form D36).

The application is posted to the court and must be accompanied by a court fee or an application for exemption.

The court staff will check that:

- no appeal has been lodged against the decree nisi;

- the correct amount of time has elapsed following the decree nisi.

If all is in order the court staff will issue the decree absolute and send a copy to both parties or their solicitors.

When the decree absolute is forwarded to the client, advice should be given on the need to keep the decree safely (in case of remarriage) and the need to consider the effect of divorce on wills and inheritance.

Although a decree absolute has been granted, the client retainer may continue with ongoing disputes about finances or children.

If the petitioner fails to apply for the decree absolute, there is provision in the rules for the respondent to apply at a later date (after three months have passed from the earliest date when the petitioner could have applied).

 Example

P received the decree nisi on 3 June 2016. P can apply for the decree to be made absolute on 15 July 2016 (six weeks later).

If P does not apply for the decree to be made absolute, R can apply three months after P would have been able to apply: six weeks *plus* three months. So six weeks after 3 June, 15 July, is the earliest time that P could have applied. R will wait a further three months, until 17 October, to apply for decree absolute.

A respondent must provide an affidavit to support their application and obtain an appointment before the court, at which the petitioner has the opportunity to show that she will suffer prejudice if a decree absolute is granted. In *Re G (Decree Absolute: Prejudice)* [2003] EWHA 2534 (Fam), the court stated that the mere fact that the financial proceedings had yet to be heard was not a sufficient reason to refuse the decree absolute. The court did not accept the wife's allegations of substantial non-disclosure by the husband within these proceedings, nor that he was likely to frustrate her claims by moving abroad. It is suggested that the outcome may have been different if the wife could have established prejudice arising from, e.g., the loss of the possibility of a widow's pension if her status was changed from that of wife to ex-wife by the grant of a decree absolute prior to the resolution of the ancillary relief proceedings.

Following the decision in *Dennis v Dennis* [2000] Fam 163, the court will not allow an application by the respondent for the decree nisi to be made absolute before the expiry of the three months after the petitioner could have applied for decree absolute.

SUMMARY POINTS

- The solicitor will take comprehensive initial instructions and advise about the appropriate divorce fact and the divorce process.

- Issue documentation will be prepared/gathered together (marriage certificate, petition, statement regarding reconciliation (if required) and application for exemption from fee (if required)).

- The documents will be signed and copies taken. If the client so instructs, proceedings will be issued at the county court.

- The divorce process is shown at **9.2**. This diagram provides a summary of the undefended divorce procedure from issue to decree absolute and you may find it useful to turn to this diagram at this stage.

SELF-TEST QUESTIONS

1. Your client is concerned that his wife (the respondent) may not cooperate with the proceedings. Describe the different methods of service that can be used to prove service of proceedings.

2. Your client wishes to have an overview of the proceedings. Describe the procedure to him as briefly as you can. List the documents required to issue proceedings in a privately funded divorce with no children involved.

3. Will your client have to attend court at any stage?

Case Study Two

In Case Study Two, your supervisor asks you to complete the divorce petition on behalf of Helena. You will find a blank form on the Online Resource Centre and a completed form.

You will also find all the documentation for an undefended divorce in this case study.

---

online
resource
centre

Answers to the questions above can be found on the Online Resource Centre:
www.oxfordtextbooks.co.uk/orc/sendall17/.

FORM 9.1 DIVORCE/DISSOLUTION/(JUDICIAL) SEPARATION PETITION

Divorce/dissolution/(judicial) separation petition

To be completed by the Court	
Name of court	
Case No.	
Date received by the court	
Date issued	
Time issued	
Fee charged/ Remission ID	

Notes to Petitioners

- This form should be used if you are making an application to the court for divorce/dissolution to end your marriage or civil partnership or (judicial) separation from your spouse or civil partner.

- Before completing this form, please read the supporting notes (D8Notes) for guidance on how to complete this form.

- Please answer all questions. If you are unsure of the answer to any question, or you do not think that it applies to you, please indicate this on the form.

- If there is not enough room on this form, you may continue on a separate sheet. Please put your name, the Respondent's (your spouse/civil partner) name, and the number of the Part the information relates to, at the top of your continuation sheet.

- If completing this form by hand, please use **black ink and BLOCK CAPITAL LETTERS** and tick the boxes that apply.

See the supporting notes for guidance on how to complete this section

I, [_____] (please state your full name)

apply for a ☐ divorce

☐ dissolution

☐ (judicial) separation

in respect of my ☐ marriage

☐ civil partnership

and give the following details in support of my application.

---

continued over the page ⇨

Part 1 About you (the Petitioner) and the Respondent (your spouse/civil partner)

See the supporting notes for guidance on how to complete this section

Petitioner	**Respondent**
My current name is First name(s) (in full)	The Respondent's current name is First name(s) (in full)
Last name	Last name
My address is (including postcode)	The Respondent's address is (including postcode)
Postcode	Postcode
My date of birth is	The Respondent's date of birth is
My occupation is	The Respondent's occupation is
I am ☐ male ☐ female	The Respondent is ☐ male ☐ female

Part 2 Details of marriage or civil partnership

See the supporting notes for guidance on how to complete this section

On the _____ day of _____ [19   ][20   ]

(insert your name exactly as it appears on your marriage/civil partnership certificate)

☐ married   ☐ formed a civil partnership with

(insert the name of the Respondent exactly as it appears on your marriage/civil partnership certificate)

at

(insert the place where the marriage/civil partnership was formed, exactly as it appears on your marriage/civil partnership certificate)

A certified copy of your marriage/civil partnership certificate must be sent to the court with this completed petition (see supporting notes for guidance).

Part 3 Jurisdiction

See the supporting notes for guidance on how to complete this section

The Respondent and I last lived together as ☐ spouses   ☐ civil partners
at

> Address

The court has jurisdiction to hear this case under

☐ Article 3(1) of the Council Regulation (EC) No 2201/2003 of 27 November 2003

or

☐ the Civil Partnership (Jurisdiction and Recognition of Judgments) Regulations 2005

or

☐ The Marriage (Same Sex Couples)(Jurisdiction and Recognition of Judgments) Regulations 2014

on the following grounds

☐ The Petitioner and Respondent are both habitually resident in England and Wales and/or

☐ Other (please state any other connection(s) on which you wish to rely)

or

☐ The court has jurisdiction other than under the Council Regulation on the basis that no court of a Contracting State has jurisdiction under the Council Regulation and the ☐ Petitioner ☐ Respondent is domiciled in England and Wales on the date when this application is issued

or

☐ The court has jurisdiction other than under the Marriage (Same Sex Couples) (Jurisdiction and Recognition of Judgments) Regulations 2014 or under the Civil Partnership (Jurisdiction and Recognition of Judgments) Regulations 2005 on the basis that no court has, or is recognised as having jurisdiction as set out in these regulations, and

either:

☐ the ☐ Petitioner ☐ or the Respondent is domiciled in England or Wales

or

☐ the Petitioner and Respondent registered as civil partners of each other in England or Wales or in, the case of a same sex couple, married each other under the law of England and Wales and it would be in the interests of justice for the court to assume jurisdiction in this case.

continued over the page ◻⇨

3

Part 4 Other proceedings or arrangements

See the supporting notes for guidance on how to complete this section

☐ There are and/or have been

☐ proceedings in any court in England and Wales or elsewhere with reference to the

☐ marriage
☐ civil partnership
☐ or to any child of the family
☐ or between the Petitioner and Respondent with reference to any property of either or both of them

(please enter details below)

or

☐ no other proceedings in any court in England and Wales or elsewhere.

☐ This is an application based on five years' separation and

☐ agreement has been made or is proposed to be made between the parties for the support of

☐ the Petitioner ☐ the Respondent ☐ and any child of the family

(please enter details below)

or

☐ no agreement has been made or is proposed to be made.

Part 5 The fact(s)

See the supporting notes for guidance on how to complete this section

I apply for a

☐ divorce on the ground that the marriage has broken down irretrievably, or
☐ dissolution on the ground that the civil partnership has broken down irretrievably, or
☐ (judicial) separation

and

I rely on the following fact(s) in support of my application:

☐ The Respondent has committed adultery and the Petitioner finds it intolerable to live with the Respondent (this fact is not applicable in relation to a civil partnership) (only conduct between the respondent and a person of the opposite sex may constitute adultery for this purpose)

☐ The Respondent has behaved in such a way that the Petitioner cannot reasonably be expected to live with the Respondent

☐ The Respondent has deserted the Petitioner for a continuous period of at least two years immediately preceding the presentation of this petition

☐ The parties to the marriage/civil partnership have lived apart for a continuous period of at least two years immediately preceding the presentation of the petition and the Respondent consents to a decree/order being granted

☐ The parties to the marriage/civil partnership have lived apart for a continuous period of at least five years immediately preceding the presentation of the petition.

4

Part 6 Statement of case

See the supporting notes for guidance on how to complete this section

(in all cases, please state briefly any relevant details about the fact(s) on which you rely)

Part 7 Details of the children

See the supporting notes for guidance on how to complete this section

If you cannot agree arrangements for your children, you can make an application under the Children Act 1989. Please see leaflets CB1 Children and the family courts and CB7 Guidance for separated parents: Children and the family courts.

Children of the family	Date of birth (or state if over 18)	Over 16 but under 18 and in education, training or working full time	(a) Child of both parties	(b) Other child of the family
Child 1	☐☐/☐☐/☐☐☐☐	☐	☐	☐
Child 2	☐☐/☐☐/☐☐☐☐	☐	☐	☐
Child 3	☐☐/☐☐/☐☐☐☐	☐	☐	☐
Child 4	☐☐/☐☐/☐☐☐☐	☐	☐	☐
Child 5	☐☐/☐☐/☐☐☐☐	☐	☐	☐
Child 6	☐☐/☐☐/☐☐☐☐	☐	☐	☐

Part 8 Special assistance or facilities if you attend court

See the supporting notes for guidance on how to complete this section

If you are required to attend court during these proceedings will you need any special assistance or facilities?

☐ Yes (please supply details below) ☐ No

Part 9 Service details

See the supporting notes for guidance on how to complete this section

☐ I am not represented by a solicitor in these proceedings

☐ I am not represented by a solicitor in these proceedings but am receiving advice from a solicitor

☐ I am represented by a solicitor in these proceedings, who has signed Part 10, and all documents for my attention should be sent to my solicitor whose details are as follows:

Box 1 Solicitor's details

Name of solicitor			
Name of firm			
Address to which all documents should be sent for service:	Telephone no.	
	Fax no.	
	DX no.	
Postcode	Your ref.	
	Fee account no.	

E-mail	

Box 2 Petitioner's address for service

Address (including postcode)

Postcode

continued over the page ⇨

Box 3 Respondent's address for service

Address (including postcode)

Postcode ☐☐☐☐ ☐☐☐☐

Box 4 Co-Respondent's details, if any

(please see the Guidance Notes for this form on the need to name the correspondent)

☐ There is no Co-Respondent

☐ There is a Co-Respondent whose details are as follows:

First Name	
Last Name	

Address (including postcode)

Postcode ☐☐☐☐ ☐☐☐☐

continued over the page ⇨

7

Part 10

See the supporting notes for guidance on how to complete this section

Prayer

The Petitioner therefore prays

(1) **The application**

☐ That the ☐ marriage ☐ civil partnership be dissolved

or

☐ That the Petitioner be (judicially) separated from the Respondent.

(2) **Costs (if you wish to claim costs from the Respondent or Co-Respondent)**

☐ That the ☐ Respondent ☐ Co-Respondent shall be ordered to pay the costs of this application

(3) **Financial Order (if you wish to make an application for a Financial Order)**

☐ (a) That the Petitioner may be granted the following Financial Order(s):

☐ an order for maintenance pending suit/outcome

☐ periodical payments order

☐ secured provision order

☐ lump sum order

☐ property adjustment order

☐ order under section 24B, 25B or 25C of the Matrimonial Causes Act of 1973/paragraph 15, 25 or 26 of Schedule 5 to the Civil Partnership Act of 2004 (Pension Sharing/Attachment Order) or section 25F or section 21B of the 1973 Act or paragraph 19B or paragraph 34A of the 2004 Act (Pension Compensation Sharing/Attachment Orders)

☐ (b) **For the children**

☐ a periodical payments order

☐ a secured provision order

☐ a lump sum order

☐ a property adjustment order

Signed ☐☐☐☐☐☐☐☐☐☐☐ Dated ☐☐/☐☐/☐☐☐☐

Petitioner ['s Solicitor]

8

10 CIVIL PARTNERSHIP ACT 2004

10.1 INTRODUCTION

This chapter will:

• discuss the Civil Partnership Act 2004.

The Civil Partnership Act 2004 (CPA 2004) came into force on 5 December 2005 and its scope is extremely wide, affecting every area of family law. It is a lengthy piece of legislation; there are 264 sections in eight parts and also 30 schedules. Despite the size of the CPA 2004, there has been very little case-law generated by the advent of civil partnerships. This chapter looks at the scope of the CPA 2004 and the impact of the Marriage (Same Sex Couples) Act 2013.

10.2 SCOPE OF THE CIVIL PARTNERSHIP ACT

The CPA 2004 enables same-sex couples to form legally recognized civil partnerships. Once a partnership has been formed, civil partners assume many legal rights and responsibilities for each other, third parties, and the State. Many of these rights and responsibilities are identical to those enjoyed by married couples.

The CPA 2004 makes many amendments to many different statutes.

The CPA 2004 amends the Children Act 1989 and the Adoption and Children Act 2002 to enable a civil partner to acquire parental responsibility (see **Chapter 25**) and the definition of a 'child of the family' includes civil partners as well as parties to a marriage. A civil partner is entitled to apply for a residence or contact order (see **Chapter 26**).

The CPA 2004 also makes wide-ranging changes to statutes as diverse as the Family Law Act 1996 to allow civil partners to apply for non-molestation orders and occupation orders (see **Chapters 33 and 34**), and the Sex Discrimination Act 1975 to allow civil partners to claim discrimination on the grounds of their civil partnership. The CPA 2004 also amends tax credits, social security, and child support legislation to ensure that civil partners are equal to married people. Wills, administration of estates, and family provision as well as intestacy are also equalized to include the same rights for civil partners.

10.3 CIVIL PARTNERSHIP AND SAME-SEX MARRIAGE

The Marriage (Same Sex Couples) Act 2013 (MSSCA 2013) has made the marriage of same-sex couples lawful. Civil partnerships are still also lawful which means that same-sex partners have a choice between marriage and civil partnership if they wish to formalize their relationships. It may be that civil partnership becomes much less relevant and s15 MSSCA 2013 has placed a duty on the Secretary of State to initiate a review of the operation and future of the CPA 2004.

Section 9 MSSCA 2013 allows a civil partnership to be converted into a marriage. There is no formal ceremony required and the conversion would be through a declaration before a superintendent registrar. As this is only in office hours, this has generated some publicity as many will wish to have a more celebratory approach.

10.4 DIFFERENCES BETWEEN CIVIL PARTNERSHIP AND MARRIAGE

There are very few differences between civil partnerships and marriage on a legal basis (although many may disagree on a political, spiritual, or religious basis).

The civil partnership is formed on the signing of the register rather than the exchange of vows. Requirements to form a valid civil partnership are similar to those for valid marriages, except that civil partners must be of the same sex (see **Chapter 5**). Further, non-consummation and venereal disease grounds are not included in the grounds for the annulment of a civil partnership (see **Chapter 5**) as they are with marriage between different sex couples.

Adultery is not a fact to establish the ground for dissolution of a civil partnership as it is in marriage (see **Chapter 6**).

Although it confers on the civil partners most of the rights and responsibility conferred by marriage, a civil partnership is not a marriage and this was confirmed in *Wilkinson v Kitzinger* [2006] EWHC 2022 (Fam). A female same-sex couple was married in British Columbia, Canada but under the CPA 2004, this was treated as a civil partnership in the UK. The petitioner sought a declaration of her marital status, but the court dismissed her application.

SUMMARY POINTS

- This is a brief introduction to civil partnerships.

- The Civil Partnership Act 2004 introduced the concept of civil partnerships.

- There are some differences between civil partnerships and marriage.

SELF-TEST QUESTIONS

1. List three differences between marriage and civil partnership.

2. Two elderly sisters share a house and all household management and bills. They wish to form a civil partnership to take advantage of inheritance provisions. Can two sisters form a civil partnership?

online resource centre

Answers to the questions above can be found on the Online Resource Centre: **www.oxfordtextbooks.co.uk/orc/sendall17/.**

Part 3

MONEY AND PROPERTY

11 FINANCIAL ORDERS FOLLOWING DIVORCE OR DISSOLUTION

11.1 Introduction to money and property

11.2 What are financial orders?

11.3 Matrimonial Causes Act 1973

11.4 Factors to be considered by the court

11.5 Section 25 Matrimonial Causes Act 1973

11.6 Clean break

11.7 *White v White*

11.8 Factors for orders involving children

11.1 INTRODUCTION TO MONEY AND PROPERTY

This chapter will:

- introduce the main concepts in proceedings for financial orders under the Matrimonial Causes Act 1973;
- examine the factors considered by the court when deciding on financial orders;
- discuss the principal case-law arising from proceedings for financial orders.

This section of the text deals with the arrangements made to divide money and property following the breakdown of a relationship. Unless a relationship has been extremely brief, money and property will be acquired during the relationship that must be divided. In this context, 'property' has a wide meaning and will include furniture, savings, antiques, shares (and many other types of property), as well as houses.

This section will look at the law relating to spouses and civil partners. There is also a great deal of guidance from the courts to be considered, as well as statutory factors. The courts are very active in this area of family practice and the Online Resource Centre will contain regularly updated cases.

online
resource
centre

The case study of Helena and David Wilson will continue throughout this section of the text to demonstrate a financial order case.

This chapter will consider the factors that a court will take into account when deciding on the division of money and property following a divorce or dissolution of a civil partnership.

11.2 WHAT ARE FINANCIAL ORDERS?

Part 9 of the Family Procedure Rules 2010 (FPR 2010) refers to proceedings for a financial remedy and replaces the old terminology of 'ancillary relief'. Part 2.3 FPR 2010 defines 'financial remedy' as:

(a) a financial order;

(b) an order under Sch 1 to the Children Act 1989;

(c) an order under Part III of the Matrimonial and Family Proceedings Act 1984;

(d) an order under Sch 7 to the Civil Partnership Act 2004;

(e) an order under s27 of the Matrimonial Causes Act 1973;

(f) an order under Part 9 of Sch 5 to the Civil Partnership Act 2004;

(g) an order under s35 of the Matrimonial Causes Act 1973;

(h) an order under para 69 of Sch 5 to the Civil Partnership Act 2004;

(i) an order under Part 1 of the Domestic Proceedings and Magistrates' Courts Act 1978;

(j) an order under Sch 6 to the Civil Partnership Act 2004;

(k) an order under s10(2) of the Matrimonial Causes Act 1973;

(l) an order under s48(2) of the Civil Partnership Act 2004.

Further, the term 'financial order' means:

(a) an avoidance of disposition order;

(b) an order for maintenance pending suit;

(c) an order for maintenance pending outcome of proceedings;

(d) an order for periodic payments or lump sum provision as mentioned in s21(1) of the Matrimonial Causes Act 1973, except an order under s27(6) of that Act;

(e) an order for periodic payments or lump sum provision as mentioned in para 2(1) of Sch 5 to the Civil Partnership Act 2004, made under Part 1 of Sch 5 to that Act;

(f) a property adjustment order;

(g) a variation order;

(h) a pension sharing order; or

(i) a pension compensation sharing order.

The term 'financial order' and 'proceedings for a financial order' will be used in this text to describe the process of sorting out money and property following the end of a civil partnership or marriage.

The term 'ancillary relief' will be seen in cases decided prior to the implementation of the FPR 2010 (in April 2010) and is still being used by practitioners and courts. It will be some time before the term falls out of use.

In the early stages of practice, proceedings for a financial order can appear overly complex and it can seem hard to know where to start. Most clients seek an opinion from their solicitor early on in the retainer.

This text will look at all the factors that a court considers in proceedings for financial orders. Many practitioners use different approaches to deciding what a client may obtain through proceedings and, when in practice, you will develop your own.

Clients frequently complain that proceedings for financial orders are not fair (on them). The courts have to make decisions that will affect your client's life for some years to come and, inevitably, neither party is generally satisfied with the outcome. The majority of clients do not have sufficient funds to approach the proceedings knowing there is enough money to meet all needs and desires of the parties. Clients may not appreciate that courts have guidance from statute and case-law and apply this guidance in their case. This chapter considers the guidance from the courts.

11.3 MATRIMONIAL CAUSES ACT 1973

The jurisdiction of the court to make financial orders is found in the Matrimonial Causes Act 1973 (MCA 1973). The orders that can be made, the scope of these orders, and the factors that the court considers when making these orders are found within MCA 1973.

The court has a duty to consider all the circumstances and so this gives the court the ability to investigate the case when making its decision. The House of Lords in *Miller v Miller; McFarlane v McFarlane* [2006] 1 FLR 1186 considered three main principles for distribution: need, compensation, and sharing with an over-arching requirement of fairness (see **11.7**). Case-law is progressing on these points and will be examined during the following chapters in Part 3.

11.4 FACTORS TO BE CONSIDERED BY THE COURT

11.4.1 ALL THE CIRCUMSTANCES OF THE CASE

Section 25(1) MCA 1973 states that it is the duty of the court in deciding whether to exercise its powers to make financial orders (see **Chapter 12**) under ss23 (periodic payments and lump sum orders), 24 (property adjustment orders), 24A (orders for the sale of property), or 24B (orders regarding pensions) to have regard to all the circumstances of the case, first consideration being given to the welfare while a minor of any child of the family who has not attained the age of 18.

All the circumstances of the case can include the existence of pre-marital agreements (sometimes called pre-nuptial agreements) and these are discussed further in **Chapter 13**.

11.4.2 CHILDREN

This differs from the Children Act 1989 (see **Chapter 24**) where the child's welfare is the court's *paramount* consideration. This must not be confused with the *first* consideration in proceedings for financial orders. In proceedings for financial orders the children's interests are not the overriding consideration of the court and the court has a general duty to consider all the circumstances of the case. The Court of Appeal in *Suter v Suter* [1987] 2 FLR 232 underlined this and stated that the court was to bear in mind the important first consideration of the welfare of the children and then to achieve an order that was just.

 Practical Considerations

In most cases, the court will have as its priority the provision of a home for the children of the family and sufficient income to maintain the home and pay bills etc. Unless the parties have a great deal of money and property, this will account for the majority of the family's assets.

11.5 SECTION 25 MATRIMONIAL CAUSES ACT 1973

When the court is considering a financial order case, the factors to be considered are found in s25(2) MCA 1973:

(2) As regards the exercise of the powers of the court under section 23(1)(*a*), (*b*) or (*c*), 24, 24A or 24B in relation to a party to the marriage, the court shall in particular have regard to the following matters—

(a) the income, earning capacity, property and other financial resources which each of the parties to the marriage has or is likely to have in the foreseeable future, including in the case of earning capacity any increase in that capacity which it would in the opinion of the court be reasonable to expect a party to the marriage to take steps to acquire;

(b) the financial needs, obligations and responsibilities which each of the parties to the marriage has or is likely to have in the foreseeable future;

(c) the standard of living enjoyed by the family before the breakdown of the marriage;

(d) the age of each party to the marriage and the duration of the marriage;

(e) any physical or mental disability of either of the parties to the marriage;

(f) the contributions which each of the parties has made or is likely in the foreseeable future to make to the welfare of the family, including any contribution by looking after the home or caring for the family;

(g) the conduct of each of the parties, if that conduct is such that it would in the opinion of the court be inequitable to disregard it;

(h) in the case of proceedings for divorce or nullity of marriage, the value to each of the parties to the marriage of any benefit which, by reason of the dissolution or annulment of the marriage, that party will lose the chance of acquiring.

Each of these factors has been considered by the courts. It is important to note that all factors are considered equally important by the courts. These factors are not exhaustive, and the courts must consider all the circumstances of the case.

11.5.1 **INCOME AND EARNING CAPACITY, PROPERTY, AND FINANCIAL RESOURCES: S25(2)(a) MCA 1973**

 Practical Considerations

Many clients are tempted to dispose of assets by selling them and hiding the money, or temporarily giving them away. Clients must be told firmly at the outset that full disclosure of all property must be made and this duty to disclose continues throughout the proceedings. If a client tells you that he intends to dispose of assets and asks for your help, there will be professional conduct issues to consider.

11.5.1.1 Income and earning capacity under s25(2)(a) MCA 1973

Evidence of income and earning capacity will be found in payslips, P60, or accounts if self-employed (see **Chapter 14** and the case study for documents required to be disclosed in financial proceedings). There may also be payments in kind to be taken into account, e.g. company car, pension contributions, or free meals.

The statute states that '… in the case of earning capacity any increase in that capacity which it would in the opinion of the court be reasonable to expect a party to the marriage to take steps to acquire'.

The court may view this as being a presumption that the court can expect the parties to become financially independent following divorce. The court will look at what employment the party to the marriage could reasonably be expected to do. The court may base an order on someone making greater efforts to obtain employment, to go back into training, or to place a limit on periodical payments to encourage someone to return to work.

 Example

Sarita and Anil are married and have two children. Sarita worked as an admin assistant in the civil service before her marriage. When the marriage ended, Sarita had not worked for 11 years as both had agreed that she should remain at home with the children. Sarita has no qualifications other than some GCSEs.

The court orders Anil to make periodical payments to Sarita for five years to enable her to retrain and gain further qualifications.

This could cover a wife who gave up work to look after children and the home. The court will probably not expect a spouse to go to work when children are under school age but once children are at school, the spouse will probably be expected to obtain employment or allow time to retrain. It is important to factor in the availability and cost of childcare when thinking about this aspect. The court may choose to make an open-ended periodical payments order leaving the onus on the paying spouse to make an application for a variation (see **Chapter 15**) should she or he believe that the receiving spouse is able to work.

The income available to the parties is important as both parties have to be able to support a home and be able to pay bills. An important consideration is whether the parties will be able to afford a mortgage.

 Practical Considerations

When applying for a mortgage, the bank or building society will look at the income of the applicant as well as any liabilities they regularly pay. The applicant's gross salary will then be multiplied by a multiplier to produce an amount which the lender feels the applicant can afford. The multiplier is usually 3 or 3.5 times the applicant's gross income.

Before the 'credit crunch' multipliers were often far higher and could be five or more times an applicant's gross income. This led to many people taking mortgages which were very large. Lenders are now much more cautious.

11.5.1.2 Property and financial resources under s25(2)(a) MCA 1973

The court will look at all of the assets of the marriage regardless of in whose name it is held or when it was acquired. This will commonly include the family home, cars, savings, stocks and shares, pensions, and valuable antiques or paintings. For clients who are wealthy, this could also include holiday homes, yachts, jewellery, land, business assets, and portfolios of investments. For many clients, there are very few assets, e.g. if the parties live in rented accommodation or have little income. An increasing feature of financial order cases is the level of debt held by the parties on credit cards, secured, or unsecured loans. All of these liabilities will be taken into account by the court.

All possible assets should be considered including the family home, holiday homes, buy-to-let property, cars, antiques, jewellery, shares, endowment policies, pensions, and all other types of assets held. A good way of ensuring that you have a complete list of all assets held by the spouses is to have a comprehensive instructions checklist. A common practice is to give the client a list to complete or to give the client a Form E (see **Chapter 14**), which is the form that gives disclosure in proceedings for financial orders. The client completes the Form E and this begins the process of working out what assets are in the matrimonial 'pot'.

Assets are valued at the time of the court hearing (*Cowan v Cowan* [2001] 2 FLR 192). The fact that an asset is not liquid (i.e. not easily realized) does not mean that it should be disregarded, but the illiquidity should be taken into account when considering fairness.

Only assets in which one or both of the parties has a legal or beneficial interest will be considered by the court to be available for distribution, or in the 'pot'. Assets owned by a third party are not able to be the subject of an order of the court. In the case of *Prest v Petrodel Resources Ltd and Others* [2013] UKSC 34 there were a number of assets held by the husband's company. The court found that in this case while it could not look behind the corporate 'veil', the company held the assets on trust for the husband and so was able to make orders concerning the assets.

11.5.1.3 Matrimonial v non-matrimonial assets? Section 25(2)(a) MCA 1973

There has been increasing discussion about whether some assets held by one spouse can be considered 'non-matrimonial' property and, as such, either not be included in 'the pot' at all, or be distributed differently to matrimonial property. For most middle- and low-income families, this is not a distinction that the court is able to make, as all assets are required so a position is reached where all parties are adequately housed and maintained. Where there are assets in excess of basic needs, this becomes more of an issue. *Jones v Jones* [2011] 1 FLR 1723 held that pre-acquired and therefore non-matrimonial assets should be apportioned in light of the 'sharing principle'. In *N v F* [2011] EWHC 586 Fam Mostyn J held that the approach to pre-acquired wealth is fact-specific to each case and, as a result, highly discretionary. The court had to balance their discretion with the desirability of consistency and predictability of outcome. Pre-marital contributions must be a contribution which is unmatched by the non-contributing spouse but the longer the marriage, the more likely that contribution will fall to be shared between the parties.

 Example

Anil and Sarita have few assets from their marriage. They own their own home which is worth £150,000, but they have a mortgage for £50,000 and so the 'equity' in the property is £100,000. Anil also has a pension but this is not worth very much at all. There are no other significant assets.

In this case, the court will not consider whether this is matrimonial or non-matrimonial property as the home is the only asset that the court can consider and so the need to provide a home for both parties will take priority.

Pre-acquired property is not the only type of property that may be considered non-matrimonial property and treated differently. In *Miller v Miller; McFarlane v McFarlane* [2006] UKHL 24 two Law Lords differed on the approach to matrimonial property. Lord Nicholls categorized non-matrimonial as property that one party brought into the marriage or acquired by inheritance or gift during the marriage, all other property being matrimonial property. Baroness Hale took a different view. She viewed as non-family property not only property brought into the marriage but also business and investment assets generated solely or mainly by the efforts of one spouse during the marriage. Lords Mance and Hoffmann agreed with Baroness Hale.

The case of *Charman v Charman* [2007] EWCA Civ 503 was heard in the Court of Appeal before England's most senior family law judges outside of the House of Lords. One commentator hoped that it would iron out the contradictions between their Lordships in *Miller; McFarlane*.

The case involved colossal sums of money from the husband's outstanding business career. In a unanimous judgment, the Court of Appeal held that, subject to needs and other factors, the sharing principle applies to all property; but there are likely to be better reasons to depart from equality with non-matrimonial property, and Baroness Hale's category of 'non-business-partnership non-family asset' cases is limited to short marriage cases and possibly dual-career families.

The classification of 'non-matrimonial property' does not mean that it is left out of account altogether; rather, the importance of the distinction is in relation to whether it is subject to equality or the sharing principle (*Norris v Norris* [2002] EWHC 2996 (Fam) and *S v S* [2007] EWHC 1975 (Fam)).

With a long marriage, the weight attached to sole contributions may diminish, though sometimes it will not. In *Miller; McFarlane*, Lord Nicholls gave the examples of modest savings introduced at the beginning of a marriage that have grown (and presumably could be split) and an inherited heirloom that should be retained in its inherited form.

Inherited wealth is a resource under s25 MCA 1973, but the nature and source of the inheritance may dictate that the court treats each inheritance differently from other assets in the 'pot'. Property inherited before the marriage may not be left with the inheriting spouse, especially in a long marriage. If an inheritance has been enjoyed by both parties it may be treated as being available to the court to meet needs. However, *Robson v Robson* [2011] 1 FLR 751 cautioned about not 'invading' inherited wealth too easily.

In *AR v AR* [2011] EWHC 2717, following a 25-year marriage there was an estimated total of between £21 and £24 million in assets, and all but £1 million were in the husband's name. Because the source of the wealth was the husband's family business, bought by his father shortly after the Second World War, the court rejected the argument for sharing and relied upon the 'needs' element of fairness (see *Miller; McFarlane*). The wife's needs were assessed at £3.2 million, so that she could have additional security during her lifetime. Her housing needs were assessed at £1.1 million and the total therefore was some £4.3 million, with the husband retaining the balance of £20 million.

There will be occasions when an asset is not easily realized, e.g. a business. The courts do not generally require such an asset to be destroyed, e.g. by forcing the business to be sold or large amounts of capital to be drawn from the business even though it is subject to be shared. In this type of case, other assets will be used to compensate the other spouse. This may take the form of an increased share of capital assets or making larger maintenance payments to increase the spousal share without compromising the asset. The courts will look carefully at business assets held by the company of one party. In *Prest v Petrodel Resources Ltd* [2013] UKSC 34 discussed earlier, valuable property was held on trust for the husband. The wife sought to include these assets in the resources available to the court. The Supreme Court held that, although entitled to do so in limited circumstances, it would not be appropriate to pierce the corporate veil based on the facts of the case, but found that these assets were available to the husband as the company held them on trust for him. The judgment is complex but worth reading.

11.5.1.4 Pre-acquired and post-separation assets

As stated above, where assets have been acquired prior to the marriage, there may be an argument for exclusion from the proceedings if the parties marry later in life or if the marriage is short. Similarly, an asset which accrues after the end of a marriage may well be excluded unless it represents the fruits of the labour of the parties whilst married (*SK v WL (Ancillary Relief: Post Separation Accrual)* [2011] 1 FLR 1471). This situation must be distinguished from an asset accruing during marriage where one party made no contribution (*Gordon (formerly Stefanou) v Stefanou* [2011] 1 FLR 1582).

11.5.1.5 Pensions

A pension is an asset that must be taken into account in the fair distribution of matrimonial property (see **Chapter 19**). The courts have either added the Cash Equivalent Transfer Value (CETV) of the pension to the 'pot' (*White*) or used a whole life fixed rate interest scheme (*Cowan v Cowan*). In *Maskell v Maskell* [2001] 3 FCR 296 the approach was simply to aggregate the pension with other assets, as only part of the pension could be taken as capital and the other part was income. The court stated that like must be compared with like. In *Martin-Dye v Martin-Dye* [2006] EWCA Civ 681 Thorpe LJ stated that the pension should not be treated as capital but as another financial resource, sitting comfortably in neither the category of 'property' nor 'income'. Pensions are often dealt with by pension sharing orders: s24B MCA 1973 (see **Chapter 19**).

 Example

The facts of *H v H* were that the husband and wife were aged 46 and 44 respectively at the time of the trial. The parties agreed on the equal division of assets totalling £2.7 million following a 20-year marriage. The couple separated in January 2005. The issue before the court was two accrued bonuses, each of about £2.4 million, and future bonuses.

Charles J held in this case that the date for the valuation of the assets was 1 January 2005, the date of the breakdown of the marriage, and so the matrimonial property did not include the bonuses. Charles J said that:

the concept of matrimonial property … is based on the concept of an equal and voluntary partnership providing mutual emotional, economic, and general support and matching contributions to it of different kinds. A point, or a line, for defining the matrimonial property is therefore a date when that mutual support ends.

11.5.2 **FINANCIAL NEEDS, OBLIGATIONS, AND RESPONSIBILITIES: S25(2)(b) MCA 1973**

online
resource
centre

The Family Justice Council have produced 'Guidance on Financial Needs on Divorce' and this can be found in the Online Resource Centre. This guide is an attempt to avoid the regional disparities in judgments, to give guidance in an area where 'needs' are not defined and to provide guidance to litigants in person.

In the majority of cases involving middle or low income families, the primary objective of the court will be to provide a home and income for the spouse with care of the children and a home and sufficient income for the other spouse. Priority will be given to the spouse with care of the children, in line with s25 MCA 1973.

 Example

Eddie and Cherry separate following a five-year marriage. They have one child, Billy, aged 4. Eddie works as a civil servant and earns £19,000 per annum. Cherry is a hairdresser and earns £16,000 per annum. The pair rent a property from a private landlord and have a few hundred pounds outstanding on a credit card. There are no other assets.

The court in this situation will have a limited set of options for the parties. The court will try to ensure that both parties have sufficient income to rent a suitable property and to meet household bills. There will be little else for the court to do. This type of case is common in practice.

The regular outgoings of both spouses will have been listed in disclosure and the court will consider whether they are reasonable for a person in their financial circumstances and the standard of living enjoyed by the parties. The court will not permit a party to live beyond their means nor condemn one spouse to unused to penury.

 Practical Considerations

The court will look for parity between the parties. One party will not be expected to live in a tiny bedsit in a dubious part of town whilst their partner lives in luxurious splendour in the nicest street imaginable. In practice, it is very unusual to find one party living on benefits with little money and the other party to be wealthy.

Most clients will have some level of debt. These are responsibilities that must be met and the court does not have the power to order one party to make payments to a creditor, who is generally not a party to the proceedings. The debt must be taken into account when the court makes its decision. In the current economic climate, it may also be difficult for clients to obtain credit or a mortgage.

Many clients will simply have insufficient assets to make a division which provides comfortably for both parties; indeed, this is the majority of cases before the courts. *A v L* [2011] EWHC 3150 (Fam) is a rare case of a set of very modest assets in a financial remedy case which has been considered by the higher courts. The case is considered more fully later in the chapter. As the judge states in his judgment, in such cases, the court has to be fair to both parties but, in one sense, the only way to do that is to balance the unfairness.

Many clients will have formed new relationships or even remarried. This will be taken into account as it will have an effect on the needs and obligations of the spouse. It may also have an effect on their resources. The new partner may have substantial resources that free up the resources of the spouse as well as reducing their needs. Alternatively, a new spouse or partner may increase the needs of the spouse if new children arrive or a larger home is required. The new partner or spouse does not become a party to proceedings but the court will take into account the effect of new relationships. It is important to realize that the resources of the new partner or spouse cannot be directly applied to meet the needs of the spouse bringing proceedings for financial orders.

Example

Eddie and Cherry separate following a five-year marriage. They have one child, Billy, aged 4. Cherry begins a new relationship with Tom almost immediately following separation and moves into Tom's flat with Billy. Cherry and Tom now have a new baby.

   Cherry now has the benefit of Tom's income and this will mean that more of her income will be available for consideration by the court. However, Cherry has both Billy and her new child to support. The court will have to consider both aspects of this new relationship carefully.

The court has the power to order a 'costs allowance' to the financially weaker party. See **Chapter 14** for further details and case-law.

11.5.2.1 'Compensation'

In *Miller v Miller; McFarlane v McFarlane*, Lord Nicholls raised a new form of needs in the shape of 'compensation'. Compensation addresses the perceived injustice of a spouse whose earning capacity is seriously depleted by the arrangements made by the parties, e.g. a wife staying at home to care for children will be disadvantaged in the labour market. The spouse may receive a fair share of the assets but has little ability to earn the same amount in the future as the spouse with the greater earning capacity. The disparity between the parties will become more apparent as time goes on. The wife sees her capital assets diminish as well as losing the ability to share in her husband's future earnings.

 Example

Katerina is a highly paid corporate lawyer when she marries Derek, a successful entrepreneur. Both agree that Katerina will stay at home with the children of the marriage until they have left home. After a 35-year marriage, Katerina and Derek separate.

   The court accepts that Katerina had a very successful career when she gave it up to look after the children. Although Derek can offer Katerina sufficient money for a comfortable life, Katerina will not regain her career and Derek will continue to accrue wealth through his business. The court may decide that Katerina has a large periodical payments order to address the disparity in wealth between the parties.

In *McFarlane*, the wife was given significant periodical payments to address this issue. Since this case, in *S v S (Non-Matrimonial Property: Conduct)* [2007] EWHC 2793 (Fam) Burton J stated that 'I do not believe that this head of loss can be said to arise in every circumstance.'

   In *RP v RP* [2007] 1 FLR 2105, Coleridge J remarked:

> The word compensation, which has been used frequently during this hearing, does not appear in the statute. Does it, I wonder, in the end, add anything to the concept of financial … obligations and responsibilities which each of the parties has deriving from s25(b)?

Coleridge J seemed to suggest that the court looks to s25(2) MCA 1973 and provide for a wife in such a situation and address the problem as a 'needs' issue.

   In *CR v CR* [2007] EWHC 3334 (Fam), Bodey J agreed with Coleridge J and warned that:

> these strands underlying fairness do not become elevated into separate 'heads of claim' or 'of loss' independent of the words of the statute … It remains the statutory criteria which ultimately guide the court's overall discretion by the exercise of which fairness is sought to be achieved.

It seems that the courts remain rooted in s25 MCA 1973 and that any perceived inequity, including the need for compensation, should be remedied through the generous interpretation of s25(2) MCA 1973.

11.5.2.2 Wealthy clients: s25(2)(a) and (b) MCA 1973

When clients are very wealthy, the court may find that there is sufficient capital and income to comfortably meet all the basic needs of the clients with much to spare. The court must then decide how to divide the remainder.

In *White v White* [2001] 1 AC 596, Lord Nicholls stated that financial needs are only one of the factors to be taken into account in arriving at the amount of the award.

McCartney v Mills-McCartney [2008] EWHC 401 (Fam) is an example of an instance when the wife was confined to her reasonable needs (albeit generously interpreted) and the husband left with a much larger balance. The husband's fortune had been made before the couple had met, the marriage was short, there was no ground for including an element of compensation in the award, and the wife's contributions had not been exceptional. Bennett J said that 'In my judgment, in this case the needs of the wife (generously interpreted) are not simply one of the factors in the case but are a factor of magnetic importance.'

In *Charman v Charman* [2007] EWCA Civ 503, the Court of Appeal considered a postscript by Coleridge J to this judgment. He asked whether there might be a threshold of wealth at which the court might consider that it was appropriate to depart from equality automatically. Neither of the leading counsel in the case could agree on what this figure should be. What would be the level of wealth at which the departure from equality would occur? The figure of £40–50 million was given, but the Court of Appeal found itself unable to identify any figure as a guideline threshold for special contribution and felt it would be dangerous to do so. The Court of Appeal felt that it might discourage a court from discerning special contribution at a lower level of wealth or that departure from equality was inevitable above that level of wealth. The court did not consider such an approach to be useful.

The problem with cases such as *Charman* is that they offer little assistance to the solicitor advising on smaller, more average cases. David Hodson commented that:

> at times higher court judges seem cocooned and exposed only to those solicitors and barristers undertaking the very big money cases. A daily diet of *Charman* does not give an appreciation of the bulk users of the family law finance resolution system, clients struggling to pay privately yet striving to reach a settlement, the middle-class disputes across the whole of England. These clients and their solicitors have suffered badly at the hands of the disputes, contradictions and conflicts between the senior judiciary of this country.

 Example

The High Court has (rarely) recently addressed a more modest case and the case *of A v L* [2011] EWHC 3150 (Fam) (Moor J) 7 December 2011 gives a little more insight into judicial thinking in 'ordinary cases'.

In the case, the wife had primarily been a housewife and mother. At the time of the case she was unemployed but had undertaken some work after the couple separated. The husband worked as a self-employed letting agent. The husband's income was unclear but was estimated to be £28,000. Even allowing for a medical condition, his earning capacity was far greater than his wife's.

The family's assets at the time of the case were:

The Former Matrimonial Home	£216,908
Egyptian properties	£45,833
Wife's accounts	£752
Husband's accounts	£5,811
Husband's debts	(£35,789)
Total	£233,515

The wife had been living in the matrimonial home since the separation in 2000 and the husband had been renting.

The judge at first instance had held that the wife needed to remain in the matrimonial home for a short period to adjust to life after separation but that it should be sold after two years. On sale, the proceeds should be divided 70:30 in the wife's favour and the husband should pay periodical pay-ments of £500 per month for four years.

Moor J held that no sufficient justification was given for the very significant departure from equal-ity at first instance. The judge had not adequately explained how the order would meet the needs of both parties rather than the wife's needs alone. There was also insufficient explanation of the interplay between the capital order and the periodical payments order.

Moor J concluded:

1. the disparity in earning capacity combined with the parties' needs was a good reason to depart from equality, but only on a clean break basis. The primary justification for the departure was the income disparity between the parties but other reasons, such as the wife's continuing responsibility for the two (adult) children, were given;

2. the former matrimonial home should be sold as soon as possible as the husband could not dis-charge his debts without this and it was doubtful whether the wife could meet the mortgage on her own;

3. the sale proceeds would be divided 70:30 in favour of the wife. It was accepted by the court that the wife would find it very difficult to buy anything other than a small flat and, once the husband had paid off his debts, he would struggle to do even that without a large mortgage.

11.5.3 STANDARD OF LIVING: S25(2)(c) MCA 1973

The courts do not have to endeavour to place the parties in the position that they would have been in had the marriage not broken down. In *Miller v Miller*, the court looked at the concept of 'legitimate expectations' and Lord Nicholls stated that 'both hopes and expectations, as such, are not an appropriate basis to assess financial needs'. The parties must be realistic about the parties' resources and both parties may have to accept a drop in the standard of living.

11.5.4 AGE OF THE PARTIES AND DURATION OF THE MARRIAGE: S25(2)(d) MCA 1973

Both the age of the parties and duration of the marriage are considered in conjunction with other s25(2) MCA 1973 factors.

If the parties are young at the time of marriage breakdown, there may be a greater argu-ment for a clean break between the parties, especially if the marriage has produced no children. Younger parties can be expected to go back to work and become financially inde-pendent once children have gone to school. Similarly, if a party has not worked for some time, there can be an expectation with a younger person that they can retrain or re-enter work with some help. Younger parties under 50 can gain a mortgage more easily than those over 50. Younger parties have scope to increase their earning capacity more easily than those towards the end of their career.

By comparison, older parties may not be expected to find a highly paid job, or any em-ployment, if they have spent the large part of their lives in the home. It may be difficult for older parties to obtain mortgages or to build up pension funds quickly.

The length of a marriage is also important. As we have seen, the longer the parties are married, the more difficult it is to untangle the finances of the parties and they will prob-ably be more financially reliant on each other than those ending a short marriage. One must not forget that, however short the marriage, any children will be the first considera-tion of the court.

In a short and childless marriage, the traditional view is that the parties can expect to exit the marriage with only what they put into it in terms of money and legal rights to property may be more important than in longer marriages. In *Miller v Miller,* a very short marriage, it was held by Lord Nicholls that a short marriage was a partnership of equals but that there may be less of a claim between parties to a short marriage. Mrs Miller received less than one-sixth of the total assets.

If there are children, this will dilute the effect of the length of the marriage as the children must be cared for and be properly housed.

11.5.5 ANY PHYSICAL OR MENTAL DISABILITY OF EITHER OF THE PARTIES TO THE MARRIAGE: S25(2)(e) MCA 1973

The court will take into account any mental or physical illness of either party as this may affect the ability of that party to earn a living or they may require a greater amount of the assets and income to meet their needs. If a party has a progressive illness, the court may require a medical report giving the party's prognosis.

11.5.6 CONTRIBUTIONS TO THE MARRIAGE: S25(2)(f) MCA 1973

It may seem incredible now, but before the seminal case of *White v White* [2001] 1 AC 596, the contribution of a wife (as it usually was the wife) to looking after children and the home was considered inferior to that of the husband (as it was usually the husband) to work and make financial contributions to the marriage.

In *White v White*, the House of Lords found that parties would make significant and different contributions to the marriage and that it was wholly wrong to discriminate against the spouse who remained at home caring for the home and children. In different spheres of financial and family activity, both contribute equally to the family and it does not matter who built up the assets and earned the money.

Section 25(2)(f) MCA 1973 refers also to contributions made in the future. This encompasses the future care of children.

In cases involving great wealth, there has been a large amount of case-law on the assumed equality of contributions to the welfare of the family. Can there be said to be 'stellar contributions' made by one party that permits the court to move away from equality? This argument is frequently used by the husband, if he has made an unmatched contribution (whether described as 'special', 'stellar', or 'exceptional').

In *Cowan v Cowan* [2001] EWCA Civ 679, this argument succeeded. Mance LJ characterized the argument as:

> a spouse exercising special skill and care had gone beyond what was expected and beyond what the other spouse could ordinarily have hoped to do for himself or herself had the parties arranged their family lives and activities differently.

The facts of the case were that during the 35-year marriage the husband built up a fortune of £11.5 million due to his 'genius' in recognizing the potential of bin-liners in his plastics business. The court praised the husband's entrepreneurial flair, although the court acknowledged the wife's full contribution to the marriage and family life. As a result of the husband's efforts, there was a departure from equality.

However, in *Lambert v Lambert* [2002] EWCA Civ 1685, the Court of Appeal retreated from this position. After a 23-year marriage, the assets amounted to £20.2 million. At first instance the court held that the wife's full contributions were not exceptional, but the husband's contributions were really special. The Court of Appeal allowed the wife's appeal and awarded her 50% of the assets. Bodey J commented that:

> it is not possible to define once and for all, by way of some formulaic label, the precise characteristics of the fortune-maker required... However, those characteristics or circumstances clearly have to be of a wholly exceptional nature that it would be inconsistent with the objective of achieving fairness for them to be ignored.

This approach was approved in *Miller; MacFarlane*.

In *H v H* [2002] 2 FLR 1021, Peter Hughes QC rejected the argument of a highly successful city solicitor that his contribution was really special and said:

it is not easy to define what may amount to a Stellar or really special contribution, but rather like the elephant, it is not difficult to spot one when you come across it.

The argument did succeed in *Sorrell v Sorrell* [2005] EWHC 1717 (Fam), where the assets were £75 million after a 32-year marriage with three children. The court described the husband's success resulting in the accrual of the assets as a result of his 'spark' or 'skill', and of the husband's genius. It held that it would be unfair to fail to recognize the exceptional circumstances and decided a 60/40 split in the husband's favour.

In *Charman v Charman (No. 4)* [2007] EWCA Civ 503, after a marriage of 28 years with two children, the assets amounted to £131 million. The wife conceded that some departure from equality should be made due to the husband's contribution; the wife was awarded 36.5% of the assets. The husband appealed and one of the grounds was that the court had not given sufficient recognition to the husband's contribution. The Court of Appeal rejected this argument and stated it would be hard to conceive that a percentage of division of matrimonial property should be further from equality than 66–33%.

The possible exception from this stated range is *McCartney v Mills-McCartney,* where the court rejected the arguments of the wife's 'exceptional' contributions. As stated at **11.5.1.3** the other factor of importance was the issue of non-matrimonial property.

In *Charman: Sharing in the Face of the Dragon*, published by Family Law Week and available at www.davidhodson.com and www.iflg.uk.com, David Hodson summarizes the impact of the *Charman* case as follows:

- equality of division is no longer just a yardstick or check; it is now a principle of financial provision law;
- since property should be shared equally unless there is good reason to depart from equality, any departure is not from the principle but takes place within the principle;
- English financial provision law is a two-stage process; first, what is the available property, income, and other resources?; secondly, how should they be distributed in accordance with s25 and case-law?;
- subject to needs and other factors, the sharing principle applies to all property, but there are likely to be better reasons to depart from equality with non-matrimonial property;
- this above comment differs from some recent cases in which non-matrimonial property tended towards equal sharing with longer marriages, greater contribution, mixing and mingling etc. Hereafter, all property starts with equality sharing;
- special contribution could be non-financial or financial, is not simply based on the level of wealth;
- the Court of Appeal preferred Baroness Hale and Lord Mance to Lord Nicholls on departing from equality in short marriage cases;
- it was dangerous to create a level of wealth above which there would be automatic departure from equality;
- special contribution was likely to lead to departure from equality of 5–16.6%;
- where there are unquantified debts at the final hearing, it was appropriate for these to be shared in accordance with the proportion of sharing the assets.

Subsequent to *Charman*, the court found in *K v L* [2012] 1 WLR 306, that 'a special contribution arises in circumstances in which a spouse's contribution, direct or indirect, to the creation of matrimonial property has been so extraordinary as to dictate a departure within the sharing principle from the ordinary consequence of its equal division' [para 21].

Evans v Evans [2013] EWHC 506 (Fam) was a 'big money' case involving in the region of £40 million of assets. There were a number of issues to be decided and they included:

- the appropriate percentage of company shares to be received by each party;
- how the available capital resources should be divided;
- whether or not there should be a clean break;
- whether the division of assets should be adjusted in the wife's favour as she alleged a 'wanton campaign of extravagance' by the husband.

The court considered in particular the allegations of financial and litigation conduct and found that it was not appropriate to consider only the husband's expenditure without also considering the wife's in the same way. There had to be clear evidence of 'wantonness', to the extent that it would be inequitable for the court to disregard it. The court had to find whether it was necessary to 'add-back' some assets to the 'pot' to make a fair consideration. The wife did establish wanton expenditure, but only partly, and so the court found there was no need to adjust the division in order to achieve fairness.

In relation to a special contribution by the husband, the court considered the fact that he had created the company that had given rise to the parties' wealth virtually from scratch. When the court considered the evidence, the case did not merit the conclusion of special contribution. In the current case, it was not possible to identify specifically what part of the wealth was not marital, but the court still had to consider the weight to give to the husband's endeavours post-marriage. Some departure from equal division was justified and would be reflected in the award.

11.5.7 CONDUCT

The courts and lawyers realistically expect that either party to a relationship breakdown will behave unpleasantly, unpredictably, or with a certain amount of negative emotion. This behaviour does not generally concern the court's consideration of the case, often to the outrage of the parties involved.

 Practical Considerations

Many clients believe that the behaviour relied upon in the divorce petition should be taken into account when considering the division of money and property, e.g. adultery or domestic abuse.

The courts consider the behaviour of the parties and 'blame' (for want of a better word) within the marriage for the principal relief under the MCA 1973, i.e. divorce. The division of money and property is therefore based on the various factors of s25 MCA 1973 and not on the factors considered in divorce. Only in very narrow circumstances can conduct be considered.

The courts have consistently held that conduct is not considered by the court unless it is 'obvious and gross' (*Wachtel v Wachtel* [1973] Fam 72). In *Miller v Miller*, their Lordships were clear that adultery did not amount to such conduct and that in most cases fairness did not require the consideration of conduct.

Examples of what has amounted to obvious and gross conduct include the case of *B v B (Financial Provision: Welfare of a Child and Conduct)* [2002] 1 FLR 555 where the husband removed money from the jurisdiction to prevent the court's consideration of its disposal and the abduction of their child resulted in a conviction for child abduction. In *H v H (Financial Relief: Attempted Murder as Conduct)* [2006] 1 FLR 990 the husband was convicted of the attempted murder of his wife and refused to sell or let the family home. The wife was awarded the majority of assets and the court held that this was conduct that could not be disregarded. In fact, the husband's conduct had resulted in harm to her mental health and almost destroyed her earning capacity and, as a result, the conduct was at the top end of the scale.

11.6 CLEAN BREAK

Under s25A MCA 1973, the court has a duty to consider whether it is appropriate to impose a clean break. A 'clean break' is a settlement that finally severs the financial ties between the parties with no continuing provision between the parties for capital or income payments.

The court is not obliged to order a clean break; it is only obliged to consider the possibility of a clean break.

Further, s25A(2) MCA 1973 obliges the court to consider the term of a periodical payments order and should consider whether it is appropriate to make an order of sufficient length to enable the spouse in whose favour the order is made to adjust without undue hardship to being financially independent of the other party. This envisages a situation where one spouse can increase their earnings and financial independence, e.g. where a spouse works part time and can increase their hours or a spouse can retrain to find work.

When there are children, it is not possible to order a complete clean break, but there is no reason why there should not be a clean break between the parties, if there are sufficient assets.

Whether or not a clean break is achievable depends entirely upon the circumstances of each individual case. There must be sufficient capital or income to enable each spouse to be financially independent of each other immediately.

 Example

In *Parlour v Parlour* [2004] 2 FLR 893 the wife was awarded periodical payments at a high rate to build a capital fund. The husband was a footballer who was expected to earn very high wages but for a limited period only. As a result, the periodical payments were made for a limited term. A clean break would be achieved at the end of the term of periodical payments.

Not many clients will be footballers, but this is applicable to clients with high earnings but little capital.

11.7 *WHITE V WHITE*

The most significant decision in recent years came from the House of Lords in *White v White* [2001] (see **11.5.6**) when guidance was given on different aspects of ancillary relief (as it was called then).

The husband appealed to the House of Lords, seeking the restoration of a lump sum order for £980,000. The wife cross-appealed and sought a higher award.

The assets of the case included a dairy farm to which the parties had contributed equally, worth £3.5 million. The husband had an interest in another farm, which was not part of the partnership assets. The marriage had lasted 30 years and the parties had worked together in partnership. Both had substantial pensions.

The award to the wife was initially based on the traditional approach of allowing the wife 'reasonable requirements' to house herself and pay reasonable outgoings. The wife argued that it was appropriate for her to receive a sum roughly equivalent to half of the assets.

The leading judgment was given by Lord Nicholls. It is essential reading for all family law students and practitioners alike and a link can be found on the Online Resource Centre. The main points of the case are discussed below.

online resource centre

The relationship between s25(2)(a) and s25(2)(b) MCA 1973 was not altogether satisfactory and the wording of the statute had led to confusion arising about 'reasonable requirements' being used as the only criterion in a big money case, when it was only one of many factors to which the court was to have regard in the overall requirement of fairness. The court in this case had fallen into error as it had confined itself to the wife's 'reasonable requirement' and ignored the fact that the husband's requirements were no greater yet awarded him the majority of the assets.

The court should not make any distinction between contributions made by running the home and caring for the family on one hand and financial contributions on the other hand. Such contributions are to be considered of equal value to the welfare of the family.

When considering the division of assets, Lord Nicholls stated that the statute did not include a presumption of equal division but gave as a general guide that only with good reason would it be sufficient for a judge to depart from the 'yardstick of equality'. In practice, this yardstick is to be applied once the s25 MCA 1973 factors have been considered as a final check in the exercise of deciding the orders. It is not the starting point.

In fact, the wife in the case received roughly two-fifths of the assets as a whole as the House of Lords departed from equality on the basis that the husband's father had contributed money to the business and had assisted the husband to buy the second farm in the husband's sole name.

In *Parra v Parra* [2003] 1 FCR 97 the Court of Appeal allowed an appeal in favour of the husband and imposed an equal division of the assets where prior to the decision the wife had been awarded 54% of the assets. The parties had ordered their lives on the basis of equality and this ought to be recognized.

Departure from equality has been allowed on the grounds of a 12-year contribution to home and family being different in quality to a marriage of 20 years or more (*GW v RW (Financial Provision: Departure from Equality)* [2003] 2 FLR 108) and in a short childless marriage where the court tried to give the parties the financial resources that they entered the marriage with (*Foster v Foster* [2003] 2 FLR 299), but see *Miller v Miller* where the House of Lords confirmed that short marriages were also subject to the yardstick of equality.

11.8 FACTORS FOR ORDERS INVOLVING CHILDREN

As will be seen in **Chapter 12**, it is possible to apply for orders for children in proceedings for financial orders. The factors that the court will take into account are found in s25(3) MCA 1973 and include:

(a) the financial needs of the child;

(b) the income, earning capacity (if any), property, and other financial resources of the child;

(c) any physical or mental disability of the child;

(d) the manner in which he was being and in which the parties to the marriage expected him to be educated or trained.

If the child is a child of the family and not the natural child of the person against whom the order is sought, the court shall also have regard:

(a) to whether that party assumed any responsibility for the child's maintenance, and, if so, to the extent to which, and the basis upon which, that party assumed such responsibility and to the length of time for which that party discharged such responsibility;

(b) to whether in assuming and discharging such responsibility that party did so knowing that the child was not his or her own;

(c) to the liability of any other person to maintain the child.

As seen in **Chapter 18**, child support maintenance is dealt with under the Child Support Act 1995 and the Child Maintenance and Other Payments Act 2008. **Chapter 18** also contains details of applications made under Sch 1 of the Children Act 1989.

SUMMARY POINTS

- Proceedings for a financial order is the term given to the proceedings to divide money and property between divorcing spouses or civil partners dissolving a partnership.

- When the court is considering how to divide the matrimonial assets between the parties, the court must follow s25 MCA 1973 and associated decisions of the court.

- The first consideration of the court is the welfare of the children of the family and it must consider all the circumstances of the case.

- The court must consider a clean break between the parties, although this is not always possible.

- The s25 MCA 1973 factors encompass the available assets, the needs of the parties, age and duration of the marriage, standard of living, and contributions to the marriage and conduct.

- Some of these issues have generated a great deal of case-law and debate.

- *White v White* was decided by the House of Lords and affirmed that the aim of the court is to ensure fairness between the parties and for assets to be shared equally unless a departure from this is required.

- Some of the recent issues considered by the courts include, when a departure from equal division is appropriate, how to classify property as matrimonial or non-matrimonial property, compensation for the ability to earn a future income, and whether 'special' contributions to marriage merit a departure from equality.

- No factor has any more importance than any other factor and the court must consider all the circumstances of the case.

SELF-TEST QUESTIONS

Matthew (aged 48) and Jilly (aged 49) have been married for 28 years and have three grown-up children. Matthew works as an accountant in a large firm and earns £250,000 per year. Jilly gave up work as a stockbroker when the first child of the marriage was born and has looked after the children and the home since then. The couple has a large comfortable home, which has been valued at £1,500,000 and is mortgage free. Matthew has a pension with a value of £250,000. The couple has some stocks and shares which, since the credit crunch, have decreased in value to around £18,000. There are no other significant assets as the couple admits that they have generally lived well, had many foreign holidays, and paid for their children to be educated privately.

The couple divorce following Matthew's adultery. Apply the s25 MCA 1973 factors to their case and draw some conclusions about how the court may divide the assets.

Case Study Two

Helena Wilson commenced divorce proceedings based on the fact of unreasonable behaviour. David has indicated that he will not defend the petition and has moved out of the family home into rented accommodation. He regularly has contact with his son Richard.

Helena comes to see you regarding financial relief. You take instructions and then receive a letter from David's solicitor giving some disclosure of his assets.

Your supervisor asks you to look at Helena's attendance note and the letter and to apply the s25 factors to the case. What are your conclusions about how the court will approach the case?

---

online resource centre

Answers to the questions above can be found on the Online Resource Centre: **www.oxfordtextbooks.co.uk/orc/sendall17/.**

12 FINANCIAL ORDERS

12.1 INTRODUCTION

This chapter will:

- discuss the principal forms of financial orders under the Matrimonial Causes Act 1973.

As you have seen in **Chapter 11**, the courts have guidelines to assist them in deciding how much of the assets each party to the case should receive. As a family law student you should apply these factors to the case in hand to understand how the court is likely to divide assets between the parties. Once you have an understanding of the factors involved in the case, it is necessary to understand which orders to make to achieve the desired result.

To reorganize the assets of the parties involved in proceedings, the court has a number of different orders at its disposal. It is important that you understand what each order can do and, equally importantly, what they cannot. You are advised to look at **Chapter 14** for a discussion on consent orders for dealing with undertakings and drafting orders. This chapter covers the principal financial orders, their scope, and how they are used. **Chapter 19** deals separately with pensions and pension orders and you are advised to read both chapters together for a full picture.

The statute that is most important to this chapter is the Matrimonial Causes Act 1973 (MCA 1973).

12.2 AVAILABILITY OF ORDERS

The financial orders are:

- under s23 MCA 1973, financial provision orders: periodical payments order, secured periodical payments order, lump sum order (including pension sharing order under s24B MCA 1973 and pension attachment order under ss25B and 25C MCA 1973);
- under s24 MCA 1973, property adjustment orders: transfer of property, settlement of property, and variation of settlement.

Section 17 Married Women's Property Act 1882 (MWPA 1882) allows the court to consider disputes concerning title to or possession of a property. Applications under this section are now rare, given the more wide-ranging powers of ss23 and 24 MCA 1973. Proceedings under s17 MWPA 1882 are rare and reference should be made to a practitioner's text.

12.2.1 WHEN ORDERS ARE AVAILABLE

The court can make the orders listed at **12.2** on the granting of decree nisi of divorce or nullity or on the grant of a legal separation (see **12.2.2** for civil partnership). Orders can only take effect on the pronouncement of decree absolute in divorce and nullity.

As orders can be applied for after decree nisi, this raises the possibility of applications being made a great deal of time after divorce or of multiple applications.

In theory a spouse could make an application for financial orders and allow it to become dormant for a number of years before reviving it. This is not likely to prove successful for a number of reasons:

- if the applicant's claim for a financial remedy is not made in the divorce petition or answer, an application must be made to the court for leave before an application can be made. Any lengthy delay between petition/answer and application will militate against the court granting leave;
- if an application is made a substantial period after a divorce has been granted, the court can take this into account when considering all the circumstances of the case under s25 MCA 1973 (see **Chapter 11**).

A successful application was made for a matrimonial order after a delay of 19 years in the case of *Wyatt v Vince* [2015] UKSC 14. The court allowed the application to proceed as Ms Wyatt's application was legally recognizable but she faced formidable difficulties in establishing an order should be made.

Repeated applications for financial orders are generally not permissible. If a financial order application is heard by a court there is usually an order with dismissal of all claims (see **Chapter 14**). No further claims can be brought in this situation. As discussed at **Chapter 14**, it is imperative that all future claims are dismissed. The court's role remains only as one of variation or enforcement (see **Chapter 15**).

In the case of one spouse inheriting or gaining a sum of money in the near future, it is possible for the court to adjourn proceedings until a date when the position will become clearer. There may, of course, be an argument about whether or not the money constitutes matrimonial property (see **Chapter 11**). The issue of adjournment was considered in the case of *MT v MT (Financial Provision: Lump Sum)* [1992] 1 FLR 362. The court held, on an application for a lump sum order, that in circumstances where there was a real possibility of a source of capital becoming available in the future, a discretionary jurisdiction to adjourn would be available where it was the only way to do justice to the parties. This also fits in with the overriding objective of fairness.

A nominal periodical payments order can also preserve the entitlement of one party to periodical payments after the dismissal of financial order claims. For a fuller discussion of nominal periodical payments orders, see **Chapter 14**.

The discussion in **Chapter 14** should also be heeded for the procedural approach of preventing multiple or late applications for financial orders.

12.2.2 CIVIL PARTNERS

Civil partners are entitled to apply for financial provision on the dissolution or annulment of a civil partnership. Under s72(1) Civil Partnership Act 2004 (CPA 2004), Sch 5 of the CPA 2004 makes provision for financial relief that corresponds with the provision made in connection with marriages by Part 2 of the MCA 1973.

All orders available to spouses are available to civil partners, with the exception of a pension attachment order. As with any proceedings for financial orders, orders will not take effect until the nullity or dissolution order has been made final or the separation order granted.

12.2.3 SPOUSES

The court can make any of the orders discussed in this chapter to the parties of a marriage.

Please note that cohabiting couples (whether same-sex or heterosexual couples) cannot apply for financial orders. For remedies available to cohabiting couples, please see **Chapters 22 and 23**.

12.2.4 CHILDREN

Under s29 MCA 1973, no provision may be made for a child of the family for financial provision or transfer of property if the child has attained the age of 18. Orders can be made for a child of the family (see **Chapter 11**) but more commonly an order will be made to one of the spouses for the benefit of the child or to achieve a situation that supports the spouse with the care of the children.

See **Chapter 18** for a discussion of Sch 1 Children Act 1989, which allows the court to make property orders for the benefit of children.

12.3 LUMP SUM ORDERS

A lump sum order, under s23(1)(c) and (f) MCA 1973, requires one party to pay a sum of money to another party (or a child of the family).

The payment can be made in one lump sum or by instalments. Instalments can be ordered to be secured to the court's satisfaction under s23(3)(c) MCA 1973. How the payments are secured will depend upon each individual case and according to the assets available to be secured. Lump sum orders are generally to be paid immediately or over a small number of instalments and so security will generally be gained by a deposit of title deeds to property, or stocks and shares, so that there is a sufficient safeguard for the recipient.

There is no power to order an interim lump sum order (*Wicks v Wicks* [1998] 1 FLR 470).

 Practical Considerations

Lump sum orders are extremely useful and are used to give one party a share of a large capital asset or as compensation for their interest in the family home, pension, shares, endowment policy, or savings. They can also be used to help one party reduce a mortgage to a more affordable level.

So, if a house is transferred to one spouse, another spouse can receive a lump sum from other assets to enable them to purchase a new property.

12.4 PROPERTY ADJUSTMENT ORDERS

Under s24(1) MCA 1973, the court may make any one or more of the following orders:

(a) an order that a party to the marriage shall transfer to the other party, to any child of the family, or to such person as may be specified in the order for the benefit of such a child such property as may be so specified, being property to which the first-mentioned party is entitled, either in possession or reversion;

(b) an order that a settlement of such property as may be so specified, being property to which a party to the marriage is so entitled, be made to the satisfaction of the court for the benefit of the other party to the marriage and of the children of the family or either or any of them;

(c) an order varying for the benefit of the parties to the marriage and of the children of the family or either or any of them any ante-nuptial or post-nuptial settlement (including such a settlement made by will or codicil) made on the parties to the marriage;

(d) an order extinguishing or reducing the interest of either of the parties to the marriage under any such settlement.

A property adjustment order is one which gives the court a great deal of scope to re-order the assets of the parties.

12.4.1 TRANSFER OF PROPERTY ORDER

Under s24(1)(a) MCA 1973 the court can order that property is transferred from one party to the other party or for the benefit of the children of the family. The party must be entitled to the property, e.g. be an owner of the property. This order is most commonly associated with the transfer of the family home. However, a transfer of property order can be used to transfer any property including cars, furniture, shares, endowment policies, holiday property or investment property, antiques, or jewellery.

Rented property can be subject to a transfer of property order as tenancies are 'property'. The court can order one party to transfer a tenancy to the other party including both private sector and council tenancies, and statutory tenancies under the Rent Act 1977. It does not matter whether the tenancy is periodic (weekly) or fixed term, although the landlord will need to consent.

Statutory tenancies can be transferred under Sch 7, para 2 of the Family Law Act 1996 and this is covered in **Chapter 34**.

12.4.2 SETTLEMENT OF PROPERTY

Under s24(1)(b) MCA 1973 the court can order one party to settle property to which he is entitled for the benefit of the other party or the children of the marriage. 'Settlement' does not mean that the person gives away the property completely. Generally, a settlement of property involves one party settling the property by way of a trust until a certain date is reached or a certain event occurs. For more discussion of this type of order, see **12.5.4**.

12.4.3 VARIATION OF SETTLEMENT

Under s24(1)(c) and (d) MCA 1973 the court can vary for the benefit of the parties or the children of the family any ante-nuptial or post-nuptial settlement including a settlement made by will or codicil.

An ante-nuptial settlement (an agreement made pre-marriage) could include a property bought in contemplation of marriage or during the engagement of the parties. If it is subsequently used as a family home, it can be regarded as an ante-nuptial settlement (*N v N and F Trust* [2006] 1 FLR 856).

In *C v C (Variations of Post-nuptial Settlement: Company Shares)* [2003] 2 FLR 493, a trust comprised the husband's shares in a company. The court varied the terms of the trust to give the wife 30% of the shares.

12.5 ORDERS CONCERNING THE FAMILY HOME

Whether owned by one or both parties, the family home is, for the majority of cases, the largest asset in financial order proceedings. As the court's first consideration are the children of the family, the court's priority will be to provide a suitable home for the children. Unless acting for wealthy clients, the central question to resolving the case is to use the family home to make an order that houses both parties adequately.

The most common orders made include the immediate sale of the property and division of proceeds, the sale of the house is postponed with the proceeds to be divided on sale, and transfer of the home into the sole name of one spouse with a charge in favour of one spouse, or immediate payment of a lump sum in compensation.

12.5.1 SALE AND DIVISION OF PROCEEDS

Under s24A MCA 1973, where the court makes an order for a lump sum, a secured periodical payments order, or a property adjustment order, on making that order or at any time afterwards, the court may make an order for sale of property specified in the order to which either or both parties have a beneficial interest. An order for sale can include an order to make a payment out of the proceeds to one of the parties. An order for sale can also be used to enforce a secured periodical payments or lump sum order.

An immediate sale may be appropriate in a number of circumstances:

- where there is sufficient equity in the family home to be divided to provide both parties with the means to purchase an adequate new home. There may not be the ability to buy a home of the same size or standard as the previous family home;

- where one party has already obtained alternative accommodation and the house proceeds are used to allow the other spouse to purchase a new property. The remainder of the proceeds can be given to the spouse with accommodation as a lump sum. This can be used as a savings 'cushion' or as a way of reducing the mortgage;

- where there is insufficient money to pay the existing mortgage and outgoings on the family home, there may be no alternative to the sale of the home if it is at risk of repossession. The proceeds of the sale can be divided between the parties, although the capital limit for certain welfare benefits must be remembered. Parties may have to seek local authority housing or housing association accommodation or private rented accommodation.

 Practical Considerations

In order to calculate the equity available in a home, the following steps must be taken:

- obtain an up-to-date valuation for the property;

- obtain the balance of any outstanding mortgage(s) and secured debts;

- take into account how much it costs to sell the home (estate agent fees, conveyancing fees, etc.) for both the sale and purchase of a new property;

- take into account any stamp duty (see **Chapter 20**) payable on the new home;

- take into account any removal fees or storage fees;

- for a publicly funded client, take into account the impact of the statutory charge.

This will give a realistic picture of the equity available to the parties when dividing sale proceeds. Advice can be taken from an independent financial adviser or mortgage adviser on the availability of mortgages and loans to purchase a new property.

12.5.2 TRANSFER INTO ONE SPOUSE'S SOLE NAME

There are some situations where the court may transfer the house into one spouse's sole name. In *S v S* [1976] Fam 18, the wife cared at home for a child with a disability and could not work full time, although she paid all mortgage and other household expenses. The house was transferred to her. Most commonly, transfer of the family home is used where the family home is the only asset and the parent with care of the children requires the property as security. This is not the only situation where the court will order a transfer and the court takes into account all the circumstances of the case. For instance in *Jones v Jones* [1976] Fam 8, the husband's assault on the wife reduced her capacity to work. The husband's conduct and the wife's inability to work led the court to transfer the house to the wife.

There are a number of variations on a transfer:

- One spouse has the family home transferred to them and the other spouse has a lump sum payment as compensation for the loss of their interest in the family home. This depends on the assets and the ability of the court to find a lump sum payment from the assets.

- The property can be transferred outright to one spouse with no lump sum payable and without any charge on the home.

If the house is sold, there may be insufficient sale proceeds for one party to receive a share of the sale proceeds. Instead of a lump sum, the spouse may receive a larger share of any pension provision or reduced or nil periodical payments. The mortgage will be transferred to the occupying spouse but it should not be assumed that this will happen automatically; the mortgage lender must agree to this. The transferring spouse is released from the commitment of the mortgage and is free to obtain one for a new property.

 Practical Considerations

One of the problems associated with transferring the family home is whether the mortgagee will consent to the transfer of the mortgage and whether the transferee can afford to take it on. One party may be willing to transfer a property to their former spouse or civil partner but if there is a mortgage, the bank or building society must agree to the mortgage being transferred too. It may also be the case that the transferee cannot afford to pay the mortgage without the assistance of the transferor. This may leave one party in the position of not being the owner of a property but still being responsible for a mortgage. This would be a difficult position for the transferee if their former spouse defaulted on the mortgage, as liability is joint and several.

This may seem a draconian measure to leave one spouse without any share of the family home, but it may be necessary to house a more vulnerable party. Alternatively, one spouse may have a high wage or excellent capacity to earn enough to provide a home for them whilst paying periodical payments—it will be a question of balancing the assets available against the needs of the parties and the overall requirement of fairness. There are some options open to the court where the spouse not living in the home retains a beneficial interest.

12.5.3 CHARGE ON THE PROPERTY

A charge is where the family home is transferred to one spouse completely with the transferring spouse receiving a proportion of the sale proceeds when the house is sold or on a specified event.

This type of order is suitable for a transferring party who is able to wait for their share and the level of the charge should be carefully considered—whether or not the money is required to pay for a new home or whether it is simply a lump sum to compensate the transferring party for the loss of the asset.

 Example

In *Browne (formerly Pritchard) v Pritchard* [1975] 3 All ER 721 the husband remained in the family home with his sons from a prior association. The wife left with the child of the marriage and remarried. At the time of the hearing (at the Court of Appeal) both parties were living on benefits and the wife had been deserted by her husband and was living in a council house.

The Court of Appeal ordered that a charge be placed on the house for one-third of the net sale proceeds in favour of the wife with the sale to be postponed until six months after the 18th birthday of the youngest son with liberty to apply for the charge to be realized earlier.

This type of order operates in a similar way to a *Mesher* order (see **12.5.4**), although the two are not identical. With a charge, one person owns the entire property with a charge against it. With *Mesher* orders, the ownership is held by both parties.

12.5.4 *MESHER* AND *MARTIN* ORDERS

If the court wishes to preserve both parties' interest in the family home but cannot immediately order a sale, a '*Mesher* order' may be suitable. A *Mesher* order is named after the case of *Mesher v Mesher and Hall* [1980] 1 All ER 126, although the case was actually decided in 1973.

A *Mesher* order is one where the family home continues to be held by both parties as trustees of land. The type of trust that is found in most *Mesher* orders is:

- one party has the sole right to occupy the property until sale;

- sale is triggered upon a particular event, e.g. the occupying spouse dies, remarries, cohabits for more than six months, voluntarily sells the property, or the youngest child of the marriage attains a certain age;

- upon sale, the net proceeds of the sale (after redeeming the mortgage and paying sale costs) are divided according to proportions agreed at the time of the order.

The occupying spouse usually gives an undertaking to the court that they will maintain and repair the property and pay all outgoings.

The advantage of a *Mesher* order is that it allows the preservation of a family home with one party retaining an interest and gives one party a future capital interest in the property. For a while, *Mesher* orders became unfashionable, as the Court of Appeal found in *Martin v Martin* [1978] Fam 12 and *Hanlon v Hanlon* [1978] 2 All ER 889. Their criticism was that a *Mesher* order stores up trouble for the future and *Mesher* orders do have some disadvantages: children may require a home longer than is allowed for in the order; the home may have decreased in value over the period of the trust, leaving parties unable to buy a property; a spouse may enter the property market in their 50s without sufficient earning capacity; and an enormous gap can be left between the order and the non-occupying spouse receiving their capital interest. However, as property prices rose throughout the early part of this century, these orders have been used increasingly to achieve equality between the spouses, even if one spouse has to wait for a capital sum.

A similar type of order is the *Martin* order from the case of *Martin v Martin*. This order allows a spouse to occupy the family home until death or remarriage and the sale is postponed until then. It is a very unusual order that is not commonly used, but will protect an older, financially vulnerable spouse with no earning capacity.

12.6 PERIODICAL PAYMENTS ORDERS

The capital orders (see **12.5**) will allow the courts to rearrange the assets between the parties, but both parties require an income.

Periodical payments orders under s23(1)(a) and (d) MCA 1973 are often referred to by clients as 'maintenance'. The order is for a regular payment of money by one party to another. The interval of payments can be weekly or monthly.

Under s23(1)(b) and (e) MCA 1973 the periodical payments can be secured in order to ensure payments are made without requiring enforcement.

The assets used as security will depend upon the assets in the case. In some cases, an asset will produce an income, e.g. savings or shares, and these will form the security. In other cases, an asset does not produce an income, e.g. a painting. The payments will be made from income as usual but in the case of non-payment, the asset will be charged with the amount of non-payment and the receiving spouse will be able to recover the charge. The assets cannot be disposed of during the life of the secured periodical payments order.

12.6.1 THE AMOUNT OF PERIODICAL PAYMENTS

There is no guidance in the MCA 1973 concerning the amount of periodical payments. There have been a number of different approaches by the courts, although there is no preferred method.

Considering the s25 MCA 1973 factors, the court will consider the children of the family (as their first consideration), the reasonable needs of the parties, as well as the standard of living of the parties. 'Needs' may also encompass a situation where one party can become financially independent through retraining or when the children go to school and, until then, periodical payments are needed to support that party.

The income of the parties is clearly relevant together with their future earning capacity. Clearly a balance must be struck between the ability of the payer to provide periodical payments with the need to maintain the payer's income at a reasonable level too. The availability of welfare benefits should also be considered (see **Chapter 21**).

One approach is to look at the 'net effect' of the proposed order and there is an example of this in the case study later in the chapter.

As seen in the case of *Parlour v Parlour* [2004] EWCA Civ 872, periodical payments may also serve the purpose of allowing the receiving party to build up a capital sum. In *McFarlane v McFarlane* [2006] UKHL 24, Baroness Hale stated that the sharing principle applied (as well as needs and compensation). The sharing principle dictates that the receiving party will share in the future surplus and share in the fruits of the matrimonial partnership. Mrs McFarlane received a periodical payments order beyond her reasonable needs. Their Lordships were clear that capital accumulation was a permissible side-effect of periodical payments. It must be borne in mind that both cases involved very high earners and most clients will not necessarily have a surplus income.

A 'nominal' periodical payments order is one where a nominal sum of money (e.g. £1 per year) is ordered either for the joint lives of the parties or for a limited term. The purpose of such an order is to allow one party to have the security of a periodical payments order that can be varied upwards in case of illness or unemployment. The periodical payment is paid at the nominal sum unless the court decides to vary the amount upwards.

 Example

In *SRJ v DWJ* [1999] 2 FLR 176, a 27-year marriage produced four children, one of whom was still dependent, with the wife unable to support herself without resort to welfare benefits. The husband was unlikely to produce sufficient income in future that would benefit the family and enable the wife to come off benefits.

The court took several factors into consideration:

- the wife still looked after a dependent child;
- the wife was unable to financially support herself but had to accept that she would have to make efforts to do so;
- this was a long marriage with four children and the wife gave up her work to look after the family.

The court made a nominal periodical payments order for £10 per annum.

12.6.2 THE TERM OF PERIODICAL PAYMENTS ORDERS

The term of the periodical payments orders is 'as the court thinks fit'. The term cannot begin any earlier than the making of the application for the order and cannot carry on after death except in the case of secured periodical payments, or (if the order is made after the grant of a divorce, nullity, or civil partnership dissolution) the remarriage or entering into a civil partnership of the party in whose favour the order has been made (s28 MCA 1973). Commonly, the term of the order will come to an end on the cohabitation, as many parties would cohabit and not marry in order to allow the payments to continue.

The courts have a number of options for the making of periodical payments orders:

- adjourn the application;

- a periodical payments order for the joint lives of the parties until death, remarriage, or entering into a civil partnership. It can be subsequently varied or discharged (see **Chapter 15**). This may be suitable where one party has an illness or disability, where they are unlikely to be able to support themselves, or where minor children are dependent on the parties. The amount of the order can be substantive or nominal;

- a periodical payments order for a limited term under s28(1A) MCA 1973 with no extension after the limited term. An application for the variation of the amount is permitted. This type of order may be made where one party requires a period of time to become financially independent but the court finds the case unsuitable for extensions, e.g. in a case where a spouse has made no effort to become financially independent;

- a periodical payments order for a limited term but with no prohibition on extension. Prior to the expiry of the limited term, an application may be made for variation, extension, or discharge. This may be used when a party seeks to become financially independent but the court wishes to give the party the opportunity for a longer period of periodical payments;

- dismiss the application.

12.7 **INTERIM ORDERS**

12.7.1 **MAINTENANCE PENDING SUIT**

Section 22 MCA 1973 allows an application for maintenance pending suit. On a petition for divorce, judicial separation, nullity, or civil partnership dissolution, the court can require either party to the marriage to pay periodical payments for his or her maintenance for such term as the court thinks reasonable. The term cannot start before the date of the presentation of a petition and ends on the date of the determination of the case.

In practice, most parties agree a form of maintenance between themselves pending resolution of the case. Sometimes the parties survive financially through a combination of earnings, welfare benefits, and loans from banks or friends.

To apply for maintenance pending suit, the applicant must issue a Form A (see **Chapter 14**).

This order addresses the problem where one spouse finds themselves in need of income following the issuing of a divorce or civil partnership dissolution. Longer term issues of capital provision or the family home are left until the final hearing. The applicant must demonstrate their specific need, usually in the form of a budget. If there is not full disclosure of the payer's income and assets at this stage of proceedings, the court will err on the side of caution if the payee's need is evident to the court. In *TL v ML* [2005] EWHC 2860 (Fam) the court noted that the approach to be applied in determining the application is 'reasonableness' under s22 MCA 1973, which was described as being synonymous with fairness.

Two new sections have been introduced by the Legal Aid, Sentencing and Punishment of Offenders Act 2012 into the Matrimonial Causes Act 1973 to help such litigants overcome this problem. They are ss22ZA and 22ZB MCA 1973 and corresponding amendments will be made to Sch 5 to the Civil Partnership Act 2004.

The amendments abolish the maintenance pending suit (MPS) 'costs allowance' provisions and create a statutory regime which provides for 'an order or orders requiring one party to the marriage to pay the other an amount for the purpose of enabling the applicant to obtain legal services for the purpose of the proceedings'. The 'Legal Services Order' amends s24A(1) MCA 1973 so that an order made for a Legal Services Order can be backed by an order for sale. It is an interim order for sale provision, for the limited purpose of giving teeth to the Legal Services Order.

Commonly this type of order will cease at the financial dispute resolution hearing (see **Chapter 14**) and this is regarded as a reasonable inducement to settle rather than improper pressure.

12.7.2 INTERIM PERIODICAL PAYMENTS ORDER

Under r9.7 FPR the court has the power to make any interim order that it sees fit. The most common such order is for periodical payments for adults. The court has limited power to make periodical payments for children.

Interim periodical payments orders for adults are generally made when proceedings for financial orders cannot be fully resolved until a substantial amount of time after decree absolute as an interim periodical payments order can only be ordered after decree nisi has been pronounced. Maintenance pending suit will end on decree absolute and interim payments will take over if the final periodical payments order is not settled. It is possible to defer application for decree absolute until the financial arrangements have been resolved to avoid this issue.

12.8 **CHILD SUPPORT**

Child support is dealt with by the Child Support Act 1991 and subsequent legislation. Please refer to **Chapter 18**.

SUMMARY POINTS

- When the courts have applied the guidance under s25 MCA 1973 to the case, a decision is made about how the assets are divided.

- There are a number of orders that allow the court to reorganize the family's money and property and they are found in ss23 and 24 MCA 1973.

- Generally orders can be made following decree nisi and come into effect on the pronouncement of decree absolute (and equivalent in civil partnerships).

- Lump sum orders can be one lump sum or by instalments and can be secured.

- Property adjustment orders are used to transfer property between parties or to vary settlements of properties.

- There are a number of orders that can be made regarding the family home, including a sale and division of proceeds, transfer to one party, a postponement with a charge, or a *Mesher* or *Martin* order attached to the home.

- Periodical payments orders provide the receiving party with an income and the orders possible vary from an order for the whole joint lives of the parties to a short, non-extendable term.

- The amount prescribed by a periodical payments order can vary from a nominal payment to a substantial sum to allow one party to build a capital sum.

- Prior to decree absolute, maintenance pending suit can be used to provide an income.

SELF-TEST QUESTIONS

1. Bilkiss and Amir divorce. Bilkiss is disabled and requires a specially adapted home and also works from home. The home has a substantial level of equity and Amir is very well paid. The couple have two children, aged 11 and 12 respectively. Bilkiss wishes to remain in the home until the children have left home and requires a large share of the equity in the house to find a suitable home. Bilkiss and Amir agree that Bilkiss can remain in the home until the youngest child is 21 years old or if Bilkiss remarries or cohabits for more than six months. Once the 'trigger' event occurs, the house will be sold and Bilkiss will receive 80% of the sale proceeds. Explain which order will be suitable to achieve this and the advantages and disadvantages of such an order.

2. Bilkiss works part time as she cares for the children. She believes that it will be very difficult for her to find full-time employment, even when the children have left home. Amir wishes to have a clean

break. What income orders may be suitable for this situation? How could the court achieve a clean break?

Case Study Two

Proceedings for financial orders have been issued by Helena and the Form A can be found on the Online Resource Centre. Helena wishes to know whether or not she can remain in the family home with Richard. Your supervisor asks you to look at the disclosure given on the Form E (on the Online Resource Centre) and details about a Form E can be found in **Chapter 14**. What possible orders can be made concerning the family home in this case and which one would you recommend for Helena?

Answers to the questions above can be found on the Online Resource Centre: **www.oxfordtextbooks.co.uk/orc/sendall17/.**

13 PRE-MARITAL AGREEMENTS

13.1 INTRODUCTION

This chapter will:

- examine the nature of pre-marital agreements;
- discuss the enforceability of pre-marital agreements in proceedings for financial orders;
- discuss the potential developments in the enforceability of pre-marital agreements.

A pre-marital agreement (PMA) is essentially a contract between the parties of a marriage that decides, in advance of the marriage, the division of money and property between the parties in the event of a divorce. There has been a great deal of discussion and case-law on whether PMAs can and should be taken into account by the courts when considering proceedings for a financial remedy.

There has been a greater public awareness of PMAs through 'celebrity' divorces. This chapter looks at features of PMAs and case-law dealing with the issue of PMAs.

13.2 WHAT ARE PRE-MARITAL AGREEMENTS?

In essence, a PMA, sometimes called an ante-nuptial agreement or a pre-nuptial agreement, is a contract made between two people before they get married. The contract generally concerns the division of money and property following divorce. There have been objections to PMAs for many years. Some of the objections made have been from a religious standpoint as it is felt that marriage is based on love and affection and should not be sullied with contracts. Others believe that PMAs discourage marriage. The courts have traditionally found that parties, as a matter of public policy, may not anticipate the end of their marriage and may not exclude the jurisdiction of the courts in deciding financial orders. **Table 13.1** sets out the advantages and disadvantages of PMAs.

13.3 ADVANTAGES AND DISADVANTAGES OF PMAs

See **Table 13.1**.

TABLE 13.1 ADVANTAGES AND DISADVANTAGES OF PMAs

Advantages	Disadvantages
Consenting, well-advised adults can decide their own outcomes on divorce and can cut costs and acrimony on divorce.	Over time, the position of the parties can change: children may be born, one party can become ill or disabled, and the initial PMA may be unfair or inadequate to deal with such changes.
	One party can unduly influence another into an unfair PMA.
PMAs encourage openness on financial issues between the parties before marriage. Many marriages end because of disagreements over family finances.	They are 'unromantic' according to Paul McCartney (!)
PMAs may encourage marriage as certainty over proceedings for financial orders when two in five marriages fail could be a wise precaution.	They may discourage marriage for fear of losing assets.
PMAs may save costs in proceedings in financial orders.	PMAs will involve the cost of independent legal advice for both parties before the marriage.
PMAs can be used to protect wealth or family assets and to preserve property for children from earlier marriages.	

13.4 THE ENFORCEABILITY OF PMAs

The traditional position of the courts in England and Wales was that pre-nuptial agreements are not enforceable. PMAs are fully enforceable in other jurisdictions, including Sweden, Canada, certain US states, New Zealand, and marriage contracts are a feature of certain religions, e.g. Islam.

In 1998, the Government produced a White Paper called 'Supporting Families'. One of the issues that the Government raised was to make agreements concerning property legally binding, albeit with safeguards to protect a vulnerable party. The consultation revealed an equal split of opinion on the issue, with the points discussed in **13.3** raised by both sides of the argument.

The Law Commission looked at PMAs as part of their review of financial needs in family cases. The final report was published in February 2014. The report recommended the introduction of 'qualifying nuptial agreements'. These would be enforceable contracts and they would enable couples to make binding arrangements for the financial consequences of divorce or dissolution. In order for an agreement to be a 'qualifying' nuptial agreement, certain procedural safeguards would have to be met. Qualifying agreements could not, however, be used by parties to contract out of meeting the 'financial needs' of each other and of any children.

In more recent cases, PMAs have been held to be influential in courts' decisions and the Supreme Court has more recently been more positive on enforceability. The following section summarizes the main case-law on PMAs.

13.4.1 *K v K*

In *K v K (Ancillary Relief: Prenuptial Agreement)* [2003] 1 FLR 120, the husband and wife separated after 14 months of marriage and the parties had one child together. Prior to the marriage the wife discovered she was pregnant and the wife's family exerted pressure on the husband to marry her. The husband had wanted a long engagement but the couple agreed to marry and entered into a PMA, mainly at the instigation of the wife's father. The wife had assets (held in trust) of about £1 million and the husband had assets of £25 million.

Both parties received independent financial advice and the solicitors were informed of the pregnancy.

The PMA was signed the day before the parties married. The terms of the PMA were that if the couple were to dissolve their marriage within five years of the date of the PMA, the wife was to receive £100,000 from the husband (to be increased by 10% pa compound) and the husband was to make reasonable financial provision for any children. There were no valuations of the husband's assets prior to the signing of the PMA and there was no reference made in the PMA to periodical payments for the wife.

When the parties divorced 14 months later, the wife sought a much larger settlement from the court with sizeable periodical payments for her and the child. She also asked the court to disregard the PMA. The husband relied upon the PMA.

The judge rejected the wife's case and held that the wife understood the agreement, she was properly advised, she was under no pressure to sign, she entered the agreement in the knowledge that there would soon be a child, and that no unforeseen changes had arisen in circumstance since the PMA was made that would make it unjust to hold the parties to it. The particular features of the case that the judge took into account included: the fact that the marriage was very short, the pressure that the husband was under from the wife's family to marry, the interference of the wife's father in controlling and manipulating the wife's finances, and that the wife had been on a spending spree. The husband was substantially wealthy and could pay a settlement that prevented the disparity in the parties' financial positions having an impact on the child. The wife had contributed nothing to the husband's wealth but she would make future contributions to the upbringing of the child.

In terms of the validity of the PMA, the wife clearly understood the PMA and had received independent legal advice. The husband had not pressured her to sign.

Whilst there had not been full disclosure, the husband did not exploit his financial position. Both knew that the wife was pregnant with their child and no circumstances had changed sufficiently that would make it unjust to hold the parties to it. The husband had been heavily pressurized into the marriage by the wife's family, and had agreed to marry on the basis that the capital sum under the PMA would be a final settlement for the wife.

The judge held that the PMA should be considered by the court as one of the circumstances of the case under s25 of the Matrimonial Causes Act 1973 (MCA 1973) (see **Chapter 11**). The PMA was clear on the issue of capital provision for the wife and there were no grounds for concluding that an injustice would be done by holding the parties to its terms. Entry into the agreement constituted conduct that it would be inequitable to disregard under s25(2)(g) of the MCA 1973.

However, the PMA could not (in this case) preclude a claim for maintenance. The wife can contribute in the future by bringing up the child with an adverse effect on her earning capacity. The judge found that it would be unjust to the wife to suggest, either because of the short duration of the marriage or because of the PMA, that she should have no maintenance. The judge awarded the wife £14,000 pa to enable her to bring up the child in comfortable circumstances.

13.4.2 *CROSSLEY v CROSSLEY*

In *Crossley v Crossley* [2007] EWCA Civ 1491, a PMA had been executed between the parties. Both were independently wealthy before the marriage; Mr Crossley had £45 million and Mrs Crossley £18 million. The PMA contained an agreement for each party to walk away with what they brought to the marriage and that neither would apply to the court. The marriage broke down after a year.

Mrs Crossley applied for ancillary relief (as it was called then). She claimed that her husband had failed to disclose assets when entering into the PMA. Mr Crossley applied to the court for a summons to show cause why Mrs Crossley's claims should not be resolved in accordance with the PMA. At the first appointment, Mr Crossley argued that the court should not simply dismiss the case and ignore the s25 MCA 1973 factors but that Mrs Crossley should be held to the PMA. Bennett J held that the exceptional facts of the case justified a departure from the usual procedure (see **Chapter 14**) and allowed a Form E, an informal questionnaire, to be completed, and set the matter down for a one-day hearing in accordance with the overriding objective found in the procedural rules.

Mrs Crossley appealed these directions to the Court of Appeal. She argued that she had been denied the right to effectively present her case and that the provisions of the procedural rules were mandatory.

The Court of Appeal dismissed the appeal. The Court of Appeal found that whilst the existence of the PMA cannot oust the court's obligation to apply the s25 MCA 1973 factors, the exceptional facts of the case gave rise to a 'very strong case that a possible result of the s25 exercise will be that the wife receives no further financial reward' and that '. . . if ever there is to be a paradigm case in which the court will look to the prenuptial agreement as . . . a factor of magnetic importance, it seems to me that this is just such a case'. Thorpe LJ also remarked that 'It does seem to me that the role of contractual dealing, the opportunity for the autonomy of the parties, is becoming increasingly important.'

Before the court could then reach a decision on what Mrs Crossley should receive, Mrs Crossley withdrew her application.

13.4.3 *MACLEOD v MACLEOD*

The Privy Council in *MacLeod v MacLeod* [2008] UKPC 64 (on appeal from the Isle of Man) was asked to rule on PMAs. The law on family finances in the Isle of Man is virtually identical to that of the MCA 1973 and so the decision can be treated as one by the House of Lords. Although there are not individual judgments given by the Privy Council, the voice of the judgment is undoubtedly Baroness Hale's.

Mr and Mrs MacLeod are both American and married in Florida in 1994. Mr MacLeod had a substantial fortune and the parties entered into a PMA on the day of the marriage. The PMA would probably have been enforceable in Florida, but would have been considered inadequate provision for the wife under English law. The parties had five children and had moved to the Isle of Man.

In July 2002, the parties entered into another agreement, which was more generous to the wife than the 1994 agreement but less generous than a court applying the MCA 1973 would have been. The court found that the wife had entered into the agreement freely, voluntarily, and with full understanding. Mrs MacLeod had taken independent legal advice, but she chose to ignore it.

The marriage broke down in 2003 and the husband complied fully with the 2002 PMA, including the transfer of a property to Mrs MacLeod. There were contested proceedings concerning the children, resulting in shared residence. The husband accepted that the property transferred to Mrs MacLeod was not suitable for times when the children lived with her.

Proceedings were issued and Mrs MacLeod sought to avoid the PMA and asked for £5 million as a lump sum. Mr MacLeod's position was that Mrs MacLeod should be held to the PMA that offered £1 million on divorce but offered a further lump sum for rehousing that would be held on trust.

At first instance the court held that Mrs MacLeod should receive £1.25 million as a housing fund in addition to the £1 million offered by the PMA (Mr MacLeod had offered £750,000) and that the housing fund should not be held in trust. At appeal the parties repeated their positions, except that the husband accepted that the additional housing fund should be £1.25 million, but his position remained that this should be held on trust. Both appeals were dismissed.

Mr MacLeod appealed to the Privy Council. The husband's appeal was allowed and a trust arrangement was substituted for the lump sum.

The Privy Council stated that 'the case is not about the validity and effect of ante-nuptial agreements as such'. It is to be regretted that the court did not take the opportunity to develop the law further on PMAs. At para 31 the Privy Council stated that:

> it is not open to them to reverse the long standing rule that ante-nuptial agreements are contrary to public policy and thus not valid or binding in the contractual sense . . . there is an enormous difference in principle and practice between an agreement providing for a present state of affairs which has developed between a married couple and an agreement made before the parties have committed themselves to the rights and responsibilities of the married state purporting to govern what may happen in an uncertain and unhoped for future.

The Privy Council drew a distinction based on the fact that any financial agreement between the parties during the marriage would be a maintenance agreement (see **Chapter 17**) capable of being varied under s35 MCA 1973, whereas one made before a marriage probably would not. Some suggest it is difficult to see the difference between an agreement made on the day before the marriage ceremony and one made after the ceremony (or indeed between one made in the throes of a disintegrating marriage), but an important point emerged from the judgment. An agreement made prior to the marriage is not valid on the basis of public policy (although the court can take it into account) whereas one made after marriage is valid subject to normal contractual considerations and the power of the court under s35 MCA 1973 to vary such an agreement. This may have the effect of making applications under s35 MCA 1973 more common than they are presently.

The Privy Council remarked in *MacLeod* that the legal status of PMAs was a matter for Parliament, to be guided by the Law Commission. The conclusion to be drawn from the case is that a PMA executed before the marriage will carry less weight and is less likely to be upheld than an agreement reached during marriage.

13.4.4 *RADMACHER v GRANATINO*

In *Radmacher v Granatino* [2009] EWCA Civ 649, the wife was a German national from a very rich family. The wife was very wealthy and her income was in the region of £2.7 million pa. The husband, a French national, who had been a City banker with earnings peaking at £300,000 gross in 2001, was by the time of the hearing studying for a doctorate at Oxford University. The parties met in 1997 in London when the wife was 28 and the husband 26 and earning £50,000 gross pa. The parties became engaged in 1998 and agreed to enter into a PMA.

The Court of Appeal, whilst acknowledging that PMAs are, as a matter of public policy, unenforceable, held that in the right circumstances they will be given such weight in the balancing exercise so as to be the decisive factor in determining an application for ancillary relief (as it was then called). Thorpe LJ highlighted the fact that the law in this area in England and Wales is increasingly out of step with the majority of countries of the European Union and Rix and Wilson LJJ also considered the need to balance the 'public interest in a fair and just exercise of the court's discretion' and the need to ensure there are safeguards in place to protect those who may enter into an agreement without a clear understanding of the possible consequences of their doing so.

The Court considered that the judge at first instance had failed to give sufficient weight to a number of factors, including: that such agreements are standard practice in France and Germany; that the husband was very able and was well established in the financial world and had had ample opportunity to take independent legal advice (although he had chosen not to do so); that the husband knew the wife was from a very wealthy family; and that the husband had chosen not to initiate negotiations. Provision for the husband should be in accordance with that envisaged by the agreement.

The husband appealed to the Supreme Court and the decision can be found at *Radmacher v Radmacher (formerly Granatino)* [2010] UKSC 42. There was an unusually large bench hearing the matter with Lord Phillips, Lord Hope, Lord Rodger, Lady Hale, Lord Brown, Lord Mance, Lord Collins, and Lord Kerr all sitting.

The judgment of the Supreme Court has given the clearest indication that there may be a significant shift in attitude by the courts towards PMAs and that there may be a change in the law. The judgment of the Supreme Court does not seek to alter the principle that it is a court, and not any prior agreement between the parties, that will determine the appropriate financial provision on divorce as this is embodied in the MCA 1973. Lord Phillips stated that 'the court should give effect to a Nuptial Agreement that is freely entered into by each party with a full appreciation of its implications unless in the circumstances prevailing it would not be fair to hold the parties to their agreement'. Applying the law to the case, Lord Phillips goes on to say in conclusion that the circumstances were such that the court felt that it 'was fair that [the husband] should be held to [the] agreement [namely, not to claim anything against the wife] and that it would be unfair to depart from it'. In short, the Court placed decisive weight on the terms of the agreement in determining the outcome.

It should be noted that Lady Hale handed down a dissenting judgment which powerfully explored the position of women when considering pre-nuptial agreements.

13.4.4.1 Case-law following *Radmacher v Granatino*

In the case of *NG v SG* [2011] EWHC 3270 (Fam), Mostyn J considered the implications of *Radmacher v Granatino*.

The parties were Italian and Swedish and entered into a pre-nuptial agreement under Swedish law at the husband's request and upon which neither took legal advice. It was a short document providing that:

1. all property owned by the husband prior to the marriage was his private property and the wife had no right to it;

2. all inherited property would remain the sole property of the recipient; and

3. all other property acquired during the marriage would be marital property.

Charles J considered that there were no vitiating factors (duress, fraud, or misrepresentation) and he disagreed with arguments that the pre-nuptial agreement should be given limited weight as:

1. whilst the parties did not receive legal advice there was nothing unfair or difficult to understand;

2. the wife was indifferent to the value of the husband's property so there was no material non-disclosure;

3. there was no finding that the wife felt under undue pressure to sign or that she was acting against her better judgement; and

4. the inequality in bargaining power did not reduce the weight to be given to the agreement.

For these reasons he concluded that the agreement was a 'good and powerful' reason for departing from an equal division and it was an important factor in assessing the overall award. Mostyn J also looked at the issue of 'need' and whether a spouse left in straitened circumstances could invalidate a PMA. Mostyn J set the level of 'need' at a fairly low level, saying that 'destitution' should be avoided. As the word 'destitution' is not mentioned in *Radmacher v Granatino*, further judicial guidance may be needed.

In *B v S (Financial Remedy: Matrimonial Property Regime)* [2012] EWHC 265 (Fam), the agreement involved was made in Catalonia. At the final hearing, there was an issue about the weight to be accorded to the 'tacit' agreement of the parties to apply the Catalonian default matrimonial property regime. Neither party was actually from Catalonia originally.

There had been no discussions between the spouses nor had either party taken independent legal advice as to the question of whether the agreement would have been influential or binding upon a court in England and Wales. Mostyn J accorded 'absolutely no weight' to the matrimonial property regime and proceeded to conduct the usual s25 MCA 1973 exercise in its absence.

In *BN v MA* [2013] EWHC 4250 (Fam) a wife applied for a full range of financial remedies (including maintenance pending suit and a legal costs order) 15 months after signing a PMA. Mostyn J considered that:

1. no agreement can be allowed to prejudice the reasonable requirements of a child;

2. respect should be accorded to the decision of a married couple as to the manner in which their financial affairs should be regulated, i.e. there should be respect for autonomy; and

3. no agreement can overreach basic need.

Mostyn J found that there was no reason to resile from the PMA and upheld it in full.

In *Luckwell v Limata* [2014] EWHC 502 (Fam), the parties had freely entered into a PMA with a raft of legal advice, disclosure, and the judge found that without the PMA, the marriage would not have occurred. The wife was from a wealthy family whilst the husband was unemployed and in debt. Holman J found that the only factor preventing the PMA being implemented fully was the husband's needs. The husband needed a home suitable for contact with the children. Holman J awarded some provision for the husband but, interestingly, made the award on the basis that the husband was housed for life but would not have access to the capital.

13.5 NEGOTIATING AND DRAFTING A PMA

Following *Radmacher* (see **13.4.4**), the Supreme Court did not discuss the circumstances in which a PMA would be considered too unfair to be upheld. The following are drawn from case-law and may assist a PMA to be considered fair:

*   the parties have confirmed that they have each received independent legal (and, if possible, accountancy) advice prior to entering into the agreement. Ideally the parties should confirm in the PMA that they intend to enter into a legally binding contract. It is also best practice for the solicitor advising the client in relation to a PMA to include a certificate of competency into the agreement, in acknowledgement that they have the relevant expertise to advise on this area of the law. If such a declaration is not made in the PMA then less weight will be given to it should it be considered at proceedings for a financial remedy;

*   there should be a minimum time for reflection, e.g. 21 days;

*   the parties have fully and frankly disclosed to each other their means and relevant circumstances, which should be set out as an attachment to the PMA;

*   clarification should be provided in relation to who would have control of assets acquired by either party prior to the marriage and furthermore how jointly acquired property should be divided;

*   the parties did not enter into the agreement less than 21 days away from the date of the marriage. If the marriage does take place shortly after the parties have signed the agreement then it is less likely to be enforced (however, see *K v K* at **13.4.1**);

*   a recital that without the PMA there would have been no marriage;

*   provision for children should be considered with a possible review of any agreement during the marriage (a post-nuptial agreement?) with generous provision for children.

From the case-law cited earlier, even following these steps does not guarantee that a PMA will be followed by the courts. The client must be fully advised of the enforceability of PMAs and the risk that the court will not take the PMA into account fully or at all. Negotiations should commence well before a wedding in order that the agreement is not rushed into or a party may claim that they were pressured into an agreement. Full and frank disclosure is essential.

SUMMARY POINTS

- Pre-marital agreements (PMAs) are contracts that allow spouses to agree how they wish their money and property to be divided after divorce.

- PMAs have traditionally been unenforceable due to public policy considerations, as they purport to oust the jurisdiction of the courts, but this position has changed with recent case-law.

- Opponents of PMAs claim that they undermine marriage and could be used against a weaker party to deprive them of a proper settlement.

- Proponents of PMAs claim that they represent an expression of a spouse's autonomous wishes, and reduce costs and acrimony following divorce.

- The courts have indicated a number of factors that assist the PMA in being recognized by the courts.

- The Law Commission issued its report on marital arrangements in 2014 but the government has thus far declined to legislate on them.

SELF-TEST QUESTIONS

Mario is a very wealthy businessman who owns several vineyards in Italy, although he spends most of his time living and working in the UK running his wine business. He meets Cordelia, who owns a large farm in Wiltshire, which she inherited from her father. The couple wish to marry but do not want to risk the other party being awarded their farm or vineyards in financial order proceedings. Neither party has children.

Cordelia's brother, Hugo, insists that Cordelia should not get married and put the farm at risk. Mario also faces pressure from his family to protect the Italian vineyards.

1. Explain the advantages and disadvantages of PMAs.

2. What steps can be taken to assist the PMA being recognized by the courts?

3. Mario and Cordelia sign a PMA after their wedding and honeymoon. The PMA states that each party should retain their own pre-marital assets and that there will be no maintenance for either party, with property accumulated during the marriage to be shared equally. Cordelia discovers that she is pregnant with twins. Advise Cordelia on the validity of the PMA once the couple have children.

online resource centre

Answers to the questions above can be found on the Online Resource Centre: **www.oxfordtextbooks.co.uk/orc/sendall17/.**

14 PROCEDURE FOR FINANCIAL ORDERS

14.1 INTRODUCTION

This chapter will:

- discuss the funding options available to clients seeking financial orders;
- discuss the protection of assets forming part of proceedings for financial orders;
- discuss the pre-action protocol;
- explore the procedure for obtaining financial orders including the first appointment, financial dispute resolution hearing, and the final hearing;
- discuss the role of consent orders in proceedings for financial orders.

In proceedings for financial orders, the party making the application for financial orders is called the 'applicant' and the party against whom the application is made is called the 'respondent'. Either party to the marriage can make an application for financial orders. It is not uncommon for the respondent to a divorce petition or civil partnership dissolution to be the applicant in proceedings for financial orders.

This chapter considers both pre-action considerations and the procedure for financial orders. It also considers funding arrangements, the pre-action protocol, as well as the drafting of consent orders and appeals.

The President of the Family Division established the Financial Remedies Working Group 'to explore ways of improving the accessibility of the system for Litigants in Person and to identify ways of further improving good practice in financial remedy cases, confined to matters of practice and procedure' in June 2014. The working group is consulting upon the Money Arrangements Programme (the MAP) and hopes to introduce greater streamlining to the process and to make proceedings more efficient.

A pilot is running at the Central Family Court involving an accelerated First Appointment procedure. In general, the view of the working group is that the current procedure of

Forms E, FDA, FDR, and final hearings works well in most cases, and will continue, but they have made some recommendations including:

- the use of one unified procedure for all financial applications;
- a review of the use of the magistrates' courts to deal with financial proceedings;
- a simplification of financial remedy forms;
- the FDR to take place on the first occasion that the parties attend at court;
- guidance for Litigants in Person (LiP) to be issued in addition to better use of the tools already available.

 There will be a period of consultation on these views but the working party has issued draft court orders which can be found on the Online Resource Centre.

14.2 FUNDING PROCEEDINGS AND THE STATUTORY CHARGE

Proceedings for financial orders are expensive as they are time consuming for solicitors and are often very complex.

14.2.1 PUBLIC FUNDING

Since April 2013, public funding for this area of work is severely restricted. It may be obtainable in a case where the person is suffering or has suffered domestic violence (see **2.1.1.2**).

Clients may use alternative forms of dispute resolution to keep costs down (see **Chapter 3**). Family help (lower) can be used to advise the client, negotiate a settlement, and to obtain a consent order (see **14.12**). If it is necessary to issue proceedings, family help (higher) will be required and this will cover all proceedings up to a final hearing. If the matter proceeds to a contested final hearing, legal representation will be required.

See **Chapter 2** for eligibility on means and merits.

Generally, clients will have to fund proceedings privately, leading to concerns that some clients may not seek advice over settlements and may not receive a fair settlement. Clients may have to resort to a variety of funding devices (see **14.2.3**).

14.2.2 STATUTORY CHARGE

The statutory charge may result when the client gains a financial benefit as a result of the proceedings and arises where the client retains their own assets or gains some of the other person's assets (see **Chapter 2** for more details). As financial order cases involve money and property, the statutory charge must be raised with the client at the start of the case and during proceedings to ensure that the client understands the impact of the statutory charge on their settlement.

14.2.3 PRIVATELY FUNDED CLIENTS

For clients ineligible for public funding, there are a variety of funding options.

 Practical Considerations

When a client consults a solicitor, one of the requirements of the Solicitors Code of Conduct is that the client is given an estimate of costs. The client should be given the best information possible about the likely overall cost of a matter and, when appropriate, as the matter progresses.

A solicitor must give the client a realistic estimate of costs at the outset of the case and must regularly update the client. This is particularly important before a major step is taken in the case, as costs will rise. Any step in proceedings for financial orders should be proportionate to the costs and assets involved.

A client who is paying privately can use funding arrangements provided by banks, e.g. loans or specially arranged finance deals. Alternatively, some firms offer a monthly direct debit payment. In **Chapter 2**, there are details of how solicitors 'unbundle' fees to enable clients to access discrete advice and assistance at different parts of a financial remedy dispute. Costs can be high in proceedings for financial orders and, although the procedure is designed to encourage early settlement, clients should be regularly advised about their costs.

There is also a 'Sears Tooth' agreement. This is where the client assigns in a deed the full settlement to the solicitor so at the end of a case the costs can be paid first. A client must gain independent legal advice before signing such a deed and be aware of its effects. A Sears Tooth agreement must be disclosed to the court and the other party.

A client can apply for a legal services order (see **Chapter 12**) in certain circumstances for the other party to pay a contribution to costs.

In the case of *Re Z* [2009] EWHC 3621 (Fam) an application was made by a husband seeking an order preventing the wife's solicitors from acting for her on the ground that the senior partner of that firm had previously acted, while at another firm, for the husband in financial proceedings with the wife.

The husband had retained the solicitor to act in connection with a freezing order to prevent the wife from disposing of assets and had regarded the solicitor as a friend. After several separations and reconciliations, the marriage broke down in 2009 and the wife approached a firm of solicitors where the husband's solicitor was now the senior partner, although the wife was being advised by another partner.

The solicitor had left her previous firm to start the new firm in concert with several colleagues although the old firm still operated and retained the relevant files. When the husband found out, he requested through his solicitors that the firm cease to act for the wife, who at first refused to do so. After a five-week wait, the husband renewed his request for the firm to cease to act. The wife's solicitors said they were prepared to put in place undertakings that the senior partner would not discuss the case with her colleagues, attend any related meetings, and the wife would not attempt to discuss the case with the solicitor. The husband applied to the court.

Bodey J identified three principal questions for the court:

- Was there a real risk of disclosure?

- If so, have the wife's solicitors refuted the burden to show that there is no risk?

- If the order is granted, what effect should the five weeks' hiatus between raising the issue and seeking this order have?

Bodey J concluded that the wife's current solicitor possessed information which is 'confidential to the husband' and that the risk is neither 'merely fanciful nor theoretical'. The judge took account of the solicitor's 'hands on' approach as senior partner and the fact that systems to prevent disclosure did not always deal with accidental or inadvertent disclosures. Bodey J granted the husband an order but ordered that the husband contribute to the wife's costs incurred during the five-week wait between requests.

14.3 PROTECTING ASSETS

Even before proceedings are issued, assets may need to be secured. In **Chapter 16**, the issue of protecting or recovering assets is dealt with in detail. It is essential that mortgage payments or rent are paid throughout the proceedings to avoid losing the asset.

14.4 APPLICABLE RULES

The Family Procedure Rules 2010 (FPR 2010) came into force in April 2011 and apply to proceedings for a financial order. The rules made changes to existing rules but did not fundamentally alter the procedures, and so cases decided prior to the change will still apply. Prior to the FPR 2010, proceedings for a financial order were called 'ancillary relief' proceedings and cases decided prior to the FPR 2010 will use this terminology.

The FPR 2010 also apply to applications under s10(2) MCA 1973 (see **Chapter 7**). Applications for financial provision made by civil partners following civil partnership dissolution under s48 Civil Partnership Act 2004 are also covered by the FPR 2010.

The FPR do not cover an application under the Trusts of Land and Appointment of Trustees Act 1996 (see **Chapter 23**).

14.5 **PRE-ACTION PROTOCOL**

The pre-action protocol can be found in PD 9A FPR 2010 at para 2.1. Attention should also be paid to PD 3A FPR 2010 which requires the parties to attend a MIAM (see **Chapter 3**). The parties should submit a form FM1 confirming attendance at the MIAM or give the reasons for not attending.

The protocol is designed to apply to all applications for financial remedies. The protocol encourages the parties (and their solicitors) to consider court proceedings as a method of starting the court timetables, controlling disclosure, and to endeavour to avoid a costly final hearing.

14.5.1 **THE FIRST LETTER**

No specimen letter of claim is given in the protocol as the circumstances of financial remedy cases are so varied. All correspondence should comply with PD 9A FPR 2010 as it states the tone of the letter is important; consideration should be given to the impact of the correspondence on the parties and should not cause the other party to adopt an entrenched, polarized, or hostile position. The first letter and subsequent correspondence should focus on relevant issues and should ideally be approved by the client. The first letter should direct the recipient to seek legal advice, provide a second copy of the letter for this end, and allow at least 14 days for a reply.

 Practical Considerations

Resolution publishes a *Guide to Good Practice* which includes a guide to correspondence. It is an excellent guide to avoiding writing letters that set an adversarial tone for proceedings and applies to all proceedings, not just proceedings for a financial order. The aim of correspondence should be to:

- address and safeguard children's needs;
- give/obtain reasonable disclosure and to identify and resolve issues;
- advance the proceedings;
- record issues of conduct and fact.

Letters must serve a constructive purpose in moving the matter forward and take into account the interests of your client and the family as a whole. Do not write a letter where the purpose is to:

- satisfy the client's feelings;
- satisfy your own feelings;
- create or perpetuate conflict between family members;
- attack the other lawyer.

14.5.2 **DISCLOSURE**

The protocol underlines the obligation on the parties to undertake full and frank disclosure of all material facts, documents, and other information relevant to the issues. This is regarded as essential to reduce costs and to clarify the issues between the parties at an early stage. This duty is ongoing and must be carefully explained to the client by their solicitor.

Form E (see **14.8.1**) can be used by the parties as a guide to the format of the disclosure and documents should only be disclosed as required by Form E. The disclosure should be made in schedules. This helps to prevent excessive or disproportionate disclosure at excessive costs.

The consequences for failing to disclose fully are severe. In *Gohil v Gohil* [2015] UKSC 61 and *Sharland v Sharland* [2015] UKSC 60, final orders were set aside after material non-disclosure. In *Gohil*, material non-disclosure was alleged at the time of the final order but the order was set aside after further evidence emerged in criminal proceedings concerning the husband. In *Sharland*, the court found that the husband had been dishonest about his financial position. In both cases, there will be a re-trial.

14.5.3 EXPERT EVIDENCE

 Practical Considerations

The value of assets within proceedings for financial orders is often in dispute. It is essential that the court has a valuation to rely upon in order that it knows how much money is available to be split between the parties. Commonly assets requiring valuation include the family home, the value of a business, or a share in a business or a valuable asset, e.g. an antique or a painting.

Experts are often used to give independent, expert valuations for the court to rely upon. For the valuation of a family home, an estate agent working the relevant local area can be relied upon to give a realistic market value. For a business, a forensic accountant may be required in order to report on the accounts of a business.

Part 25 FPR 2010 covers the use of expert evidence. Expert evidence should only be required when the parties do not know or cannot agree the value of a significant asset. Rule 25.4 FPR 2010 states that the court should only allow expert evidence when it is necessary to resolve proceedings.

The cost of valuation should be proportionate to the sums in dispute. Rule 25.11 directs that the court has power to direct that evidence can be given by a single joint expert. A single joint expert should be instructed in accordance with r25.12 FPR 2010 including a jointly agreed letter of instruction. This method of valuation is also considerably cheaper than both parties instructing experts.

In order for parties to agree an expert, one party should give the other party a list of the names of one or more experts in the relevant specialty. Within 14 days, the other party must indicate any objection to the experts and, if so, should supply names of experts considered suitable. There should be a joint letter of instruction, which is disclosed to the court, and all meetings and conferences should be attended by both parties. If the parties cannot agree, the parties must carefully consider the cost implications of instructing their own individual expert and should consider whether to disclose the reports produced.

14.5.4 OVERRIDING OBJECTIVE

Part 1 FPR 2010 has an overriding objective, which applies to all proceedings. The court must give effect to the overriding objective when it exercises powers given to it by financial order rules or when it interprets any rule. The parties are also required to help the court to further the overriding objective.

In so far as is practical, dealing with a case justly involves:

- ensuring the parties are on an equal footing;
- saving expense;

- dealing with the case in ways that are proportionate to the amount of money involved, the importance of the case, and the complexity of the issues;
- ensuring the case is dealt with expeditiously and fairly; and
- allotting a fair share of the court's resources.

The court is also given a duty of 'active case management'. This includes:

- encouraging the parties to cooperate and to resolve disputes through mediation where appropriate;
- identifying the issues at an early stage;
- regulating the extent of disclosure of documents and expert evidence to be proportionate to the issues in question;
- helping the parties settle part or the whole of the case;
- fixing timetables and controlling the progress of the case;
- giving directions to ensure that the trial of the case proceeds quickly.

The aim of the protocol is to ensure that pre-application disclosure and negotiation takes place in appropriate cases and that it is cost effective.

14.6 **PROCEDURE**

Figure 14.1 is a diagram showing the overview of the procedure for financial orders.

FIGURE 14.1 AN OVERVIEW OF PROCEDURE FOR FINANCIAL ORDERS

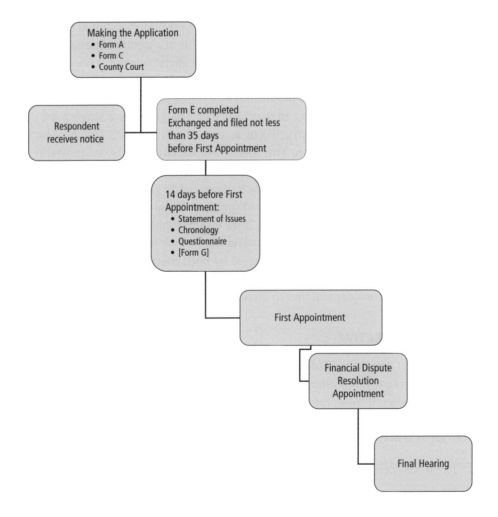

14.7 COMMENCING PROCEEDINGS

14.7.1 MAKING AN APPLICATION FOR FINANCIAL ORDERS

As seen in **Chapter 9**, the divorce petition contains a prayer, which asks for the various forms of financial orders (apart from an order for sale under s24A MCA 1973) and this is made operational by the petitioner in the divorce suit filing a Form A at court. A copy of Form A can be found in the case study. In addition to the Form A, the following documents must also be filed:

- if the client is publicly funded, a copy of the funding notice;
- Form FM1;
- notice of acting if the solicitor is not already on the court record;
- a fee or fee exemption.

Section 26 MCA 1973 allows applications for financial remedies to be made at any time following the presentation of the petition for divorce, nullity, or judicial separation.

Applications for a pension sharing or pension attachment order must be included either in general terms or specifically if the client is in a position to do so.

The Form A is served on the respondent by the court. The acting solicitor must also serve any pension provider where there is an application for a pension sharing or pension attachment order and a copy of the draft order must be filed with the Form A. If an application is made in respect of property subject to a mortgage, a copy of the Form A should be served on the mortgagees as soon as possible and in any event within 14 days.

14.7.1.1 Respondent's application

Under r9.4 FPR 2010 a respondent to a divorce suit can apply for financial orders through an answer to the petition and an answer is discussed at **9.10**. The respondent should make his financial relief claims in the answer.

If the respondent does not file an answer, then he can make an application for financial orders by filing a Form A at the county court where the divorce is being conducted.

14.7.1.2 Application with leave

If no claim has been made in the divorce petition or an answer, an application must be made with the leave of the court. If an order has been agreed by the parties, no leave is required (r9.4 FPR 2010).

14.7.2 PROTECTING THE CLIENT

The full range of orders should be applied for in the petition or answer or in Form A. It may seem strange to ask for some orders, e.g. a lump sum where the spouse is on income support, but circumstances of the parties can change. The common example is usually that a spouse may win the lottery. It is important that the court can use their full powers to make a suitable set of orders.

There is also a 'remarriage trap' (and a re-civil partnership trap too). Section 28(3) MCA 1973 states that a party cannot apply for a financial provision order or a property adjustment order following the grant of a decree of divorce or nullity or the dissolution of a civil partnership. If a client wishes to preserve their claim, they should make their claim before the marriage or civil partnership is dissolved. In *Re G (Financial Provision: Liberty to Restore Application for Lump Sum)* [2004] 1 FLR 997, the wife's application for a lump sum was adjourned by the court for several years in anticipation of the husband's significant inheritance. The wife was permitted to claim against the inheritance when it was received on the basis of her reasonable need, a new car, and discharge of her debts. The exception to this is periodical payments (see **Chapter 12**), which end on marriage or civil partnership (s28 MCA 1973).

14.7.3 **STEPS TAKEN BY THE COURT FOLLOWING APPLICATION FOR FINANCIAL ORDERS**

Once a Form A has been filed, the court fixes a first appointment not less than 12 weeks and no more than 16 weeks from the date of filing. Notice of this date is given to the applicant and the respondent is served with a copy of that notice not less than four days from the date of filing of that notice (r9.12(1) FPR 2010). Once the first appointment date has been set by the court, it cannot be cancelled unless the court gives permission (r9.12(3) FPR 2010).

14.8 **FIRST APPOINTMENT**

14.8.1 **FORM E**

Under r 9.14 FPR 2010, both parties must, at the same time, exchange with each other, and each file with the court, a statement in Form E. This must be signed by the party who made the statement, sworn to be true, and contain and attach the information required by Form E.

The timing is important. Form E must be exchanged and filed not less than 35 days before the date of the first appointment. The Form E contains details of income and capital assets of each party as well as the outstanding liabilities and the income requirements of each party. Towards the end of the Form E, there is a section that allows each party to state which orders they are seeking and the contributions made to the marriage.

Form E is a large document and requires practice in completion. There are many IT applications available to firms to make this process more straightforward. A copy of a Form E can be found at the end of this chapter as well as on the Online Resource Centre. Unfortunately, in December 2015 it was found that there was a software error which meant that there were errors in calculating assets. Although the fault has now been corrected, there could up to 2,000 cases which could be affected.

online
resource
centre

14.8.2 **PREPARATION FOR THE FIRST APPOINTMENT**

A good deal of preparation is required for the first appointment, which continues the procedural aim of identifying issues early in proceedings, thereby hopefully reducing costs.

Rule 9.14(5) FPR 2010 requires both parties to simultaneously exchange and file at court the following documents at least 14 days before the hearing of the first appointment:

- a concise statement of issues between the parties;

- a chronology;

- a questionnaire setting out by reference to the concise statement of issues any further information and documents requested from the other party or a statement that no information and documents are required;

- a notice in Form G stating whether that party will be in a position at the first appointment to proceed on that occasion to an FDR appointment.

14.8.2.1 Statement of issues

The statement of issues is described in the FPR 2010 as 'concise' and should not be unduly long or complex. This document enables the parties and the court to define at an early point in proceedings the matters in issue between the parties.

As discussed at **14.8.1**, the parties indicate on Form E the orders sought and this is a good place to look first when compiling the statement of issues. Other issues will become apparent when both parties' Form E and other information are examined closely.

An example of such an issue may be where one party wishes to sell the family home and the other party wishes to have it transferred to them. An example of a statement of issues can be found in Case Study One.

14.8.2.2 The chronology

The chronology sets out the personal details of the parties and any children, e.g. dates of birth, employment details, and details of ill health or disability. Important dates should be included of cohabitation prior to marriage, dates of marriage, separation, and key dates within the divorce and associated cases.

14.8.2.3 The questionnaire

Rule 1 FPR 2010 included a duty of active case management by the court. The court and parties must ensure that disclosure of documents is managed properly and the amount of disclosure is sufficient to enable the court to decide the case but that it is also proportionate to the case. The parties are not permitted to ask informally for disclosure of documents once proceedings for financial orders are commenced. As a result, the questionnaire is extremely important at this early stage in proceedings.

Again, the Form E is the starting point for examination of the issues raised by the parties and the information required to resolve them. Firstly, check whether all the documentation required by Form E has in fact been disclosed. Concentrate on the relevant issues of the case rather than undertaking fishing expeditions for information that may be old or not entirely relevant.

14.8.2.4 Form G

There is a procedural mechanism that allows cases to use the date of the first appointment if the parties are in a position to proceed straight to an FDR on that date and there is adequate disclosure in Form E. This is a feature of the court process established in part 9 of the FPR.

14.8.3 **THE FIRST APPOINTMENT**

The conduct of the first appointment is governed by r9.15 FPR 2010. The objective of the first appointment is to define issues and save costs. It is the first opportunity for a district judge to examine the case. The parties must attend the hearing personally. This hearing is a good opportunity for negotiations between the parties.

 Practical Considerations

In addition to the documents considered in previous paragraphs, many solicitors also prepare a summary of the income, assets, and liabilities of the parties and provide details of any large discrepancies in valuations between the parties. This document is helpful to the court and para 4.1 PD 9A FPR 2010 states that 'if possible' it should be filed along with a case summary.

There are a number of issues to be resolved during the first appointment.

The district judge must determine the extent to which any questions seeking information must be answered and which documents requested must be produced. The district judge may also give directions for the production of further documents as may be necessary. The overriding objective seems to indicate that disclosure should only be allowed if it is relevant and proportionate to the issues between the parties. It is important to note that under r9.15 FPR 2010, after the first appointment a party is not entitled to production of any further documents except in accordance with directions given in the first appointment or with the permission of the court. If permission of the court is sought for disclosure after the first appointment, the district judge will seek to understand why permission was not requested at the first appointment. There may also be adverse costs consequences for that party.

In *Tchenguiz v Imerman; Imerman v Imerman* [2010] EWCA Civ 908 the court examined the position where one party resorts to 'self-help'. This is where one party removed documents in paper or electronic form belonging to the other party without their knowledge or permission.

In a case involving large sums of money and property, the documents were removed from the husband's computer. He shared a work office and computer system with his wife's brothers. As she commenced divorce and ancillary relief proceedings against the husband, one of her brothers (possibly with others) accessed and copied information and documents of the husband's from a server in the office, and passed them to their (the brothers') solicitor. These solicitors had a barrister assess all documents for possibly privileged material, leaving seven files of documents which were then passed to the wife's matrimonial solicitors. An order was obtained to prevent disclosure of the material.

In the initial decision, the High Court gave judgment in the husband's favour and granted him an injunction against the brothers and their solicitor requiring them to return all copies of the documents and against disclosing anything obtained from the server to any third party including the wife or her solicitors. The Court of Appeal upheld this order.

The Court of Appeal held that there is a need to ensure that a husband does not avoid his liability on divorce by concealing assets. However, that does not entitle a wife, or some other person on her behalf, to breach the husband's rights to protect the confidentiality of his documents and information. It does not entitle her or another to breach any statutory duty or the criminal law.

It is an actionable breach of confidence for a person, without the authority of another to whom a document is confidential, to examine, or to make, retain, or supply to a third party a copy of, or to use the information contained in, such a document. Confidence in principle exists between a husband and a wife. It might be lost in relation to a bank statement left lying around open in the matrimonial home, or in relation to information shared between the particular spouses. However, if information is confidential, it is entitled to protection.

The court commented that illegal 'self-help disclosure' is not to be condoned. It is only at the point at which a party is required to file and serve Form E that his duty arises to give disclosure of his assets. At that point, indeed throughout an application for financial orders, the FPR 2010 and the court closely regulate the process of discovery of documents. It is a matter for the court to determine what evidence is admissible, and whether it should be admitted, balancing one spouse's rights under the European Convention on Human Rights (under Arts 6 and 10) against the other's (under Arts 6 and 8) and applying the provisions of the FPR 2010. It is not open to a wife to pre-empt consideration of a husband's Form E (or other) disclosure by self-help.

The difficulty of this decision may be felt in 'ordinary' cases where the sums of money involved are considerably smaller. In such cases, parties do not have the luxury of separate studies at home to keep documents (as the Court of Appeal discussed) and parties will often keep personal documents in easily accessible parts of the family home. The Online Resource Centre will contain updates on cases arising from this judgment.

The district judge can give directions on:

- the valuation of assets (including the joint instruction of joint experts);
- obtaining and exchanging expert evidence, if required;
- evidence to be adduced by each party and, where appropriate, further chronologies or schedules.

If the parties fail to settle at the first appointment or if there are outstanding disclosure-issues, the district judge must direct that the case should be referred to a financial dispute resolution hearing, unless it is not appropriate. There may be cases when moving to an FDR is not appropriate. In *Crossley v Crossley* [2008] FCR 323, the case required argument on the validity of pre-nuptial agreements (see **Chapter 13**) and required a modified approach to the rules.

The district judge may also make a number of orders, including an order for maintenance pending suit or a legal services order (see **Chapter 12**) for the filing of a pension inquiry form.

There may also be a decision on costs. Although costs are more fully discussed at **14.11**, the court can make a costs order. In deciding whether to do so, the court must consider the conduct of the parties including whether the parties have complied with their duty of disclosure with the Form E.

At every hearing, there is a requirement for both parties to produce an estimate of costs in Form H. Form H must contain an estimate of costs and disbursements incurred up to the date of hearing. This enables the parties to understand the level of costs incurred in proportion to the assets in question.

14.9 **FINANCIAL DISPUTE RESOLUTION**

The financial dispute resolution (FDR) hearing is designed as a forum for negotiation and discussion between the parties.

14.9.1 **PREPARING FOR THE FDR**

One week before the FDR, the applicant must file a schedule of offers and counter offers and any responses to offers between the parties (r9.17(3) FPR 2010). These are returned to the parties at the end of the FDR. This includes without prejudice documents.

 Practical Considerations

'Privilege' is a legal concept that allows certain documents not to be revealed to the courts during proceedings. There are a number of forms of privilege. The form most relevant to financial remedy proceedings is legal professional privilege. Legal professional privilege concerns communications between client and lawyer for the purposes of legal advice or for the purposes of litigation. The letters and documents produced under such privilege are protected and will generally not be shown to a court.

The court sees all offers made but, as explained later, should the matter not settle, the documents are not seen by the district judge at a final hearing.

14.9.2 **FDR**

The purpose of the FDR, as stated in r9.17(1) FPR 2010, is to meet to discuss and negotiate. There are important procedural devices that enable this.

 Practical Considerations

The Law Society Protocol recommends that a solicitor must:

- ensure clients are aware of the need to attend the FDR hearing and that it can last all day;
- encourage clients to make and consider offers and proposals in advance of the FDR;
- if offers are made, ensure the recipients give them proper consideration and reply promptly where possible;
- be clear what the client's 'bottom line' is to aid settlement, bearing in mind delays and cost involved in prolonging the proceedings;
- explain to clients the requirement to use their best endeavours to reach agreement bearing in mind the court's sanctions if one party does not make or receive proposals;
- not pressure clients to accept offers that they are not satisfied with.

A solicitor or fee earner attending the FDR must have full knowledge of the case and be able to conduct the case personally. An FDR may overrun and it may not be wise to attempt to attend more than one in a day.

The district judge who hears the FDR will have no further involvement in the case other than to conduct other FDRs, to make consent orders, or a further directions order. The parties must attend in person and use their best endeavours to reach agreement on the matters in issue between them (r9.17(6) FPR 2010). As a result, the parties can approach the FDR openly and the court expects the parties to 'place their cards on the table'. The role of the district judge in the FDR is to hear the parties' arguments and put their respective positions. The district judge will then give what recommendations and comments are necessary to assist the parties to come to an agreement. It is the author's experience that exactly the same advice given by you (but ignored) is taken very seriously when it comes from the district judge.

In *Myerson v Myerson* [2008] EWCA Civ 1376, the case was brought before the Court of Appeal as the husband sought to exclude Baron J from hearing the husband's application for variation of a consent order (see **14.12**). Baron J had presided over the FDR where the consent order was drawn up. Baron J refused to excuse herself from the husband's application and an application was made to the Court of Appeal.

Thorpe LJ considered the equivalent of r9.17(2) FPR 2010, which provides:

> The district judge or judge hearing the FDR appointment must have no further involvement with the application, other than to conduct any further FDR appointment or to make a consent order or a further directions order.

The court held that this Rule should be strictly interpreted. A judge presiding over an FDR cannot deal with any subsequent applications, since she had been privy to without prejudice material. If the agreement was incomplete or peripheral issues remained, these needed to be dealt with by a different judge.

The FDR is conducted without prejudice (see **14.9.1**) and the parties must be aware that anything said during the FDR will not be part of the final hearing.

If the matter settles, a consent order can be made (r9.17(8) FPR 2010). If the matter does not settle, the court can make directions for the future course of proceedings and, if appropriate, the filing of evidence and fixing of a final hearing date (r.9.17(9) FPR 2010).

14.10 **FINAL HEARING**

14.10.1 **PREPARATION AND BUNDLES**

All directions made at the FDR must be complied with or there may be cost consequences (see **14.11**). For a final hearing, bundles must be prepared in compliance with PD 27A FPR 2010.

 Practical Considerations

'Bundle' is the term used for the collated documents prepared by solicitors for the court hearing. Unless the hearing is very short, some form of bundle will be required. Bundles are agreed between the parties and are indexed and numbered in order to allow all parties to find and use documents easily. Bundles and the preparation of bundles is a key job for paralegals, trainee solicitors, and junior solicitors. Ultimately, it is the responsibility of the person with conduct of the case to ensure that the bundle is correct. If a bundle is incorrect or sloppily compiled, the court will at least be very displeased and, at worst, cost consequences can follow.

 online resource centre

Preparation of bundles is governed by PD 27A FPR 2010 which reproduces the Practice Direction (Family Proceedings: Court Bundles) (Universal Practice to be Applied in All Courts other than Family Proceedings Court) [2006] 2 FLR 199. The Practice Direction can be found on the Online Resource Centre.

The Practice Direction applies to hearings in the High Court and in hearings in all family proceedings except for the Single Family Court. A hearing includes all appearances before a judge or district judge whether with or without notice and whether for directions or substantive relief. It does not apply to cases under one hour or an urgent hearing where it is impossible to comply.

The main features of the Practice Direction (PD) are:

- the responsibility for preparation of the bundle lies with the applicant or the respondent if the applicant is a Litigant in Person;
- if possible, the content of the bundle should be agreed between the parties;
- the bundle should be paginated and indexed and the files should be clearly marked on the front and spine to identify the court case;
- the documents should be in chronological order and divided into sections as listed in the PD;
- preliminary documents (listed in the PD) should be inserted at the start of the bundle.

In the case of *Re X and Y (Bundles: Failure to Comply with Practice Direction)* [2008] EWHC 2058 (Fam), Munby J commented that:

> Too often bundles arrive late or not at all. Too often bundles are incomplete or not up to date. Too often skeleton arguments and other preliminary documents (see para 4.2 of the Practice Direction) are handed in on the morning of the hearing—at 10 am, 10.15, or even later—and at a time when the judge is already sitting or is struggling to assimilate other documents which have also been handed in late. The problem, in my experience, is particularly acute when the judge is sitting as urgent applications judge and, in those circumstances, particularly serious in its consequences.

Munby J suggested that defaulters could be publicly named and shamed in particularly egregious cases.

14.10.2 THE HEARING

Following all the disclosure that the parties have given, the court will already be in possession of a great deal of information about the case. The hearing will be in private in the judge's chambers. The case can be heard by either a district judge or a district judge can refer the matter to a judge.

The district judge will decide how she wishes to conduct the hearing and may decide to outline to the parties her own view of the case and to invite comment from the parties (sometimes a district judge does this by calling the advocates for a meeting before the hearing starts and the advocates communicate these views to the parties as an attempt to settle the matter). The district judge may also decide to run the case in the normal fashion, as any other hearing.

The applicant's advocate will generally open the proceedings succinctly and guide the judge through the history of the case, although the district judge will have had the chance to read the bundle in advance. The district judge may hear evidence from the parties. Advocates may outline their own proposals for orders.

The district judge will make her decision and communicate this to the parties. A careful note of the decision should be made to explain to the client and in case of possible appeal. Your client may not have achieved the result that they wanted and you may have to explain the decision carefully.

14.11 ORDERS FOR COSTS

'Costs' refers to the legal costs of your client including solicitors' and barristers' fees, disbursements, court fees etc. Both during a case and at the end, someone has to pay these costs. An order for costs describes the decision of the court about who has to pay which costs and it is possible that one client becomes responsible for paying the other party's costs.

14.11.1 MONITORING COSTS DURING THE CASE

At every hearing a Form H must be completed by both parties (r9.27 FPR 2010). Form H details the costs incurred by that party up to the date of the hearing. The parties can see how much is being spent on proceedings and this may encourage a settlement.

14.11.2 **COSTS ORDERS AT THE END OF THE CASE**

No fewer than 14 days before the final hearing, both parties must file and serve a Form H1 (r9.27(2) FPR 2010). Form H1 gives full particulars of all costs incurred or that are expected to be incurred during proceedings and allows the district judge to take account of the parties' liabilities when deciding what order to make.

The overall position on costs is found under r28.1 FPR 2010: the court may at any time make such an order as to costs as it thinks just. Under r28.3 FPR 2010, there is a general rule that the court will not make an order as to costs in proceedings for financial orders (with an exception for maintenance pending suit and interim periodical payments).

The court will only have the power to make a costs order when this is justified by the litigation conduct of one of the parties. Rule 28.7 FPR 2010 allows the court to have regard to:

- any failure by a party to comply with the rules, any order of the court, or practice direction that the court considers relevant;
- any open offer to settle made by the party;
- whether it is reasonable for a party to raise, pursue, or contest a particular allegation or issue;
- the manner in which a party has pursued or responded to the application or a particular issue;
- any other aspect of a party's conduct that the court considers relevant;
- the financial effect on the parties of any costs order.

An open offer is one that is made in open correspondence between the parties and is not marked without prejudice. Most offers made in proceedings for financial relief are now open offers.

The starting point for costs orders is that parties will pay their own costs and only in the circumstances listed above will an order be made that one party pay the whole or part of the other party's costs.

 Practical Considerations

A client may allege that his ex-spouse has been taking money from the joint accounts and putting it in another bank account. You check the bank statements supplied with the Form E and can find no evidence for this. Your client insists on seeking bank statements for the past ten years, despite your advice to the contrary. The court agrees on allowing disclosure of bank statements for the past three years. Following close examination, you still cannot find any evidence for your client's allegation. At the final hearing (as the parties have refused to settle), the district judge makes an order that your client pays the costs of the application for the additional disclosure as this was an unreasonable point to raise.

Another common example is wishing to spend many hours arguing over a relatively inexpensive asset. When a client wishes to argue over a dinner service or set of cutlery (both occurred in the author's practice), unless the asset has great sentimental value or is unique, it may simply be a waste of fees. In practice, the author would find out the value of the disputed item (most memorably a commonly available dinner service) and tell the client how many hours of solicitor's time was represented by the value of the asset—usually no more than one or two hours. Compared with several hours of time paid to argue about the asset, the client usually opted to spend the money on buying a new dinner service!

In *KSO v MJO* [2008] EWHC 3031 (Fam) the costs of the case amounted to £430,000 equivalent to 71% of the assets. Eventually, the husband became bankrupt.

The judgment is worth reading as a cautionary tale. Munby J commented:

Not for the first time I have here been faced with ancillary relief litigation conducted at ruinous expense to the parties. I should like to think it will be the last time, but I doubt it. The picture is deeply dispiriting. And it is not as if it is only the adults who suffer from the consequences of such folly. The luckless children do as well. The present case is a sobering, and for me deeply saddening, example. If, instead of spending—squandering—over £430,000 in costs, the wife and the husband had been able to resolve their differences at a more modest and, dare I say it, more seemly level of costs, there might very well have been enough left in the matrimonial 'pot' to house the wife and children and to enable the children to remain at their school, whilst still leaving something more than a mere consolation prize over for the husband. As it is, it is hard to see much being left from the wreck, not least after the trustee in bankruptcy has had his costs, expenses, and remuneration. And the wife and the husband—and for this purpose I refer to them as the mother and the father, for that is what they are—are faced now with the wretched and thankless task of trying to explain to their daughters how it has all come to this.

14.12 CONSENT ORDERS

If an application for a financial order is settled without a contested hearing, a consent order records the details of the settlement and is approved by the court.

14.12.1 PROCEDURE FOR CONSENT ORDERS

The first point to note is that the duty of full disclosure applies to consent orders (*Livesey v Jenkins* [1985] 2 WLR 47) and the procedure attempts to ensure this is achieved.

Rule 9.26 FPR 2010 states that if the parties wish to apply for a consent order before financial order proceedings have been issued, an application can be made by either party in Form A with two copies of the draft order (one of which must be signed by the respondent giving their consent). If proceedings have been issued, two copies of the consent order should be filed together with a request for the judge to make the order as requested, and a pension sharing annexe if applicable. The court should make the order unless they believe that circumstances exist that should be examined further, e.g. if the court feels that inadequate provision has been made for one spouse.

In addition, r9.26 FPR 2010 also requires a statement of information to be lodged with the draft orders and this should be done in Form D81. This form gives the court details about the parties, children of the marriage, a summary of the parties' capital and income resources, as well as pension provision, details of the family home, and any plans for remarriage or new civil partnership.

A copy of a Form D81 can be seen in Case Study One.

14.12.2 DRAFTING CONSENT ORDERS

Drafting a consent order is a skill required of all lawyers dealing with financial matters as well as being able to analyse a consent order drafted by another lawyer.

A consent order has a number of parts and each is examined later in the chapter. The order should set out the title of the case fully.

The preamble to the order records the parts of the agreement that the court has no power to order under the MCA 1973.

 Practical Considerations

A court can make orders only where the law gives it the power to do so. A court in financial proceedings may desire an order to force one party to make mortgage payments but there is no power under the MCA 1973 to make this order. The preamble is used to record agreements that cannot be the subject of an order.

The preamble can include a record of the basis upon which the order is made, e.g. that a lump sum is made to pay off a debt.

Undertakings form part of the preamble and will generally cover aspects of an agreement that are not covered by the MCA 1973, e.g. paying a mortgage.

 Practical Considerations

An undertaking is a promise to do something. An undertaking can be drafted to achieve a particular outcome, e.g. to pay off a debt. Alternatively, an undertaking can be drafted for a party to try to achieve a specific outcome using their 'best endeavours'. This form of drafting is used to avoid the situation where a promise is made that subsequently proves to be impossible, e.g. obtaining the release of one party from a mortgage. It is better to draft this as using a party's best endeavours as there is no guarantee that a mortgagee will release one party to a mortgage. If the consent order includes an undertaking, it is endorsed with a notice which states:

You may be sent to prison for contempt of court if you break the promises you have given to the court.

This is signed by the person giving the undertaking.

The operative part of the law (BY CONSENT IT IS ORDERED) must be present. The author once conducted three years of litigation when this was omitted by another solicitor, leading to severe consequences for the client.

The body of the consent order contains the orders including periodical payments, lump sum orders, orders for sale, pension orders, and property adjustment orders. The consent order must go on to dismiss any further claims between the parties now and in the future e.g. an application for maintenance under the MCA 1973.

The consent order should contain a 'Liberty to Apply' clause as this allows the parties to apply to resolve any difficulties in implementing the order; it does not operate to vary the order.

Costs should be dealt with, including any recovery of the statutory charge.

14.12.3 SETTING ASIDE A CONSENT ORDER

Consent orders cannot be easily set aside. The court would have to be satisfied that the agreement was reached on the basis of a serious mistake by one of the parties, as a result of fraud or serious misrepresentation, or through non-disclosure of material facts that would have led the court to make a substantially different order than it would have otherwise (see *T v T (Consent Order: Procedure to Set Aside)* [1997] 1 FLR 205).

Practice Direction 30A FPR 2010 is the rule that now applies. In *TF v PJ* [2014] EWHC 1780 (Fam), a children case, Mostyn J applied r4.1(6) FPR 2010 and the Supreme Court's judgment in *Re L-B (Reversal of Judgment)* [2013] 2 FLR 859, also a children case. Mostyn J stressed the importance of consistency between children proceedings and ancillary relief proceedings in considering applications to set aside orders where there has been a supervening change of circumstances which destroys the basis on which the previous order was made.

When the appeal is out of time, it is generally only very recent events that can be relied upon to set aside a consent order. The criteria for application are found in *Barder v Barder (Caluori intervening)* [1988] AC 20:

- new events have occurred since the making of the order that invalidate the basis or fundamental assumptions upon which the order was made;
- the new events have occurred within a relatively short period of time of the order being made;
- application for permission to appeal has been made promptly in the circumstances of the case;
- the granting of permission should not prejudice third parties who have acquired in good faith, for valuable consideration, interests in a property that is the subject matter of the dispute.

In *Myerson v Myerson* [2009] EWCA Civ 282, the appellant husband was seeking to appeal an order on the grounds that the fall in value of his shares caused by the financial crisis constituted a *Barder* event that undermined the basis of the order.

Thorpe LJ dismissed the appeal and stated that the order was not imposed but was the product of the will of the parties. The husband, with all knowledge both public and private, agreed to an asset division that left him 'captain of the ship', and certain to keep for himself whatever profits or gains his enterprise and experience would achieve in the years ahead. When a businessman takes a speculative position in compromising his wife's claims, the court asked whether the court should subsequently relieve him of the consequences of his speculation by rewriting the bargain at his behest. As the payment of the lump sum was spread over five instalments there exists, and the appellant husband had invoked, the statutory power of variation. Given that the outstanding instalments amounted to £2.5 million this was much more than token relief, albeit subject to the exercise of the judicial discretion. Thorpe LJ held that:

> the appellant fails to satisfy the court that the appeal would be certain, or very likely, to succeed. Given the width of the discretion given to the judge deciding the application for variation in the exercise of statutory powers, an appeal directed to the majority of the lump sum already paid and/or the transfer of property order would seem to me to have most uncertain prospects of success.

14.13 **APPEALS**

Rule 30.5(4) FPR 2010 sets out the appeal period as 14 days from the date of the district judge's order. The appeal would be heard before open court.

A party cannot appeal simply because they disagree with the decision made. Many clients do not appreciate this. The order made should be carefully explained to the client and should directly address grounds of appeal as soon as possible in order to either settle the grounds for appeal or to implement the order. Under r30 FPR 2010, permission to appeal is required. The details of procedure can be found in PD 30A FPR 2010, which is, unfortunately, extremely complex. Permission to appeal under r30.3 FPR 2010 will only be given if there are real prospects of success or there is a compelling reason why the appeal should be heard.

The grounds for appeal can be found in r30.12 FPR 2010:

- the appeal should be limited to a review of the decision or order of the district judge unless the judge considers that in the circumstances of the case it would be in the interests of justice to have a rehearing.

Grounds for appeal are that the court was wrong on:

- the law;
- fact (to a more limited degree (see *Piglowska v Piglowska* [1999] 2 FLR 763)).

Where the order was based on judicial discretion, the decision must be shown to be 'plainly wrong'. In *V v V (Financial Relief)* [2005] 2 FLR 697, it was held that any appeal should be allowed only if it had been demonstrated that there had been some form of procedural irregularity or that, in conducting the necessary balancing exercise, the district judge had taken into account matters that were irrelevant, or ignored matters that were relevant, or had otherwise arrived at a conclusion that was plainly wrong.

▌ SUMMARY POINTS

- Prior to commencing proceedings, clients should consider how to fund the proceedings and the impact of the statutory charge.
- Careful consideration should be given to the protection of any vulnerable assets.

- There is a pre-action protocol that should be followed, with care being given to the beginning of correspondence, disclosure, and expert evidence.

- The overriding objective of proceedings for financial orders is to be just and for the court to actively manage the case.

- Proceedings are commenced by a Form A and either party to the divorce can apply.

- Between the commencement of proceedings and the first appointment, the Form E must be filed and served.

- A statement of issues, chronology, questionnaire, and Form G must also be completed.

- The first appointment is where the court defines issues and resolves the extent to which disclosure should be ordered in an attempt to save costs.

- If settlement is not reached, the parties prepare to attend a financial dispute resolution (FDR) and negotiations must continue.

- The FDR is privileged and is heard by a judge who will have no further involvement with the case and will give the parties a realistic view of the case to assist settlement.

- If settlement is not reached at the FDR, the case will proceed to a final hearing.

- Costs orders are unusual as the starting position is that each party will pay their own costs. The court can make a costs order where a party's conduct of the proceedings requires sanction.

- Consent orders are used where the parties reach agreement to formalize orders and agreements.

SELF-TEST QUESTIONS

1. Draw a diagram to illustrate the order of proceedings for a financial order.

2. Explain the differences between the first appointment and FDR.

3. Your client, Miranda, has instructed you in proceedings for financial orders. She reluctantly disclosed assets following an order from the district judge at the first appointment. At the FDR you inadvertently discover that Miranda has concealed £300,000 in savings in a previously undiscovered bank account. Advise Miranda on the potential consequences of non-disclosure.

Case Study Two

Helena has decided that she wishes to have the house transferred to her as she does not wish to disrupt Richard's life any further. However, David does not agree and wishes to sell the family home. Using the Form E on the Online Resource Centre, find the part of the Form E dealing with this and draft that part of the Form E on behalf of Helena.

Look at the statement of issues and questionnaire in the case and Helena's instructions. Draft the reply to David's questionnaire for your supervisor and then look at the documents on the Online Resource Centre.

The first appointment passes without agreement and the court sets a date for the FDR. Draft a letter to Helena explaining what will happen at the FDR. Will Helena have to attend? Look at the Online Resource Centre for a letter to Helena.

Finally at FDR, an agreement is reached. Take a look at the draft consent order on the Online Resource Centre. Can you suggest any improvements?

Answers to the questions above can be found on the Online Resource Centre:
www.oxfordtextbooks.co.uk/orc/sendall17/.

online
resource
centre

FORM 14.1 FINANCIAL STATEMENT FOR A FINANCIAL ORDER OR FOR FINANCIAL RELIEF AFTER AN OVERSEAS DIVORCE OR DISSOLUTION ETC

	Click here to reset form

Financial statement for a financial order or for financial relief after an overseas divorce or dissolution etc

of

_____

☐ Husband ☐ Wife ☐ Civil partner

Dated ☐ ☐ / ☐ ☐ / ☐ ☐ ☐ ☐

To be completed by the relevant party

Name of court	Case No.
Name of Applicant	
Name of Respondent	

(please tick appropriate boxes)

The parties are

_____ and _____

Who is the

☐ husband ☐ wife ☐ civil partner
☐ Petitioner ☐ Applicant ☐ Respondent in the
☐ divorce ☐ dissolution ☐ nullity
☐ (judicial) separation ☐ financial relief application

Applicant in this matter

Who is the

☐ husband ☐ wife ☐ civil partner
☐ Petitioner ☐ Applicant ☐ Respondent in the
☐ divorce ☐ dissolution ☐ nullity
☐ (judicial) separation ☐ financial relief application

Respondent in this matter

This form should only be completed in applications for a financial order or for financial relief after an overseas divorce/dissolution etc. If the application is for any other financial remedy in the county court please complete Form E1. If the application is for a financial remedy in the magistrates court please complete Form E2.

Please fill in this form fully and accurately. Where any box is not applicable, write 'N/A'.

You have a duty to the court to give a full, frank and clear disclosure of all your financial and other relevant circumstances.

A failure to give full and accurate disclosure may result in any order the court makes being set aside.

If you are found to have been deliberately untruthful, criminal proceedings may be brought against you for fraud under the Fraud Act 2006.

The information given in this form must be confirmed by an affidavit. Proceedings for perjury may be brought against a person who makes or causes to be made, a false statement in a document confirmed by an affidavit.

You must attach documents to the form where they are specifically sought and you may attach other documents where it is necessary to explain or clarify any of the information that you give.

Essential documents that must accompany this statement are detailed in the form.

If there is not enough room on the form for any particular piece of information, you may continue on an attached sheet of paper.

If you are in doubt about how to complete any part of this form you should seek legal advice.

This statement is filed by

_____

Name and address of solicitor

Form E Financial statement for a financial order or for financial
relief after an overseas divorce or dissolution etc (04.11)

1 General Information

1.1 Full name

1.2 Date of birth

Date	Month	Year

1.3 Date of the marriage/ civil partnership

Date	Month	Year

1.4 Occupation

1.5 Date of the separation

Date	Month	Year

Tick here if not applicable ☐

1.6 Date of the

Petition for divorce/ dissolution/nullity/ (judicial) separation			Decree nisi/ conditional order/ (judicial) separation order			Decree absolute/ final order (if applicable)		
Date	Month	Year	Date	Month	Year	Date	Month	Year

1.7 If you have subsequently married or formed a civil partnership, or will do so, state the date

Date	Month	Year

1.8 Are you living with a new partner?   Yes ☐ No ☐

1.9 Do you intend to live with a new partner within the next six months?   Yes ☐ No ☐

1.10 Details of any children of the family

Full names	Date of birth			With whom does the child live?
	Date	Month	Year	

1.11 Details of the state of health of yourself and the children if you think this should be taken into account

Yourself	Children

2

1.12 Details of the present and proposed future educational arrangements for the children.

Present arrangements	Future arrangements

1.13 Details of any child support maintenance calculation or any maintenance order or agreement made in respect of any children of the family. If no calculation, order or agreement has been made, give an estimate of the liability of the non-resident parent in respect of the children of the family under the Child Support Act 1991.

1.14 If this application is to vary an order, attach a copy of the order and give details of the part that is to be varied and the changes sought. You may need to continue on a separate sheet.

1.15 Details of any other court cases between you and your spouse/civil partner, whether in relation to money, property, children or anything else.

Case No	Court	Type of proceedings

1.16 Your present residence and the occupants of it and on what terms you occupy it (e.g. tenant, owner-occupier).

Address	Occupants	Terms of occupation

3

2 Financial Details

Part 1   Real Property (land and buildings) and Personal Assets

2.1   Complete this section in respect of the family home (the last family home occupied by you and your spouse/civil partner) if it remains unsold.

> Documentation required for attachment to this section:
>
> a)   A copy of any valuation of the property obtained within the last six months. If you cannot provide this document, please give your own realistic estimate of the current market value
>
> b)   A recent mortgage statement confirming the sum outstanding on **each** mortgage

Property name and address	
Land Registry title number	
Mortgage company name(s) and address(es) and account number(s)	
Type of mortgage	
Details of who owns the property and the extent of your legal and beneficial interest in it (i.e. state if it is owned by you solely or jointly owned with your spouse/civil partner or with others)	
If you consider that the legal ownership as recorded at the Land Registry does not reflect the true position, state why	
Current market value of the property	
Balance outstanding on any mortgage(s)	
If a sale at this stage would result in penalties payable under the mortgage, state amount	
Estimate the costs of sale of the property	
Total equity in the property (i.e. market value less outstanding mortgage(s), penalties if any and the costs of sale)	

TOTAL value of your interest in the family home: Total A   £   0.00

4

2.2 Details of your interest in any other property, land or buildings. Complete one page for each property you have an interest in.

Documentation required for attachment to this section:
a) A copy of any valuation of the property obtained within the last six months. If you cannot provide this document, please give your own realistic estimate of the current market value
b) A recent mortgage statement confirming the sum outstanding on **each** mortgage

Property name and address	
Land Registry title number	
Mortgage company name(s) and address(es) and account number(s)	
Type of mortgage	
Details of who owns the property and the extent of your legal and beneficial interest in it (i.e. state if it is owned by you solely or jointly owned with your spouse/civil partner or with others)	
If you consider that the legal ownership as recorded at the Land Registry does not reflect the true position, state why	
Current market value of the property	
Balance outstanding on any mortgage(s)	
If a sale at this stage would result in penalties payable under the mortgage, state amount	
Estimate the costs of sale of the property	
Total equity in the property (i.e. market value less outstanding mortgage(s), penalties if any and the costs of sale)	
Total value of your interest in this property	

TOTAL value of your interest in ALL other property: Total B   £

5

2.3 Details of all personal bank, building society and National Savings Accounts that you hold or have held at any time in the last twelve months and which are or were either in your own name or in which you have or have had any interest. This applies whether any such account is in credit or in debit. For joint accounts give your interest and the name of the other account holder. If the account is overdrawn, show a minus figure.

> Documentation required for attachment to this section:
> For each account listed, all statements covering the last 12 months.

Name of bank or building society, including branch name	Type of account (e.g. current)	Account number	Name of other account holder (if applicable)	Balance at the date of this statement	Total current value of your interest

TOTAL value of your interest in ALL accounts: (C1)   £

2.4 Details of all investments, including shares, PEPs, ISAs, TESSAs, National Savings Investments (other than already shown above), bonds, stocks, unit trusts, investment trusts, gilts and other quoted securities that you hold or have an interest in. (Do not include dividend income as this will be dealt with separately later on.)

> Documentation required for attachment to this section:
> Latest statement or dividend counterfoil relating to each investment.

Name	Type of Investment	Size of Holding	Current value	Name of any other account holder (if applicable)	Total current value of your interest

TOTAL value of your interest in ALL holdings: (C2)   £

6

2.5 Details of all life insurance policies including endowment policies that you hold or have an interest in. Include those that do not have a surrender value. Complete one page for each policy.

> Documentation required for attachment to this section:
> A surrender valuation of each policy that has a surrender value.

Name of company			
Policy type			
Policy number			
If policy is assigned, state in whose favour and amount of charge			
Name of any other owner and the extent of your interest in the policy			
Maturity date (if applicable)	Date	Month	Year
Current surrender value (if applicable)			
If policy includes life insurance, the amount of the insurance and the name of the person whose life is insured			
Total current surrender value of your interest in this policy			

TOTAL value of your interest in ALL policies: (C3) £

2.6 Details of all monies that are OWED TO YOU. Do not include sums owed in director's or partnership accounts which should be included at section 2.11.

Brief description of money owed and by whom	Balance outstanding	Total current value of your interest

TOTAL value of your interest in ALL debts owed to you: (C4) £ 0.00

7

2.7 Details of all cash sums held in excess of £500. You must state where it is held and the currency it is held in.

Where held	Amount	Currency	Total current value of your interest

TOTAL value of your interest in ALL cash sums: (C5)	£

2.8 Details of personal belongings individually worth more than £500.

INCLUDE:

- Cars (gross value)
- Collections, pictures and jewellery
- Furniture and house contents

Brief description of item	Total current value of your interest

TOTAL value of your interest in ALL personal belongings: (C6)	£	0.00
Add together all the figures in boxes C1 to C6 to give the TOTAL current value of your interest in personal assets: TOTAL C	£	0.00

8

2 Financial Details   Part 2   Capital: Liabilities and Capital Gains Tax

2.9   Details of any liabilities you have.

EXCLUDE liabilities already shown such as:
- Mortgages
- Any overdrawn bank, building society or National Savings accounts

INCLUDE:
- Money owed on credit cards and store cards
- Bank loans
- Hire purchase agreements

List all credit and store cards held including those with a nil or positive balance. Where the liability is not solely your own, give the name(s) of the other account holder(s) and the amount of your share of the liability.

Liability	Name(s) of other account holder(s) (if applicable)	Total liability	Total current value of your interest in the liability
TOTAL value of your interest in ALL liabilities: (D1)			£ 0.00

2.10   If any Capital Gains Tax would be payable on the disposal now of any of your real property or personal assets, give your estimate of the tax liability.

Asset	Total Capital Gains Tax liability
TOTAL value of ALL your potential Capital Gains Tax liabilities: (D2)	£
Add together D1 and D2 to give the TOTAL value of your liabilities: TOTAL D	£ 0.00

9

2 Financial Details   Part 3 Capital: Business assets and directorships

2.11 Details of all your business interests. Complete one page for each business you have an interest in.

> Documentation required for attachment to this section:
> a) Copies of the business accounts for the last two financial years
> b) Any documentation, if available at this stage, upon which you have based your estimate of the current value of your interest in this business, for example a letter from an accountant or a formal valuation.
>   It is not essential to obtain a formal valuation at this stage

Name of the business	
Briefly describe the nature of the business	
Are you (please tick appropriate box)	☐ Sole trader ☐ Partner in a partnership with others ☐ Shareholder in a limited company
If you are a partner or a shareholder, state the extent of your interest in the business (i.e. partnership share or the extent of your shareholding compared to the overall shares issued)	
State when your next set of accounts will be available	
If any of the figures in the last accounts are not an accurate reflection of the current position, state why. For example, if there has been a material change since the last accounts, or if the valuations of the assets are not a true reflection of their value (e.g. because property or other assets have not been re-valued in recent years or because they are shown at a book value)	
Total amount of any sums owed to you by the business by way of a director's loan account, partnership capital or current accounts or the like. Identify where these appear in the business accounts	
Your estimate of the current value of your business interest. Explain briefly the basis upon which you have reached that figure	
Your estimate of any Capital Gains Tax that would be payable if you were to dispose of your business now	
Net value of your interest in this business after any Capital Gains Tax liability	

TOTAL value of ALL your interests in business assets: TOTAL E | £ |

2.12 List any directorships you hold or have held in the last 12 months (other than those already disclosed in Section 2.11).

2 Financial Details

Part 4 Capital: Pensions and Pension Protection Fund (PPF) Compensation

2.13 Give details of all your pension rights and all PPF compensation entitlements, including prospective entitlements. Complete a separate page for each pension or PPF compensation entitlement.

EXCLUDE:

- Basic State Pension

INCLUDE (complete a separate page for each one):

- Additional State Pension (SERPS and State Second Pension (S2P))
- Free Standing Additional Voluntary Contribution Schemes (FSAVC) separate from the scheme of your employer
- Membership of ALL pension plans or schemes
- PPF compensation entitlement for each scheme you were a member of which has transferred to PPF

Documentation required for attachment to this section:

a) A recent statement showing the cash equivalent (CE) provided by the trustees or managers of each pension arrangement; for the additional state pension, a valuation of these rights or for PPF a valuation of PPF compensation entitlement

b) If any valuation is not available, give the estimated date when it will be available and attach a copy of your letter to the pension company, administrators, or PPF Board from whom the information was sought and/or state the date on which an application for a valuation of an Additional State Pension was submitted to the Department of Work and Pensions

---

Name and address of pension arrangement or PPF Board	
Your National Insurance Number	
Number of pension arrangement or reference number or PPF compensation reference number	
Type of scheme e.g. occupational or personal, final salary, money purchase, additional state pension, PPF or other (if other, please give details)	
Date the CE, PPF compensation or additional state pension was calculated	Date / Month / Year
Is the pension in payment or drawdown? (please answer Yes or No)	☐ Yes ☐ No
State the CE quotation, the additional state pension valuation or PPF valuation of those rights	
If the arrangement is an occupational pension arrangement that is paying reduced CEs, please quote what the CE would have been if not reduced. If this is not possible, please indicate if the CE quoted is a reduced CE	
Is the PPF compensation capped? (please answer Yes or No)	☐ Yes ☐ No

TOTAL value of ALL your pension assets: TOTAL F   £

2 Financial Details   Part 5 Capital: Other assets

2.14 Give details of any other assets not listed in Parts 1 to 4 above.

INCLUDE (the following list is not exhaustive):

- Any personal or business assets not yet disclosed
- Unrealisable assets
- Share option schemes, stating the estimated net sale proceeds of the shares if the options were capable of exercise now, and whether Capital Gains Tax or income tax would be payable
- Business expansion schemes
- Futures
- Commodities
- Trust interests (including interests under a discretionary trust), stating your estimate of the value of the interest and when it is likely to become realisable. If you say it will never be realisable, or has no value, give your reasons
- Any asset that is likely to be received in the foreseeable future
- Any asset held on your behalf by a third party
- Any asset not disclosed elsewhere on this form even if held outside England and Wales You are reminded of your obligation to disclose all your financial assets and interests of ANY nature.

Type of asset	Value	Total NET value of your interest

TOTAL value of ALL your other assets: TOTAL G	£

13

2 Financial Details Part 6 Income: Earned income from employment

2.15 Details of earned income from employment. Complete one page for each employment.

Documentation required for attachment to this section:
a) P60 for the last financial year (you should have received this from your employer shortly after the last 5th April)
b) Your last three payslips
c) Your last Form P11D if you have been issued with one

Name and address of your employer	
Job title and brief details of the type of work you do	
Hours worked per week in this employment	
How long have you been with this employer?	
Explain the basis of your income i.e. state whether it is based on an annual salary or an hourly rate of pay and whether it includes commissions or bonuses	
Gross income for the last financial year as shown on your P60	
Net income for the last financial year i.e. gross income less income tax and national insurance	
Average net income for the last three months i.e. total income less income tax and national insurance divided by three	
Briefly explain any other entries on the attached payslips other than basic income, income tax and national insurance	
If the payslips attached for the last three months are not an accurate reflection of your normal income briefly explain why	
Details and value of any bonuses or other occasional payments that you receive from this employment not otherwise already shown, including the basis upon which they are paid	
Details and value of any benefits in kind, perks or other remuneration received from this employer in the last year (e.g. provision of a car, payment of travel, accommodation, meal expenses, etc.)	
Your estimate of your net income from this employment for the next 12 months. If this differs significantly from your current income explain why in box 4.1.2	

Estimated TOTAL of ALL net earned income from employment for the next 12 months: TOTAL H £

14

2 Financial Details   Part 7   Income: Income from self-employment or partnership

2.16 You will have already given details of your business and provided the last two years accounts at section 2.11. Complete this section giving details of your income from your business. Complete one page for each business.

> Documentation required for attachment to this section:
> a)   A copy of your last tax assessment or, if that is not available, a letter from your accountant confirming your tax liability
> b)   If net income from the last financial year and estimated net income for the next 12 months is significantly different, a copy of management accounts for the period since your last account

Name of the business	
Date to which your last accounts were completed	
Your share of gross business profit from the last completed accounts	
Income tax and national insurance payable on your share of gross business profit above	
Net income for that year (using the two figures directly above, gross business profit less income tax and national insurance payable)	
Details and value of any benefits in kind, perks or other remuneration received from this business in the last year e.g. provision of a car, payment of travel, accommodation, meal expenses, etc.	
Amount of any regular monthly or other drawings that you take from this business	
If the estimated figure directly below is different from the net income as at the end date of the last completed accounts, briefly explain the reason(s)	
Your estimate of your net annual income for the next 12 months	

Estimated TOTAL of ALL net income from self-employment or partnership for the next 12 months: TOTAL I   £

15

2 Financial Details

Part 8 Income: Income from investments
e.g. dividends, interest or rental income

2.17 Details of income received in the last financial year (the year ended last 5th April), and your estimate of your income for the current financial year. Indicate whether the income was paid gross or net of income tax. You are not required to calculate any tax payable that may arise.

Nature of income and the asset from which it derived	Paid gross or net	Income received in the last financial year	Estimated income for the next 12 months

Estimated TOTAL investment income for the next 12 months: TOTAL J   £

16

2 Financial Details

Part 9 Income: Income from state benefits (including state pension and child benefit)

2.18 Details of all state benefits that you are currently receiving.

Name of benefit	Amount paid	Frequency of payment	Estimated income for the next 12 months

Estimated TOTAL benefit income for the next 12 months: TOTAL K	£

17

2 Financial Details   Part 10   Income: Any other income

2.19 Details of any other income not disclosed above.

INCLUDE:

Any source including a Pension (excluding State Pension), and Pension Protection Fund (PPF) compensation

- from which income has been received during the last 12 months (even if it has now ceased)
- from which income is likely to be received during the next 12 months

You are reminded of your obligation to give full disclosure of your financial circumstances

Nature of income	Paid gross or net	Income received in the last financial year	Estimated income for the next 12 months

Estimated TOTAL other income for the next 12 months: TOTAL L   £

2 Financial Details   Summaries

2.20 Summary of your capital (Parts 1 to 5).

Description	Reference of the section on this statement	Value
Current value of your interest in the family home	A	
Current value of your interest in all other property	B	
Current value of your interest in personal assets	C	0.00
Current value of your liabilities	D	0.00
Current value of your interest in business assets	E	
Current value of your pension and PPF compensation assets	F	
Current value of all your other assets	G	
TOTAL value of your assets (Totals A to G less D):		£ 0.00

2.21 Summary of your estimated income for the next 12 months (Parts 6 to 10).

Description	Reference of the section on this statement	Value
Estimated net total of income from employment	H	
Estimated net total of income from self-employment or partnership	I	
Estimated net total of investment income	J	
Estimated state benefit receipts	K	
Estimated net total of all other income	L	
Estimated TOTAL income for the next 12 months (Totals H to L):		£ 0.00

19

3 Financial Requirements   Part 1   Income needs

3.1   Income needs for yourself and for any children living with you or provided for by you. ALL figures should be annual, monthly or weekly (state which). You *must not* use a combination of these periods. State your current income needs and, if these are likely to change in the near future, explain the anticipated change and give an estimate of the future cost.

The income needs below are: (delete those not applicable)	Weekly	Monthly	Annual
I anticipate my income needs are going to change because			

3.1.1   Income needs for yourself.

INCLUDE:

- All income needs for yourself
- Income needs for any children living with you or provided for by you only if these form part of your total income needs (e.g. housing, fuel, car expenses, holidays, etc)

Item	Current cost	Estimated future cost
SUB-TOTAL your income needs		£

3.1.2   Income needs for children living with you or provided for by you.

INCLUDE:
- Only those income needs that are different to those of your household shown above

Item	Current cost	Estimated future cost
SUB-TOTAL children's income needs:		£
TOTAL of ALL income needs:		£ 0.00

20

3 Financial Requirements   Part 2   Capital needs

3.2   Set out below the reasonable future capital needs for yourself and for any children living with you or provided for by you.

3.2.1 Capital needs for yourself.

INCLUDE:
- All capital needs for yourself
- Capital needs for any children living with you or provided for by you only if these form part of your total capital needs (e.g. housing, car, etc.)

Item	Cost
SUB-TOTAL your capital needs:	£

3.2.2 Capital needs for children living with you or provided for by you.

INCLUDE:
- Only those capital needs that are different to those of your household shown above

Item	Cost
SUB-TOTAL your children's capital needs	£
TOTAL of ALL capital needs:	£ 0.00

21

4 Other Information

4.1 Details of any significant changes in your assets or income.

At both sections 4.1.1 and 4.1.2, INCLUDE:
- ALL assets held both within and outside England and Wales
- The disposal of any asset

4.1.1 Significant changes in assets or income during the LAST 12 months.

4.1.2 Significant changes in assets or income likely to occur during the NEXT 12 months.

4.2 Brief details of the standard of living enjoyed by you and your spouse/civil partner during the marriage/civil partnership.

22

4.3 Are there any particular contributions to the family property and assets or outgoings, or to family life, or the welfare of the family that have been made by you, your partner or anyone else that you think should be taken into account? If there are any such items, briefly describe the contribution and state the amount, when it was made and by whom.
INCLUDE:

- Contributions already made
- Contributions that will be made in the foreseeable future

4.4 Bad behaviour or conduct by the other party will only be taken into account in very exceptional circumstances when deciding how assets should be shared after divorce/dissolution. If you feel it should be taken into account in your case, identify the nature of the behaviour or conduct below.

4.5 Give details of any other circumstances that you consider could significantly affect the extent of the financial provision to be made by or for you or any child of the family.
INCLUDE (the following list is not exhaustive):

- Earning capacity
- Disability
- Inheritance prospects
- Redundancy
- Retirement
- Any agreement made between you and your spouse/civil partner before or after your marriage/civil partnership stating whether or not you rely upon the agreement giving your reasons
- Any plans to marry, form a civil partnership or live with a new partner
- Any contingent liabilities

23

4.6 If you have subsequently married or formed a civil partnership (or intend to) or are living with another person (or intend to), give brief details, so far as they are known to you, of his or her income, assets and liabilities.

Annual Income		Assets and Liabilities	
Nature of income	Value (if known, state whether gross or net)	Item	Value (if known)
Total income:	£	Total assets/liabilities:	£

24

5 Order Sought

5.1 If you are able at this stage, specify what kind of orders you are asking the court to make. Even if you cannot be specific at this stage, if you are able to do so, indicate:

    a) If the family home is still owned, whether you are asking for it to be transferred to yourself or your spouse/civil partner or whether you are saying it should be sold

    b) Whether you consider this is a case for continuing spousal maintenance/maintenance for your civil partner or whether you see the case as being appropriate for a 'clean break' *(A 'clean break' means a settlement or order which provides amongst other things, that neither you nor your spouse/civil partner will have any further claim against the income or capital of the other party. A 'clean break' does not terminate the responsibility of a parent to a child.)*

    c) Whether you are seeking a
       i) pension sharing order
       ii) pension attachment order
       iii) pension compensation sharing order
       iv) pension compensation attachment order

    d) If you are seeking a transfer or settlement of any property or assets, identify the property or assets in question

5.2 If you are seeking a variation of an ante-nuptial or post-nuptial settlement or a relevant settlement made during, or in anticipation of, a civil partnership, identify the settlement, by whom it was made, its trustees and beneficiaries and state why you allege it is a settlement which the court can vary.

5.3 If you are seeking an avoidance of disposition order, or if you have already applied for such an order, identify the property to which the disposition relates and the person or body in whose favour the disposition is alleged to have been made.

25

Sworn confirmation of the information

I, [   ] Enter your full name

of [   ] Enter your full residential address

The above named ☐ Applicant
☐ Respondent

☐ make oath
☐ affirm

and confirm that the information given above is a full, frank, clear and accurate disclosure of my financial and other relevant circumstances.

SWORN/AFFIRMED
at [   ]

in the County of [   ]

on [D D / M M / Y Y Y Y]

[   ]

Before me, [   ]

☐ A Commissioner for Oaths
☐ Officer of the Court appointed by the Judge to take Affidavits

---

Address all communications to the Court Manager of the Court and quote the case number.
If you do not quote this number, your correspondence may be returned.

26

Schedule of Documents to accompany Form E

The following list shows the documents you must attach to your Form E if applicable. You may attach other documents where it is necessary to explain or clarify any of the information that you give in the Form E.

Form E paragraph	Document	Please tick		
		Attached	Not applicable	To follow
1.14	**Application to vary an order:** if applicable, attach a copy of the relevant order.	☐	☐	☐
2.1	**Matrimonial home valuation:** a copy of any valuation relating to the matrimonial home that has been obtained in the last six months.	☐	☐	☐
2.1	**Matrimonial home mortgage(s):** a recent mortgage statement in respect of each mortgage on the matrimonial home confirming the amount outstanding.	☐	☐	☐
2.2	**Any other property:** a copy of any valuation relating to each other property disclosed that has been obtained in the last six months.	☐	☐	☐
2.2	**Any other property:** a recent mortgage statement in respect of each mortgage on each other property disclosed confirming the amount outstanding.	☐	☐	☐
2.3	**Personal bank, building society and National Savings accounts:** copies of statements for the last 12 months for each account that has been held in the last twelve months, either in your own name or in which you have or have had any interest.	☐	☐	☐
2.4	**Other investments:** the latest statement or dividend counterfoil relating to each investment as disclosed in paragraph 2.4.	☐	☐	☐
2.5	**Life insurance (including endowment) policies:** a surrender valuation for each policy that has a surrender value as disclosed under paragraph 2.5.	☐	☐	☐
2.11	**Business interests:** a copy of the business accounts for the last two financial years for each business interest disclosed.	☐	☐	☐
2.11	**Business interests:** any documentation that is available to confirm the estimate of the current value of the business, for example, a letter from an accountant or formal valuation if that has been obtained.	☐	☐	☐
2.13	**Pension and PPF compensation:** a recent statement showing the cash equivalent (CE) provided by the trustees or managers of each pension arrangement or valuation of each PPF entitlement provided by the PPF Board that you have disclosed (or, in the case of the additional state pension, a valuation of these rights). If not yet available, attach a copy of the letter sent to the pension company, administrators or the PPF Board requesting the information.	☐	☐	☐

2.15	**Employment income:** your P60 for the last financial year in respect of each employment that you have.	☐	☐	☐
2.15	**Employment income:** your last three payslips in respect of each employment that you have.	☐	☐	☐
2.15	**Employment income:** your last form P11D if you have been issued with one.	☐	☐	☐
2.16	**Self-employment or partnership income:** a copy of your last tax assessment or if that is not available, a letter from your accountant confirming your tax liability.	☐	☐	☐
2.16	**Self-employment or partnership income:** if net income from the last financial year and the estimated income for the next twelve months is significantly different, a copy of the management accounts for the period since your last accounts.	☐	☐	☐
State relevant Form E paragraph	Description of other documents attached:	☐	☐	☐

Form E Financial statement for a financial order or for financial relief after an overseas divorce or dissolution etc (04.11)

VARIATION, COLLECTION, AND ENFORCEMENT OF FINANCIAL ORDERS

15.1 INTRODUCTION

This chapter will:

- discuss the circumstances in which a financial order can be varied;
- discuss the collection of monies due under financial orders;
- discuss the enforcement of financial orders.

To clients' immense frustration, gaining a financial order is sometimes not the end of proceedings. It is tempting to close a file at the end of a financial order hearing, but it is essential that compliance is carefully monitored until all orders are fully complied with by all parties. It is not uncommon for a disgruntled spouse or civil partner to refuse to comply with the terms of an order, even a consent order, and so a family law solicitor must be able to use enforcement mechanisms to enforce the court order. The Law Commission has held a consultation on the current law as the current law is often difficult to understand and can be frustratingly ineffective. The Law Commission consulted on proposals including simplification of existing enforcement methods, and the introduction of 'coercive' orders including disqualification from driving. The consultation closed in July 2015 and a report is expected in 2017. The Online Resource Centre will contain updates on any changes to the law.

online
resource
centre

Some orders made by the court may be in force for a number of years, e.g. a periodical payments order. Circumstances within clients' lives change through, e.g., remarriage or the loss of a job. There is scope within financial orders for the court to reconsider such an order and this will be discussed in this chapter. All methods of variation, collection, and enforcement apply equally to civil partners as well as spouses.

15.2 VARIATION OF FINANCIAL ORDERS

15.2.1 ORDERS SUBJECT TO VARIATION

Section 31 of the Matrimonial Causes Act 1973 (MCA 1973) states the orders made in financial proceedings that can be varied:

- order for maintenance pending suit or an interim maintenance order;
- any periodical payments order or secured periodical payments order;
- lump sum by instalments;
- a pension attachment order (income or lump sum from the pension) made under s25B(4) or s25C MCA 1973;

- an order for sale under s24A MCA 1973;

- a pension sharing order under s24B MCA 1973 if made before decree absolute.

Some orders cannot be varied and these include a transfer of property under s24(1)(a) MCA 1973 (although there are a limited set of circumstances where a property transfer order is made following judicial separation). There is no power to vary the amount of a lump sum order, only to adjust the arrangements if payable by instalments.

15.2.2 APPLICATIONS FOR VARIATION

When a party applies for variation of an order, the court can vary, discharge, or suspend the order. The order most commonly varied is periodical payments following a change in circumstances of either the payer or payee.

In an application for the variation of a periodical payments order, the court has the power under s31(7C) and (7D) MCA 1973 to commute the order into a lump sum, a property adjustment order, or a pension sharing order. This is often described in practice as a 'capitalization' of a periodical payments order and allows the parties to have a clean break. The court must decide how much could be paid under a periodical payments order and then balance the harm to the spouse in the termination of the payments against the desirability of a clean break (*Boylan v Boylan* [1988] 1 FLR 282). The calculation of the lump sum capitalization is complex and students are referred to practitioner texts.

The factors that the court takes into account when considering an application for variation are found in s31(7) MCA 1973 and include:

- all the circumstances of the case with first consideration to the children of the family;

- any change in any of the matters which the court was required to consider when making the order to which the application relates.

The court has the power to end the order or to limit the term of the order to enable one party to adjust to the end of payments.

In terms of a variation of the amount of the payments, it is vital to advise clients that the court can look at capital accumulated since the order was made, to look afresh at the evidence of parties' means, and to vary the order down as well as up. Clients should be aware that the court may decide to look afresh at the issue of periodical payments to the detriment of the client.

 Example

Millie and Lucas divorce in 2010. The court ordered that Millie pay Lucas £125 per week as she was the higher earning spouse and Lucas needed to retrain after looking after the children for a number of years. In 2016 Lucas applies for an upward variation of periodical payments following a rise in the cost of living.

However, in the intervening years, Millie has lost her highly paid job and has taken a less well-paid job. Lucas has bought a house, inherited a large sum, and has a very well-paid job. At the hearing the district judge decides that Lucas no longer requires periodical payments and discharges the order.

15.3 COLLECTION OF FINANCIAL ORDERS

The main issue with collection of financial orders is when periodical payments are not paid. It is a source of immense frustration for clients as collection procedures are slow and complex.

15.3.1 COLLECTION OF PERIODICAL PAYMENTS

As payments are directly between parties, clients are advised to keep a record of payments made. The permission of the court is required to enforce arrears over 12 months old under s32 MCA 1973. An application can also be made for an oral examination before a district judge to find out the financial position of a non-paying spouse.

15.4 ENFORCEMENT OF FINANCIAL ORDERS

One of the major benefits of the new Family Procedure Rules 2010 (FPR 2010) has been the introduction of a harmonized enforcement procedure under Part 33. Applications are now made on one form, the D50K, for all types of enforcement. The form allows the applicant to specify the type of method of enforcement or to apply for such order as the court considers appropriate.

15.4.1 PERIODICAL PAYMENTS

For periodical payments, methods of enforcement include a judgment summons requiring the non-payer to attend court and be examined on their means. The district judge makes an order based on this information. A non-payer can be committed to prison but this is generally suspended on the basis that the payments are made. See, e.g. *Prest v Prest* [2015] EWCA Civ 674. The procedure for such an order can be found in a practitioner civil procedure text.

In addition, the Maintenance Enforcement Act 1991 allows the High Court or county court to specify that periodical payments are paid by standing order or through an attachment of earnings (the employer sends the payment directly from the non-payer's wages). Payments may also be made through the court.

Periodical payments can also be registered with the court. The payments will be collected and enforced through the court. A new EU Regulation No. 4/2009 of 18 December 2008 on jurisdiction, applicable law, recognition, and decisions, and cooperation in matters relating to maintenance obligations came into force in June 2011. The regulation covers a situation where maintenance is owed by someone living in another jurisdiction. A maintenance creditor should be able to obtain easily in a member state a decision which will be automatically enforceable in another member state without further formalities. This may change as the UK leaves the EU.

If the non-payer is not within the jurisdiction, there are mechanisms for recovery but this is beyond the scope of this text.

15.4.2 ENFORCEMENT OF OTHER ORDERS

 Example

Anoushka and Pavel agree a consent order during the financial dispute resolution. One of the orders made was for Pavel to transfer £20,000 to Anoushka within 14 days of the order. Six months after the order, Pavel has failed to make the transfer. Anoushka cannot purchase a new property as she was relying on the money as a deposit.

Anoushka will have to rely on the normal methods of civil enforcement to force Pavel to give her the money.

In some cases, the final order is not the final step of the proceedings. Some spouses fail to implement the orders of the court and the receiving spouse has to enforce the order. As the order is made in the county court, the receiving spouse will have to rely on civil procedure enforcement, e.g. judgment summons or attachment of earnings. A civil procedure text should be consulted.

The receiving spouse could apply to make the non-payer bankrupt. The problem with this is that the unpaid periodical payments will be only one debt amongst many others and the spouse may only receive a proportion of the actual amount owed to them.

For lump sum orders, an order for sale under s24A MCA 1973 can be made with a direction that part of the proceeds are directed to pay off arrears.

Property adjustment orders are generally concerned with the family home. Occasionally, spouses or civil partners may refuse to execute the documentation to complete the property adjustment order. The answer lies within s38 County Courts Act 1984 (for county courts) or occasionally s39 Senior Courts Act 1981 (in the High Court). Orders under these sections allow the court to require the offender to complete the act (e.g. signing the contract of sale) within a prescribed time. If the act is not done, the district judge can execute the necessary documentation to complete the transaction. This is often a surprise to recalcitrant clients! Orders can also be made to require a party to vacate a property. The author once had to use several bailiffs to complete this type of order.

There are also a range of enforcement methods used in civil litigation, including enforcement of undertakings, attachment of earnings, and charging orders. Details of these orders can be found in most good civil procedure texts.

SUMMARY POINTS

- Not all orders are complied with and it is essential that compliance with orders is carefully monitored.

- Only some orders are able to be varied by the court, including periodical payments and lump sums by instalments.

- Care must be taken when applying for variation as the court has the ability to consider matters afresh.

- Periodical payments are paid directly between the parties in most cases.

- There are a variety of methods for enforcement of periodical payments, including a judgment summons or attachment of earnings.

- Property adjustment orders can be completed by a district judge if one party fails to complete the transaction.

- All methods of civil enforcement are available in family proceedings.

SELF-TEST QUESTIONS

1. Your client has not been receiving their periodical payments for the past six months. Describe one method of enforcement. Would your answer be any different if the arrears were over two years old?

2. Sam and Gene's case was heard in the county court. A property adjustment order was made about their home and Gene was ordered to transfer it to Sam. Gene is refusing to sign the contract for sale. Can you suggest the next steps to take?

online resource centre

Answers to the questions above can be found on the Online Resource Centre: **www.oxfordtextbooks.co.uk/orc/sendall17/.**

PROTECTING ASSETS AND THE FAMILY HOME IN FINANCIAL ORDER PROCEEDINGS

16.1 INTRODUCTION

This chapter will:

- examine whether a client can protect assets in financial order proceedings;

- examine the provisions of s37 Matrimonial Causes Act 1973;

- discuss the availability of 'home rights' under the Family Law Act 1996.

Every family law solicitor will have been asked by a client about hiding or disposing of assets in financial proceedings. Apart from the professional conduct issues involved in such an issue, the courts will take such attempts to hide or dispose of assets in proceedings very seriously. It is tempting for clients to minimize the assets available to the court, but the Matrimonial Causes Act 1973 (MCA 1973) has the power to prevent and recover such disposals. This chapter will look at the scope of the court's power, as well as considering the procedural and evidential issues in making or defending such an application.

16.2 SCOPE OF THE LAW

Section 37 MCA 1973 gives the court the power to make orders concerning the disposal of property to prevent or reduce financial relief. 'Financial relief' means relief under any of the provisions of ss22, 23, 24, 24B, 27, 31 (except sub-s (6)), and 35 of the MCA 1973. As in **Chapter 14**, these are applications for maintenance pending suit, financial provision, property adjustment, wilful neglect to maintain, or a variation application.

Defeating a claim for financial relief is a reference to preventing financial relief from being granted to that person, or to that person for the benefit of a child of the family, or reducing the amount of any financial relief which might be so granted, or frustrating or impeding the enforcement of any order which might be or has been made at his instance under any of those provisions under s37(1) MCA 1973.

A 'disposition' is defined in s37(6) MCA 1973. It does not include any provision contained in a will or codicil but (with that exception) includes any conveyance, assurance, or gift of property of any description. The courts have defined the term widely. Lord Hoffmann described 'disposition' as a 'familiar enough word in the law of property and ordinarily means an act by which someone ceases to be the owner of that property in law or in equity'

(*Newlon Housing Trust v Alsulaimen* [1999] 1 AC 313). Section 37 MCA 1973 also applies to property held abroad (*Hamlin v Hamlin* [1986] Fam 11).

 Example

Xavier separates from Yolande and commences proceedings for divorce and financial relief. Yolande and Xavier have considerable savings in SaverBank. Xavier checks the balance one morning and finds that the savings have gone. Yolande tells him that she gave the money to her sister, Maria, as a gift. Xavier believes that Maria will give the money back once the financial order proceedings are finished. Xavier could apply for an order under s37 MCA 1973 as Yolande has disposed of savings in an attempt to reduce the amount of money available to the court in financial relief.

In order for the court to consider an application, proceedings for financial orders must be in existence. There must be sufficient evidence for the court to believe an order is necessary to prevent a disposition or to review a disposition that has already occurred. The vague suspicion of a client is not sufficient. An application should be proportionate according to the amount of money and other disputed issues in a case.

 Example

From the earlier example, consider instead that Xavier and Yolande have savings of just £400. Although Yolande has removed the savings in the same circumstances, it would probably not be a proportionate step to institute proceedings under s37 MCA 1973 due to the relatively small sum of money involved.

16.2.1 CIVIL PROCEEDINGS UNDER THE CPR

In some circumstances, freezing orders and search orders may be available under the Civil Procedure Rules (CPR). A freezing order does what is indicated by its name and freezes assets enabling the court to prevent their dispersal. A search order allows the applicant to enter premises and search for documents. These orders are complex and draconian. Reference should be made to a specialist practitioner civil litigation text.

16.3 WHAT CAN THE COURT DO?

Section 37 MCA 1973 has two functions. Firstly, the section allows the court to prevent a future disposal or further dealings with property. It states:

(2) Where proceedings for financial relief are brought by one person against another, the court may, on the application of the first-mentioned person—

(a) if it is satisfied that the other party to the proceedings is, with the intention of defeating the claim for financial relief, about to make any disposition or to transfer out of the jurisdiction or otherwise deal with any property, make such order as it thinks fit for restraining the other party from so doing or otherwise for protecting the claim.

 Example

Martin and Becky are married and own several rental properties. Most of the properties are in Martin's sole name. Following an application for financial relief by Becky, Martin arranges to sell two properties and Becky only becomes aware of this when she comes across a letter from an estate agent.

Becky applies for an order under s37 MCA 1973 and the court makes an order forbidding Martin from selling any of the rental properties.

Secondly, s37 MCA 1973 allows the court to set aside dispositions that have already been made where, if the disposition were set aside, different financial relief would be granted to the applicant. The court may also make an order where a disposition impedes the operation of an enforcement order.

Section 37(2)(b) and (c) MCA 1973 states:

(b) if it is satisfied that the other party has, with that intention, made a reviewable disposition and that if the disposition were set aside financial relief or different financial relief would be granted to the applicant, make an order setting aside the disposition;

(c) if it is satisfied, in a case where an order has been obtained under any of the provisions mentioned in subsection (1) above by the applicant against the other party, that the other party has, with that intention, made a reviewable disposition, make an order setting aside the disposition;

and an application for the purposes of paragraph (b) shall be made in the proceedings for the financial relief in question.

 Example

Hari and Saira are in the middle of financial order proceedings. Hari's solicitors have discovered that Saira has 'donated' her collection of rare paintings to her uncle, which were valued at £100,000 and was one of the largest assets within the proceedings.

On an application by Hari, the 'donation' is set aside by the court.

16.4 PROVING INTENTION TO DEFEAT FINANCIAL RELIEF

Any application must show that the act of the respondent was made with the intention of defeating the claim for financial relief. Section 37(5) MCA 1973 assists the applicant if the act in question took place less than three years ago: if the court is satisfied that the disposition would have the consequence of defeating the applicant's claim for financial relief, it shall be presumed, unless the contrary is shown, that the person who disposed of or is about to dispose of or deal with the property did so or is about to do so with the intention of defeating the applicant's claim for financial relief.

The court must have some evidence of intention; a mere suspicion will not suffice.

16.5 THIRD PARTIES

Third parties may be affected by an order either by having taken ownership of the property in question or by being served with an order to disclose documents.

In terms of third parties taking ownership of property, s37(4) MCA 1973 makes all dispositions reviewable unless made for valuable consideration (other than marriage) to a person who, at the time of the disposition, acted in relation to it in good faith and without notice of any intention on the part of the other party to defeat the applicant's claim for financial relief. Thus third parties who give valuable consideration in good faith will not be deprived of the property. The valuable consideration given to the person making the disposition may become the subject of a s37 MCA 1973 order.

 Example

Miriam sells a holiday cottage she bought before her marriage to Leslie. The couple are now divorcing. The house was in her sole name but Leslie has spent a great deal of money renovating the property and it is one of the assets being considered by the court in financial order proceedings. Miriam sells the property for valuable consideration of £125,000.

The court makes an order that the third party keeps the house but the £125,000 becomes the subject of an order.

An order under s37 MCA 1973 may require a third party, e.g. a bank, to disclose documents or information. This information can be given to the court in affidavits. It is a breach of Art. 6 of the European Convention on Human Rights (ECHR) to give the court information following a without notice order if that information cannot be revealed to the respondent party to the application (*C v C (Without Notice Orders)* [2006] 1 FLR 936).

In *Ansari v Ansari & Ors* [2008] EWCA Civ 1456, the husband had left the matrimonial home, which was in his sole name, and the wife registered her home rights under ss30–33 of the Family Law Act 1996. The husband then proceeded to sell the house although the wife remained in occupation. The solicitors acting for the purchasers and the mortgage bank had requested that the notice be removed but this was not completed. The wife then started proceedings to prevent the husband dealing with the sale proceeds but did not seek any relief against the bank's charge. At first instance, the district judge set aside the sale and the charge as a reviewable disposition under s37 MCA 1973. On appeal, the Circuit Judge allowed the bank's appeal against setting aside the charge so the wife appealed that decision.

In the Court of Appeal, Longmore LJ identified three questions:

 (i) was the transaction a reviewable disposition under s37?

 (ii) could the bank claim that it had acted in good faith and with no notice of the husband's intention to defeat the wife's claims? and

(iii) was setting aside the charge consequential on setting aside the sale?

He found that the disposition was not reviewable, as only dispositions made by the respondent to the financial order proceedings (i.e. the husband) can be reviewed. Secondly, even if it was a reviewable disposition, the bank had acted in good faith (under s37(4)) and notice of the wife's rights was not the same as notice of the husband's intention to defeat her claims. Finally, the charge could not be set aside as a consequence of setting aside the sale, again as the bank had acted in good faith.

16.6 CIVIL PARTNERS

Section 74 of and Sch 5 to the Civil Partnership Act 2004 (CPA 2004) gives the court analogous powers to s37 MCA 1973 to review dispositions made to prevent or reduce financial relief.

16.7 PROCEDURE FOR AN APPLICATION UNDER S37 MCA 1973

Rule 9.6 Family Procedure Rules 2010 (FPR 2010) governs the procedure for application. Applications are made to a district judge under Part 17 FPR 2010 and proceedings for financial relief must be in existence. The application is made by filing an application notice D50G together with a draft order. The FPR 2010 do not specify whether a sworn statement should be attached. The application will most probably be made without notice in order to avoid alerting the respondent to the application.

If the application is successful and the district judge makes an order, a return date must be given and the respondent be at liberty, on two days' notice, to make an application to discharge the order.

16.8 **THE FAMILY HOME**

The family home is generally the largest asset in financial proceedings. It may be held in the name of one spouse only and, as such, is vulnerable to sale without the other spouse having notice unless his or her interest is registered.

16.8.1 JOINT NAMES

If the house is in joint names, the property cannot be transferred or conveyed without both owners' consent.

16.8.2 HOME RIGHTS

If the home is owned in the sole name of a spouse or civil partner, they can, theoretically, sell the property without the consent of the other spouse or civil partner. However, a spouse or civil partner has 'home rights' under s30 Family Law Act 1996 (FLA 1996) (as amended by the Domestic Violence, Crime and Victims Act 2004).

Home rights under s30(1) FLA 1996 encompass one spouse or civil partner occupying a dwelling house by virtue of:

- a beneficial estate or interest or contract; or
- any enactment giving 'A' the right to remain in occupation; and where
- the other spouse or civil partner 'B' is not so entitled.

The spouse or civil partner in the position of 'B' has the right under s30(2) FLA 1996 not to be evicted or excluded from the house by 'A' except with the leave of the court. If 'B' is not in occupation, they have the right to enter and occupy the house. If the person in position of spouse 'B' pays the rent or mortgage, this will be accepted as if made by 'A' (s30(3) FLA 1996). The dwelling house must have been or must have been intended to be the matrimonial or civil partnership home (s30(7) FLA 1996). Under s63(1) FLA 1996, a dwelling house can include a caravan or a houseboat. These rights subsist as long as the marriage or civil partnership. These rights do not extend to cohabitants.

Home rights are a charge (see the **Glossary**) on the estate or interest under s31 FLA 1996. Home rights should be registered as a charge against the property and a solicitor should do this as soon as possible. In unregistered land, a Class F land charge should be registered against the spouse or civil partner's name in the register of land charges (s2 Land Charges Act 1972). In the case of registered land, a notice should be entered into the charges register under the Land Registration Act 1925. Please note, such a registration will lead to a notice being issued by the Land Registry and there is no provision for this to be withheld. If this is likely to provoke a strong reaction from the other spouse or civil partner, please consider the methods of protection available under the FLA 1996 (see **Chapter 33** onwards). The protection afforded by registration is lost once decree absolute is granted and this may be a reason to delay an application for a decree.

Spouses with only an equitable interest in the property fall under s30(9) FLA 1996. This is beyond the scope of this text and reference should be made to a specialist text.

SUMMARY POINTS

- Assets must be protected during financial proceedings in order that they are available to the court for division between the parties.

- Section 37 MCA 1973 assists the parties and the courts to prevent the disposition of any assets by either party to the proceedings.

- Proceedings for financial relief must be in existence before an application can be made.

- An order can be made preventing a party from making a disposition with the intention of defeating the claim for financial relief or an order reviewing a disposition that has already been made.

- Property is widely defined as is the concept of a 'disposition'.

- Third parties can be the subject of orders for information, although a bona fide purchaser for money's worth will not lose their property—the consideration for the transaction will form the subject of the order.

- The procedure for such an application is found in r9.6 and Part 17 FPR 2010.

- The family home can be protected using 'home rights' under s30 FLA 1996.

- Home rights protect the right of occupation of a spouse or civil partner in the family home and can be registered as a notice in registered land or as a Class F land charge in unregistered land.

SELF-TEST QUESTIONS

1. Martine and Malcolm are in the middle of divorce and financial order proceedings. The couple are very wealthy and each spouse owns a number of valuable assets as well as the joint family home. During the course of the proceedings, Martine finds that Malcolm has been selling his collection of valuable paintings over the past six months and putting the money into a secret bank account. The buyers of the paintings have paid the market price. Malcolm has six more paintings and she worries that he will sell these too. Martine also finds that Malcolm sold his yacht four years ago for £1 million.

   (a) Describe the concept of 'disposition' to Martine.

   (b) Advise whether Martine can recover the paintings. If not, how would you advise her to proceed?

   (c) Can Martine recover the yacht or the sale proceeds?

online resource centre

Answers to the questions above can be found on the Online Resource Centre: **www.oxfordtextbooks.co.uk/orc/sendall17/.**

17.1 INTRODUCTION

This chapter will:

- examine the use of separation and maintenance agreements and the essential features of both types of agreements;

- discuss the advantages and disadvantages of separation and maintenance agreements.

If parties wish to avoid expensive, time-consuming, and emotionally draining litigation, a separation or maintenance agreement can be drawn up. Such agreements can include a wide variety of terms and are a useful tool for family lawyers.

This chapter looks briefly at separation and maintenance agreements: their form, drafting, and enforcement.

There is a distinction between separation and maintenance agreements. Separation agreements essentially record that the parties wish to live apart and can include terms about children, property, and maintenance. Maintenance agreements deal with the payment of maintenance to or for the benefit of spouses, civil partners, or children, but do not deal with the separation of the parties; they can include other terms.

17.2 SEPARATION AGREEMENTS

There are very few limitations on the terms that the parties can agree to include in a separation agreement. The wishes of the parties should be explored fully when advising. As with any agreement concerning money and property on relationship breakdown, the agreement should be comprehensive and realistic.

 Practical Considerations

The terms that are common to separation agreements include:

- arrangements for contact and where the children of the family shall live;

- the arrangements for the family home and other assets; but parties would be advised to agree only following full and frank disclosure of all assets;

- an agreement to live apart and not to molest each other;

- an agreement that one spouse or civil partner will pay maintenance for the benefit of the other spouse or civil partner or the children. As noted in **Chapter 18**, parties are now free to agree child support maintenance even when on benefits. The agreement would not prevent the resident parent with care from applying to the Child Maintenance Agency. See **17.4** for further considerations on drafting maintenance agreements.

Sections 34–36 Matrimonial Causes Act 1973 (MCA 1973) deal with maintenance agreements. Section 34(2) MCA 1973 defines a maintenance agreement as either an agreement containing financial arrangements or a separation agreement that contains no such financial information. Section 34(1) MCA 1973 states that any provision in a maintenance agreement seeking to restrict the right to apply to court is void, but other terms will remain valid. Parties can apply under ss35–36 MCA 1973 for a variation of the agreement during their joint lives or following the death of one of the parties. These provisions are very rarely used in practice.

17.3 ADVANTAGES AND DISADVANTAGES OF SEPARATION AND MAINTENANCE AGREEMENTS

Not many clients are aware of the availability of such agreements. It is worth understanding the possible advantages and disadvantages of separation and maintenance agreements in order to advise clients fully. See **Table 17.1**.

TABLE 17.1 ADVANTAGES AND DISADVANTAGES OF SEPARATION AND MAINTENANCE AGREEMENTS

Advantages	Disadvantages
Agreements are flexible and can address the client's need specifically.	Although the agreement is given great weight, it is not final; the parties cannot exclude the court's jurisdiction and so parties may still seek an order through the courts.
The parties retain control of the process and this can help to preserve good relations. The parties do not have to adopt an adversarial stance and so can avoid becoming entrenched in a dispute.	It is a contract and so the enforcement procedures are not easy and can be costly.
As court processes are avoided, costs can be lower.	Maintenance orders can be varied in certain circumstances but if the agreement falls outside this exception, variation can only occur by consent.

17.4 DRAFTING MAINTENANCE AGREEMENTS

Great care should be taken when drafting maintenance agreements. Clients need to be advised on the issue of the termination of maintenance payments. Options include drafting an agreement that continues even following divorce, remarriage, or cohabitation of the receiving spouse or civil partner or the death of the paying spouse or civil partner. If this is not what the parties want, the agreement should be drafted to address when payments will be terminated.

 Example

Hari and Saira separate as they no longer love each other and do not want to remain living in the same house. They intend to wait for two years in order to use s1(2)(d) MCA 1973 (two years' separation plus consent) as the basis of their divorce.

Hari does not wish Saira to struggle with money as he has a well-paid job, whereas Saira is pursuing a full-time degree. Hari asks you to draw up a maintenance agreement for the sum of £750 per month to be paid to Saira. He is concerned that once Saira leaves university, she should get a job and he does not want to support her if she meets someone else. A maintenance agreement is drafted where maintenance will cease upon Saira finishing her undergraduate degree or if she cohabits with someone for more than three months.

17.5 FORM OF SEPARATION AND MAINTENANCE AGREEMENTS

Like PMAs (see **Chapter 13**), separation and maintenance agreements are contracts and will require an offer, acceptance, and intention to create legal relations. There may be difficulty with consideration and so the agreement is generally embodied in a deed (see the **Glossary**). Agreements can be made in writing or orally, although an oral agreement may attract evidential difficulties. As with all contracts, separation and maintenance agreements can be set aside for duress, undue influence, or misrepresentation. In order to prevent any accusations, it is desirable that both parties receive independent legal advice.

17.5.1 EXCLUDING THE MCA 1973

It is not possible for either party to exclude the other's right to apply to the courts for financial relief under s34 MCA 1973 and also *de Lasala v de Lasala* [1980] AC 546. This may appear to a client to make a maintenance or separation agreement rather pointless. A separation agreement is useful if the parties separate but do not intend to divorce immediately and such an agreement records the parties' agreement. Should the parties divorce in the future, this agreement can be formalized in a consent order. The parties would save a great deal of money in legal costs and avoid the need to take adversarial proceedings in court.

17.6 ENFORCEMENT

As stated earlier, separation and maintenance agreements are contracts and are enforceable as such. Civil litigation methods of enforcement are expensive and are often very frustrating. For more information consult a civil procedure text.

SUMMARY POINTS

- Separation and maintenance agreements are a commonly used device for separating parties to draw up in binding form any agreement reached between the parties.

- As long as full disclosure is given and independent legal advice is obtained, these agreements have many advantages.

- Such agreements are contracts and must have all the legal elements of a contract. They are best contained in a deed.

- The jurisdiction of the court cannot be excluded.

- Maintenance agreements can be altered under ss34–35 MCA 1973 but it is a rare application.

- Agreements are enforced by usual civil enforcement methods.

SELF-TEST QUESTIONS

1. Advise your client Hari on the following terms in a separation agreement for Saira requested by your client:

(a) maintenance is agreed at £750 per month and child maintenance is agreed at £250 per month for their three children;

(b) the provisions of the MCA 1973 are to be ousted by the agreement;

(c) Hari will have contact with the children of the family from 10am Saturday until 4pm Sunday;

(d) Saira has made full and frank disclosure of all of her assets and has sought independent legal advice before signing the agreement.

online
resource
centre

Answers to the questions above can be found on the Online Resource Centre: **www.oxfordtextbooks.co.uk/orc/sendall17/.**

18 CHILD SUPPORT

18.1 INTRODUCTION

This chapter will:

- examine the system for the payment of child support maintenance;
- examine the Child Support Act 1991 and subsequent legislation;
- examine the changes currently being made to child support maintenance.

The Child Support Act 1991 (CSA 1991) introduced a mechanism to recover maintenance from absent parents for their children. It is a controversial area of family law that raises strong feelings in clients. The CSA 1991 created the Child Support Agency (CSA) as the organization responsible for the collection of child support maintenance. It has not been a popular organization amongst some and has been heavily criticized.

The CSA has been heavily criticized as just one in three parents with care of the child receive child support maintenance through the CSA, and although the purpose of the CSA was to save taxpayers money, the CSA actually costs £20 million net per year.

This chapter will look at the framework of child support, when a client may be required to pay child support, what a client can do if they do not receive child support, and the future of child support. This chapter will cover the Child Maintenance Scheme which started in 2013, and brief mention will be made of the 2003 CSA as its operation ceases in 2017.

Chapter 24 looks at the position where a parent can make a claim under Sch 1 Children Act 1989 and **Chapter 14** contains details of orders a court can make for children under the Matrimonial Causes Act 1973 (MCA 1973).

18.2 **CHILD SUPPORT ACT 1991**

The CSA 1991 was enacted to introduce a new regime for the maintenance of children, which previously had been within the purview of the courts. Section 8 CSA 1991 states that where the CMS has actual or potential jurisdiction the courts have no power to order periodic payments of child maintenance, unless exceptional circumstances apply. The CSA 1991 came into force on 5 April 1993. It introduced responsibility for parents to maintain their children, which means that there can never be a clean break between parents and children (see **Chapter 12** for clean break between parents). The CSA 1991 was amended first by the Child Support Act 1995 and then by the Child Support, Pensions and Social Security Act 2000 (CSPSSA 2000). The CSPSSA 2000 simplified the system of calculating child support and made some fairly radical changes. The Child Maintenance and Other Payments Act 2008 makes even more changes, which are discussed at **18.9**.

18.3 **2003 SCHEME—THE BASIC PRINCIPLES**

Section 1 CSA 1991 makes a natural parent of a qualifying child responsible for maintaining them. A 'qualifying child' is defined in s3 CSA 1991 as a child where one or more of his parents are 'non-resident' parents. The parent is the biological parent of the child. A non-resident parent shall be taken to have met his responsibility to maintain the qualifying child by making periodical payments of maintenance. The CSA 1991 describes these payments as 'child support maintenance'.

A 'non-resident' parent is also defined in s3 CSA 1991 where the parent is not living in the same household as the child and the child has his home with a person who is, in relation to the child, a person with care. A 'person with care' is defined by s3(3) CSA 1991 as a person with whom the child has his home, who provides day-to-day care for the child (whether exclusively or with another person), and is not within a prescribed category of persons (e.g. a foster parent or a local authority).

18.3.1 **NET INCOME**

The calculation for child support maintenance is based on net weekly income. Net weekly income is calculated with reference to the Schedule to the Child Support (Maintenance Calculation and Special Cases) Regulations 2000.

For those who are employed, earnings include all wages, overtime, bonus, commissions, statutory sick pay, and regular payments made in addition to wages. Income tax, national insurance, and pension payments (including personal pension payments) are disregarded.

Self-employed net weekly income is based on the total taxable profits that are taken into account by HMRC with the deduction of tax and national insurance together with pension contributions.

For both categories of earners, other income can be taken into account including pensions payments (net of tax) and working tax credit.

 Example

Pavel earns £300 per week, net of income tax and national insurance (NI) payments. He contributes £56 to his pension but receives £80 (net of tax and NI) overtime.

Pavel's net weekly income will be as follows:

$$£300 (- £56 + £80) = £324.00$$

18.4 **THE CHILD SUPPORT CALCULATION**

The person with care of the child or the non-resident parent can apply for a child support maintenance calculation and this will be calculated using a set formula. The child support maintenance is currently collected and enforced by the CSA.

The CSPSSA 2000 simplified a previously very complex way of calculating child support maintenance and this came into operation in March 2003. There will, therefore, still be cases where the calculation dates back to the original calculation and reference should be made to a specialist text.

The calculation follows a number of stages. Based on the number of children and the net earned income of the non-resident parent, four rates are applicable.

18.4.1 **BASIC RATE**

Where the non-resident's weekly net income is £200–2,000, the child support maintenance payable is:

- 15% of net income for one child;
- 20% of net income for two children;
- 25% of net income for three or more children.

Where the non-resident parent has one or more 'relevant other children', then the following percentages are applied to the non-resident parent's net weekly income before the calculation for qualifying children is performed:

- 15% of net income for one relevant other child;
- 20% of net income for two relevant other children;
- 25% of net income for three or more relevant other children.

'Relevant other children' are children other than qualifying children in respect of whom the non-resident parent or his partner receives child benefit.

 Example

Pavel has a daughter with his new partner and she is a relevant other child. His income will be reduced by 15% to take account of this child:

$$£324 \times 15\% = £48.60.$$

Pavel's net weekly income will be reduced by £48.60 and his net weekly income for the purposes of the basic rate calculation will be:

$$£324 - £48.60 = £275.40.$$

As Pavel has three qualifying children with Anoushka, his liability for these children will be 25% of his net income:

$$£275.40 \times 25\% = £68.85.$$

Anoushka will receive £68.85 in child support maintenance.

18.4.2 **REDUCED RATE**

Where weekly net income is over £100 but less than £200, the non-resident parent pays £5 on the first £100 and a percentage of the income over £100 but less than £200. This percentage is calculated using the formula shown in **Table 18.1**:

TABLE 18.1 REDUCED RATE

Number of qualifying children	One				Two				Three or more			
Number of relevant other children of the non-resident parent	0	1	2	3 or more	0	1	2	3 or more	0	1	2	3 or more
Percentage payable	25%	20.5%	19%	17.5%	35%	29%	27%	25%	45%	37.5%	35%	32.5%

18.4.3 FLAT RATE

There is a flat rate of £5 per week where weekly net income is less than £100 or if the non-resident parent is on certain benefits or is in receipt of the state pension.

18.4.4 NIL RATE

The non-resident parent will pay no child support maintenance (the nil rate) where s/he is:

- a student;
- a prisoner;
- a child (see s55 CSA 1991);
- a person who is 16 or 17 years old in receipt of income support or jobseeker's allowance.

A full list of those paying the nil rate can be found at reg 5 of the Child Support (Maintenance Calculation and Special Cases) Regulations 2000.

18.4.5 REDUCTION FOR SHARED CARE

If the non-resident parent shares care with the resident parent, adjustments are made. The more nights spent with the non-resident parent, the greater the reduction as shown in **Table 18.2**:

18.4.6 VARIATIONS

Under the Child Support (Variations) Regulations 2000, the non-resident parent may apply for a variation (often referred to as 'departure directions') according to circumstances, which have the effect of notionally increasing or decreasing the non-resident parent's weekly income for these purposes. As these are complex, reference should be made to a specialist text.

18.5 BENEFIT CASES

It used to be the case that if a parent with care was in receipt of income support, income-based jobseeker's allowance or a prescribed benefit, the CSA 1991 treated them as having applied for a maintenance calculation and the parent with care was required to supply

TABLE 18.2 REDUCTION FOR STAYING CONTACT

Number of nights	Fraction to subtract
52–103	1/7
104–155	2/7
156–174	3/7
175 or more	1/2

information to allow the non-resident parent to be traced or identified (unless the parent requests otherwise).

18.6 DISPUTES ABOUT PARENTAGE

When a person is alleged to be the parent of a qualifying child and denies this, a maintenance calculation should not be made unless:

- the person was married to the mother at some time in the period beginning with conception and ending with the birth of the child;
- the person is registered as the father on the birth certificate;
- the alleged parent refuses to take a scientific test (a paternity test by DNA samples) or a test shows he is the parent;
- a parent has adopted the child;
- there has been a previous declaration of parentage;
- the parent has been adjudged to be the father in other court proceedings.

An application for a declaration of parentage can be made under s55A Family Law Act 1986 if parentage is disputed. A specialist practitioner text should be consulted.

18.7 COURT INVOLVEMENT

As a result of s8 CSA 1991, the courts lost their general jurisdiction over the issue of child support maintenance. The courts have not been completely ousted however.

Section 23 MCA 1973 and ss2, 6, and 7 of the Domestic Proceedings and Magistrates' Courts Act 1978 (DPMCA 1978) allow an application to be made for periodical payments for a stepchild who has been treated as a child of the family. As discussed in **Chapter 12**, a lump sum, property adjustment order, or transfer or settlement of property can be ordered for the benefit of a child under Sch 1 of the Children Act 1989, the DPMCA 1978, and MCA 1973.

A court can make a 'Segal' order where an order is made through financial proceedings for the maintenance of the payee and child with the understanding that if a child support maintenance calculation is made, the amount paid will be reduced by that amount. In *Dorney-Kingdom v Dorney-Kingdom* [2000] 2 FLR 855, the court warned that courts had no jurisdiction where the mother only had a nominal claim to financial support herself.

18.8 COLLECTION AND ENFORCEMENT

One of the most contentious areas of child support has been the enforcement of unpaid child support maintenance. There have been problems with parents with care not receiving child support with the result that the poorest of families go without much-needed income.

The methods available to the CSA for the collection and enforcement of child support maintenance include:

- deduction from earnings;
- liability orders;
- removal of passport.

18.9 **CHANGES TO CHILD SUPPORT—2008**

Sir David Henshaw was asked to report on the CSA, as it has been heavily criticized. His report was unambiguous that the current system of child support maintenance was failing to deliver. Although the report was clear that the ultimate responsibility for child support remained with parents, the CSA had suffered policy and operational failures.

The Henshaw Report made many recommendations, the result of which was the Child Maintenance and Other Payments Act 2008 (CMOPA 2008). The 'Other Payments' refers to claims made by people with mesothelioma and has nothing to do with family law.

The CMOPA 2008 contains measures to reform the policy and delivery of child maintenance. One change was the introduction of the Child Maintenance Service.

18.10 **CHILD MAINTENANCE SERVICE—2013 REGIME**

The Child Maintenance Service (CMS) opened its doors on 29 July 2013. There are some transitional arrangements in place to move already existing clients of the CSA to the new service, which is expected to take over by 2017. The underlying aim of the CMS is to encourage parents to agree their own maintenance arrangements by way of a Family-Based Arrangement (FBA) rather than using the statutory framework. Before the CMS can be used, parents have to go through a 'gateway' telephone service to see if they can agree maintenance privately in such a Family-Based Arrangement.

There is a bewildering array of legislation which applies to the new scheme and this can be found mainly in the Child Maintenance and Other Payments Act 2008 (Commencement No. 11 and Transitional Provisions) Order 2013 and Child Support Maintenance Calculation Regulations 2012.

18.10.1 **CHARGES FOR PARENTS**

One aspect of the CMS scheme is that applicants are charged for its use.

There is a £20 application fee, a 20% collection charge for non-resident parents on top of their calculation, and a 4% charge on payments for parents with care of the child. These ongoing charges can be avoided if parents opt for direct pay, where parents pay each other directly at arm's length from the CMS. If payments stop, the CMS will step in and enforce payments.

18.10.2 **THE FORMULA**

The CMS also updates the formula which applies to child support maintenance. The gross weekly income of the paying parent is now the starting point (as opposed to net under the CSA) and a sliding scale is applied. The gross income is a change introduced by the CMOPA 2008 and which languished on the statute books for some time. HMRC will provide details of a paying parent's gross income to CMS directly. Even though parents with one child are not included in the scheme, the rates are included for sake of completeness.

If the gross weekly income of the paying parent is less than £800, the maintenance payable is calculated using the following formula:

    (a) one child—12% of gross income;

    (b) two children—16% of gross income;

    (c) three or more children—19% of gross income.

Where the paying parent earns more than £800 per week gross to £3,000, the amount of maintenance is calculated by applying the above formula to the first £800 and then adding the following percentage on the remainder:

    (a) one child—9% of gross income;

(b) two children—12% of gross income;

(c) three or more children—15% of gross income.

Where a paying parent's gross weekly income is less than £100 they will pay a flat rate of £7 per week (paying parents who earn less than £10 per week will be 'nil assessed').

Any income above £3,000 gross per week is ignored for the purpose of calculating the level of maintenance payable (parents will still be able to use Sch 1 Children Act 1989 (see **18.11**) for applications for 'top-up' orders if the paying parent has a very high income). The threshold for a top-up award is now £156,000 gross per annum. In the same way as the 2003 scheme, it is possible to apply to the court if the payer's income exceeds this threshold.

If the non-resident parent has the child/children staying with them overnight, the reduction of maintenance payable will be in 1/7 increments as before.

If there are other children living with the parent paying the maintenance, they will be entitled to reduce their gross weekly income as follows:

(a) one child—12%;

(b) two children—16%;

(c) three or more children—19%.

Unless there is a significant drop or rise in the paying parent's income, the liability will be fixed for a term of 12 months to prevent frequent applications for variation.

18.10.3 CALCULATING GROSS INCOME

Regulations deal with the calculation of gross income; the non-resident parent's total income from employment, self-employment, and pensions (although it is possible to deduct pension contributions from the gross income). This information is taken from a self-assessment tax return or information provided to HMRC under the PAYE scheme. It is possible to apply for a calculation based on current income if their historic income differs by at least 25%.

18.11 FINANCIAL PROVISION FOR CHILDREN UNDER THE CHILDREN ACT 1989

Section 15(1), Sch 1 to the CA 1989 gives the courts the power to make orders for financial provision for children where the CMS does not have jurisdiction. This is considered in this chapter as most spouses or civil partners receive provision for the person caring for children of the family through the Matrimonial Causes Act 1973. The schedule states that on an application made by a parent or guardian of a child, or by any person in whose favour a residence order is in force with respect to a child, the court may make one or more of the following orders:

(a) an order requiring either or both parents of a child to make to the applicant for the benefit of the child; or to make to the child himself, such periodical payments, for such term, as may be specified in the order;

(b) an order requiring either or both parents of a child to secure to the applicant for the benefit of the child; or to secure to the child himself, such periodical payments, for such term, as may be so specified;

(c) an order requiring either or both parents of a child to pay to the applicant for the benefit of the child; or to pay to the child himself, such lump sum as may be so specified;

(d) an order requiring a settlement to be made for the benefit of the child, and to the satisfaction of the court, of property to which either parent is entitled (either in possession or in reversion); and which is specified in the order;

(e) an order requiring either or both parents of a child to transfer to the applicant, for the benefit of the child; or to transfer to the child himself, such property to which the parent is, or the parents are, entitled (either in possession or in reversion) as may be specified in the order.

18.11.1 **WHO IS A PARENT?**

Parents include the child's natural mother and father and any party to a marriage or civil partnership in relation to whom the child is a child of the family. This therefore includes step-parents. A child of the family is defined in s105(1) CA 1989 as being, in regard to the parties to a marriage or a civil partnership:

- a child of both those parties;

- any other child, not being a child who is placed with those parties as foster parents by a local authority or voluntary organization, who has been treated by both of those parties as a child of a family.

In deciding whether to exercise their powers, para 4 of Sch 1 CA 1989 requires the court to have regard to all the circumstances, including:

(a) the income, earning capacity, property, and other financial resources which each person mentioned in sub-paragraph (4) has or is likely to have in the foreseeable future;

(b) the financial needs, obligations, and responsibilities which each person mentioned in sub-paragraph (4) has or is likely to have in the foreseeable future;

(c) the financial needs of the child;

(d) the income, earning capacity (if any), property, and other financial resources of the child;

(e) any physical or mental disability of the child;

(f) the manner in which the child was being, or was expected to be, educated or trained.

In deciding whether to exercise its powers under para 1 against a person who is not the mother or father of the child, and if so in what manner, the court shall in addition have regard to:

(a) whether that person had assumed responsibility for the maintenance of the child and, if so, the extent to which and basis on which he assumed that responsibility and the length of the period during which he met that responsibility;

(b) whether he did so knowing that the child was not his child;

(c) the liability of any other person to maintain the child.

Parent includes unmarried mothers, unmarried fathers without parental responsibility (see **Chapter 25**), guardians, or special guardians or those with a residence order (see **Chapter 26**).

18.11.2 **CASE-LAW CONCERNING SCH 1 CA 1989**

There has been a proliferation of applications under Sch 1 CA 1989, especially in cases involving wealthy parents.

The Court of Appeal gave a landmark decision in *Re P (Child: Financial Provision)* [2003] EWCA Civ 837. A two-year-old child had parents who had not cohabited. The husband described himself as fabulously wealthy. At first instance, the mother was awarded £450,000 for a house, £30,000 for furnishings, and periodical payments of £35,560 to be reduced to £9,333 on the child's ninth birthday. On appeal, the Court of Appeal increased the housing fund to £1 million, furnishings to £100,000, and periodical payments to £70,000. The following points arose from the judgment:

- children should not suffer just because their parents had (for whatever reason) not been married to one another;

- the child's welfare should come before that of the adults;

- no great significance should be attached to whether or not the pregnancy was planned;

- the child in question was entitled to be brought up in circumstances that bore some sort of relationship to the father's current resources and standard of living, although the court should guard against unreasonable claims;
- the child's home should be set up on the basis of a settlement of property during the child's minority.

It should be noted that once the child reaches 18 years, the home or property settled during the child's minority will revert back to the parent who owns it. The property is held on trust by the parent caring for the child. The parent caring for the child does not ultimately gain from the order.

In *F v G* [2004] EWHC 1848 (Fam), Singer J looked at the issue of standard of living and held that the court should be cognizant of the child's current standard of living if there has been a long separation from the other parent. If the mother develops a new relationship, the contribution of the new partner does not detract from the value of the mother as a primary carer. If and when any relationship of the mother has an impact on her domestic economy, that will be the time for consequential amendments to the father's contributions to be discussed.

SUMMARY POINTS

- Child support maintenance is governed by the Child Support Act 1991 and is administered by the Child Support Agency.

- Non-resident parents must pay child support maintenance for qualifying children to the parent with care from their net income.

- There are four different rates depending upon the circumstances of the non-resident parent:
  - the basic rate which is a percentage of income according to the number of qualifying children. This can also be reduced to take into account the non-resident parent's relevant other children;
  - the reduced rate for net income between £100 and £200;
  - the flat rate and nil rate for those with little or no income.

- Parents are now free to decide whether to apply to the CSA, even if the parent with care is in receipt of benefits.

- The CSA has a wide range of enforcement powers for those parents who fail to pay child support maintenance.

- The CMS started operations in 2013, applying a new scheme for those applying for child support maintenance.

- The Children Act 1989 can be used to provide a range of orders for the benefit of children.

SELF-TEST QUESTIONS

Barry and Sharon have two children, Emma aged 3 and Louis aged 2. Barry had a previous marriage to Maisie and they had two children, Sam and Ellie, aged 6 and 7. The children live with their mother, Sandra. Barry has contact with Sam and Ellie two nights per week.

Barry works as a sheet metal welder and earns £299 per week after tax and national insurance and he pays £50 per week into a private pension. Barry earns a bonus monthly, which works out at around £25 per week.

1. Sandra applies to the CMS. Advise Barry on how much the CMS are likely to ask for.

2. Would your answer change if Barry became unemployed and claimed jobseeker's allowance?

Case Study Two

Helena wishes to know how much David should pay in child support maintenance for Richard. On the Online Resource Centre, check David's net income on the Form E and advise Helena.

Answers to the questions above can be found on the Online Resource Centre: **www.oxfordtextbooks.co.uk/orc/sendall17/.**

19 PENSIONS IN FINANCIAL PROCEEDINGS

19.1 Introduction

19.2 What is a pension?

19.3 How is a pension valued?

19.4 Options for pensions in financial proceedings

19.1 INTRODUCTION

This chapter will:

- discuss pensions as a financial instrument;
- discuss how pensions are dealt with following divorce or dissolution.

Pensions can seem something of a mystery to most people new to proceedings for financial orders and clients often do not understand how the courts deal with pensions. In most 'average' cases, pensions can be one of the larger assets held by the parties and can be pivotal to obtaining a settlement. There have been many changes to legislation in relation to pensions and that will be covered in this chapter as well as the orders that a court can make in relation to pensions.

Pensions are an extremely complex area within proceedings for financial orders. This chapter provides a basic outline of pensions and pension orders available to the court. Practitioner texts provide greater detail and, in practice, pension specialists, such as independent financial advisers, are often instructed to provide expert advice.

This chapter *must* be read in conjunction with **Chapter 12** as pension orders are orders that are available to the court when considering financial orders, as well as **Chapter 14** for the procedural aspects involving pensions.

19.2 WHAT IS A PENSION?

One of the many skills that a solicitor dealing with finances must have is the ability to understand common financial instruments (e.g. pensions, endowment policies etc.) and to explain to a client how they work and how the court can deal with them. Pension legislation was simplified fairly recently and came into force on 6 April 2006: this is referred to as 'A' Day.

A pension provides a regular source of income when a person retires. As people are living longer, a pension provides income for a large proportion of a person's life. A pension is a long-term investment, and during their working life a person pays a proportion of their income into a pension fund. There is a state pension, where the Government takes money from wages (national insurance), and also private pension funds, e.g. occupational pensions (work or company pensions) or personal pensions. Tax relief is paid on contributions to a pension.

The fund cannot be accessed until retirement and so is not like a savings account. It is rather a valuable intangible asset whose value builds over working life until it becomes realizable upon retirement. How the pension fund is converted into an income depends upon the type of pension.

The Online Resource Centre contains further sources of information.

online resource centre

19.3 **HOW IS A PENSION VALUED?**

It is usually the case that a pension has to be valued during the financial proceedings and the method of valuation requires further examination.

A cash equivalent transfer value (CETV) is the prescribed method of valuing a pension, irrespective of the pension order made (see **19.4**). The CETV is the capital value of the pension rights calculated by the pension scheme provider. Further details of how this is done can be found in the Pension Sharing (Valuation) Regulations 2000. The CETV relates only to pensionable service up to the date of the calculation and does not take into account future salary increases. The CETV gives an idea of how much the pension is currently worth but may be challenged if it is felt to be unfair, because, for example, of anticipated salary increases. Pension valuation can be complex and requires specialist actuarial assistance.

In financial proceedings, s25B(1) Matrimonial Causes Act 1973 (MCA 1973) states that the matters to which the court must have regard under s25(2) include any benefit under a pension arrangement that a party has or is likely to have and any benefits under a pension arrangement which, by reason of the dissolution or annulment of the marriage, a party to the marriage will lose the chance of acquiring. The most common benefit in practice for this purpose is widows' benefit or death in service benefit, which benefit spouses if the pension holder dies before retirement.

Form P is used to acquire more information from pension providers and is a standard form. Not all information required is free and a charge may be levied.

19.4 **OPTIONS FOR PENSIONS IN FINANCIAL PROCEEDINGS**

19.4.1 **OFFSETTING**

Pension offsetting is less complex than attachment or sharing orders. The parties look at all available assets including pensions and offset one party retaining a pension by compensating the other with assets.

 Example

David and Christine divorce. They have no children, are young, and own few assets. There is a family property, a car, and David has an occupational pension, which he has paid into for some years. A CETV of the pension is obtained and it is found to be roughly the same as the available equity in the family home.

David retains his pension and Christine retains the family home. The pension is 'offset' by the equity in the family home.

It should be noted that the pension should be correctly valued and that a pension is a long-term investment that will grow in time. Offsetting may be useful in situations where a pension is too small to be attached or shared, if the parties have equal pensions of their own, where the greatest priority is to house the children of the marriage/civil partnership, or where the parties are very young and will be able to build up their own pensions.

19.4.2 **PENSION ATTACHMENT**

Under s23 MCA 1973, attachment orders allow the court to order the pension provider to pay all or part of the pension scheme member's benefit to their ex-spouse on retirement or death, i.e. when the pension becomes payable. The order should be worded carefully to make clear whether the order attaches to the income of the pension, retirement lump sum, or lump sum payment on death. Any order made against income benefits will cease on re-marriage as attachment orders are a form of deferred spousal maintenance (see **Chapter 12**).

This order was introduced by s166 Pensions Act 1995 on 1 August 1996, amending the MCA 1973 to include ss25B, 25C, and 25D.

In *T v T* [1998] 1 FLR 1072, Singer J stated that the MCA 1973 does not compel the court to compensate for pension loss and the court's obligations are limited to considering orders for periodical payments, lump sum orders, and then to look at pension considerations. An attachment order does not transfer legal ownership of the benefits from the member to the ex-spouse.

Attachment orders may be useful to provide lump sum life cover, as maintenance in retirement, without ownership being transferred.

 Practical Considerations

There have been problems with attachment orders as some people have delayed retirement to delay the payment of the pension to the other party or have stopped paying into the fund. This results in the party with the pension attachment order being in a vulnerable position if they are relying on the income. It does not achieve a clean break between the parties.

19.4.3 PENSION SHARING

A solution to the problems and unpopularity of pension attachment orders is the pension sharing order introduced by the Welfare Reform and Pensions Act 1999. This came into force on 1 December 2000. A pension sharing order divides pension benefits between the parties at the time of divorce and there is a transfer of legal ownership of benefits. This is expressed as a percentage of the CETV. There are some types of pension that cannot be shared including the state pension and any lump sum payable on death. The order takes effect on decree absolute. Research from Cardiff University has suggested that pension sharing orders are not common, with more offsetting of pensions in financial remedy cases.

Once a pension sharing order has been made, the recipient (if the pension is a private pension or a funded occupational scheme) may transfer their share into a new pension fund or remain with the present scheme, but with that share of the pension held in their own right. If the pension is an unfunded and a public service pension scheme, transfer is not possible.

Sharing orders may be useful where it is the only major asset, one party has no pension and is unlikely to be able to build one up, and the pension is very large and can withstand sharing, where there are no other assets that can be offset. Please note that it is not possible to make both a pension attachment order and a pension sharing order in respect of the same pension.

 Example

Hari works for Good Company plc and has done since the start of his career. Good Company offer a very good pension scheme and Hari has contributed the maximum amount possible to his pension fund for 35 years. Unfortunately, Hari and his wife Suzi divorce when both are 59. Suzi has a very low-paid job following years at home looking after the house. The court orders that the family home is sold as there is sufficient capital to house both parties in modest accommodation. The only other asset of the marriage is Hari's pension. The pension is subject to a pension sharing order where Suzi receives 50% of the pension to give her an income in retirement.

SUMMARY POINTS

- A pension is a long-term investment which provides income during retirement.

- The court must consider a pension when considering the case under s25(2) MCA 1973.

- A pension is valued using the cash equivalent transfer value (CETV).

- A pension can be offset against other assets as part of a settlement.

- A pension attachment order can be used to attach part of a pension to give the recipient a share of the pension on retirement.

- A pension sharing order allows a share of the pension to be given to the recipient to be transferred into a new scheme or retained in the same scheme and title to the share is transferred to the recipient.

SELF-TEST QUESTIONS

1. Explain what a pension is and name two different types of pension schemes.

2. There have been some problems with pension attachment orders—what are they?

3. Explain when a pension sharing order may be used within financial proceedings and its advantage over pension attachment orders.

Case Study Two

David has a pension and this has been disclosed in the proceedings. On the Online Resource Centre, find the CETV in the Form E and comment on the size of the pension fund. What pension orders are available to Helena and David? Explain to your supervisor which order David may prefer in this case.

online resource centre

Answers to the questions above can be found on the Online Resource Centre: **www.oxfordtextbooks.co.uk/orc/sendall17/.**

20 TAXATION IN FAMILY LAW

20.1 INTRODUCTION

This chapter will:

- examine the types of tax most relevant to family law including income tax, capital gains tax, inheritance tax, and stamp duty land tax.

Family law students are often surprised to be told that tax is part of the study of family law. Tax is more often associated with business law or private client practice but it is also essential that a family law practitioner is aware of the tax implications of any financial settlement and to make it tax efficient for the client. As we have seen with pensions (see **Chapter 19**) this is an area where it may be necessary to involve other professionals, e.g. an accountant, to give expert advice.

This chapter gives a basic outline of income tax, capital gains tax, and inheritance tax as it applies to the practice of family law, rather than as a general consideration of tax rules. For further details, it is recommended that the student consult a practitioner text. Tax rates, schemes and allowances change with the Budget in April every year and updates will be available on the Online Resource Centre.

 online resource centre

20.2 INCOME TAX

Income tax is paid on taxable income. Everyone has a basic personal allowance which in the 2016–17 tax year is £11,000. Section 55B Finance Act 2014 will allow basic-rate married couples and civil partners to transfer up to £1,060 of their personal allowances to each other, with effect from April 2015.

The rates for income tax in the tax year 2016–17 are as follows:

- basic rate (20%) £0–32,000;
- higher rate (40%) on taxable income between £32,000 and £150,000;
- from April 2013, a further rate of 45% on taxable income over £150,000.

 Example

Jennie works in a cake shop and earns £15,250 pa. She is married to William who works as a family lawyer and earns £46,000 pa.

Jennie and William both have a personal allowance of £11,000.

Jennie has the following taxable income: £15,250 − £11,000 = £4,250.

Jennie does not earn enough to pay higher rate tax and so will pay tax on £4,250 at the rate of 20%.

William has the following taxable income: £46,000 – £11,000 = £35,000.

William will pay the first £32,000 at 20% and the remaining £3,000 at 40%.

This is a simplified tax calculation for illustrative purposes.

20.2.1 MAINTENANCE AND INCOME TAX

When a person pays maintenance, there is no longer any tax relief available and maintenance is paid from the payer's net income. This is irrespective of the way that maintenance is paid, e.g. through the Child Support Agency, as a result of a court order, or by agreement. If a party pays towards household expenses directly to the suppliers, no tax relief is available.

20.3 CAPITAL GAINS TAX

Capital gains tax (CGT) arises on the disposal of an asset or the receipt of money in respect of an asset if there is a 'chargeable gain'. A chargeable gain may arise if a person:

- sells, gives away, exchanges, or transfers—disposes of—all or part of an asset;
- receives a capital sum, such as an insurance payout for a damaged asset.

Assets that commonly attract CGT include:

- land;
- buildings, for example a second home;
- personal possessions such as a painting worth more than £6,000;
- shares or securities;
- business assets, e.g. business premises or goodwill.

You work out CGT by:

- working out separately the gain or loss for each asset you sell or dispose of, taking off any allowable expenses and reliefs;
- taking away your total allowable losses from your total gains—this gives you your net gain or loss;
- taking off allowable losses brought forward from an earlier year;
- taking off the annual tax-free allowance (known as the 'annual exempt amount'). This is £11,100 for an individual for 2016–17;
- a net gain will be subject to CGT and the rates of CGT are 10% (18% on residential property) or 20% (28% on residential property) depending upon the amount of total taxable income and your tax bracket.

 Example

Jennie and William own a holiday cottage in the Yorkshire Dales, which they bought five years ago for £200,000. In the time since the purchase, the BBC have filmed a popular costume drama and the village has become a major tourist attraction. The cottage is sold for £400,000. The chargeable gain is £200,000 less £11,100 = £188,900.

Tax will be paid at 18% or 28% depending upon their total taxable income as it is residential property.

There have been recent changes in relief available on chargeable gains for disposals made before 6 April 2008. For further details, refer to a specialist practitioner text.

20.3.1 CGT AND SPOUSES/CIVIL PARTNERS

Spouses and civil partners, if living together, will generally not pay CGT on transfers between one another, as they are treated as one person. The transfer is not treated as a chargeable gain or loss (the exception is trading stock).

If the spouses or civil partners are separated, then they are not treated as one person for the purposes of CGT and so a chargeable gain may arise.

The issue of transfers of assets between separated spouses or civil partners arises when the parties agree a settlement or an order is made under s24 Matrimonial Causes Act 1973 (MCA 1973) in financial order proceedings as they may give rise to CGT liability.

20.3.2 FAMILY ASSETS AND CGT

There is no CGT liability on certain assets including premium bonds, a private car, and cash. Other assets that do not attract CGT include tangible moveable property that is a wasting asset (has less than 50 years of useful life or less). One of the most important exceptions to CGT is the family home.

However, a party may have to dispose of an asset to raise cash and so this would attract CGT.

Most disposals of the family home are covered by the private residence exception. Any gain accruing to an individual on a disposal of a dwelling house that is or has been at any time in his period of ownership the only or main residence will be wholly or partly exempt from CGT by virtue of the private residence exemption provided by ss222 and 223 of the Taxation of Chargeable Gains Act 1992 (TCGA 1992). If a person occupies the property as his home for the whole period of ownership, the whole gain will be CGT exempt, otherwise the gain will be apportioned to the portion for which he was not in occupation. However, an individual will be treated as having been in residence during their final 36 months of ownership, whether s/he was actually there or not. There are also exception where the house has been rented out, used as a business, or is very large.

Statutory Instrument 2009/730, The Enactment of Extra-Statutory Concessions Order 2009, implemented a concession to spouses and civil partners under s215B TCGA 1992 and is important in a case where a party transfers his share in the family home when he has been out of occupation for more than three years (18 months from April 2014).

This concession applies to a situation where a spouse transfers an interest in the family home to the other spouse as part of a financial settlement on divorce or separation, and:

- the other spouse continues to occupy the family home as her only or main residence; and
- the transferring spouse has not elected to treat any other property as his only or main residence.

The transferring spouse is deemed to continue in occupation of the home until the date of the transfer, however long it is since they left. Other assets may also attract CGT, e.g. a holiday home or company shares, and it is important to be vigilant for assets attracting a chargeable gain. However, from April 2014, the period of occupation has been reduced to 18 months.

20.4 INHERITANCE TAX

Inheritance tax was introduced by the Finance Act 1975 and substantial changes have been made to the inheritance tax regime by the Finance Act 2006. The general rule is that inheritance tax may be payable on any transfer of value made by a person while that person is alive. On death, a person is deemed to make a transfer of value equal to the value of his entire estate immediately before death.

An individual is entitled to a 'nil rate band' within which transfers of value made within a seven-year period will be free of tax. The nil rate band announced for the tax year 2016–17 is £325,000.

20.4.1 INHERITANCE TAX DURING MARRIAGE/CIVIL PARTNERSHIP

During a marriage or civil partnership transfers of assets are exempt from inheritance tax (IHT) until the date of decree absolute: s18 Inheritance Tax Act 1984 (IHTA 1984).

Following divorce or dissolution, spouses or civil partners have fewer opportunities to make exempt transfers. If a transfer is made pursuant to an order of the court following a decree of divorce or nullity, it will generally be regarded as a transaction at arm's length not intended to confer gratuitous benefit (Senior Registrar of the Family Division statement (1975) 119 SJ 596). It would appear that this will extend to transfers made pursuant to an agreed settlement.

20.5 STAMP DUTY LAND TAX

Stamp duty is charged in respect of 'land transactions', which are broadly the transfer of interests of land. The amount of stamp duty is based on the amount of consideration provided for the land. Most commonly, this tax is encountered during house sales and purchases and should be taken into account when calculating the money available to the parties.

The rates are as follows:

Residential property—purchase price	Rate of stamp duty land tax
up to £125,000	0%
£125,001–£250,000	2%
£250,001–£925,000	5%
£925,001–£1.5 m	10%
£1.5 m +	12%

The rate for first time buyers is nil if the property is sold for less than £250,000.

SUMMARY POINTS

- Tax must be taken into account when considering a settlement between the parties.

- Income tax is relevant where a party will start work and a client may need to understand the net income available.

- If the parties transfer or sell assets, there may be liability for either CGT or IHT.

- When buying and selling property, stamp duty land tax will be paid.

SELF-TEST QUESTIONS

1. Minnie and Boris divorce. Boris earns £100,000 per year and Minnie earns £150,000. As part of their financial proceedings they sell their family home, a yacht, and a very valuable painting that Boris bought in 1999. Minnie buys a new house worth £489,000. Advise Minnie and Boris on any potential tax issues.

Case Study Two

David has a small fishing boat that he bought for £1,000 in 1980. He has restored it to bring it back to life as a fishing vessel, as it was a shell when he bought it. It has been valued as being worth £25,000. David will sell the boat as part of the financial proceedings. Advise on the tax implications of this sale.

Answers to the questions above can be found on the Online Resource Centre: **www.oxfordtextbooks.co.uk/orc/sendall17/.**

online
resource
centre

21

WELFARE BENEFITS

21.1 INTRODUCTION

This chapter will:

• discuss the main forms of welfare benefits available to family law clients.

As well as being able to advise on the law and procedure involved with proceedings for a financial remedy, a family lawyer must have a working knowledge of welfare benefits. In **Chapter 2**, it was seen that some welfare benefits 'passport' the client into certain forms of public funding. You are unlikely to find situations in practice where one party is on welfare benefits and another is earning a large salary. In practice, it is more likely that one party is on welfare benefits and the other party is earning a low wage. For this reason, it is very important to understand your client's potential eligibility for welfare benefits and the effect on their eligibility of any financial change in circumstances.

In this chapter we will look in outline at the main types of welfare benefit that a new family lawyer will come across in their practice. This is not a comprehensive account of all welfare benefits available but does cover most benefits commonly encountered by family lawyers. The welfare benefits system is currently undergoing a series of changes and therefore it would be wise to keep an eye on the news and the Online Resource Centre. What follows is the situation currently in effect and those changes anticipated to come into effect in 2016 and 2017.

21.2 INCOME SUPPORT

Income support is available for those who are financially eligible and cannot be available for work full time but do not have sufficient money to live on, e.g. lone parents, registered sick or disabled, or a student who is a lone parent or disabled or caring for someone who is elderly or sick.

21.2.1 **ELIGIBILITY**

Clients should be habitually resident and present in the UK, be aged between 18 and 60, and not engaged in remunerative work for more than 24 hours a week (or have a partner engaged in remunerative work for more than 24 hours a week). Students in 'relevant education' will not be eligible.

The first £6,000 of capital is disregarded, but clients will be ineligible if they have capital of £16,000, and must work less than 16 hours per week. If a client's partner works more than 24 hours per week, then they will be ineligible. The client's income must be below the amount necessary to live on (the 'applicable amount').

Income is calculated according to the family income and this includes spouses, civil partners, and cohabitants (including same-sex couples). The first £10 of child mainte-nance is disregarded, as well as lump sum orders, statutory sick pay, statutory maternity payments, part-time earnings, and child benefit as well as income from capital sums over £6,000.

21.2.2 **WHAT WILL THE CLIENTS RECEIVE?**

What the clients receive will depend on a number of factors including:

- age;
- whether they live alone or as a couple;
- age and income of dependants;
- disability;
- earnings.

The rate of benefit changes frequently although in the 2015 Budget it was announced that it would be frozen for four years. For 2016–17 it is:

- single people—aged 16–24: £57.90, aged 25 or over: £73.10;
- couple—both aged 18 and over: £114.85;
- lone parents—aged 16–17: £57.90, aged 18 and over: £73.10.

Those in receipt of income support will automatically gain the following benefits:

- free dental care;
- free prescriptions;
- free school meals;
- housing benefit;
- council tax benefit.

These are described as 'passport benefits' and their value to the client should be remem-bered when advising on the level of maintenance. To set the level of maintenance at exactly the same monetary level as income support may mean the person is worse off, as they lose entitlement to passport benefits.

 Example

Helen and Seamus have one child together. Seamus leaves Helen to live with another woman. Sea-mus works out that Helen would be entitled to income support and other benefits. Seamus pays this amount in maintenance to Helen. Unfortunately, this means that Helen has to pay for her own prescriptions and her child's school meals and loses some entitlement to housing benefit. Helen is financially worse off as a result.

21.2.3 SUPPORT FOR MORTGAGE INTEREST

Support for mortgage interest (SMI) can be paid to people on income support, income-based jobseeker's allowance, income-related employment and support allowance, and pension credit, if they are experiencing problems with the interest payments on their mortgage. No payment is made towards the endowment or repayment element of a mortgage.

The support available:

- the waiting period for homeowners is 13 weeks for all working age claims;
- the capital limit on loans for which SMI can be paid is £200,000 for new working age claims.

Pensioners getting pension credit are limited to £100,000. The standard interest rate used to calculate SMI is currently 3.63%. SMI cannot help to pay the capital element of the mortgage (only the interest), insurance policies, or any missed mortgage payments. In the 2015 Budget it was announced that from 2018 SMI will be treated as a loan only.

21.3 JOBSEEKER'S ALLOWANCE

Jobseeker's allowance is the main benefit for people who are out of work. There are two types of jobseeker's allowance. The first is called 'contribution-based jobseeker's allowance'. A client may receive contribution-based jobseeker's allowance if they have paid or been credited with class 1 national insurance (NI) contributions in the relevant tax years. Self-employed contributions will not generally qualify for contribution-based jobseeker's allowance.

The other form of jobseeker's allowance is based on income and savings. This is called 'income-based jobseeker's allowance'.

21.3.1 WHAT ARE THE BENEFIT RATES (WEEKLY)?

- Contribution-based jobseeker's allowance:
  - single person:
    person aged 16–24: £57.90;
    person aged 25 or over: £73.10.

- Income-based jobseeker's allowance:
  - single person:
    person aged 16–24: £57.90;
    person aged 25 or over: £73.10.
  - couples:
    both aged 18 or over: £114.85.

Like income support, jobseeker's allowance will be frozen in 2016 for four years.

21.4 TAX CREDITS

A client may be able to claim two tax credits, child tax credit and working tax credit, which have been payable since April 2003 under the Tax Credits Act 2002. The administration of tax credits has not been straightforward as the system is complex and clients must keep HMRC up to date with changes in circumstances. An outline of the system follows; for further information see the Online Resource Centre.

Tax credits are based on the claimant's income (please note that income for tax credits differs from income tax calculations). The first award is based on the previous year's income, which is then revised to the current year's income (this is either when the claimant provides an estimate or when the award is finalized at the year end). The personal circumstances on which the award is based are those of the current tax year but the award can be changed during that year or the year end to reflect any change in circumstances.

The general rule is that to qualify for tax credits the applicant must be aged 16 or over and usually live in the UK. Spouses and civil partners are required to make joint claims. The amounts of credits will depend upon the income of the applicant as the tax credit operates to increase the income available. If the applicant is on certain benefits, the maximum credit will be received. The amount of credit available decreases as the applicant's income increases. This chapter will look briefly at child tax credit and working tax credit. Pension credits are also available for people of retirement age. Tax credits are subject to the benefits cap.

21.4.1 CHILD TAX CREDIT

Child tax credit is for people who are responsible for at least one child or qualifying young person. Child tax credit is paid directly to the person who is mainly responsible for caring for the child or children or directly to a lone parent. An applicant does not have to be working to claim.

The rules for entitlement to child tax credit are found in the imaginatively titled Child Tax Credit Regulations 2002. Further information can be found on the Online Resource Centre.

A basic element of up to £545 can be paid and then a family element up to £2,780 can be paid, according to eligibility. An additional element of child tax credit can be paid for each child for whom the claimant has responsibility if:

- receiving disability living allowance for the child; or
- the child is registered blind.

21.4.2 WORKING TAX CREDIT

Working tax credit is for people who are employed or self-employed (either on their own or in a partnership), who:

- usually work 16 hours or more a week;
- are paid for that work; and
- expect to work for at least four weeks;

and who are:

- aged 16 or over and responsible for at least one child; or
- aged 16 or over and disabled; or
- aged 25 or over and usually work at least 30 hours a week.

Working tax credit is paid to the person who is working 16 hours or more a week (and responsible for at least one child), and where the applicants are a couple, if both are working 16 hours or more a week, one must choose which will receive it. Working tax credit cannot be claimed if an applicant is not working. If a person is not responsible for a child, they must be working over 30 hours per week and be over the age of 25.

As part of working tax credit, an applicant may qualify for help towards the costs of childcare. If the applicant receives the childcare element of working tax credit, this will always be paid direct to the person who is mainly responsible for caring for the child or children, alongside payments of child tax credit.

Working tax credit is made up of the following elements:

- basic element:

this is paid to any working person who meets the conditions;

- lone parent element (if applicable);

- couples element (if applicable);

- 30-hour element:

this is paid to people who work at least 30 hours a week. Couples with at least one child can claim the 30-hour element if they work at least 30 hours a week between them providing at least one of them works 16 hours or more a week;

- disability and severe disability element:

for people who have a disability or severe disability;

- 50 plus element:

paid to people aged 50 or over and who are starting work after a period on benefits.

The rules regarding working tax credit can be found in the Working Tax Credit (Entitlement and Maximum Rate) Regulations 2002. The Online Resource Centre contains more information.

21.5 EMPLOYMENT AND SUPPORT ALLOWANCE

Employment and Support Allowance (ESA) replaced Incapacity Benefit and provides financial help to those who cannot work due to illness or disability. The Online Resource Centre has more details about this benefit.

21.6 HOUSING BENEFIT

Housing benefit helps those on a low income to pay for rental accommodation. An applicant may be entitled to housing benefit if they pay rent and their income and capital (savings and investments) are below a certain level. For all new tenancies, local housing allowance will be granted, especially for private tenancies. It is a more generous benefit than housing benefit and is paid directly to the client. Different rates are payable in different local authorities. For more information see the Online Resource Centre.

The housing benefit available is the same as 'eligible' rent. This is the amount used to work out the benefit but may not be the same as the full rent. Eligible rent may be limited to an amount that is reasonable for a suitably sized property and will depend on whether in the area the applicant lives:

- the amount of rent is reasonable for the particular home;

- the home is a reasonable size for the applicant and their family;

- the amount of rent is reasonable for the area where the applicant lives.

Eligible rent includes:

- rent for the accommodation;

- charges for some services, such as lifts, communal laundry facilities, or play areas.

21.6.1 WHO IS ELIGIBLE?

If the client has capital between £6,000 and £16,000, a 'tariff' is applied where £1 = £250 and housing benefit will not be available if:

- there are savings of over £16,000, unless the applicant is aged 60 or over and getting the 'guarantee credit' of pension credit;

- the applicant lives in the home of a close relative;
- the applicant is a full-time student (unless disabled or has children);
- the applicant is an asylum seeker or is sponsored to be in the UK.

Further, if the applicant lives with a partner or civil partner only one can get housing benefit. If the applicant is single and aged under 25, housing benefit is only available for bed-sit accommodation or one room in shared accommodation. From 2017, those between the ages of 18 and 21 will no longer be eligible for housing benefit.

21.6.2 'BEDROOM TAX'

Subject to much publicity have been the changes to housing benefit for those with spare rooms, dubbed the 'bedroom tax'. From April 2013, if a claimant lives in council accommodation or other social housing and is assessed as having at least one extra bedroom in the house, housing benefit could be reduced by:

- 14% of the 'eligible rent' if you have one extra bedroom;
- 25% of the 'eligible rent' if you have two or more extra bedrooms.

 Example

Eligible rent is £100 per week. Of this, housing benefit pays £50 and the claimant pays £50. There is one extra bedroom so the reduction is 14%. Housing benefit will be reduced by £14 per week.

21.7 COUNCIL TAX REDUCTION

Until April 2013, the benefit was known as council tax benefit. The benefit is now known as council tax reduction. It is available if the applicant pays council tax and their income and capital (savings and investments) are below a certain level. Every council will run their own scheme and so each may be slightly different.

Rebates are available for a second adult if the home is shared with a person who is not their partner or civil partner, is aged 18 or over, is not paying rent or council tax themselves, and is on low income. A person living alone will receive a 25% reduction.

21.7.1 WHO IS NOT ELIGIBLE?

Council tax reduction is administered by local councils and they will look at:

- income, including earnings, some benefits and tax credits, and occupational pensions;
- savings;
- family circumstances including age, the size of the family and their ages, and disability.

The most council tax reduction obtainable is 100%.

21.8 CHILD BENEFIT

Child benefit is a tax-free payment that is claimed for a child. It is usually paid every four weeks but in some cases can be paid weekly, and there are separate rates for each child. The payment can be claimed by anyone who qualifies, whatever their income or savings.

A person is eligible for child benefit if any of the following apply:

- the child is under 16;

- the child is over 16 and in relevant education or training;
- the child is 16 or 17, has left relevant education or training, and is registered for work, education, or training with an approved body.

There are two separate amounts, with a higher amount for the eldest (or only) child. The rate is £20.70 a week for the oldest child and £13.70 a week for each of the other children.

Child benefit can be paid into any bank or building society and is usually paid every four weeks, but it can be paid weekly if the claimant is in receipt of income support or income-based jobseeker's allowance. Since January 2013, any family with an individual earner with an income over £50,000 will be subject to a tax charge administered by HMRC.

21.9 **UNIVERSAL CREDIT**

Universal credit is a single monthly payment which will, eventually, replace the following benefits:

- income-based jobseeker's allowance;
- income-related employment and support allowance;
- income support;
- child tax credit;
- working tax credit;
- housing benefit.

The benefit is being introduced in a phased roll-out and currently ten areas in the UK have universal credit. The benefit is being rolled out in stages across the country and there are now 279,000 claimants claiming universal credit. However, its roll-out will not be complete until 2022. Universal credit is a 'passporting' benefit for public funding (see **Chapter 2**).

▌SUMMARY POINTS

- It is important to be able to give basic advice on welfare benefits and be aware of the main types of welfare benefits to clients.
- A knowledge of welfare benefits is also essential when considering eligibility for public funding (see **Chapter 2**).
- It is also important to understand how benefits can assist those on low incomes as well as those who have lost an income and also the 'passport' benefits that some forms of welfare benefits bring and the impact that their loss has on a family's income.
- This chapter gives a brief overview of the main benefits that are encountered in practice. The Online Resource Centre gives more information on calculating eligibility.

online
resource
centre

▌SELF-TEST QUESTIONS

1. Margaret and Nick live in rented accommodation with their two children. Nick decides that he cannot live with Margaret any longer and leaves the home. Margaret works 12 hours per week as a cleaner but is worried that she may lose her job in the recession. She earns £66.76 per week and has no savings.
   (a) Advise Margaret if she may be able to claim any welfare benefits.
   (b) Would your advice change if Margaret were to lose her job?

Case Study Two

Helena is concerned that she is not claiming all the benefits that she is entitled to. Look at the case study documents on the Online Resource Centre and advise Helena. You will find an email in the case study materials giving you a solution.

online
resource
centre

Answers to the questions above can be found on the Online Resource Centre: **www.oxfordtextbooks.co.uk/orc/sendall17/.**

Part 4

COHABITATION

22 COHABITATION

22.1 INTRODUCTION

This chapter will:

- make a comparison between marriage, civil partnership, and cohabitation;
- examine the law on cohabitation contracts;
- examine future developments on cohabitation.

Part 4 deals with the legal position of cohabitant families. The current estimate is that in 2013 there were 2.9 million people in cohabiting relationships. Families are amazingly diverse and do not always fall within the neat categories of spouses and civil partners, and as a result, the law does not deal well with cohabitant families. This is partly as a result of social policy not recognizing families who have chosen not to enter into legally recognized relationships. It is important to consider the law that exists for cohabitants, as many clients will consult a solicitor when their cohabiting relationships have broken down.

When a cohabiting relationship ends, there is not the same coherent body of law available to married couples or civil partners. Many cohabitants mistakenly believe that they acquire legal rights after a number of years of cohabiting, but this is incorrect. The myth of the 'common law wife/husband' persists, despite having no legal foundation. Many clients are shocked to find they have few legal remedies and those available are far from straightforward.

In this chapter, 'cohabitation' includes couples living together, both opposite- and same-sex couples. This chapter will compare remedies available to married couples, civil partners, and cohabitants as well as the emerging law on cohabitation contracts. The legal remedies available to cohabitants will be further considered in **Chapter 23** in much more detail.

22.2 COMPARISON OF COHABITATION, MARRIAGE, AND CIVIL PARTNERSHIPS

See Table 22.1.

22.3 COHABITATION CONTRACTS

Cohabitation contracts have been traditionally regarded as void on the grounds of public policy as they undermined the status of marriage and were considered sexually immoral. As the numbers of people living together outside of marriage (or civil partnerships) have increased, the courts appear to be taking a less absolute view. The courts have drawn

TABLE 22.1 COMPARISON OF COHABITATION, MARRIAGE, AND CIVIL PARTNERSHIPS

Issue	Marriage	Civil partnerships	Cohabitants
Legal process to end relationship?	Divorce under MCA 1973.	Dissolution under the CPA 2004.	None required.
Duty to provide financial support during relationship?	Spouses must provide financial support during the marriage.	Partners must provide financial support during the civil partnership.	No legal duty to provide financial support to cohabitant.
Finance and property division following relationship breakdown.	Financial relief under MCA 1973 and under the Domestic Proceedings and Magistrates' Courts Act 1978.	Financial resolution under the CPA 2004 equivalent to financial relief under the MCA 1973.	No specific rights or remedies. Parties may negotiate and reach an agreement. No right to maintenance for either party. Proceedings may be taken in property and trust law.
Parental responsibility (PR) for children.	Both parents automatically gain PR for their natural child (from 1 December 2003).	Natural mother automatically has PR. Civil partners can acquire PR by agreement or court order.	Natural mother will have automatic PR but father does not acquire PR unless on the child's birth certificate, by agreement or court order.
Children (disputes about where a child lives or with whom they shall have contact).	Proceedings can be taken under the CA 1989 and both natural parents may apply.	Proceedings can be taken under the CA 1989 and the natural parent may apply for a s8 order but the civil partner may apply only if he has PR, and child arrangement orders if not a natural parent but child is the child of the family.	Proceedings can be taken under the CA 1989 and both parents may apply for a s8 order if natural parents.
Financial support for children.	Spouses have a duty to maintain their children.	Both partners have a duty to maintain a child of the family.	Both parents have a duty to maintain their children.
	May apply for child support from the Child Support Agency or Child Maintenance Service.	May apply for child support from the Child Support Agency, Child Maintenance Service and under Sch 1 CA 1989.	May apply for child support from the Child Support Agency, Child Maintenance Service and under Sch 1 CA 1989.
Wills and probate.	Married couples will be treated as having pre-deceased the spouse in a will when divorced and there may be a partial intestacy.	Civil partners will be treated as having pre-deceased the civil partner in a will once the partnership has been dissolved and there may be a partial intestacy.	Breakdown of a cohabiting relationship has no effect on existing wills.
	Once divorced, the spouse will not inherit under the Intestacy Rules.	Once the civil partnership has been dissolved, the civil partner will not inherit under the Intestacy Rules.	Cohabiting couples have no right to inherit each other's property under the Intestacy Rules.

	A claim may be made under the Inheritance (Provision for Family and Dependants) Act 1975 (I(PFD)A 1975).	A claim may be made under the I(PFD)A 1975.	A claim may be made under the I(PFD)A 1975 if the requirements of the Act are satisfied.
Domestic violence.	Proceedings under the Family Law Act 1996 (FLA 1996) as spouses are associated persons.	Proceedings under the FLA 1996 as civil partners are associated persons.	Proceedings under the FLA 1996 if the parties are associated persons.
The family home.	Section 33 FLA 1996 gives spouses 'home rights' that entitle the spouse to live in the family home.	Section 33 FLA 1996 gives civil partners 'home rights' that entitle the civil partner to live in the family home.	No statutory right to occupy the family home.

a distinction between a 'contract for cohabitation' and a 'contract for the regulation of property and financial matters between cohabitants'.

In *Sutton v Mishcon de Reya and Gawor & Co* [2004] 1 FLR 837 a cohabitation contract was drafted for a gay couple. The contract concerned a 'master and servant' relationship. The claimant was to be the 'master' and the other man to be the 'servant'. The 'servant' agreed to transfer his considerable property and wealth to the 'master'. The 'servant' changed his mind with the parties never having cohabited. The men negotiated a settlement through the defendant solicitors that was considerably less advantageous than the original cohabitation contract.

The claimant sued the solicitors for negligence in drafting. The court held that the contract was for cohabitation and therefore void.

Hart J, in his judgment, indicated that there is nothing contrary to public policy in a cohabitation agreement governing the property relationship between adults who intend to cohabit or who are cohabiting for the purposes of enjoying a sexual relationship.

The defendant solicitors had advised their client that the agreement would be unenforceable and so they were not negligent for alleged errors of drafting. The court further held that the instant cohabitation agreement could not have withstood further scrutiny of the parties' legal intention to create the agreement; particularly undue influence or misrepresentation.

Cohabitation contracts may not be void for public policy if they regulate the property and financial relationship of cohabitants but the courts will scrutinize such agreements carefully and parties should seek professional advice.

22.4 LAW COMMISSION PROPOSALS AND FUTURE DEVELOPMENTS

Many solicitors encounter cases where cohabitants are left without a home following the end of a relationship and many clients must use remedies that were not designed to resolve family relationships. The remedies available to resolve property and financial affairs between cohabitants are considered in more detail in **Chapter 23**.

The Law Commission published a report, 'Cohabitation: The Financial Consequences of Relationship Breakdown', in July 2007. The Law Commission looked at the financial consequences of the end of a cohabiting relationship by separation or death and the adequacy of existing remedies. It found that a majority of people supported the availability of legal remedies for cohabitants.

The Law Commission did not believe that cohabitants should have the same remedies as married couples or civil partners due to the lack of distinctive public and formal commitment between cohabitants. The Law Commission's proposals would be to extend financial relief to cohabitants who:

- had satisfied certain eligibility criteria;
- had not opted out of the scheme; and
- made certain financial contributions to the relationship giving rise to certain enduring consequences at the end of the relationship.

The details of the proposed scheme can be found in **Chapter 23**. There is currently no move by the Government to make legislation to enact the Law Commission proposals.

Lord Lester of Herne Hill introduced the Cohabitation Bill into the House of Lords in 2008 and the Bill reached committee stage. The Cohabitation Bill was largely based on the Law Commission's proposals. The Cohabitation Bill did attract some wide support from family lawyers but also had some significant opponents. The Bill failed to become law. In 2012, Lord Lester introduced a private member's Bill, the Inheritance (Cohabitants) Bill, with assistance from the Law Commission. The Bill has not become law.

SUMMARY POINTS

- Cohabitants will often seek legal advice at the end of a relationship but the legal remedies are not straightforward.
- There are differences in law between married couples, civil partners, and cohabitants, including the availability of financial support and the rules on inheritance.
- Contracts to regulate property and financial arrangements between cohabitants are beginning to receive judicial acceptance.
- The Law Commission has made proposals for the reform of the law concerning cohabitants but no legislation has been proposed by the Government.

SELF-TEST QUESTIONS

1. A client tells you that after she has lived with her partner for two years, she is a 'common law wife'. Is she correct?

2. Does a cohabitant have the right to maintenance for herself after the end of a relationship?

3. Your cohabitant client wishes to have a contract drawn up to deal with the family home following any relationship breakdown. Explain whether this is permitted.

online resource centre

Answers to the questions above can be found on the Online Resource Centre: **www.oxfordtextbooks.co.uk/orc/sendall17/.**

23

COHABITATION AND FINANCE

23.1 INTRODUCTION

This chapter will:

- discuss the legal position of cohabitants;
- discuss the legal remedies available to separating cohabitants;
- examine the position of cohabitants in relation to the family home.

There is a very persistent myth that once a couple have lived together for a number of years (curiously, most clients put this at about two years) a cohabitant gains the status of a 'common law' wife/husband. Further, once a person becomes a 'common law' wife/husband, they gain a number of rights including a 'right' to part of the family home or other assets.

This is a myth and there is no such thing as a 'common law' wife/husband. Your clients will often argue with you and tell you that you are wrong. In 1753, Lord Hardwicke's Marriage Act legislated that no other marriage other than one presided over by an Anglican clergyman would be valid (although now one can marry in a register office or in a civil ceremony). The Online Resource Centre gives a fuller picture of the history of the law of marriage. Suffice to say that your clients must be firmly advised that no rights of 'common law marriage' exist. Clients must be married before home rights are accrued or relief can be given under the Matrimonial Causes Act 1973 (MCA 1973). Similarly, same-sex cohabiting couples have no legal rights over one another unless they marry or enter a civil partnership.

So, where does this leave cohabitants? This chapter will discuss the rights and remedies available to cohabiting couples in terms of money and property. In this chapter, the term 'cohabitant' will include both same-sex and heterosexual couples.

23.2 COHABITANTS AND FINANCIAL REMEDIES

In the introduction (see **23.1**), we see that cohabitants have no rights inherent in the fact that they live together. There is no right to maintenance for cohabitants other than that of child support maintenance for the natural children of the couple. Property disputes between cohabitants are resolved using existing property and trusts law and not the MCA 1973 or any other family law.

The difficulty that cohabitants face is that the law is a patchwork of remedies and lacks the cohesion of the law relating to spouses or civil partners. The law is complex, uncertain, and expensive to litigate and not designed for families. There are often very unjust conclusions to such proceedings.

Cohabitation contracts are discussed fully at **22.3**. The court may become more sympathetic to cohabitation contracts in the future.

If the cohabitants require protection from domestic abuse, the Family Law Act 1996 can be used (see **Chapter 33** onwards). If there are disputes involving children, the Children Act 1989 (CA 1989) will apply (see **Chapter 24** onwards).

This chapter will concentrate on the availability of financial remedies for cohabitants.

23.2.1 LAW COMMISSION PROPOSALS

The Law Commission considered the hardships faced by cohabitants following the breakdown in a cohabiting relationship. The Law Commission recognized that simply improving public awareness would be insufficient, as many people cannot 'simply get married' as their partners might refuse to and that person is faced with remaining with the status quo or leaving the relationship. The Law Commission did not agree that cohabitants should have the same legal rights as spouses and civil partners as there are a broad range of cohabiting relationships.

The Law Commission proposed a scheme where cohabitants can gain some financial relief but remedies should only be available where:

- the couple satisfy certain eligibility requirements (having a child or living together for a specified number of years);
- the couple had agreed not to disapply the scheme; and
- the applicant had made certain qualifying financial contributions to the relationship giving rise to certain enduring consequences.

Since the publication of the report by the Law Commission in July 2007, there has been no move on the part of the Government to pass legislation enacting the recommendations.

 The Online Resource Centre has more details.

23.3 JOINTLY HELD PROPERTY

If property is held by both parties jointly as legal co-owners, then the property cannot be sold or transferred without the consent of both parties. If the parties do not intend the property to be shared 50/50 on sale, then the parties should execute a declaration of trust. A declaration of trust is a document that states the shares in which each joint owner holds the property, e.g. 50/50 or some other proportion. Unfortunately, not everyone is advised about the importance of making such a declaration when purchasing a home.

Completion of the TR1 form in the conveyance of a house is crucial and parties buying a house should be fully advised on how the property is held and to properly execute the form and/or execute a declaration of trust to be held with the deeds. A problem can arise (with either married/civil partners or cohabitants) where the property is held jointly but a dispute arises concerning the shares the parties have on sale of the property.

The extent of the shares in jointly held property was considered by the House of Lords in *Stack v Dowden* [2007] UKHL 17. Baroness Hale (who gave the leading judgment) commented that it was the first time that the question had come before the House of Lords.

The facts of the case are worth noting. The parties, Mr Stack and Ms Dowden, met as teenagers and began to live together in their mid 20s in 1983. They had four children and separated in 2002. The house at the centre of the dispute (in Chatsworth Road) had been bought in joint names in 1993 and sold in November 2005 for £746,245. The conveyance contained no deed of trust. Prior to purchasing this house the parties had lived in a property (in Purves Road) in the sole name of Ms Dowden. She paid all the mortgage and bills. The house in Purves Road was held to be Ms Dowden's entirely.

The Chatsworth Road property cost £190,000. £128,813 came from Ms Dowden's savings and a mortgage in joint names. By the time of the sale, Mr Stack had paid £27,000 towards reducing the mortgage and Ms Dowden had paid £38,345. Mr Stack paid the premiums of a joint endowment policy and Ms Dowden paid household bills. Both parties kept their finances absolutely separate.

At first instance the court held that the property was held 50/50. Ms Dowden appealed. The Court of Appeal upheld Ms Dowden's appeal and held that the interests of the property were held 65% to Ms Dowden and 35% to Mr Stack. The House of Lords upheld the Court of Appeal's decision. Their Lordships found that the property was held in joint names but that the proceeds should be divided in the proportions decided by the Court of Appeal. Ms Dowden could demonstrate that the shares were not equal as a result of the unequal contributions to the property and the fact that the parties had not pooled their resources.

The assumption would be that beneficial interests would follow legal title unless the contrary is proved. Joint legal owners will be assumed to hold the property as beneficial joint tenants and sole legal owners will be assumed to hold the beneficial interest unless the contrary is proved. The contrary is established by the parties' express, implied, and imputed intentions. Baroness Hale gave the following guidance:

- each case will turn on its own facts;
- advice or discussions at the time of transfer that cast light on parties' intentions;
- the reasons why the home was acquired in joint names;
- the purpose for which the home was acquired and the nature of the parties' relationship and children;
- how the purchase was financed both initially and subsequently;
- how the parties arranged their finances.

The onus is on the person seeking to show that the beneficial ownership is different from the legal ownership.

In *Kernott v Jones* [2010] EWCA Civ 578, a cohabitants' property dispute was heard by the Court of Appeal. The principal issue at trial before the court was whether and, if so, to what extent the equal beneficial interests of the co-owners had been varied after their separation.

In May 1985 the parties, who had an infant child, purchased the property in joint names for £30,000. The woman, Jones, contributed £6,000 and the balance of the purchase price was raised by means of an endowment mortgage. In 1986 a further loan of £2,000 was taken out for an extension, built and paid for largely by Kernott, enhancing the value of the house from about £30,000 to £44,000. The parties' second child was born that year. Jones and Kernott shared household bills including mortgage payments. They separated in 1993, Jones and the children staying in the property. It was common ground at trial that at that time their beneficial interests were equal. Thereafter, Jones assumed sole responsibility for the outgoings on the property and the children's maintenance.

In May 1996 Kernott bought another property for £57,000. He raised the deposit, with Jones' agreement, by cashing in a separate life policy which they owned, whose proceeds they divided equally. The trial judge ruled that Jones' investment towards the purchase of the property, particularly since separation, meant that she was entitled to a greater share. In addition she received very little contribution from Kernott to the maintenance and support of the two children.

He found that at the outset the parties' intentions may well have been to provide a home for them and their children, but they had altered since separation to the extent that Kernott demonstrated that he had no intention until recently of availing himself of the beneficial ownership, having ignored it completely by way of any investment in it or attempt to maintain or repair it whilst he had his own property upon which he concentrated.

The judge turned to assess the altered shares on the basis of what was 'fair and just'. He fixed the beneficial interests at: Jones, 90%; Kernott, 10%.

The Court of Appeal dismissed Kernott's appeal. It was held that, so far as the intention of the parties cannot be inferred, the court is free to impute a common intention to them. The judge was quite right to infer or impute the parties' intention to change their beneficial interests. 'Fair and just' was the appropriate criterion to quantify the varied interests by imputation.

The Court of Appeal allowed Kernott's second appeal, by a 2–1 majority (Jacob LJ dissenting). The judge had identified no evidence from which could properly be inferred a common intention to vary the equal beneficial interests held on separation. The parties' beneficial interests were equal. The case was heard by the Supreme Court and the question to be resolved by their Lordships was 'whether a court can properly infer an agreement by an unmarried couple, who hold a property in equal shares at the date of their separation, to the effect that thereafter their respective beneficial interests should alter'.

In the Supreme Court at [2011] SC 53, their Lordships restored the judgment made at first instance and awarded Mrs Jones 90% of the proceeds of the property. The presumption of equal beneficial ownership can be rebutted by the demonstration that the parties had different common intention as to the quantum of their respective shares in a property, either at the time of acquisition or at a later date. These intentions as to shares can change over time and can be ambulatory in nature.

The method by which the court divines the parties' intention was considered by the court and their Lordships exhorted the need to use best efforts at this stage and not to shrink from making inferences from disputed evidence. Differences arose between their Lordships on the issue of whether it is possible to draw inferences as to a change over time in the parties' intention to the shares in the disputed property. The majority (with Lord Kerr and Lord Wilson dissenting) held that such a change can be inferred.

There arises a question about whether the court can *impute* such an intention if the court is unable to infer the parties' common intention from the evidence. This is done by looking at the whole course of dealing between the parties. Lord Kerr emphasized the dichotomy between inferring intention and imputing intention and Lord Kerr felt that there had to be strong demarcation between the two. Lord Kerr questioned the aptness of imputation but considered that it may not be practicable to discard it. Lord Collins was robust in that he held that the difference 'will hardly ever matter'.

The main conclusion to draw from this case is that their Lordships were able to find that the parties' interests in the property had changed over time and their Lordships were willing to embrace 'fair and just' as an appropriate measure of assessing those interests.

This decision may be problematic for practitioners as it does appear to give a great deal of discretion to district judges in such cases and makes the predicted outcomes of cases less certain. The Online Resource Centre contains more information on this case.

23.4 PROPERTY OWNED BY ONE PARTY

The law in England and Wales has never developed a system of law to deal with family property. The law of property is applied to family property, often with harsh results. The reason for this is possibly that, until relatively recently, cohabitation was uncommon and divorce rates were low. Family property division following breakdown of a cohabiting relationship has come before the court increasingly since post-war societal changes.

The law is completely different to that of the MCA 1973 and the CPA 2004. There is no statutory guidance for the distribution of family property and there is no doctrine of community of property. As a result, the only way that a cohabitant can seek a beneficial interest in a property where the legal title is vested in another is to demonstrate that the legal owner holds the property in trust for the person claiming the interest. Orders for the benefit of children are available under Sch 1 CA 1989 (see **11.8**).

23.4.1 ESTABLISHING LEGAL TITLE

The conveyance of a property will indicate not only the legal owner of a property, but also the beneficial interests of the property. The title deeds to the property should be carefully checked.

23.4.2 **ESTABLISHING A BENEFICIAL INTEREST**

The person claiming an interest is called a 'claimant' as proceedings will be in the civil courts, not family courts. In order to claim a share of the property the claimant will have to demonstrate that a legal owner holds the property in trust for the claimant. The establishment of such a trust depends upon the parties' intention. Establishing the common intention can be extremely problematic.

In *Gissing v Gissing* [1971] AC 886, Lord Diplock stated that a party's intention means that both words and conduct led the other to believe that he holds a beneficial interest in the property.

In *Midland Bank v Cooke* [1995] 4 All ER 562, the court held that even if both parties admit that neither had discussed nor intended any agreement as to the proportion of their interests, this did not preclude the court from inferring one.

Section 53(1)(b) Law of Property Act 1925 (LPA 1925) requires that a valid declaration of a trust of a beneficial interest in land must be in writing. If one partner buys the home out of their own money and has it conveyed into their sole name, any oral agreement between the parties for one to take a beneficial share will not (per se) give that person an entitlement. The agreement will amount to an imperfect gift, which equity will not perfect. However, s53(2) LPA 1925 does not require the creation or operation of resulting, implied, or constructive trusts to be evidenced in writing. In *Gissing v Gissing*, Lord Diplock stated that in the absence of writing, the claimant to a beneficial interest will need to establish an interest under a resulting, implied, or constructive trust. The classification of trusts can be problematic, but it is important to do so as this may impact the quantum of interest available.

Whilst the creation of a trust requires the parties to have a common intention, the court will not find a trust when the intention does not exist. The court does not devise or invent a legal result, according to Lord Morris in *Pettitt v Pettitt* [1970] AC 777. An agreement may be inferred from conduct or words as they would be reasonably understood by the parties.

23.4.2.1 Resulting trusts

A resulting trust arises when property is bought by one party and put into the name of the other; the property is presumptively held on a resulting trust by the latter for the purchaser. If one person puts money into the property at the time of purchase (and it is not a gift), a trust is created to recognize this fact and is called a resulting trust. The person's beneficial interest will consist of the amount of money which they have paid into the property where their name is not on the deeds as a legal owner. Case-law suggests that resulting trusts arise only at the time of the purchase of the property. Resulting trusts are fairly easy to prove as there is a direct financial contribution to the purchase of the property.

 Example

The facts of the case in *Carleton v Goodman* [2002] EWCA Civ 545 are a good illustration of a resulting trust in real life.

Mr Goodman wished to buy a house but lacked sufficient income to finance a mortgage. He was in a relationship with Ms Carleton but did not live with her. Mr Goodman and Ms Carleton applied for a mortgage based on their joint income and the house was conveyed into their joint names. The deposit and mortgage payments were all met by Mr Goodman. Mr Goodman died without making a will and a dispute arose concerning whether Ms Carleton had a beneficial interest in the property.

It was held that the presumption that the joint owners held the property on trust absolutely for Mr Goodman, on the basis of his having made all the payments, was not rebutted. The court held that, on the facts, the parties had not intended to allow Ms Carleton a share.

The shares that the parties will receive from the property will depend upon their contributions.

 Example

Hilary and Denny decide to live together and buy a house together jointly for £100,000. Hilary provides £79,000 from her savings. The remaining £21,000 is obtained from a joint repayment mortgage. Hilary is doing a degree as a mature student and has no income and so Denny makes all of the mortgage repayments until the mortgage is paid off in full. The relationship subsequently breaks down. Denny seeks clarification of how the property was held and the shares each party are entitled to on sale.

The property will be held as a resulting trust. Hilary will be treated as having contributed her cash contribution and Denny will be treated as having made a cash contribution and the house was owned in proportionate shares to the contribution made. Hilary will own 79% and Denny will own 21%.

23.4.2.2 Constructive trusts

Where there is no evidence of direct contributions made to the purchase price giving rise to the presumption of a resulting trust, there may be a constructive trust between the parties. This is a much 'looser' type of trust but is often difficult to establish. There are two hurdles for a client to establish:

1. there must be evidence of common intention between the parties to share in the ownership of a property, and

2. there must also be evidence of a detrimental reliance by the party on this common intention seeking to establish the trust.

This would establish a constructive trust.

There are two ways of demonstrating a constructive trust; first by evidence of agreement between the parties, and secondly, where there is no evidence of a common agreement, the court may infer common intention.

Where there is evidence of an agreement between the parties to share the property, this will establish the first limb of a constructive trust. The evidence may be that of a written deed (the author never found this in practice!) or evidence of an oral agreement or discussions about a common intention to share the property. This is also uncommon in practice and is often simply contradictory evidence. If there is no common agreement between the parties, then the court will look for evidence of inferred (or indirect) intention.

23.4.2.3 Evidence of common intention

In *Lloyds Bank plc v Rossett* [1991] 1 AC 107, Lord Bridge stated that the question that must be resolved is whether the parties at the time of acquisition of the property (or exceptionally at a later date) agreed, arranged, or came to an understanding that the property is to be shared beneficially.

There must be evidence of an express agreement between the parties based on discussion between the parties. This is clearly problematic, as discussions may have been held some time ago and may have been vague or not felt to be serious at the time. The courts have generally looked for clear evidence. In *Hammond v Mitchell* [1992] 2 All ER 109, the man said to the woman shortly after completion, 'don't worry about the future because when we are married [the home] will be half yours and I'll always look after you'. This was held to be sufficiently clear to establish a constructive trust.

In *Springette v Defoe* [1992] 2 FLR 388, the court held that it was not sufficient to have a mutual but an uncommunicated intention to share the property. Steyn LJ commented that 'law does not allow property rights to be affected by telepathy'.

Example

A communicated intention has been found by the courts in the following circumstances:

- a woman was assured her partner would put her name on the title deeds 'when he had time';
- a woman helping a man with his business when he was in prison was promised an (unclear) share of assets;
- a woman was assured that her assumption of a joint liability for a mortgage would be sufficient proof of her entitlement to a share of the property.

Two cases are very good examples of the court finding a trust through expressly declared intention.

In *Eves v Eves* [1975] 3 All ER 768, the couple were cohabitants. The man told the woman that as she was under 21, the house had to be in his sole name and that but for her age he would have put the house into joint names. The woman did a great deal of heavy manual work on the house including demolishing a shed, breaking up concrete, painting woodwork, and stripping wallpaper. All this work helped to renovate the property from an initially dilapidated state.

In *Grant v Edwards* [1986] Ch 638, the man told his cohabitant that she should not have her name on the deed as this would prejudice her ongoing matrimonial proceedings. The woman made no financial contribution to the purchase price but went out to work and looked after four children. The woman's wages allowed the mortgage to be paid whilst leaving sufficient for the family to live on.

Both cases demonstrate contributions made that amounted to the second limb of the test for a constructive trust: conduct on which they could not reasonably have been expected to embark unless they were to have an interest in the house. This conduct was a detrimental reliance even where a share had been stated in advance. The conduct demonstrated more than simply living in the property and caring for the home and family. As we will see, this conduct (considered to demonstrate a detrimental reliance) was subject to a less rigorous test as there had been prior agreement to share. In order to establish a constructive trust, the client will have to show detrimental reliance as well as common intention.

Where there is no prior agreement to share the home, the test for common intention is more difficult to establish.

23.4.2.4 No evidence of common intention

Where there is no evidence for the court to find that the parties agreed or arranged or came to an understanding that the property was to be shared, the court must rely entirely on the conduct of the parties to see if an intention to share can be inferred from the evidence. If an intention to share can be inferred from the conduct of the parties, the court may find a constructive trust. As will be seen from the case-law, the courts have been very reluctant to infer an intention from anything less than a contribution to the purchase price of the house.

The leading case is *Lloyds Bank plc v Rossett* [1991] 1 All ER 1111, where neither the wife's extensive renovations of the house nor a common intention to share the family home was enough to indicate that both parties were to have an interest. The court held that her work was that which could be expected of a wife to do with no expectation of a beneficial interest.

This case was preceded by cases with similar decisions. In *Pettitt v Pettitt* [1970] AC 777, unusually the house was in the wife's name and the husband failed to establish an interest by reason of home improvements, e.g. internal decorating, laying a lawn, and building a wall in the garden. In *Gissing v Gissing* [1971] AC 886, Mrs Gissing's payments for household expenses and family clothing did not amount to a beneficial interest. Both parties would have been better off paying mortgage repayments.

Practical Considerations

The case of *Burns v Burns* [1984] Ch 317 is strongly reminiscent of cases the author has seen in practice. Mrs Burns lived with her partner for 19 years, although they never married. Mrs Burns gave up her job to take care of the family's two children and then contributed her wages on return to work to the household expenses, family clothing, and fixtures and fittings in the house. This was not a sufficient contribution for the court to find a beneficial interest. Even the indirect contributions to the mortgage contributions through paying household expenses to free up the partner's income for mortgage payments will not suffice if there is no express agreement to share the property.

Clients in Mrs Burns' position are often very distressed, firstly at the break-up of a relationship, but then to find themselves in straitened financial circumstances as a result of having made no provision for housing during the life of their relationship. Clients who are coming to the end of their working life are particularly vulnerable. Advice is vital on welfare benefit and housing entitlement and any provision available for child support maintenance or orders for children under Sch 1 CA 1989 (see **11.8**).

The other problem that clients face is that these types of proceedings are taken in civil courts, not family courts, and are subject to the Civil Procedure Rules with associated risks on costs.

There is a glimmer of hope for clients in Mrs Burns' position in *Le Foe v Le Foe and Woolwich plc* [2001] 2 FLR 970. Following comments made in the case of *Bernard v Josephs* [1982] Ch 391, the trial judge found that an inference that the parties intended to share can be drawn from indirect contributions to the mortgage, thus enabling the family economy to function. This was a first instance decision only, however. In *Stack v Dowden*, discussed earlier, Baroness Hale stated that the law had moved on since *Pettitt* and *Gissing* in response to changing social and economic conditions. Lord Walker commented that the court should take into account a broad view of the contributions. He referred to the Court of Appeal's decision in *Oxley v Hiscock* [2005] Fam 211 with approval. In this case, it was held that the court should refer to 'the whole course of dealing between them in relation to the property'. However, their Lordships failed to elaborate fully on the status of the inferred common intention constructive trust.

For those advising clients in this position, a careful reading of case-law is essential. It is to be hoped that either the courts or Parliament will provide greater clarity in due course.

23.4.2.5 Quantification of the shares

In cases of an express trust, the shares will be as agreed by the parties. If the court finds or infers a common intention, it has a wide discretion when deciding the shares of the parties.

In *Oxley v Hiscock* (see **23.4.2.4**), it was held that the parties are entitled to that share which the court considers fair having regard to the whole course of dealing between them in relation to the property. In that context, the whole course of dealing includes the arrangements that they make from time to time in order to meet the outgoings that have to be met (mortgage contributions, council tax and utilities, repairs, insurance, and housekeeping). The court will look at the evidence of any discussions between the parties regarding the amount of shares that each was to have.

This approach in *Oxley v Hiscock* to looking at the 'whole course of dealing' was approved in *Stack v Dowden*.

23.5 TRUSTS OF LAND AND APPOINTMENT OF TRUSTEES ACT 1996

The Trusts of Land and Appointment of Trustees Act 1996 (TOLATA 1996) has an impact on property held by cohabitants.

Section 12 TOLATA 1996 gives any beneficiary who is beneficially entitled to an interest in possession in land subject to a trust in land a right to occupy the land at any time (unless it is unavailable or unsuitable for occupation by him). Of course, the beneficial entitlement must first be established.

The more common use of TOLATA 1996 within family law is the power contained in s14 TOLATA 1996 for the court to hear an application for a trustee of the land relating to the exercise of their function or to declare the nature or extent of a person's interest in property. Commonly the function of cohabitant trustees concerns the sale of the property. A cohabitant with an interest in a property can apply under s14 TOLATA 1996 for an order to sell the property.

If an application is brought under s14 TOLATA 1996, the matters to which the court must have regard are found in s15 TOLATA 1996. These matters include:

- the intentions of the person or persons who created the trust;
- the purposes for which the property subject to the trust is held;
- the welfare of any minor who occupies or might reasonably be expected to occupy any land subject to the trust as his home; and
- the interest of any secured creditor of any beneficiary.

 Example

Margaret and Peter bought a property jointly to live together and are tenants in common in equal shares in 2002. They have two children (aged 10 and 11). They separate in 2010 and Peter moves out. In 2013 Peter decides that he needs the money from his share of the house to buy his own property and applies for an order for sale under s14 TOLATA 1996 on the basis that the intention and purpose behind the purchase was for their cohabitation and that cohabitation is at an end. Margaret resists the application on the basis that the children require a home and that the trust was for the purpose of a family home including the children of the family.

SUMMARY POINTS

- Cohabiting couples do not have any intrinsic legal rights by simply cohabiting. The 'common law wife/husband' does not exist in law.

- Cohabitants must rely on a mixture of property and trust law to resolve property disputes.

- The Law Commission has reported on potential reforms to the law relating to cohabitants but there appears to be no move to legislate on the part of the Government.

- When property is held jointly, the court will presume that the beneficial interests reflect the legal ownership and the onus is on the party who wishes to prove otherwise unless there is a valid deed of trust.

- If a property is owned by one party solely, the other party may have to establish a beneficial interest through an express, resulting, or constructive trust.

- A resulting trust is established through contributions made directly to the purchase of a property.

- A constructive trust is established through either a directly expressed common intention to share the property or an inferred intention to share the property coupled with detrimental reliance upon that common intention.

- The court can be asked for an order for sale under s14 TOLATA 1996.

SELF-TEST QUESTIONS

1. Ellie moved in with her girlfriend Lucy into Lucy's flat. Lucy is having difficulties paying her mortgage and asks Ellie to pay off her mortgage arrears of £7,000. Lucy says that banks discriminate against lesbians and so Ellie cannot put her name on the deeds. Lucy and Ellie live

together for ten years with Ellie making more than half of the total mortgage payments. The house was bought by Lucy for £100,000 with Lucy paying £20,000 as a deposit and sells for £200,000 with Ellie contributing £30,000 to the repayments. Advise Ellie on whether she would be able to recover any of her money if she and Lucy separated.

2. Martin and Luke buy a house together. Luke contributes 25% of the deposit and pays only 25% of the mortgage payments as he is in a low-paid job. A deed of trust was not executed and the property is held as joint tenants. Luke and Martin separate. Martin wishes to know if he can claim 75% of the sale proceeds of the house. Advise Martin.

3. Henrik meets Abri during a business trip. Henrik is a very wealthy businessman whose personal wealth runs into many millions of pounds. They meet up for drinks and have a brief relationship. Henrik thinks of their relationship as a 'fling' and does not plan to see Abri again. Four months later, Abri contacts Henrik to tell him that she is pregnant with his child and that she wants him to support her and the child. Advise Henrik on the claims, if any, that Abri can make on behalf of the child and for herself.

4. Describe the proposals made by the Law Commission to reform the law on cohabitation.

online
resource
centre

Answers to the questions above can be found on the Online Resource Centre: **www.oxfordtextbooks.co.uk/orc/sendall17/.**

Part 5

CHILDREN

24 INTRODUCTION TO THE CHILDREN ACT 1989

24.1 INTRODUCTION

This chapter will:

- examine the principles the court will follow in private children law proceedings;
- discuss the content of the 'welfare principle' and the 'welfare checklist' under the Children Act 1989;
- discuss the principles of 'no order' and 'no delay'.

This part of the text deals with the law and practice relating to children. When family members cannot agree about the upbringing or arrangements concerning where a child shall live or with whom they shall have contact, this is described as 'private' children proceedings. When a child is subject to intervention by the local authority out of concern for the child's safety, development, or health, these proceedings are described as 'public' children proceedings. A family lawyer in practice will see both types of proceedings, although lawyers conducting public children proceedings are specialist lawyers who have many years of experience.

This part of the text will examine the law and practice for both types of proceedings. This chapter will look at the Children Act 1989 (CA 1989), the Child and Families Act 2014 (CFA 2014) which has made recent significant amendments to the CA 1989, and the main principles upon which Children Act proceedings are conducted.

A case study will continue to look at the ongoing proceedings of Helena and David Wilson in private Children Act proceedings.

24.1.1 FAMILY JUSTICE REVIEW

The Family Justice Review was commissioned by the Ministry of Justice to examine issues of delay and other problems within the family justice system. The report's author was David Norgrove and his report was highly critical and made a number of wide-ranging suggestions for reform. The final report was given in November 2011 and subsequently Ryder J was appointed to make suggestions about its implementation. Ryder J's report into the modernization of family justice contained a series of proposals to improve the workings of family courts and covers most of family law but made particular reference to cases involving children.

A principal area for the review and Ryder J was private Children Act proceedings. Private law proceedings range from the most complex family breakdowns, involving intractable disputes and serious safeguarding issues, to relatively modest disagreements about when and how children maintain contact with separated parents. Most private law parties, i.e. parents, who seek to resolve their differences about the plans for their children now have little access to public funding (see **Chapter 2**) and the majority of parties are unrepresented. Ryder J recommended that the judiciary must take steps to ensure that those who are entitled to family justice are provided with access to it, whether represented or not. This sentiment was echoed by the President in *Q v Q; Re B; Re C* [2014] EWFC 31. As the courts deal with greater volumes of Litigants in Person (LiP) (see **Chapter 2**) this will lead to greater delays as LiP have not had the benefit of legal advice to identify solutions or the merits or demerits of their proposals. Before their arrival at the court door they may not have had identified to them the issues the court can address. Many LiP will have no idea what a conventional court process entails and some will have difficulty understanding its rules.

The CFA 2014 has enacted many of the reforms recommended by the Norgrove Report and the main provisions came into force on 22 April 2014. It contains a number of important changes to private law regarding children and those include a change to residence and contact orders as well as a change in the statutory basis of shared parenting and a new procedure for private Children Act proceedings.

24.2 **CHILDREN ACT 1989**

The CA 1989 was passed to reform the law relating to children and also to provide for local authority services for children in need and others, to amend the law with respect to children's homes, community homes, voluntary homes and voluntary organizations, and to make provision with respect to fostering, child minding, and day care for young children and adoption. The CA 1989 has been amended, most recently by the CFA 2014, and these amendments will be dealt with in the text.

A child is defined in s105 CA 1989 as a person under the age of 18.

24.3 **WELFARE PRINCIPLE**

Section 1(1) of the CA 1989 states that:

> When a court determines any question with respect to—
>
> (a) the upbringing of a child; or
>
> (b) the administration of a child's property or the application of any income arising from it, the child's welfare shall be the court's paramount consideration.

This is described variously as the 'welfare' or 'paramountcy' principle. The effect of this section is to place the child's welfare before and above any other consideration when deciding whether to make an order.

 Practical Considerations

When advising clients, it is essential to tell the client about the welfare principle and how the court will use this principle to place the children's interests ahead of their own. When a client is in the middle of stressful (and possibly antagonistic) proceedings, it may be difficult for them to place the children's interests first and they must be prepared to accept that the court will do this. Some clients feel that a court has not listened to their wishes sufficiently and may be dissatisfied with the court's decision and, possibly, their adviser's advice.

24.3.1 **PRESUMPTION OF PARENTAL INVOLVEMENT**

The CFA 2014 introduces a new s1(2A) into the Children Act 1989 as follows:

(2A) A court, in the circumstances mentioned in…, is as respects each parent… to presume, unless the contrary is shown, that involvement of that parent in the life of the child concerned will further the child's welfare.

(2B) In subsection (2A) 'involvement' means involvement of some kind, either direct or indirect, but not any particular division of a child's time.

The effect of this amendment is to require the court, when determining contested applications for the variation or discharge of a s8 order or when considering the award or removal of parental responsibility, to presume, unless the contrary is shown, that involvement of each of the relevant child's parents in his or her life will further the child's welfare. However a parent only comes within new s1(2A) if under s1(6) CA 1989 in certain circumstances:

In subsection (2A) 'parent' means parent of the child concerned; and, for the purposes of that subsection, a parent of the child concerned—

(a) is within this paragraph if that parent can be involved in the child's life in a way that does not put the child at risk of suffering harm; and

(b) the parent is to be treated as being within paragraph (a) unless there is some evidence before the court in the particular proceedings to suggest that involvement of that parent in the child's life would put the child at risk of suffering harm whatever the form of the involvement.

This is a significant change to the CA 1989. During the consideration of family justice, there was a proposal that the law enshrined a right to shared parenting. This was ultimately rejected and the law has been changed to reflect the view that parental involvement is generally better for children. The important caveat is that the parent must not put the child at risk of significant harm. For some, this is a positive statement which legislates the rights of all parents. For other commentators, it is an irrelevance as the law has always presumed that children benefit from the involvement of both partners. It may assist to allay the often stated, and unfair, myth that the courts favour mothers over fathers.

24.4 **NO ORDER**

Section 1(5) CA 1989 states that:

where a court is considering whether or not to make one or more orders under this Act with respect to a child, it shall not make the order or any of the orders unless it considers that doing so would be better for the child than making no order at all.

This section does not create a presumption that the court should or should not make an order. The section requires the court to ask 'will it be better for the child to make the order than making no order at all?' (*Re G (Children)* [2006] 1 FLR 771). An example of the court's approach can be found in *Re K (Supervision Orders)* [1999] 2 FLR 303 where Wall J found that 'there must be something in the making or operation of an [order] which makes it better for the children for an order to be made'. In *Re X and Y (Leave to Remove from the Jurisdiction: No Order Principle)* [2001] 2 FLR 118, the court required that the party applying for the order has the burden of proof to make out a positive case on the balance of probabilities that it is in the interests of the child that the order be made.

Example

Meera is the two-year-old child of Anil and Sarita. Anil and Sarita separate and Meera lives with Sarita. The pair initially cannot agree about how much time Meera spends with Anil and proceedings are commenced. During the proceedings, they agree the amount of contact. As they appear to have reached an agreement, there would not appear to be any need for the court to make this agreement into an order.

It is generally better for the parties to agree, as agreements are more likely to be adhered to than a court-imposed settlement. If the agreed arrangements fail, then the matter can return to the court and an order may have to be made. An order is sometimes necessary. If a child lives with someone who has no formal status as a parent or carer, it may be necessary to have an order for others, e.g. hospitals or schools, to recognize their status.

24.5 NO DELAY

Section 1(2) CA 1989 states that in any proceedings in which any question with respect to the upbringing of a child arises, the court shall have regard to the general principle that any delay in determining the question is likely to prejudice the welfare of the child.

The duty to avoid delay falls both upon the court and practitioners. The welfare principle states that the court's paramount consideration is the welfare of the child and it may be the case that the proper consideration of a case involves some delay, e.g. for experts to report or for further investigations.

Children progress quickly through development milestones and even a short delay can mean that a child who does not see a parent for a while will have undergone developmental changes. Avoiding delay will help to avoid disruption in a child's life. As will be seen in **Chapter 27**, a timetable is imposed by the court in CA 1989 proceedings to assist in minimizing delay.

24.6 WELFARE CHECKLIST

There is no definition of 'welfare' within the CA 1989. There have been many judicial statements about it, with the most recent comprehensive review by the President of the Family Division in *Re G* [2012] EWCA Civ 1233. The CA 1989 does, however, provide a 'welfare' or 'statutory' checklist for the court to consider when the court is considering whether to make, vary, or discharge a s8 order or whether to make, vary, or discharge an order under Part IV CA 1989. These orders will be explained in **Chapters 26** and **29**.

Section 1(3) of the CA 1989 states that:

A court shall have regard in particular to:

(a) the ascertainable wishes and feelings of the child concerned (considered in the light of his age and understanding);

(b) his physical, emotional, and educational needs;

(c) the likely effect on him of any change in his circumstances;

(d) his age, sex, background, and any characteristics of his which the court considers relevant;

(e) any harm which he has suffered or is at risk of suffering;

(f) how capable each of his parents, and any other person in relation to whom the court considers the question to be relevant, is of meeting his needs;

(g) the range of powers available to the court under this Act in the proceedings in question.

The checklist is not in any order of importance and the full circumstances of the case must be considered.

Practical Considerations

The checklist is at the heart of decisions made by the courts concerning children. It is extremely important that the checklist is applied fully to the client's case as the court will make decisions based on it and may expect a lawyer to address the court on the checklist.

24.6.1 WISHES AND FEELINGS OF THE CHILD (S1(3)(a) CA 1989)

When a child expresses their wishes and feelings, the court will try to give them their due weight. The court will be conscious that their wishes and feelings may be influenced deliberately or unconsciously by their parents, that the child's views may be influenced by the desire to please one parent or to avoid hurting another, or by saying what they believe the adults involved in proceedings wish to hear.

The court rarely seeks the child's opinions directly (see **Chapter 27**) and the views of the child can become known through the evidence of parents. The better way of seeking evidence is through the Child and Family Court Advisory and Support Service (CAFCASS) report (see **Chapter 27**). The CAFCASS officer will report what he has heard from the child during his investigations or, with older children, he may ask them directly. Rarely, the judge can hear evidence from the child directly.

 Example

In the case of *Re P (A Minor) (Education: Child's Views)* [1992] 1 FLR 316, the court was asked to decide where a child should go to school. The child in question was 14 years old and mature. He expressed a wish to go to a local day school instead of an expensive boarding school and the court listened to his wishes.

24.6.2 CHILD'S PHYSICAL, EMOTIONAL, AND EDUCATIONAL NEEDS (S1(3)(b) CA 1989)

The level of material comfort offered by a parent has little influence over the court's decision—a fear often expressed by clients. The courts will strive to use their powers in proceedings for financial orders to provide both parents with suitable homes. Cohabitant parents may find that child support maintenance equalizes parties' positions. Clearly, unsatisfactory accommodation because of poorly maintained or damp conditions or being in a dangerous area will influence the court's decision and the information provided by the CAFCASS officer will contain information on parties' living situations.

If a move is proposed to a new place by either party, the court will take this into account. Even if the proposed accommodation is suitable, a move to a new area will involve the removal of the child from their school and friends, and the child will have to make friends again and form new relationships following a move. A parent contemplating such a move should make investigations concerning schools and affordable accommodation in the new area in good time for the court (and the other parent) to consider the move.

More importantly, the standard of day-to-day care offered by either parent in caring for a child's physical and emotional needs will be considered by the courts. Although no party's care can be beyond any criticism, minor issues or grumbles will not be entertained as a reason to deny a parent to care for a child.

 Example

Anil has criticized Sarita's care of Meera. He claims that Sarita allows Meera to eat sweets (of which he disapproves), that she should be sent to bed at 7pm rather than 7.30pm, and that she should not be allowed to watch any television at all.

These criticisms are minor and a matter of personal choice. Meera will not suffer from Sarita's choices and the court will disregard these criticisms.

The child's emotional ties to parents and siblings will carry a great deal of weight with the court and courts are reluctant to split up siblings (*Re P (Custody of Children: Split Custody Order)* [1991] 1 FLR 337) as this can create lasting damage. But there have been cases where this has been ordered (*B v B (Residence Order: Restricting Applications)* [1997] 1 FLR 139).

Contrary to many clients' beliefs, the court does not favour the care of a mother over that of a father. On the Online Resource Centre, you can find details of research done into contact applications.

In reality most separating parents agree that the mother will remain as the principal carer of children and court orders simply reflect this arrangement. Where one parent is working and the other cares for the children, the caring parent has a greater advantage as they have the greater experience of day-to-day care. As children get older, they rely less and less on having a parent at home all day and so this perceived advantage diminishes.

Educational needs can also prove decisive when the court decides an order. Educational needs can encompass a wide variety of situations. If a parent proposes a move away from a particular school at a crucial time in a child's education, e.g. when they are taking GCSEs or A-levels, the parent offering the least disruption to schooling may have an advantage, although this is less important when a child is at an earlier stage in their education.

24.6.3 LIKELY EFFECT ON THE CHILD OF A CHANGE IN CIRCUMSTANCES (S1(3)(c) CA 1989)

The court will seek to avoid any major disruption within the child's life; this is known as keeping the 'status quo'. This is particularly important when the question is where the child shall live. In this situation, the parent with the child's current care has the greater advantage. The longer any situation continues, the greater the status quo of a situation becomes. This is only one factor in the checklist and other factors may outweigh this factor when the court is weighing its decision.

 Example

Meera lives with Sarita and has done since Anil and Sarita's separation. She attends a local nursery and Sarita regularly attends a mother and toddler group. Anil proposes that Meera comes to live with him. The disruption caused to Meera would be considerable and she may suffer harm as a result. The status quo is for Meera to remain with Sarita.

24.6.4 THE CHILD'S AGE, SEX, BACKGROUND, AND ANY RELEVANT CHARACTERISTICS (S1(3)(d) CA 1989)

This can cover a multitude of factors within a child's life.

The age of a child can be crucial; if the child is very young, their needs may be best met by their mother. As a child becomes more mature, it matters less which parent cares for them and their views will become more important. The sex of the child can be important as a child may benefit from being with the parent of the same sex as they approach puberty and may benefit from a role model. The background of a child can cover many factors including religious upbringing, race, nationality, cultural background, disability, or illness.

Where a child grows up with a background of a mixed heritage, the court will look at the characteristics of both parents and will try to keep the child in touch with all aspects of their parents' different backgrounds.

24.6.5 ANY HARM WHICH THE CHILD HAS SUFFERED OR IS AT RISK OF SUFFERING (S1(3)(e) CA 1989)

Harm can cover physical, mental, or emotional harm. The Adoption and Children Act 2002 amended the CA 1989 to extend the definition of harm to include the impairment suffered from seeing or hearing the ill-treatment of another. This will encompass the child who witnesses domestic abuse.

24.6.6 THE CAPABILITY OF THE PARENTS OF MEETING THE CHILD'S NEEDS (S1(3)(f) CA 1989)

When a parent applies to the court to have their child(ren) live with them or applies to have contact that involves their sole care of the child(ren) for any period, the court will consider whether the parent can care for the child(ren) properly.

The court may have to consider very serious questions of a parent's capability. A parent may have previously harmed the child and this will prejudice a claim for their child to live with them. A parent who fails to prevent their child from harm from another may similarly struggle to convince the court that they are a capable parent.

The religious views of a parent are not often considered under this factor but the court may be reluctant to allow a child to remain with a parent belonging to a sect or group with extreme views harmful to a child. A court can allay some fears by attaching conditions to orders.

 Example

A child is living with a parent whose religious views do not permit inoculations against common diseases. A condition is attached to the order requiring the parent to take the child for inoculations.

Some parents may have mental or physical illnesses that are relevant to the care of the child. The court may require medical evidence to explain the impact of the illness on the parent's ability to care for the child. If there is evidence that the illness may place the child at risk of harm, where a parent may require regular in-patient treatment at hospital, or the child has an inappropriate level of responsibility for the care of the parent, the court may decide that the illness affects the capability of the parent to care for the child. The evidence may equally reveal that the illness does not affect the parent's capability.

This factor covers the capability of any other person in relation to whom the court considers the question to be relevant. This may include the new partner of one parent, the child's grandparents, extended family, nurseries, and child minders. Family solicitors are used to allegations that the other parent's new partner or friends are unsuitable for a number of reasons. These allegations should be investigated thoroughly.

24.6.7 RANGE OF POWERS AVAILABLE TO THE COURT (S1(3)(g) CA 1989)

The court has a wide range of powers under the CA 1989 and can make an order if they believe it is appropriate to the case, even if none of the parties have applied for that particular order. The court has a great deal of control over the proceedings and can grant orders where it is in the interests of the children.

 Example

Anil and Sarita make very serious allegations about each other's care of Meera. The court receives evidence that both parties' behaviour is having a very bad emotional impact on Meera and that she is at risk of psychological harm. Although Meera's grandparents are not parties to the court proceedings, the court hears evidence of their capability as carers for Meera. The court uses its power under the CA 1989 to order that Meera live with her grandparents.

The court also has the power under s91(14) CA 1989 to prevent a party making repeated applications, e.g. parental responsibility, without the permission of the court.

24.7 **GOOD PRACTICE**

It is particularly important that proceedings are conducted sensitively and within good practice guidelines. The Law Society's Family Law Protocol offers guidance on the correct approach to mediation and the need to be mindful of the need to attempt to reach an early resolution of any dispute.

SUMMARY POINTS

- The CA 1989 is the principal Act concerning the law on children.

- Private children proceedings involve disputes between individual members of a family.

- Public children proceedings involve the intervention by the local authority to safeguard a child.

- The child's welfare is the paramount consideration when the court is deciding whether to make an order.

- The court must also ensure that it is in the child's interest to make an order.

- The court and parties must seek to avoid delay in the proceedings.

- The court must also have regard to a 'welfare checklist' that lists a number of important considerations to a child's life including the child's wishes and feelings, their physical, emotional, and educational needs and any change of circumstances, the child's age, sex, background, and other characteristics, any harm that the child is at risk of suffering, and the parents' capability.

- It is important to remember that the child should be at the centre of a case and clients should be encouraged to make decisions accordingly.

SELF-TEST QUESTION

1. Imagine that you are advising a client on the CA 1989. Explain to them what the central principles of the CA 1989 are in language that a non-lawyer would understand.

Case Study Two

Following their divorce, Helena and David Wilson are having some further difficulties. Their child, Richard, has remained with Helena, and David has been having regular contact; for about the last nine months this system has worked very well.

However, Helena seeks your advice. David has moved in with a new partner, Anna. Anna already has two children. Richard gets on very well with Anna and Helena has been quite happy to allow David to have generous contact as she believes that it is in Richard's best interests for everyone to get along.

Last week, Richard came home from David's house and told Helena that his father had told him that it would be nicer if he could live with him and Anna as a 'proper family'. Helena was very upset by this and telephoned David. David told her that he felt he could offer Richard a better home with him and Anna and that he wanted Richard to come and live with him. Helena was so upset that she has told David that he cannot have contact with Richard.

Yesterday, Helena received a letter from David's solicitors stating that David wished Richard to come and live with him (see the Online Resource Centre for document CA 1). Helena is very upset and asks what the court will decide. Helena admits that David's decision has probably arisen as she has started a new relationship with Phillip and that David is simply being difficult. Phillip does not live with Helena and Richard.

The child is the paramount consideration of the court. When the court is deciding whether to make an order, they will consider the welfare checklist under s1(3) CA 1989. Your supervisor asks you to consider the information and the documents on the Online Resource Centre and apply the checklist to the case.

---

online
resource
centre

Answers to the questions above can be found on the Online Resource Centre:
www.oxfordtextbooks.co.uk/orc/sendall17/.

25.1   INTRODUCTION

This chapter will:

- examine the concept of parental responsibility;

- discuss the circumstances in which a parent has parental responsibility and how parental responsibility can be gained by a parent.

Parental responsibility (PR) is one of the most important concepts in the Children Act 1989 (CA 1989) and was introduced by the CA 1989. Clients must be advised about what PR is and its effects and whether or not they have PR for their children. The Law Society Family Law Protocol recommends that clients are always advised on who has PR for a particular child as part of the general advice given to a client. Whether or not a parent has PR can also affect the orders for which they are able to apply (see **Chapters 26 and 27**). PR is also an important consideration in public children law (see **Chapters 29–32**). PR usually, but not always runs with the legal status 'parent'.

This chapter examines the nature and scope of PR and how it is acquired.

25.2   WHAT IS PARENTAL RESPONSIBILITY?

Section 3 CA 1989 defines PR as 'all the rights, duties, powers, responsibilities and authority that by law a parent of a child has in relation to the child and his property.'

 Practical Considerations

Many clients do not understand the scope of PR when faced with the above definition and often clients focus on the rights and powers parts of the definition. It is important to be able to describe what PR is and how the law views the client's duties and responsibilities.

PR covers all the decisions and responsibilities that a parent may make on behalf of their child during their childhood and can include:

- access to the child's medical records;

- access to a child's school reports;

- consenting to medical treatment;

- deciding where a child is educated;

PARENTAL RESPONSIBILITY | 241

- teaching a child about the family's religion or culture;
- providing suitable food, clothing, and discipline;
- deciding where a child shall live.

Clearly, when a child is very young, PR will encompass most, if not all of the decisions made on behalf of a child. As the child gets older and more able to make decisions concerning their own lives, PR applies more to the larger decisions in a child's life. This reflects the approach of the court in *Gillick v West Norfolk and Wisbech Area Health Authority* [1985] 3 All ER 402. The case dealt with a mother who objected to her teenage daughter being prescribed the contraceptive pill without the mother's knowledge or consent. The House of Lords held that a child had sufficient competency to consent if the child had sufficient maturity and understanding of the issues involved. This is often referred to as 'Gillick' competency.

Under s2(5) CA 1989 more than one person may have PR for the same child at the same time and s2(6) CA 1989 states that a person who has PR for a child at any time shall not cease to have that responsibility solely because some other person subsequently acquires PR for the child.

Therefore two (or more) people may share PR for a child and they all have an equal say about the child's upbringing. **Chapter 26** gives details of orders that the court can make should parents disagree. The parent with day-to-day care of the child will make ordinary decisions concerning the child and should be allowed to do so without undue interference from those with PR who do not live with the child (see *D v S (Parental Responsibility)* [1995] 3 FLR 783). PR is delegable under s2(9) CA 1989 and one person can meet the responsibilities of PR for a child with the others with PR having delegated PR to them. This may occur when a child goes on holiday with one person with PR and the others with PR delegate PR during the period of the holiday.

There are some very important decisions that should not be made by one person with PR alone. Although s2(9) CA 1989 states that a person who has PR for a child may not surrender or transfer any part of that responsibility to another but may arrange for some or all of it to be met by one or more persons acting on his behalf, the Court of Appeal held in *Re J (Specific Issue Orders: Muslim Upbringing and Circumcision)* [2000] 1 FLR 571 that there are a small group of decisions made on behalf of a child which, in the absence of agreement of those with PR, ought not to be carried out by one person.

The CA 1989 also provides for someone who cares for a child and does not have PR for that child. Section 3(5) CA 1989 states that a person who does not have PR for a particular child but has care of the child may do what is reasonable in all the circumstances of the case for the purpose of safeguarding or promoting the child's welfare.

25.3 AUTOMATIC PARENTAL RESPONSIBILITY

Section 4 CA 1989 states that:

(1) Where a child's father and mother were married to each other at the time of his birth, they shall each have parental responsibility for the child.

(2) Where a child's father and mother were not married to each other at the time of his birth—

    (a) the mother shall have parental responsibility for the child;

    (b) the father shall not have parental responsibility for the child, unless he acquires it in accordance with the provisions of this Act.

A mother of a child will automatically have PR for the child irrespective of her marital status.

A father will automatically have PR if he was married to the mother at the time of the child's birth or subsequently marries the mother of his child as s2(3) CA 1989 imports ss1 and 10 Family Law Reform Act 1987, which deals with the legitimacy of children.

PR is lost when a child is adopted and is acquired by the adoptive parents.

25.4 **UNMARRIED FATHERS**

As noted in **25.3**, only mothers and married fathers have automatic PR. Unmarried fathers can acquire PR in a number of ways. See **Figure 25.1**.

Section 111 Adoption and Children Act 2002 amended s4 CA 1989 so that a father who was not married to the mother at the time of the child's birth has PR if his name is placed on the birth certificate at registration or re-registration of the birth under the Births and Deaths Registration Act 1953. In reality the father cannot register his name without the consent of the mother. Once an unmarried father gains PR by registration, it can only be removed by order of the court, on application by a person with PR for the child, or by the child (with leave of the court) if they have sufficient understanding. This amendment came into force on 1 December 2003 and so children born before that date will not be covered by this amendment.

Section 4(1) CA 1989 states that:

> where a child's father and mother were not married to each other at the time of his birth the court may, on the application of the father, order that he shall have parental responsibility for the child or the father and mother may by agreement ('a parental responsibility agreement') provide for the father to have parental responsibility for the child.

This means that there are a number of options for an unmarried father. Where the parents agree that the father should have PR, they can enter into a PR agreement. A PR agreement is a straightforward document that the parents can obtain from and complete at a family proceedings court.

FIGURE 25.1 HOW A FATHER CAN OBTAIN PR

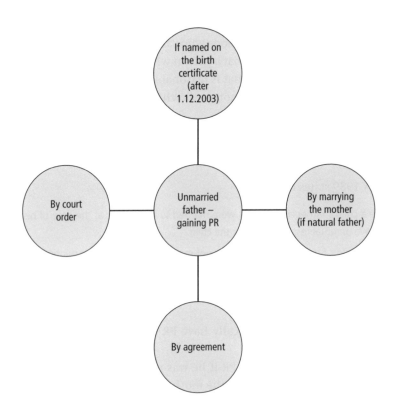

If the mother of the child will not agree to the father having PR, he will have to apply for a PR order from the court. The procedure for obtaining orders under the CA 1989 can be found in **Chapter 27**.

As seen in **Chapter 24**, the welfare of the child is the paramount consideration of the court. The court must be satisfied that the applicant is the father of the child before granting him PR. Section 55A Family Law Act 1986 provides for a party to apply for a declaration of parentage to confirm whether or not the person making the application is the parent of the child named in the application.

The court will always consider the commitment of the applicant father to the child, the degree of attachment between father and child, and the father's reasons for applying for PR (see *Re P (A Minor) (Parental Responsibility Order)* [1994] 1 FLR 578). These factors are not exhaustive and the court must take into account all relevant circumstances including a lack of a responsible attitude towards the child or evidence that the grant of PR will be used to undermine the mother's care of the child. In these circumstances the court may refuse to make an order (see *Re H (Parental Responsibility)* [1998] 1 FLR 855 and *Re P (Parental Responsibility)* [1998] 2 FLR 96). The court will also consider the welfare checklist under s1(3) CA 1989 (see **Chapter 24**).

 Practical Considerations

It is important to establish as early as possible in the case who has PR for a child. This is important as a father may need advice on how to obtain PR and those with PR may need advice on how it is shared and exercised with respect to a child. The ability to apply for orders under the CA 1989 is affected by whether a person has PR.

25.4.1 TERMINATION OF PR ORDERS AND AGREEMENTS

A PR order or agreement will end automatically upon the child reaching the age of 18 (s91(7) and (8) CA 1989). A PR order or agreement can be discharged by the court under s4(2A) and (3). The court will have the welfare of the child as the paramount consideration when considering making such an order.

Any person with PR can apply for such an order, as can the child if they are of sufficient age and understanding and the court gives leave (s4(3)(b) and (4) CA 1989). The exception to this is where a person is granted PR during the currency of a residence order (see **Chapter 26**) and PR will continue as long as the residence order (s12(2) CA 1989).

Examples of PR being removed by courts usually involve serious harm to the child; e.g. in *Re P (Terminating Parental Responsibility)* [1995] 1 FLR 1048, where the father seriously injured the child causing lasting physical and mental disability. The court held that the normal presumption was that once an agreement had been entered into it would remain in force until the welfare of the child requires its termination. In this case, the court considered whether it would have made a PR order had one not been in force already and held that there was no aspect of PR that this father could have exercised in a way that would be beneficial to the child and the existing PR agreement was terminated. This approach was confirmed by the Court of Appeal in *CW v SG* [2013] EWCA Civ 335.

In *Re F (Indirect Contact)* [2007] 1 FLR 1015, there was a history of domestic abuse with the father breaching a non-molestation order 68 times. The family moved ten times to escape the father and he served two terms of imprisonment. The court terminated the father's PR agreement on the basis that it did not benefit the child.

In *Re D (A Child)* [2014] EWCA Civ 315, the father had been convicted of serious sexual offences against two of the mother's children. The mother applied for the termination of PR in respect of child D and the father sought specific issue orders (see **Chapter 26**) for annual reports on the child's progress. At first instance, Baker J had found no reason to depart from *Re P* (discussed earlier) and the father appealed on the basis that the court had failed to take into account the Human Rights Act 1998 in his application of *Re P* and, in any event, had failed to make a proportionate order. This was upheld by the Court of Appeal.

The Court of Appeal found that the concept of paramountcy of welfare remained the governing principle to be applied. The Court of Appeal considered the principle of proportionality in light of the availability of less draconian orders that could be made. The Court of Appeal found that the court was right to terminate PR as the father was unlikely to be able to exercise his PR consistently with the welfare of the child. However, Ryder LJ warned that this case was not to be construed as allowing it to become easier to remove PR from a parent; it would be hoped that the court would be wary when considering applications of this sort.

25.5 PARENTAL RESPONSIBILITY FOR NON-BIOLOGICAL PARENTS

Others can apply for PR for a child. Under the CA 1989, the following people can gain PR:

- guardians under s5(6) CA 1989;
- adopters who acquire PR on the passing of an adoption order;
- step-parents (see **25.5.1**);
- local authorities when a care order is made (see **Chapter 29**), although parents do not lose PR, it is shared;
- a person with a residence order, or child arrangements order setting out residence, who will have PR for the duration of the order (see **Chapter 26**);
- a person with a special guardianship order (see **Chapter 26**);
- certain partners of those who have children after assisted reproduction measures (see Human Fertilisation and Embryology Act 2008 (HFEA 2008));
- those who have in their favour a parental order under s54 HFEA 2008.

25.5.1 STEP-PARENTS

If a step-parent becomes a guardian of the child or has a residence order granted in their favour or adopts a child, they will acquire PR in the same way as any other person. This is the same for a person who obtains a special guardianship order.

Section 4A CA 1989 allows a step-parent to acquire PR either with the agreement of those parents with PR for the child concerned or by order of the court. Section 4A CA 1989 requires that the step-parent be married to or in a civil partnership with the parent of the child concerned; being a cohabitant will not suffice. PR acquired in this way can be ended by a court order on the application of a person with PR or the child itself (with the leave of the court).

Step-parents without PR still have duties toward the child. As seen at **25.2**, s3(5) CA 1989 provides a duty for anyone without PR with the care of a child to do what is reasonable to safeguard and promote the child's welfare.

SUMMARY POINTS

- PR is a concept introduced by the CA 1989.
- PR encompasses the rights, duties, powers, responsibilities, and authority that by law a parent of a child has in relation to the child.
- PR covers all the decisions that are made concerning a child as well as the duty to care for the child.

SELF-TEST QUESTIONS

1. Feli and Abdul have two children, Miri (born 1 March 2003) and Kim (born 3 July 2007). Abdul is named as the children's father on their birth certificates. Feli and Abdul are not married and separate. Feli refuses to allow Abdul to see the children. Advise Abdul on whether he has PR for the children and, if not, how he may acquire it.

2. Advise Abdul on what the effect of having PR will be. Abdul wishes to receive school reports and to go to hospital appointments. How does having PR affect these wishes?

Case Study Two

Look at the documents contained on the Online Resource Centre. Who has PR for Richard?

David has now moved in with Anna and her children. Anna's ex-partner, William, is the children's natural father but they were not married and the children were born before 2003; William's name is not registered on their birth certificates. William does not approve of David and he has decided to apply for PR. Who has PR for Anna's children and how could William gain PR?

---

online resource centre

Answers to the questions above can be found on the Online Resource Centre: **www.oxfordtextbooks.co.uk/orc/sendall17/.**

26 PRIVATE CHILDREN LAW

26.1 INTRODUCTION

This chapter will:

- discuss the orders available under s8 of the Children Act 1989 to resolve disagreements between parents;
- discuss special guardianship orders.

As explained in **Chapter 24**, private children law concerns disputes between family members about children; generally parents' disputes about children. Private children law concerns itself with whom a child shall live, with whom they should have contact, and what steps a parent can take in their exercise of parental responsibility. The Children Act 1989 (CA 1989) has orders that the court can make to help to resolve these disputes and the principles discussed in **Chapter 24** will be taken into account when the court is deciding which order to make or whether to make an order. This chapter will look at the orders available in private children proceedings, who can apply for them, and the individual considerations of each order.

Private children proceedings can be very emotionally charged as they are a continued reminder of the end of a relationship and unresolved disputes. There are often entrenched positions maintained by either party which can be difficult to resolve. The problems faced by some parents in terms of maintaining contact with children after separation are a topic of some controversy and the perceived faults of private children proceedings have also produced campaigning groups such as Fathers 4 Justice. More details can be found on the Online Resource Centre. This chapter will consider the enforcement of orders for contact and residence.

It should be noted that all of the principles discussed in **Chapter 24** apply when the court is considering orders described in this chapter. Orders discussed in this chapter also have relevance in public children law proceedings as a court can make an order for a child arrangement order or special guardianship in care proceedings (see **Chapters 29–32**).

The Family Justice Review led to the enactment of the Children and Families Act 2014 (CFA 2014), which amends the CA 1989 substantively and procedurally. This chapter will look at the changes made to the CA 1989 and **Chapter 27** covers the substantial changes to procedure.

26.2 CHILD ARRANGEMENT ORDERS

The CFA 2014 has amended the CA 1989 to replace two orders with one. Prior to the CFA 2014, a residence order was the order used to settle the arrangements to be made as to the person with whom a child is to live and a contact order settled who a child had contact with. Both of these orders have been replaced in the CA 1989 by a child arrangements order (CAO) as s12 CFA 2014 amends s8 CA 1989 to define a CAO as:

'child arrangements order' means an order regulating arrangements relating to any of the following—

(a) with whom a child is to live, spend time or otherwise have contact, and

(b) when a child is to live, spend time or otherwise have contact with any person.

The rest of this section will examine the issues arising from where a child lives and with whom they should have contact.

26.2.1 **WHERE A CHILD SHALL LIVE**

A CAO which deals with where a child shall live does not affect the existing PR held by parents or others but under s12(1) CA 1989, if a court makes a CAO in favour of the father of the child, the father is granted PR if he did not already have it by the court making an order under s4 CA 1989 (see **Chapter 25**). Section 12(2) CA 1989 grants PR to any person who is not the parent or guardian of the child for the duration of the CAO. Once the CAO lapses, PR is lost.

 Example

Mario and Honore separate. After some disagreement the couple both apply to the court to resolve where their children shall live. The court decides that the children shall live with Mario and make a CAO accordingly. If Mario did not have PR before the CAO, he will have PR during the life of the order.

The importance of biological parentage was highlighted in the case of *Re G (Children)* [2006] 2 FLR 629. The House of Lords found that where an applicant is both the psychological and biological parent of a child, this is an important and significant factor in determining what would be best for the children in the long and short term. This case concerned children of a lesbian couple. The House of Lords awarded residence (as it was then) to the natural mother of the children.

 Practical Considerations

'Custody' and 'access' are emotive words commonly used in the media or in soap operas to describe where a child lives or with whom they should have contact. It is important that you use the correct terminology with clients and doubly important that you use the correct terms in court or you will be sharply corrected!

26.2.1.1 Change of surname

Under s13(1) CA 1989, where a CAO is in force with respect to a child, no person may cause the child to be known by a new surname. The House of Lords found in *Dawson v Wearmouth* [1997] 2 FLR 629 that the change of a child's surname has been viewed as a profound and not merely formal issue by the courts, whatever the age of the child. They ruled that any dispute should be referred to the courts for determination, whether or not there is a CAO in existence and whomsoever has or does not have PR.

When a child is born, he or she must be registered in accordance with the Births and Deaths Registration Act 1953 (BDRA 1953). If the parents are married, the duty to register lies with both the mother and father. If the parents are not married, the duty is on the mother alone. The surname registered is to be the one by which the child is intended to be known. Once the surname has been registered, there is nothing in the BDRA 1953 to permit it to be changed and this point was extensively considered in the case of *Dawson v Wearmouth* (discussed earlier). The court's powers are limited to those contained in s13(1) CA 1989 when the surname can be changed with the written consent of every person who has PR for the child or by the leave of the court.

A change of name is generally evidenced by a deed poll. Informal steps to change the child's name are prohibited.

 Example

Asha has separated from the father of her children. She wishes to change the children's surname to hers but knows that their father will not agree (he has PR). Instead of changing the children's surname formally by deed poll, Asha asks the children's school to call the children by her surname and registers the children in her surname at the GP and dentist. By these informal (and inadvisable) steps, the children are generally known by Asha's surname.

If the requirements of s1(5) CA 1989 mean that a CAO is not made, Practice Direction (1994) [1995] 1 FLR 458 is important. Any application for the registration of a deed poll to change the surname of a child under the age of 18 must be supported by the production of the consent in writing of every person having responsibility for the child or leave of the court (see also the Enrolment of Deeds (Change of Name) Regulations 1994 and *Re T (Change of Surname)* [1998] 2 FLR 620).

 Practical Considerations

From case-law, it appears that the proper approach in all cases for seeking a change of name will be as follows:

- everyone with PR should be consulted, whether or not a CAO is in force (*Re PC (Change of Surname)* [1997] 2 FLR 730);

- if a father does not have PR, there is some uncertainty about the extent to which he is entitled to be consulted. Section 13 CA 1989 refers to those with PR giving consent and so one may infer that a father without PR has no right of consultation. However, case-law suggests that a father without PR can object to the proposed name change if he learns of it (*Dawson v Wearmouth*). In *Re C (Change of Surname)* [1998] 2 FLR 656, the court held that at the first sign of a dispute, the court should become involved. It is wise, therefore, to consult a father without PR before attempting to make a change in surname;

- if consent is obtained from all with PR, it is probably wise to gain such consent in writing;

- if the proposed change of name is disputed, the case should be referred to the courts under s13 CA 1989 if there is a CAO in force and under s8 CA 1989 for a specific issue order (see **26.3**) if there is no CAO in force.

The welfare principle was demonstrated in *Re S (Change of Names: Cultural Factors)* [2001] 2 FLR 1005. A child's name was changed with the court's permission from a recognizably Sikh name to a recognizably Muslim name, in order to allow the mother and child to integrate fully into the Muslim community. However, the change of surname was to be used for school and registration with a GP but would not be completed by deed poll and so the change of name was essentially informal to prevent the child's Sikh identity being eliminated altogether.

In the case of *Re W; Re A; Re B (Change of Name)* [1999] 2 FLR 930, Butler-Sloss LJ gave guidelines for cases (although warned that these are not exhaustive). Each case should be decided on its own facts with the welfare of the child being the paramount consideration and all relevant factors weighed in the balance. The guidelines are as follows:

- if parents are married, they both have the power and duty to register their child's name;
- if not married, only the mother has the power and duty to do so;
- following registration of the child's name, if a CAO is granted any person wishing to change the child's surname must obtain the permission of the court or written consent of all with PR;
- if there is no CAO in existence, a person wishing to change a child's surname should obtain the written consent of those with PR or apply for a specific issue order to gain the permission of the court;
- when considering any application, the welfare of the child is paramount and the court must have regard to s1(3) CA 1989 factors;
- the court should have regard to the registered surname and the reasons for registration (e.g. the recognition of the biological link with the father). Registration is always important but not in itself decisive and the weight given to it by the court will depend upon the other relevant factors or valid countervailing reasons;
- the considerations include factors that may arise in the future;
- reasons given for changing or seeking to change a child's name based on the fact that the child's name is or is not the same as a parent making the application do not generally carry much weight;
- the reasons for a prior unilateral decision to change the child's name may be relevant;
- any change of circumstances of the child since original registration may be relevant;
- if a child's parents were married, the fact of the marriage is important and there would have to be strong reasons to change the name from the father's surname if that was the surname that was registered;
- if the child's parents were not married, the mother has the sole power to register the child's name. On an application to change the name of a child, the court will consider the commitment shown by the father to the child: quality of contact (if any) between father and child and the existence or absence of PR are all relevant factors to be taken into account.

26.2.1.2 Removal from the jurisdiction

The right to remove the child from the jurisdiction is covered extensively in **Chapter 28**.

Section 13 CA 1989 states that where a CAO is in place no person may remove a child from the UK without the written consent of every person who has PR or leave of the court, but that a person named in the CAO as the person with whom the child lives may remove the child for up to one month.

26.2.1.3 Removing the child from the jurisdiction to live elsewhere

Occasionally a parent may wish to move to a different country for work, to be nearer family, or for a better life. Unless those with PR agree to the move, the court's permission will be required (see **Chapter 28**).

The principle that the welfare of the child is the paramount consideration will apply. The general approach of the courts is to grant permission to the parent wishing to move unless the reasons for the move are unreasonable and there are compelling reasons to refuse. The court will look at the reasons for wishing to move and the plans for contact between the child and parent in the other jurisdiction to see if the child's welfare is safeguarded.

There are human rights implications concerning a decision to allow a child to be removed from the jurisdiction as this interferes with one parent's right to family life under Art. 8 of the European Convention on Human Rights (ECHR). In *Payne v Payne* [2001] 1 FLR 1052, the Court of Appeal ruled that all parties had rights under Art. 8 and when such rights conflicted, the rights of the parties had to be balanced against each other. The child's welfare is of crucial importance and if in conflict with a parent's rights would override the parent's rights. Article 8(2) ECHR allows a public authority to interfere with the right to family life where it is necessary to protect the rights and freedoms of others and where the need is proportionate to the need demonstrated. The court must consider the effect of the application on the applicant proposing the move and the respondent who opposes it. If this is properly done, then there will be no appeal. This case has been the focus of increasing criticism both judicially and academically.

This issue has been re-examined in *K v K (Children)* [2011] EWCA Civ 793. In this case, the parents of two children had a shared residence arrangement but the Canadian mother wished to relocate the children to Canada so she could live with her parents and maintained that she would have greater support there. The father opposed the application as he wished to avoid losing close contact with the children. This is an unremarkable case and reflects the position which occurs most commonly in practice.

At first instance, the judge followed the guidance given in *Payne v Payne*. At the Court of Appeal, their Lordships agreed that the only principle to come from *Payne* was that the welfare of the child is paramount. The rest is guidance to be applied or distinguished depending on the circumstances. The judge should apply the statutory checklist in s1(3) of the CA 1989 in order to exercise his discretion. All the facts of the case must be considered.

A very useful overview of the law can be found in *S v G* [2015] EWFC 4. In an application concerning the proposed removal of a Russian child from the UK, Jackson J reminded the courts that they should carefully scrutinize proposals of those wishing to remove a child, that going to an established home is less arduous than creating a new life, and to consider whether there is a motivation to exclude the other parent from the child's life, but similarly, any objection should be child-centred and not part of an ongoing dispute between parents. Any relocation proposal should be scrutinized for the impact on the parent left behind and the wider family whilst recognizing that relocation can also result in widening of the extended family in the country of return.

26.2.1.4 Internal relocation

Often, a dispute will arise where one person wishes to move with a child within the jurisdiction. A move of hundreds of miles can prove problematic for regular contact, as work or transport restrictions may mean that travel is difficult.

In *Re C (Internal Relocation)* [2015] EWCA 1305 the Court of Appeal confirmed that the governing principle of the child's welfare is the same for both internal and external relocation cases. There is no rule that moves can only be prevented in exceptional cases and guidance from the case of *Payne* (above) can be useful in helping judges to identify issues arising in the case.

26.2.2 WHEN AND WITH WHOM A CHILD SHALL HAVE CONTACT

Unfortunately when arguments develop about who a child shall see, this is often described as 'access', which is an overly emotive term. A CAO regulates when and with whom a child shall have contact. It is instructive to note that the law is drafted to state that the child is to have contact with the other person and contact is often stated as being the right of the child. Usually the court expects parents to resolve issues surrounding where and with whom a child spends time between themselves and to be flexible. However, when parents cannot agree about the level of contact and even whether contact should occur, the courts may become involved.

There is no presumption about the right to have contact between parents and adult children.

Contact between parent and child can take the form of staying overnight, visiting, meeting for a meal or activity, telephone calls, emails, and birthday cards. Contact can be direct or indirect. Direct contact is where the child has contact with the person by visiting or staying with them, whereas 'indirect' contact is where the contact takes place via letters, telephone calls, or emails. Indirect contact is generally ordered when it is not suitable or appropriate for the child to see the person directly. Contact can be supervised if there is any risk to the child of unsuitable or inappropriate behaviour and indirect contact can be supervised as well as direct contact. The usual order is 'reasonable contact', which is usually direct contact between the child and the person concerned with the arrangements and frequency agreed between the parties. If there are some difficulties concerning agreement or the arrangements being made, then a more defined order may be made. This either sets out the actual times/places for contact to take place or it can resolve particular disputes, e.g. where a child should spend school holidays or Christmas Day.

 Example

Bill and Melissa have three children. Neither party can agree when the children should have contact with Bill and, as a result of the dispute, Bill does not see the children for some time. The court makes an order that Bill telephones the children three times a week to reintroduce himself and then the contact progresses to the children meeting Bill for tea twice a week. After six months contact is going very well and so the children stay with Bill at the weekend.

26.2.2.1 Child contact centres

Where contact between a parent and child requires careful reintroduction or security for one party, child contact centres can be extremely useful. Most child contact centres do not offer supervised contact but do offer supported contact. The National Association of Child Contact Centres (NACCC) describes supported contact as taking place in a variety of neutral community venues where there are facilities that enable children to develop and maintain positive relationships with non-resident parents and other family members. Supported child contact centres are suitable for families when no significant risk to the child or those around the child has been identified. Sadly, due to funding issues, many contact centres are closing.

 Example

If Bill from the earlier example had lost touch with his children, a contact centre may have been a useful way of reintroducing their relationship in a neutral, safe place.

The basic elements of supported contact between child and parent are:

- impartiality;
- staff and volunteers are available for assistance but there is no close observation;
- monitoring or evaluation of individual contacts/conversations;
- several families are usually together in one or a number of rooms;
- encouragement for families to develop mutual trust and consider more satisfactory family venues.

NACCC has issued a protocol, which can be found on the Online Resource Centre, concerning the use of contact centres in terms of the categories of cases that are suitable for these centres and the practical steps to be taken to get in touch with an appropriate centre.

 Practical Considerations

The following matters should be checked:

1. that the child contact centre coordinator has been contacted and has confirmed:
   - the referral appears to be suitable for that particular centre. Child contact centres can refuse to accept families if the circumstances appear inappropriate for the centre;

- the intended day and times are available at the particular centre concerned;
- a vacancy is available or a place on the waiting list has been allocated;

2. that it has been agreed who will have the responsibility for completing and returning the centre's referral form. Solicitors for both parties should agree the contents and it should be forwarded to the child contact centre within 24 hours of the court hearing;

3. if contact is to be observed at the child contact centre by a family court welfare officer (CAFCASS officer) or other third party that this is a facility offered by that centre and that the centre has agreed to this course of action (many do not permit such attendance);

4. that the parties understand whether the centre offers supported or supervised contact and appreciate the difference;

5. that it is agreed who is going to tell the children where and when they will see their non-resident parent.

26.2.2.2 Contact between parent and child and human rights

Unmarried fathers have used the Human Rights Act 1998 (HRA 1998) and the European Convention on Human Rights (ECHR) to complain that the refusal of a court to order contact with their children is a breach of Art. 8 ECHR, the right to family life.

The European Court of Human Rights upheld complaints by unmarried fathers in *Elsholz v Germany* [2000] 2 FLR 486. In *Hendriks v Netherlands* [1982] 5 D&R 225, it was stated:

> the Commission has consistently held that, in assessing the question of whether or not the refusal of the right of access to the non-custodial parent was in conformity with article 8 of the Convention, the interests of the child will predominate.

26.2.2.3 Child arrangements and CAO and domestic violence

In many cases there are allegations of domestic abuse and practitioners will come across clients who allege that a CAO application is a device by which a person can continue abuse through continued contact between parents. Equally, many clients will instruct you that allegations of domestic abuse are simply a device to prevent contact with children.

This issue was considered by the Court of Appeal in the case of *Re L (Contact: Domestic Violence); Re V (Contact: Domestic Violence); Re M (Contact: Domestic Violence); Re H (Contact: Domestic Violence)* [2000] 2 FLR 334.

The Court of Appeal requested that the Official Solicitor act as an amicus in each case and the Official Solicitor commissioned a report by Dr Sturge and Dr Glaser. This can be found at [2000] Fam Law 615 and it is suggested that all practitioners should read it carefully.

The President said:

> The family judges and magistrates need to have a heightened awareness of the existence of and consequences, (some long-term), on children of exposure to domestic violence between their parents or other partners. There has, perhaps, been a tendency in the past for courts not to tackle allegations of violence and to leave them in the background on the premise that they were matters affecting the adults and not relevant to issues regarding the children. The general principle that contact with the non-resident parent is in the interests of the child may sometimes have discouraged sufficient attention being paid to the adverse effects on children living in the household where violence has occurred. It may not necessarily be widely appreciated that violence to a partner involves a significant failure in parenting—failure to protect the child's carer and failure to protect the child emotionally.
>
> In both contact and other section 8 applications, where allegations of domestic violence are made which might have an effect on the outcome, those allegations must be adjudicated upon and found proved or not proved. It will be necessary to scrutinise such allegations which may not always be true or may be grossly exaggerated. If however there is a firm basis for finding that violence has occurred, the psychiatric advice becomes very important. There is not, however, nor should there be, any presumption that, on proof of domestic violence, the offending parent has to surmount a prima facie

barrier of no contact. As a matter of principle, domestic violence of itself cannot constitute a bar to contact. It is one factor in the difficult and delicate balancing exercise of discretion. The court deals with the facts of a specific case in which the degree of violence and the seriousness of the impact on the child and on the resident parent have to be taken into account. In cases of proved domestic violence, as in cases of other proved harm or risk of harm to the child, the court has the task of weighing in the balance the seriousness of the domestic violence, the risks involved and the impact on the child against the positive factors, (if any), of contact between the parent found to have been violent and the child. In this context, the ability of the offending parent to recognize his past conduct, be aware of the need to change and make genuine efforts to do so, will be likely to be an important consideration.

The court must refer to the welfare principle and the checklist in s1(3) CA 1989. **Chapter 27** contains further information on how the courts screen all applications for domestic abuse and how the courts deal with disputed allegations between parties.

26.2.2.4 Activity directions and conditions

There are sometimes difficulties in enforcing CAOs concerning contact. The traditional method of enforcing orders made under the CA 1989, under the laws of contempt of court, is problematic for the courts. Contempt of court is not really effective in enforcing CAOs as the choice of the court to fine or imprison the parent with care of the child is most probably not in the best interests of that child. The courts give parents many opportunities to comply with the order, which is time-consuming and very frustrating for a parent who is anxious to see their child.

online resource centre

The Online Resource Centre contains links to organizations that have campaigned on this issue.

The CA 1989 has been amended by the Children and Adoption Act 2006 (CAA 2006) to introduce an activity direction in ss11A–H CA 1989. These activity directions and conditions are part of a strategy to encourage better adherence to CAOs and came into force on 8 December 2008.

26.2.2.4.1 *Activity directions*

Directions can be made when the court is considering whether to make (or to vary or discharge) a CAO.

Section 11A(3) CA 1989 states that an activity direction is a direction requiring an individual who is a party to the proceedings to take part in an activity that in the court's opinion would help to establish or maintain or improve the involvement in the life of the child concerned of the individual concerned. The direction is to specify the activity and the person providing the activity.

The activities under s11A CA 1989 that may be required include:

(a) programmes, classes, and counselling or guidance sessions of a kind that—

    (i) may assist a person as regards establishing, maintaining, or improving involvement in a child's life;

    (ii) may, by addressing a person's violent behaviour, enable or facilitate involvement with a child's life;

(f) sessions in which information or advice is given as regards making or operating arrangements for involvement in a child's life, including making arrangements by means of mediation.

It is likely that a report will be required on whether there has been compliance with the direction and to assess the effectiveness of the directions in resolving difficulties before the court decides whether to make a CAO.

26.2.2.4.2 *Activity conditions*

An activity condition may only be attached to a final CAO and is enforceable in contempt proceedings in the event of a breach.

Section 11C(2) CA 1989 allows the imposition of an activity condition requiring an individual falling within sub-s (3) to take part in an activity that would, in the court's opinion, help to establish, maintain, or improve the involvement in the life of the child concerned of that individual, or another individual who is a party to the proceedings.

A CAO may not impose an activity condition on an individual who is a child unless the individual is a parent of the child concerned.

The CAA 2006 does not develop any further the type of conditions that would in the court's opinion, help to establish, maintain, or improve the involvement in the life of the child concerned, but presumably attendance at a contact centre or some form of parenting guidance may feature in activity conditions.

26.2.2.5 The imposition of activity directions and conditions

Section 11E(2) CA 1989 states that the first matter is that the activity proposed to be specified is appropriate in the circumstances of the case. In considering whether to make an activity *direction*, the welfare of the child concerned is to be the court's paramount consideration. However, there is no express provision for the child's welfare when making any activity *condition*.

A court may not make an activity direction in any proceedings unless there is a dispute as regards the provision in the CAO that the court is considering whether to make in the proceedings. For activity conditions, there appears to be no such requirement.

26.2.2.6 Monitoring contact and enforcing activities

Under s11H CA 1989, a CAFCASS officer can be asked to monitor the provisions of the CAO and report on compliance with the order. A warning notice can be attached to an order warning of the consequences of a failure to comply. Under s11J CA 1989, if the court is satisfied beyond reasonable doubt that a person has failed to comply with the contact order, it may make an enforcement order imposing on the person an unpaid work requirement.

These provisions are very new and it is anticipated that it will be some time before there is a clear idea of the types of orders being made by the courts and an evaluation of their effectiveness.

26.3 SPECIFIC ISSUE ORDERS

A specific issue order can be made as a free-standing order or in concert with a child arrangement order. This order allows the court to make an order concerning an issue that has arisen in connection with the exercise of PR.

 Example

Semaab and Sean separate and their daughter lives with Semaab. Sean wishes to bring the child up as a Catholic and Semaab wishes to raise the child as a Muslim. The couple cannot agree about this and apply to the court for a specific issue order. The court orders that the child is exposed to both religious cultures until such time as the child can make up their own mind.

The courts can become involved where those with PR simply cannot agree on a major aspect of a child's upbringing. The court will place a great deal of pressure on parties to agree such issues, as an imposed decision is often unsuccessful.

Local authorities can apply for a specific issue order for a decision involving a child in care. In **Chapter 29** you will see that when a care order is made a local authority gains PR for the child.

26.4 **PROHIBITED STEPS ORDERS**

A prohibited steps order allows a court to prevent a person taking a step that could be taken in meeting PR for a child. The step may only be taken with the permission of the court.

 Example

Martin is worried that his ex-wife Soraya will take their children to live outside of the UK. He obtains a prohibited steps order to prevent her from removing the children from the UK.

The order will specify the action or steps that are prohibited by the court. The order can be made as a free-standing order or in concert with a CAO.

Prohibited steps orders are discussed in connection with parental child abduction in **Chapter 28**.

26.4.1 **RESTRICTIONS ON PROHIBITED STEPS AND SPECIFIC ISSUE ORDERS**

Neither a prohibited steps nor a specific issue order may be made in relation to a child over the age of 16 (ss9(7) and 12(5) CA 1989).

Importantly, neither of these orders can be used to achieve a CAO by the 'back door' under s9(5)(a) CA 1989.

 Example

Mandy and Isobel have two children but decide to separate. Mandy decides to represent herself and applies for a specific issue order to settle where the children shall live. This is not the correct order. The correct order is a CAO.

26.4.2 **DIRECTIONS**

Section 11(7) CA 1989 allows the court to attach directions to a s8 order about how it is to be carried into effect and impose conditions that must be complied with by any person in whose favour the order is made or by a parent of the child or any person who has PR for the child.

26.5 **SPECIAL GUARDIANSHIP ORDERS**

Special guardianship orders (SGOs) are private children law orders which give the special guardian PR for the child subject to the order. It is an order that allows a child to be cared for by someone other than their parents but avoids the need for care proceedings. The order is designed to give a child permanence and security where adoption is not appropriate but where it is not appropriate that they live with their natural parents. The legal links between the child and their parents is preserved. A special guardian cannot be a parent of the child.

SGOs were introduced by the Adoption and Children Act 2002 and the provisions are in s14A CA 1989. The same regime of eligibility for s8 CA 1989 also applies to an application for an SGO (s14A(5) CA 1989). An applicant must give three months' notice to the relevant local authority so that a report can be prepared about the applicant's suitability and the court will not make an SGO unless the report is made (s14A(11) CA 1989).

The effect of an SGO under s14C CA 1989 is that while it remains in force:

- the special guardian has PR for the child;
- the special guardian is entitled to exercise PR for the child to the exclusion of any other person with PR for the child;

- an SGO differs from a CAO as the court may give leave for the child to have a new surname, whereas for a CAO, this is not encouraged;
- the guardians can act to the exclusion of anyone else who has PR for the child and can be characterized as the exclusive exercise of PR (rather than a CAO which is concurrent) but this does not extend to major decisions, e.g. immunization or changes in education.

Section 14F CA 1989 provides that the local authority must provide special guardianship support services including counselling, advice, and information. The local authority must put into place a range of support services, including financial support. At the request of the guardian, the local authority must carry out an assessment of the person's needs and s14G CA 1989 requires a local authority to put in place a procedure, including a complaints procedure, in respect of these support services. These services can include therapeutic services and assistance in preserving the relationship between the child and her parent(s). Financial support can assist guardians with the cost of accommodating a child, adaptations of the home, furniture, and clothing and toys. The guardian may also receive a remuneration element which will cease once the child reaches 18, ceases education, or obtains full-time employment.

SUMMARY POINTS

- Section 8 CA 1989 provides a set of orders to assist the courts in resolving disputes arising between parents and carers.
- All of the usual principles in the CA 1989 apply when considering s8 CA 1989 orders including the welfare principle, the no order principle, no delay, and the welfare checklist.
- A CAO decides where and with whom a child shall live.
- Whilst a CAO is in force a child should not have their surname changed and should not be removed from the jurisdiction (except in certain circumstances).
- A CAO decides with whom a child shall have contact.
- Contact comes in many forms: direct and indirect, by direct visits, letters, cards, and emails.
- The court can make an order for reasonable contact where the parties agree when contact will take place. Alternatively the court can make an order for defined contact where the court specifies when contact will take place.
- Where there are allegations of domestic violence then the court must first of all make a finding on the allegations and then consider the impact of the violence on the child and what the impact will be of continuing contact.
- The CA 1989 has been amended to include contact activity directions and conditions in order to promote and encourage contact. These provisions are very new and as yet untested.
- Specific issue orders resolve disputes between all those people who have PR for a child. The order resolves disputes over a step which can be taken in the exercise of PR.
- A prohibited steps order prevents someone from taking a step in the exercise of PR and can be used to prevent a child being removed from the jurisdiction.
- A special guardianship order allows someone other than a parent of the child to gain and exercise PR for the child to the exclusion of anyone else with PR.

SELF-TEST QUESTIONS

1. Albert Morton has a residence order for his daughter, Maddie Phelps, and Maddie spends time with her mother every weekend. Albert wishes to take her on holiday to France for two weeks

and to change her surname to Morton. Advise Albert on whether this is possible and the steps he should take.

2. Sarah is the daughter of a French mother and Italian father who have recently divorced. Both parents wish their daughter to come and live with them in their respective countries of origin. Advise which orders will be necessary should the parties be unable to agree and the factors that the court will consider when deciding.

3. Would your answer to question 2 above be any different if there were allegations of domestic violence?

Case Study Two

David has made an application to the court for an order (see the **Case Study to Chapter 27** for details of forms and procedure). He wishes Richard to live with him and states that he is willing to allow contact with Helena. Helena then issues an application for an order as she wishes Richard to continue living with her.

Which orders should (a) Helena and (b) David apply for?

See **Chapter 27** for a discussion of the procedural aspects of the case study.

---

online resource centre

Answers to the questions above can be found on the Online Resource Centre: **www.oxfordtextbooks.co.uk/orc/sendall17/.**

27 PRIVATE CHILDREN LAW PROCEDURE

27.1 INTRODUCTION

This chapter will:

- describe who is entitled to apply for an order under s8 Children Act 1989;
- explore public funding available for proceedings under the Children Act 1989;
- examine the procedure for obtaining an order under the Children Act 1989 in private law proceedings.

Many trainee solicitors and paralegals advise upon and run private children law cases and gain experience of court advocacy and also negotiating child arrangement orders (CAOs) between clients. The procedure is not complex but it is worth understanding all the guidance from the courts and practice directions concerning aspects of procedure. Private children law cases often run during or after other proceedings, such as divorce or applications for domestic violence injunctions, and emotions often run very high. It is essential that clients are properly advised on the opportunities to enter into conciliation or mediation and that proceedings are conducted sensitively and within good practice guidelines within a system that is struggling with scarce resources. The Children and Families Act 2014 (CFA 2014) has made sweeping changes both to s8 CA 1989 and to the procedure for obtaining orders, which is known as the Child Arrangements Programme (CAP). This chapter will discuss the procedure in full.

As stated in **Chapter 2**, public funding has been withdrawn from private children proceedings except in cases of child abuse or domestic violence, which means that many parents may come to court unrepresented. This presents challenges to both courts and family lawyers. As stated by Ryder J, many parents will not have had the opportunity to learn about the approach of the courts to disputes and may need to take a greater amount of court time to engage fully in their case. **Chapter 2** also contains a discussion of dealing with unrepresented parties.

This chapter covers the basic procedure for a s8 CA 1989 order. See **Figure 27.1** for a simple procedural flowchart provided with the CAP Practice Direction.

27.2 WHO IS ELIGIBLE TO APPLY FOR A S8 ORDER?

Chapter 26 outlined the orders available under s8 CA 1989 and **Chapter 25** discussed parental responsibility (PR) and its importance in private children work. As stated in **Chapter 25**, it is important to identify at the earliest opportunity which parents or carers

FIGURE 27.1 FLOWCHART OF PROCEDURE IN PRIVATE CHILDREN CASES

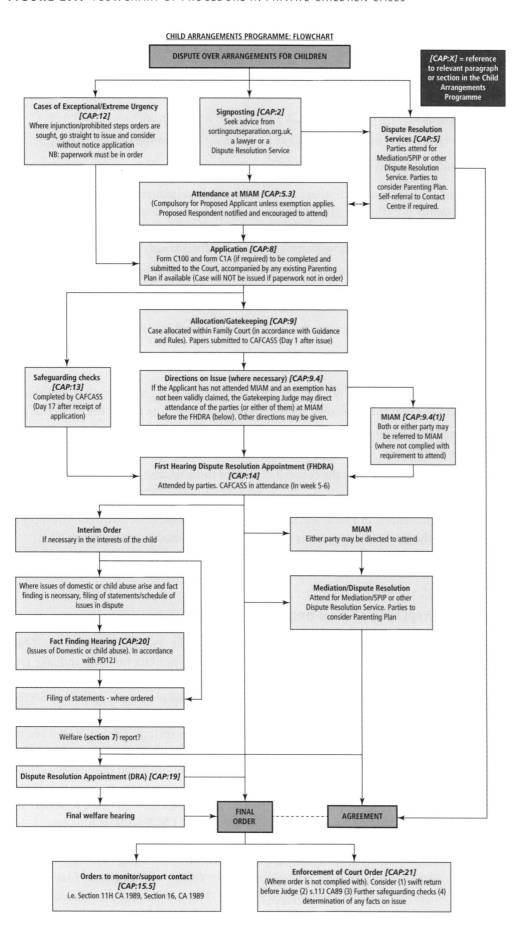

CHILD ARRANGEMENTS PROGRAMME: FLOWCHART

DISPUTE OVER ARRANGEMENTS FOR CHILDREN

[CAP:X] = reference to relevant paragraph or section in the Child Arrangements Programme

Cases of Exceptional/Extreme Urgency [CAP:12]
Where injunction/prohibited steps orders are sought, go straight to issue and consider without notice application
NB: paperwork must be in order

Signposting [CAP:2]
Seek advice from sortingoutseparation.org.uk, a lawyer or a Dispute Resolution Service

Dispute Resolution Services [CAP:5]
Parties attend for Mediation/SPIP or other Dispute Resolution Service. Parties to consider Parenting Plan. Self-referral to Contact Centre if required.

Attendance at MIAM [CAP:5.3]
(Compulsory for Proposed Applicant unless exemption applies. Proposed Respondent notified and encouraged to attend)

Application [CAP:8]
Form C100 and form C1A (if required) to be completed and submitted to the Court, accompanied by any existing Parenting Plan if available (Case will NOT be issued if paperwork not in order)

Allocation/Gatekeeping [CAP:9]
Case allocated within Family Court (in accordance with Guidance and Rules). Papers submitted to CAFCASS (Day 1 after issue)

Safeguarding checks [CAP:13]
Completed by CAFCASS (Day 17 after receipt of application)

Directions on Issue (where necessary) [CAP:9.4]
If the Applicant has not attended MIAM and an exemption has not been validly claimed, the Gatekeeping Judge may direct attendance of the parties (or either of them) at MIAM before the FHDRA (below). Other directions may be given.

MIAM [CAP:9.4(1)]
Both or either party may be referred to MIAM (where not complied with requirement to attend)

First Hearing Dispute Resolution Appointment (FHDRA) [CAP:14]
Attended by parties. CAFCASS in attendance (In week 5-6)

Interim Order
If necessary in the interests of the child

MIAM
Either party may be directed to attend

Where issues of domestic or child abuse arise and fact finding is necessary, filing of statements/schedule of issues in dispute

Mediation/Dispute Resolution
Attend for Mediation/SPIP or other Dispute Resolution Service. Parties to consider Parenting Plan

Fact Finding Hearing [CAP:20]
(Issues of Domestic or child abuse). In accordance with PD12J

Filing of statements - where ordered

Welfare (**section 7**) report?

Dispute Resolution Appointment (DRA) [CAP:19]

Final welfare hearing

FINAL ORDER

AGREEMENT

Orders to monitor/support contact [CAP:15.5]
i.e. Section 11H CA 1989, Section 16, CA 1989

Enforcement of Court Order [CAP:21]
(Where order is not complied with). Consider (1) swift return before Judge (2) s.11J CA89 (3) Further safeguarding checks (4) determination of any facts on issue

have PR as this will affect who can apply for which orders and the procedure followed in the application for an order.

There are differences between the categories of people who can apply for s8 orders. Under s10(4) CA 1989, the following persons are entitled to apply to the court for any s8 order with respect to a child:

- any parent, guardian, or special guardian of the child;
- any person who by virtue of s4A CA 1989 has PR for the child;
- any person who is named in a CAO as a person with whom the child is to live.

The following persons can apply for a CAO with respect to a child under s10(5) CA 1989:

- any party to a marriage (whether or not subsisting) in relation to whom the child is a child of the family. A child is a child of the family in relation to the parties to a marriage, which means a child of both of those parties and any other child, except a foster child, who has been treated by both of those parties as a child of their family under s10(5) CA 1989;
- any person with whom the child has lived for a period of at least three years. The period of three years need not be continuous but must not have begun more than five years before, or ended more than three months before, the making of the application;
- local authority foster carers who have had the child living with them for one year prior to the application;
- any person who:
    (i) in any case where a CAO is in force and regulates arrangements with whom the child is to live, has the consent of each of the persons in whose favour the order was made;
    (ii) in any case where the child is in the care of a local authority, has the consent of that authority; or
    (iii) in any other case, has the consent of each of those (if any) who have parental responsibility for the child.

In limited circumstances a local authority foster carer and a special guardian can apply for a CAO under the CA 1989 and further reference should be made to practitioner texts.

If a client does not fall into the above categories, they must apply to the court for leave to apply for an order under s10(2) CA 1989.

27.2.1 CHILDREN APPLYING FOR AN ORDER

A child can apply for leave to apply for a s8 CA 1989 order (see the **Glossary** for 'Leave'). Leave is the permission of the court. Where the person applying for leave to make an application for a s8 CA 1989 order is the child concerned, the court may only grant leave if it is satisfied that he has sufficient understanding to make the proposed application for the s8 CA 1989 order.

Even if the child has sufficient understanding, the granting of leave by the court remains a discretion only and the child's welfare is not paramount (*M v Warwickshire County Council* [2007] EWCA Civ 1084). Applications should be approached cautiously as the parents are in conflict and the child may be exposed to evidence of the parents that it would be better for them not to hear and may have to be cross-examined (*Re N (Contact: Minor Seeking Leave to Defend and Removal of Guardian)* [2003] 1 FLR 652). Whilst the s1(3) CA 1989 checklist does not specifically apply, the court may consider other matters as being relevant to deliberations about granting leave to a child. The leading case for the approach that the court should take is *Re H (Residence Order: Child's Application for Leave)* [2000] I FLR 780, where a 12-year-old boy applied for leave. The application was refused as the son wished to live with the father and the father could advance the son's wishes through his own application.

27.2.2 OTHER POTENTIAL APPLICANTS

Where a person does not fit into any of the categories listed earlier, an application for leave will have to be made.

 Practical Considerations

Grandparents are a category of applicants who wish to apply for a s8 CA 1989 order and will have to apply for leave. When families separate, often grandparents lose contact as their son or daughter ceases to have contact with their child or relationships break down and contact becomes very difficult. Sometimes a grandparent will apply for a CAO to have the child live with them should neither parent prove capable of caring for the child. Grandparents will have to apply for leave to apply for a CAO but it is the author's experience that leave is rarely refused in such circumstances.

Section 10(9) CA 1989 states that where the person applying for leave to make an application for a s8 order is not the child concerned, the court shall, in deciding whether or not to grant leave, have particular regard to:

- the nature of the proposed application for the s8 order;
- the applicant's connection with the child;
- any risk there might be of that proposed application disrupting the child's life to such an extent that he would be harmed by it; and
- where the child is being looked after by a local authority:
  - the authority's plans for the child's future; and
  - the wishes and feelings of the child's parents.

Other factors may also be relevant but the child's welfare is not the paramount consideration as stated in *G v F (Contact and Shared Residence: Application for Leave)* [1998] 2 FLR 799 and the court must have regard to the merits of the proposed application (*M v Warwickshire County Council* [2007] EWCA Civ 1084). In considering the risk of disruption, it is not only the risk of disruption from the making of the substantive application that is relevant, but also the disruption that there may be to the child's life if the application succeeds (*Re M (Care: Contact: Grandmother's Application)* [1995] 2 FLR 86). However, in *Re H (Children)* [2003] EWCA Civ 369, the Court of Appeal stated that the test used should be that found in s10(9) CA 1989 and that the question for the court was whether the application was disruptive to the litigation process.

27.2.3 PROCEDURE FOR OBTAINING LEAVE

The party wishing to apply for leave should file:

- Form C2 requesting permission setting out the reasons for the application; and
- Form C100 stating the s8 order applied for (assuming leave is granted to proceed) (reproduced at the end of this chapter).

Once leave is granted, the procedure for the consideration of the application is as described at **27.5**.

27.2.4 EXISTING PROCEEDINGS

One of the aims of the CA 1989 was to avoid the duplication of proceedings concerning children and the CA 1989 tries to ensure that orders concerning children can be made within existing proceedings. The court can make a s8 CA 1989 order within the following existing proceedings under s8(3) and (4) CA 1989 in 'family proceedings'. Family proceedings are any proceedings under:

- the inherent jurisdiction (see **Glossary**) of the High Court in relation to children;
- Parts I, II, and IV of the Children Act 1989;
- the Matrimonial Causes Act 1973;
- Schs 5 and 6 to the Civil Partnership Act 2004;
- the Adoption and Children Act 2002;
- the Domestic Proceedings and Magistrates' Courts Act 1978;
- Part III of the Matrimonial and Family Proceedings Act 1984;
- the Family Law Act 1996;
- ss11 and 12 of the Crime and Disorder Act 1998.

27.3 FUNDING AND ADR

After April 2013, a limited number of cases involving child abuse or domestic violence may attract some funding. **Chapter 2** contains details of the evidence required in such an application. If public funding is granted, initial advice and assistance can be secured through legal help if the client is eligible. Should the case require funding for further negotiation, family help (lower) can fund further negotiation, subject to eligibility. If it is necessary to issue proceedings, family help (higher) will be required, again subject to eligibility. It is important to advise clients that application for family help (higher) will require attendance at a meeting with a mediator (unless the case is deemed unsuitable) before any application can be processed. Usually the funding is restricted to commencing proceedings in the family proceedings courts, as this is a cheaper option. If there are existing proceedings, these proceedings should be consolidated to be heard together. Funding may be available for mediation.

Clients should also be encouraged to attempt to settle any dispute about children informally through mediation, arbitration, or collaborative law (see **Chapter 3**).

27.4 RULES

For applications under the CA 1989, the rules for applications are found in the Family Procedure Rules 2010 (FPR 2010). Prior to this set of rules, there were a number of complex sets of rules. The FPR 2010 aims to combine most types of proceedings concerning children into Part 12 (save for a few rare and unusual applications). Adoption is covered in Part 14 FPR 2010 (and is not covered by this text) and rules regarding the representation of children are found in Part 15 FPR.

The CAP can be found in PD 12B which was issued on the 22 April 2014.

Since April 2014, the Single Family Court was created and **Chapter 4** contains fuller details. Applications are now made to the Family Court sitting at the parent's local court and then the case will be allocated to the appropriate level of judiciary.

27.5 PROCEDURE FOR A S8 CA 1989 ORDER

27.5.1 ISSUING THE APPLICATION

Where the application is for a free-standing order (see **Glossary**), the Form C100 is completed to commence proceedings for a s8 CA 1989 order. A Form C110 is used for all other applications (see **Chapter 31** for an example). The form is long and may be daunting for Litigants in Person (LiP). The form seeks details on any potential exemption from a MIAM (see **Chapter 3** for more details).

Form C100 is straightforward to complete, although the following guidance is offered on the following paragraphs:

Page 1 of the C100 asks whether the children named have experienced or are at risk of experiencing, harm from any of the following by any person who has contact with the child:

- any form of domestic abuse;
- child abuse;
- child abduction;
- drugs, alcohol, or substance abuse;
- other safety or welfare concerns.

If the applicant answers 'yes', the Supplemental Information Form C1A must be completed. The procedure to be adopted in cases of domestic abuse is dealt with at **27.6**.

Section 3 of Form C100 must also be completed with care. The form asks for brief reasons for the application and to indicate the order sought from the court. Avoid the temptation to write a full statement in this part of the form. The information required should address the no order principle as stated in s1(5) CA 1989 but not give a huge amount of detail.

27.5.2 RESPONDENTS

There are a number of people who must be made respondents to an application for a s8 CA 1989 order and these are found in Appendix 3 CA 1989:

- every person the applicant believes to have PR for the child;
- where the child is subject to a care order, every person the applicant believes to have PR immediately prior to the making of the care order;
- if the application is to vary, extend, or to discharge an order, the parties to the proceedings leading to the original order that the applicant wishes to vary, extend, or discharge.

27.5.3 JOINING IN OTHER PARTIES

If a person wishes to become a party or cease to be a party, this is done by filing a Form C2. If a person has PR, the court must grant their request (r12.3(2) FPR 2010). For a person without PR, the court can grant the order without a hearing or representations or have a hearing where parties can make representations.

 Practical Considerations

If acting for an unmarried father without PR, an application for PR should in most cases be made should proceedings commence.

27.5.4 SERVICE

The application must be served on the respondent(s) together with Form C6. Form C6 sets out the time, date, and place of the hearing or directions appointment. These must be served on all respondents at least 14 days before the hearing or directions appointment. Rule 12.8 FPR 2010 deals with service. The customary method of service is by first class post to the respondent(s) or their solicitor, if they are represented.

27.5.5 URGENT AND WITHOUT NOTICE APPLICATIONS

An application may be made without notice in cases of emergency and the rules are found at r12.16 FPR 2010. An application may be made to the court for an emergency order without the requirement for the applicant to have attended a MIAM. The categories of an urgent situation requiring an emergency application can be found at r3.8 FPR and may include cases in which:

- there is a risk to the life, liberty, or the physical safety of the prospective applicant, or his or her family;
- any delay in attending at a MIAM would cause risk of harm to a child, risk of unlawful removal of a child or unlawful retention of a child who is outside England and Wales, significant risk of miscarriage of justice, unreasonable hardship, or irretrievable problems in dealing with the dispute.

Without notice orders should only be made exceptionally. In para 12.3 PD 12B FPR 2010, the circumstances include:

1. if the applicant were to give notice to the respondent(s) this would enable the respondent(s) to take steps to defeat the purpose of the injunction; cases where the application is brought without notice in order to conceal the step from the respondent(s) are very rare indeed; or

2. the case is one of exceptional urgency; that is to say, that there has been literally no time to give notice (either by telephone, text or email or otherwise) before the injunction is required to prevent the threatened wrongful act; or

3. if the applicant gives notice to the respondent(s), this would be likely to expose the applicant or relevant child to unnecessary risk of physical or emotional harm.

Any order made following a without notice order should state the reason why it has made the order, the outline facts which have been relied upon, and the right of the respondent to apply to vary or discharge the order.

In *Note: Re J (Children: Ex Parte Orders)* [1997] 1 FLR 606, Hale J made some observations regarding the care required when making without notice orders. Courts have a special responsibility to ensure that ex parte orders that can harm the interests of a child or an adult are not made without good reason. An order forcing a child to be handed over to a parent they do not know well should only be made in exceptional circumstances. Practitioners should take scrupulous care in relation to the application and the implementation of any order.

27.5.6 ACKNOWLEDGEMENT

Each respondent to the application is required to complete and file a Form C7 (and a C1A if necessary) in acknowledgement within 14 days of being served with the application.

Form C7 requires the respondent to give details identifying him and whether he has a solicitor (and details of that solicitor) and an address to where correspondence may be sent. The respondent must state whether he has received the application, whether he opposes it, and whether he intends to apply for an order. Indicating such an intention is not sufficient to commence an application and proceedings for an order should be commenced in the usual way (see **27.5.1**).

If a Form C1A has been served, the C7 asks if this has been received and whether the respondent wishes to comment on any of the statements made by the applicant. This is done by completing a Form C1A. If the respondent believes that the child has suffered harm as described at **27.5.1**, the respondent should complete and file his own Form C1A.

27.5.7 GATEKEEPING AND ALLOCATION

An application will be considered by gatekeepers (usually a nominated legal adviser and/or district judge) who will allocate it according to the principles found in the Allocation and Gatekeeping for Proceedings under Part II of the Children Act 1989 (Private Law Proceedings) and the Family Court (Composition and Distribution of Business) Rules 2014 together with the Allocation Schedule. The gatekeepers will consider:

- the need to make the most efficient and effective use of the local judicial resources that is appropriate, given the nature and type of application;
- the need to avoid delay;
- the need for judicial continuity;
- the location of the parties/any relevant child;
- complexity.

Most cases should be allocated to the lay justices at a magistrates' court unless the case has features found in Parts 1–3 of the Allocation Schedule. A case may be allocated to a district judge if there are allegations of significant harm or emotional or sexual abuse which have caused or are at risk of causing significant harm. A case may be referred to a circuit judge in cases where there are significant factual disputes where a fact-finding hearing may last more than three days and it is likely that more than one expert may be involved. A case will be referred to the High Court where there are issues of child abduction or an application for wardship. These are just examples and the whole schedule should be read carefully.

On allocation, the gatekeepers can issue directions. This may be if the exemption from attending a MIAM has not been validly claimed or an accelerated hearing is required. Draft directions can be found in Directions for Issue (CAP01) and this can be found on the Online Resource Centre.

online resource centre

27.5.8 FIRST HEARING DISPUTE RESOLUTION APPOINTMENT (FHDRA)

The FHDRA may take place within four weeks if time for service has been abridged but should ordinarily take place in week five following the issue of the application (at the latest six weeks). The respondent should have ten working days' notice of the hearing where practicable. Unless the court directs, any party to proceedings, including litigation friends, must attend the hearing.

A CAFCASS officer (see **27.5.11**) should attend the hearing in order to speak (where practicable) separately to each party.

27.5.8.1 Safeguarding

An application for a CAO will be sent to CAFCASS who will undertake safeguarding enquiries, the outcome of which is to be contained in a safeguarding letter (or report in Wales) and is to be sent to the court within 17 working days of receipt of the application and no later than three days prior to the hearing.

A safeguarding check will comprise CAFCASS making enquiries with local authorities and carrying out police checks on the parties. Where possible CAFCASS will undertake telephone risk identification interviews with the parties and if risks of harm are identified, may invite the parties to meet separately with the CAFCASS officer.

 Practical Considerations

A check will be made to find out if the parties to proceedings are a risk to the child. For instance, the local authority may have concerns about a parent's ability to be a safe and suitable parent for a child or the police may identify convictions which are relevant to the proceedings. The safeguarding procedure means that the court finds out about such issues early in proceedings rather than after an interim order has been made.

There generally should be no contact with the child before the FHDRA. CAFCASS are required under s16A CA 1989 to undertake and provide to the court risk assessments where the CAFCASS officer suspects that a child is at risk of harm. The FHDRA should be adjourned if the safeguarding letter is not available and interim orders should not be made in the absence of safeguarding checks.

The FHDRA is not privileged and so will refer to any evidence at a later hearing.

27.5.8.2 Purpose of FHDRA

At the FHDRA the judge, working with the CAFCASS officer, will seek to assist the parties in conciliation and in resolution of all or any of the issues between them. Any remaining issues will be identified, the CAFCASS officer will advise the court of any recommended means of resolving such issues, and directions will be given for the future resolution of such issues. At all times the decisions of the court and the work of the CAFCASS officer will take account of any risk or safeguarding issues that have been identified. The court will consider the following matters:

- safeguarding:
  - whether a fact-finding hearing is needed to determine allegations which are not accepted;
  - risk identification and risk management;
- MIAMs:
  - whether the applicant has validly claimed an exemption;
  - whether the respondent has attended a MIAM;
- mediation:
  - whether the parties can safely resolve some of their issues with the assistance of a CAFCASS officer;
  - whether a referral to mediation should be made or whether collaborative law is appropriate;
- consent orders:
  - no order will be made without scrutiny by the court;
- reports:
  - reports may be ordered where there are welfare issues or other specific considerations which should be addressed in a report by CAFCASS or the local authority;
  - general requests for reports should be avoided; a report should direct which specific considerations relating to the welfare of the child are to be addressed;
  - the court should consider if expert evidence is needed (see **27.5.12**);
- wishes and feelings of the child:
  - the child shall be at the centre of all proceedings;
  - a child's wishes should be considered in light of their age and understanding;
- allocation:
  - the allocation decision should be considered and if it is necessary to transfer the case, the court shall give the reasons for the transfer and make directions for the next hearing in the court.

The court must consider case management and the following are issues for the court to consider:

(a) What, if any, issues are agreed and what are the key issues to be determined?

(b) Should the matter be listed for a fact-finding hearing?

(c) Are there any interim orders which can usefully be made (e.g. indirect, supported, or supervised contact) pending Dispute Resolution Appointment or final hearing?

(d) What directions are required to ensure the application is ready for a Dispute Resolution Appointment or final hearing—statements, reports etc?

(e) Should the application be listed for a Dispute Resolution Appointment (it is envisaged that most cases will be so listed)?

(f) Should the application be listed straightaway for a final hearing?

(g) Judicial continuity should be actively considered (especially if there has been or is to be a fact-finding hearing or a contested interim hearing).

Where no final agreement is reached, the court will have to make an order to progress the case towards resolution. A draft order template is available on the Online Resource Centre but broadly, the court will consider the following issues:

(a) the issues about which the parties are agreed;

(b) the issues that remain to be resolved;

(c) the steps that are planned to resolve the issues;

(d) any interim arrangements pending such resolution, including arrangements for the involvement of children;

(e) the timetable for such steps and, where this involves further hearings, the date of such hearings;

(f) a statement as to any facts relating to risk or safety; in so far as they are resolved the result will be stated and, in so far as not resolved, the steps to be taken to resolve them will be stated;

(g) whether the parties are to be assisted by participation in mediation, Separated Parents Information Programme, WT4C, or other types of parenting intervention, and to detail any activity directions or conditions imposed by the court;

(h) the date, time, and venue of the next hearing;

(i) whether the author of any section 7 report is required to attend the hearing, in order to give oral evidence. A direction for the CAFCASS officer to attend court will not be made without first considering the reason why attendance is necessary, and upon what issues the CAFCASS officer will be providing evidence;

(j) where both parties are LiP, the court may direct HMCTS to produce a LiP Person bundle;

(k) the judge will, as far as possible, provide a copy of the order to both parties before they leave the courtroom, and will, if necessary, go through and explain the contents of the order to ensure they are clearly understood by both parties. The parties should know the date, time, and venue of any further hearing before they leave the court.

27.5.9 TIMETABLES

Section 1(2) CA 1989 states that the court should avoid delay as this is detrimental to the child and para 15 PD 12B FPR 2010 states that court proceedings should be timetabled so that the dispute can be resolved as soon as safe and possible in the interests of the child.

The judge shall, at all times during the proceedings, have regard to the impact which the court timetable will have on the welfare and development of the child to whom the application relates. The judge and the parties shall pay particular attention to the child's age, and important landmarks in the immediate life of the child, including:

(a) the child's birthday;

(b) the start of nursery/schooling;

(c) the start/end of a school term/year;

(d) any proposed change of school;

and/or

(e) any significant change in the child's family, or social, circumstances.

27.5.10 **DOCUMENTARY EVIDENCE**

Evidence can only be submitted in s8 CA 1989 proceedings with the permission of the court (r12.19(2) FPR 2010). This is to prevent a multiplicity of documents that may only increase the dispute and add to the time that the court must use to consider the proceedings. Where documentary evidence is required by the courts, it is clear that advance disclosure should be given. Evidence cannot be admitted or relied upon unless it has been disclosed to the other parties, unless the court gives permission.

Practical Considerations

When drafting a statement, the client's position should be made clear and the statement should be drafted with the principles of the CA 1989 in mind. Restraint should be practised if the client suggests that material should be included in the statement that attacks the other party gratuitously or seeks to inflame the situation further.

As well as statements, thought should be given to any other supporting evidence required by the client's case. Independent witnesses can offer evidence on a party's lifestyle or unsavoury associations. Care should be taken when a client suggests a number of witnesses claiming to support their case, as the client may be overly optimistic about the client's evidence or it may merely repeat evidence stated elsewhere.

27.5.11 **CAFCASS**

The Children and Family Court Advisory and Support Service (CAFCASS) was set up on 1 April 2001 under the provisions of the Criminal Justice and Court Services Act 2000, which brought together the family court services previously provided by the Family Court Welfare Service, the Guardian ad Litem Service, and the Children's Division of the Official Solicitor's Office. CAFCASS is independent of the courts, social services, education and health authorities, and all similar agencies.

Its role is to:

- safeguard and promote the welfare of children;
- give advice to the family courts;
- make provision for children to be represented;
- provide information, advice, and support to children and their families.

online resource centre

Its website address can be found on the Online Resource Centre.

In s8 CA 1989 disputes, the court may under s7 CA 1989 order a report, commonly known as a welfare report, to be compiled by CAFCASS.

A CAFCASS officer will have access to all of the court files and documents and will be aware of the issues between the parties. The CAFCASS officer will visit both parents (and all other parties to the proceedings) in their homes, if possible. The CAFCASS officer will also expect to see the parties with the child(ren) and observe how they interact. If the children are old enough and have sufficient maturity, the CAFCASS officer may meet the children separately to gain their views. The CAFCASS officer may also make other enquiries that are necessary for the report, including of the children's teacher, GP, or social workers. The CAFCASS officer will use all of this information to compile her report and the report may make recommendations concerning the application before the court.

The gathering of this information will take some time and the wait for a CAFCASS report can be quite lengthy. The expected wait for a report can be between 12 and 18 weeks. Any report should be requested early in proceedings if the court does not order one of its own right. To ask for a CAFCASS report late in proceedings may run the risk that the court considers that the harm caused by the delay outweighs the benefit of the court having the report.

The CAFCASS report will inevitably contain some evidence that would normally be considered to be hearsay, e.g. 'Sarah's primary school teacher, Mrs Billings, told me that Sarah is very disruptive following contact with her father.' Courts will accept this evidence and attach the weight that they feel to be appropriate.

Once a CAFCASS report is received, it is essential to gain clients' instructions on it and to gain their reaction to the comments and recommendations made by the CAFCASS officer. Clients should take a realistic view of their case if the CAFCASS officer makes a recommendation in favour of the other parent or party. The court greatly values the CAFCASS report as the CAFCASS officer has seen the parties, children, and others at first hand, unlike the court, and as a result the report carries great weight. A client needs to be given realistic advice if the recommendation in the report does not support their position. In *Re M (Residence)* [2005] 1 FLR 656, it was stated that the court should not depart from the recommendations of the CAFCASS officer without first giving them the opportunity to respond to any misgivings held by the court.

The CAFCASS officer can be cross-examined by either party if there are flaws in the reporting of evidence or recommendations that are unsound given the evidence of the case and this was confirmed in *Re I and H (Contact: Right to Give Evidence)* [1998] 1 FLR 876.

27.5.12 EXPERT EVIDENCE

Section 13 Children and Families Act 2014 and Part 25 FPR 2010 must be adhered to. Expert evidence is permitted if it is necessary to assist the court to resolve proceedings. Should either party wish to introduce medical or psychological evidence concerning a child, they will have to gain the permission of the court under r12.19(2) FPR 2010. The child may not be examined without the court's permission for the purposes of compiling expert evidence and any such evidence will not be admitted without the court's permission.

Part 25.6 FPR 2010 states that permission for an expert must be applied for no later than the FHDRA. The court has a power under Part 25.11 FPR 2010 to direct that evidence is given by a single joint expert.

This may produce difficulty. If an expert is necessary to resolve proceedings but the parties are unable to pay for it, the practical question of how the dispute will be resolved arises. The President of the Family Division, Sir James Munby, has considered the issue in the case *Q v Q; Re B (a Child); Re C (a Child)* [2014] EWFC 31 at para 54, when he asked 'How can the court deal with a case justly if, having determined that the instruction of an expert is "necessary" to achieve that objective, the absence of funding makes what is necessary impossible?' The President answered this question at paras 56–57:

> In principle, the first question in that situation must be, is it, in the view of the court, 'necessary', if the proceedings are to be resolved 'justly', to have the expert in court to answer questions, or will it suffice for the court to be able to read the expert's report? If the proceedings can be resolved 'justly' without requiring the expert's attendance, then there is no reason why public funds should be spent on something which is, on this hypothesis, unnecessary. If, on the other hand, it is necessary for the expert to attend court to enable the proceedings to be resolved justly—and that must always be a question for determination by the case management judge, not for mere agreement between the parties—then it follows, in my judgment, that the obligation is on the State to provide the necessary funding if a litigant through poverty is unable to pay the cost.
>
> In the final analysis, if there is no other properly available public purse, that cost has, in my judgment to be borne by the court, by HMCTS. It is, after all, the court which, in accordance with FPR 1.1, has imposed on it the duty of dealing with the case justly. And, in the final analysis, it is the court which has the duty of ensuring compliance with Articles 6 and 8 in relation to the proceedings before it.

27.5.13 ATTENDANCE AT HEARINGS

All parties must attend the hearing of which they have had notice unless the court directs otherwise under r12.14 FPR 2010. If the child is a party, they should attend unless the court believes that the child should be absent having regard to the matters being discussed or evidence to be given at the hearing, or if the child is represented by a children's guardian or solicitor.

If a respondent is absent, the court may only proceed in their absence if it is proved that he had reasonable notice and the circumstances of the case justify proceeding. If the applicant does not appear, the case can proceed if the court has sufficient evidence or can refuse the application. If neither party appears, the court may refuse the application.

27.5.14 DISPUTE RESOLUTION APPOINTMENT (DRA)

A DRA should follow the preparation of s7 or other expert report, or Separated Parenting Information Programme (SPIP) if this is considered likely to be helpful in the interests of the child. The author of the section 7 report will only attend this hearing if directed to do so by the court.

At the DRA the court will:

(a) identify the key issue(s) (if any) to be determined and the extent to which those issues can be resolved or narrowed at the DRA;

(b) consider whether the DRA can be used as a final hearing;

(c) resolve or narrow the issues by hearing evidence;

(d) identify the evidence to be heard on the issues which remain to be resolved at the final hearing;

(e) give final case management directions including:

    (i) filing of further evidence;

    (ii) filing of a statement of facts/issues remaining to be determined;

    (iii) filing of a witness template and/or skeleton arguments;

    (iv) ensuring compliance with PD 27A (the Bundles Practice Direction);

    (v) listing the final hearing.

A draft order template (CAP03) is available and can be found on the Online Resource Centre.

27.5.15 THE FINAL HEARING

The final hearing follows the normal course of a trial with evidence introduced and then witnesses cross-examined. The decision of the court should be made as soon as practicable after the final hearing of proceedings (r29.11). The order shall be recorded by an officer of the court in the proper form and the draft order template (CAP04) can be found on the Online Resource Centre. The order shall be served as soon as practicable by the proper officer on the parties to the proceedings and on anyone with whom the child is living.

27.5.16 APPEALS

An appeal from the magistrates' court is heard in the High Court (s91(4) CA 1989) and will be heard by a High Court judge of the Family Division who will generally sit in public.

An appeal from the county court or the High Court will be directly to the Court of Appeal. An appeal against the decision of a district judge will usually be made to the judge of the court in which the decision is made (r30 FPR 2010) but it is not a rehearing.

The time-limits for filing and serving a notice of appeal are:

• 14 days after the decision against which the appeal is brought; or

• as the court may direct.

27.6 **ALLEGATIONS OF HARM**

The C100 asks if the child is experiencing or is at risk of suffering various forms of harm. The procedure to be adopted if allegations of harm are made are found in PD 12J FPR 2010. The purpose of the Practice Direction is to set out what the Family Court should do in any case in which it is alleged or admitted, or there is other reason to believe, that the child or a party has experienced domestic violence or abuse perpetrated by another party or that there is a risk of such violence or abuse. PD 12J FPR 2010 is an admirable attempt to organize an early decision on whether domestic abuse (and other forms of behaviour harmful to children) are being perpetrated. The terms of the PD 12J are very clear and so the majority of the PD is set out here with limited commentary.

In PD 12J:

'Domestic violence' includes any incident or pattern of incidents of controlling, coercive, or threatening behaviour, violence or abuse between those aged 16 or over who are or have been intimate partners or family members regardless of gender or sexuality. This can encompass, but is not limited to, psychological, physical, sexual, financial, or emotional abuse.

'Controlling behaviour' means an act or pattern of acts designed to make a person subordinate and/or dependent by isolating them from sources of support, exploiting their resources and capacities for personal gain, depriving them of the means needed for independence, resistance and escape, and regulating their everyday behaviour.

'Coercive behaviour' means an act or a pattern of acts of assault, threats, humiliation and intimidation or other abuse that is used to harm, punish, or frighten the victim.

An adverse finding does not necessarily end a parent's involvement with their child. The Family Court presumes that the involvement of a parent in a child's life will further the child's welfare, so long as the parent can be involved in a way that does not put the child or other parent at risk of suffering harm.

The court must, at all stages of the proceedings, and specifically at the First Hearing Dispute Resolution Appointment (FHDRA), consider whether domestic violence is raised as an issue, either by the parties or by CAFCASS and if so must:

- identify at the earliest opportunity (usually at the FHDRA) the factual and welfare issues involved;

- consider the nature of any allegation, admission or evidence of domestic violence or abuse, and the extent to which it would be likely to be relevant in deciding whether to make a child arrangements order and, if so, in what terms;

- give directions to enable contested relevant factual and welfare issues to be tried as soon as possible and fairly;

- ensure that where violence or abuse is admitted or proven, that any child arrangements order in place protects the safety and wellbeing of the child and the parent with whom the child is living, and does not expose them to the risk of further harm. In particular, the court must be satisfied that any contact ordered with a parent who has perpetrated violence or abuse is safe and in the best interests of the child; and

- ensure that any interim child arrangements order (i.e. considered by the court before determination of the facts, and in the absence of admission) is only made having followed the guidance in paragraphs 25–27 below.

27.6.1 **INTERIM ORDERS**

In all cases it is for the court to decide whether a child arrangements order accords with s1(1) Children Act 1989; any proposed CAO, whether to be made by agreement between the parties or otherwise must be scrutinized by the court accordingly. The court shall not make a CAO by consent or give permission for an application for a CAO to be withdrawn, unless the parties are present in court, all initial safeguarding checks have been obtained by the court, and an officer of CAFCASS has spoken to the parties separately, except where it is satisfied that there is no risk of harm to the child in so doing. This prevents a parent being pushed into a potentially unsafe order when a full risk assessment has not been completed.

Paragraphs 25–27 include more guidance:

25. Where the court gives directions for a fact-finding hearing, the court should consider whether an interim child arrangements order is in the interests of the child; and in particular whether the safety of the child and (bearing in mind the impact which domestic violence against a parent can have on the emotional well-being of the child) the parent who has made the allegation and is at any time caring for the child can be secured before, during and after any contact.

26. In deciding any interim child arrangements question pending a full hearing the court should—

(a) take into account the matters set out in section 1(3) of the Children Act 1989 or section 1(4) of the Adoption and Children Act 2002 (the welfare check-list), as appropriate; and

(b) give particular consideration to the likely effect on the child, and on the care given to the child by the parent who has made the allegation of domestic violence, of any contact and any risk of harm, whether physical, emotional or psychological, which the child and that parent is likely to suffer as a consequence of making or declining to make an order.

27. Where the court is considering whether to make an order for interim contact, it should in addition consider—

(a) the arrangements required to ensure, as far as possible, that any risk of harm to the child and the parent who is at any time caring for the child is minimised and that the safety of the child and the parties is secured; and in particular:

(i) whether the contact should be supervised or supported, and if so, where and by whom;

(ii) the availability of appropriate facilities for that purpose;

(b) if direct contact is not appropriate, whether it is in the best interests of the child to make an order for indirect contact; and

(c) whether contact will be beneficial for the child.

27.6.2 FHDRA

Where any information provided to the court before the FHDRA or other first hearing (whether as a result of initial safeguarding enquiries by CAFCASS or on Form C1A or otherwise) indicates that there are issues of domestic violence or abuse which may be relevant to the court's determination, the court must ensure that the issues are addressed at the hearing, and that the parties are not expected to engage in conciliation or other forms of dispute resolution which are not suitable.

If at any stage the court is advised by the applicant, by CAFCASS, or otherwise that there is a need for special arrangements to secure the safety of any party or child attending any hearing, the court shall ensure that appropriate arrangements are made for the hearing and for all subsequent hearings in the case, unless it considers that these are no longer necessary.

The court must ascertain at the earliest opportunity whether domestic violence or abuse is raised as an issue of risk of harm to the child which is likely to be relevant to any decision of the court relating to the welfare of the child, and specifically on the making of any child arrangements order.

27.6.3 DIRECTIONS FOR A FACT-FINDING HEARING

The court should determine as soon as possible whether it is necessary to conduct a fact-finding hearing in relation to any disputed allegation of domestic violence or abuse:

(a) in order to provide a factual basis for any welfare report or for assessment of the factors set out in paragraphs 36 and 37 (below);

(b) in order to provide a basis for an accurate assessment of risk; or

(c) before it can consider any final welfare-based order(s) in relation to child arrangements; or

(d) before it considers the need for a domestic violence-related activity.

In determining whether it is necessary to conduct a fact-finding hearing, the court should consider—

(a) the views of the parties and of Cafcass;

(b) whether there are admissions by a party which provide a sufficient factual basis on which to proceed;

(c) if a party is in receipt of legal aid, whether the evidence required to be provided to obtain legal aid provides a sufficient factual basis on which to proceed;

(d) whether there is other evidence available to the court that provides a sufficient factual basis on which to proceed;

(e) whether the factors set out in paragraphs 36 and 37 below can be determined without a fact-finding hearing;

(f) the nature of the evidence required to resolve disputed allegations;

(g) whether the nature and extent of the allegations, if proved, would be relevant to the issue before the court; and

(h) whether a separate fact-finding hearing would be necessary and proportionate in all the circumstances of the case.

Where the court determines that a finding of fact hearing is not necessary, the order shall record the reasons for that decision.

Where the court considers that a fact-finding hearing is necessary, it must give directions as to how the proceedings are to be conducted to ensure that the matters in issue are determined as soon as possible, fairly and proportionately, and within the capabilities of the parties. In particular it should consider—

(a) what are the key facts in dispute;

(b) whether it is necessary for the fact-finding to take place at a separate (and earlier) hearing than the welfare hearing;

(c) whether the key facts in dispute can be contained in a schedule or a table (known as a Scott Schedule) which sets out what the applicant complains of or alleges, what the respondent says in relation to each individual allegation or complaint; the allegations in the schedule should be focused on the factual issues to be tried; and if so, whether it is practicable for this schedule to be completed at the first hearing, with the assistance of the judge;

(d) what evidence is required in order to determine the existence of a pattern of coercive, controlling or threatening behaviour, violence or abuse;

(e) directing the parties to file written statements giving details of such behaviour and of any response;

(f) whether documents are required from third parties such as the police or health services and giving directions for those documents to be obtained;

(g) whether oral evidence may be required from third parties and if so, giving directions for the filing of written statements from such third parties;

(h) whether any other evidence is required to enable the court to decide the key issues and giving directions for that evidence to be provided;

(i) what evidence the alleged victim of violence is able to give and what support the alleged victim may require at the fact-finding hearing in order to give that evidence;

(j) what support the alleged perpetrator may need in order to have a reasonable opportunity to challenge the evidence; and

(k) whether a pre-hearing review would be useful prior to the fact-finding hearing to ensure directions have been complied with and all the required evidence is available.

27.6.4 THE FACT-FINDING HEARING

While ensuring that the allegations are properly put and responded to, the fact-finding hearing can be an inquisitorial (or investigative) process, which at all times must protect the interests of all involved. At the fact-finding hearing:

- Each party can be asked to identify what questions they wish to ask of the other party, and to set out or confirm in sworn evidence their version of the disputed key facts.

- The judge or lay justices should be prepared where necessary and appropriate to conduct the questioning of the witnesses on behalf of the parties, focusing on the key issues in the case.

Victims of violence are likely to find direct cross-examination by their alleged abuser frightening and intimidating, and thus it may be particularly appropriate for the judge or lay justices to conduct the questioning on behalf of the other party in these circumstances, in order to ensure both parties are able to give their best evidence:

> The court should, wherever practicable, make findings of fact as to the nature and degree of any domestic violence or abuse which is established and its effect on the child, the child's parents and any other relevant person. The court shall record its findings in writing, and shall serve a copy on the parties. A copy of any record of findings of fact or of admissions must be sent to any officer preparing a report under section 7 of the 1989 Act.
>
> At the conclusion of any fact-finding hearing, the court shall consider, notwithstanding any earlier direction for a section 7 report, whether it is in the best interests of the child for the court to give further directions about the preparation or scope of any report under section 7; where necessary, it may adjourn the proceedings for a brief period to enable the officer to make representations about the preparation or scope of any further enquiries. The court should also consider whether it would be assisted by any social work, psychiatric, psychological or other assessment of any party or the child (such as an expert risk assessment), and if so (subject to any necessary consent) make directions for such assessment to be undertaken and for the filing of any consequent report.
>
> Where the court has made findings of fact on disputed allegations, any subsequent hearing in the proceedings should be conducted by the same judge or by at least the same chairperson of the justices. Exceptions may be made only where observing this requirement would result in delay to the planned timetable and the judge or chairperson is satisfied, for reasons recorded in writing, that the detriment to the welfare of the child would outweigh the detriment to the fair trial of the proceedings.

27.6.5 IN ALL CASES WHERE DOMESTIC VIOLENCE OR ABUSE HAS OCCURRED

The court should take steps to obtain (or direct the parties or an Officer of CAFCASS to obtain) information about the facilities available locally to assist any party or the child in cases where domestic violence or abuse has occurred:

> Following any determination of the nature and extent of domestic violence or abuse, whether or not following a fact-finding hearing, the court should consider whether any party should seek advice, treatment or other intervention as a precondition to any child arrangements order being made or as a means of assisting the court in ascertaining the likely risk of harm to the child and to the parent with whom the child is living from that person, and may (with the consent of that party) give directions for such attendance and the filing of any consequent report.
>
> Further or as an alternative to the advice, treatment or other intervention, the court may make an Activity Direction under section 11A and 11B Children Act 1989. Any intervention directed pursuant to this provision should be one commissioned and approved by CAFCASS. It is acknowledged that acceptance on a DVPP is subject to a suitability assessment by the service provider, and that completion of the programme will take time in order to achieve the aim of risk-reduction for the long-term benefit of the child and the parent with whom the child is living.

27.6.6 FACTORS TO BE TAKEN INTO ACCOUNT WHEN DETERMINING WHETHER TO MAKE CAOs IN ALL CASES WHERE DOMESTIC VIOLENCE OR ABUSE HAS OCCURRED

When deciding the issue of child arrangements the court should ensure that any CAO including an order for children to spend time with a parent will be safe and in the best interests of the child.

In the light of any findings of fact the court should apply the individual matters in the welfare checklist with reference to those findings; in particular, where relevant findings of domestic violence or abuse have been made, the court should in every case consider any harm which the child and the parent with whom the child is living has suffered as a consequence of that violence or abuse, and any harm which the child and the parent with whom the child is living, is at risk of suffering if a child arrangements order is made. The court should only make a CAO if it can be satisfied that the physical and emotional safety of the child and the parent with whom the child is living can, as far as possible, be secured before, during, and after contact, and that the parent with whom the child is living will not be subjected to further controlling or coercive behaviour by the other parent:

In every case where a finding of domestic violence or abuse is made, the court should consider the conduct of both parents towards each other and towards the child; in particular, the court should consider—

(a) the effect of the domestic violence or abuse on the child and on the arrangements for where the child is living;

(b) the effect of the domestic violence or abuse on the child and its effect on the child's relationship with the parents;

(c) whether the applicant parent is motivated by a desire to promote the best interests of the child or is using the process to continue a process of violence, abuse, intimidation or harassment or controlling or coercive behaviour against the other parent;

(d) the likely behaviour during contact of the parent against whom findings are made and its effect on the child; and

(e) the capacity of the parents to appreciate the effect of past violence or abuse and the potential for future violence or abuse.

Where the court has made findings of domestic violence or abuse but, having applied the welfare checklist, nonetheless considers that direct contact is safe and beneficial for the child, the court should consider what, if any, directions or conditions are required to enable the order to be carried into effect and in particular should consider—

(a) whether or not contact between parent and child should be supervised, and if so, where and by whom;

(b) whether to impose any conditions to be complied with by the party in whose favour the order for contact has been made and if so, the nature of those conditions, for example by way of seeking intervention (subject to any necessary consent);

(c) whether such contact between parent and child should be for a specified period or should contain provisions which are to have effect for a specified period; and

(d) whether it will be necessary, in the child's best interests, to review the operation of the order; if so the court should set a date for the review consistent with the timetable for the child, and shall give directions to ensure that at the review the court has full information about the operation of the order.

In its judgment or reasons the court should always make clear how its findings on the issue of domestic violence or abuse have influenced its decision on the issue of arrangements for the child. In particular, where the court has found domestic violence or abuse proved but nonetheless makes an order which results in the child having future contact with the perpetrator of domestic violence or abuse, the court should always explain, whether by way of reference to the welfare checklist the factors in paragraphs 36 and 37 or otherwise, why it takes the view that the order which it has made is safe and beneficial for the child.

SUMMARY POINTS

- Section 10(4) CA 1989 outlines those people who can apply for any order and s10(5) CA 1989 those people who can apply for a CAO. Those not covered by these provisions must apply for the leave of the court.

- The court will consider the nature of the application, the applicant's connection with the child, and the risk of disruption to the child's life when considering an application for leave.

- An application for a s8 order is made on a Form C100 and for all other applications the Form C1 is completed. A Form C1A should be completed in addition if there are allegations of domestic violence or other harm to the child.

- The respondent will acknowledge the application on Form C7 and the court will set a date for a conciliation/directions.

- The parties will be expected to negotiate or enter into some form of mediation, conciliation, or ADR.

- The court will make directions to allow the case to be fully explored including a timetable of the proceedings and a report from a CAFCASS officer.

- If there are allegations of domestic violence made during the proceedings, the court must follow the procedure set out in the Practice Direction: Residence and Contact Orders: Domestic Violence and Harm.

SELF-TEST QUESTIONS

1. Mary (born 3 June 2000) is the daughter of Simon and Katie, who are unmarried. Simon was arrested after assaulting Katie and was given community service. Katie is having difficulty coping on her own and asks her parents, Tim and Annie, to look after Mary.

    (a) Advise Tim and Annie whether they can apply for a residence order and the procedure that will be followed.

    (b) Advise Simon whether he can apply for a contact order and whether there are any other orders that he should apply for at the time of applying for a contact order.

    (c) Advise Katie how the court will deal with her allegations of domestic violence.

Case Study Two

David and Helena have both applied for a CAO to resolve living arrangements (see Documents CA 2 and 3) at the local county court. Helena acknowledges David's application on a Form C7 (Document CA 4) and the court confirms the first hearing resolution dispute hearing (FHDRA) on Form C6 and David files a C9, a statement of service.

David's instructions to his solicitor are that Richard should be brought up with a father in order for him to have a male role model. He and Anna have created a loving home with two parents to care for Richard. David is concerned that Richard attends nursery for three mornings a week and that he should not be out of the home as much. David has moved away from Longtown, England to London and he acknowledges that Richard would have to move away from his nursery and his friends. David is convinced that Helena's new boyfriend is unsuitable company for Richard, but gives no reasons why.

Helena's instructions are that Richard is settled with her and has a routine that he enjoys. He attends an excellent nursery that he enjoys. Helena felt that Richard needs more stimulation as he is a bright child. Richard has made many friends and Helena believes that the disruption of a move would be very damaging, given that the divorce was fairly recent.

At the FHDRA, David and Helena both speak to the CAFCASS officer in an attempt to settle the case. Both parties are adamant that they wish Richard to live with them and that it would be in his best interests. Neither Helena nor David will attend mediation.

At the FHDRA, the court makes a set of directions including a report from CAFCASS (Document CA 6 gives the full set of directions) and, after 16 weeks, the report is filed at court (see Document CA 6). To find out what happens in the case, see the case study on the Online Resource Centre!

---

online
resource
centre

Answers to the questions above can be found on the Online Resource Centre:
www.oxfordtextbooks.co.uk/orc/sendall17/.

FORM 27.1 C100: APPLICATION UNDER S8 OF THE CHILDREN ACT 1989 FOR A CHILD ARRANGEMENTS, PROHIBITED STEPS, SPECIFIC ISSUE ORDER OR TO VARY OR DISCHARGE OR ASK PERMISSION TO MAKE A S8 ORDER

C100

Application under section 8 of the Children Act 1989 for a child arrangements, prohibited steps, specific issue order or to vary or discharge or ask permission to make a section 8 order

To be completed by the court	
The family court sitting at	
Case number	Date issued
Fee charged/Remission ID	

Before completing this form please read the leaflet 'CB1 – Making an application – Children and the Family Courts' and the leaflet CB7 - Guide for separated parents: children and the family courts. These leaflets are available from your local court or online at hmctsformfinder.justice.gov.uk

Full name of applicant(s)

Full name of respondent(s)

Nature of application

What order(s) are you applying for?

☐ Child Arrangements Order

☐ Prohibited Steps Order

☐ Specific Issue Order

Please specify the nature of the order you seek. *For example, an order about with whom a child is to live, or how often they spend time with the applicant and for how long.*

Concerns about risk of harm

Are you alleging that the child(ren) named in Section 1 of this form have experienced, or are at risk of experiencing, harm from any of the following by any person who has had contact with the child?

any form of domestic violence	☐ Yes	☐ No
child abduction	☐ Yes	☐ No
child abuse	☐ Yes	☐ No
drugs, alcohol or substance abuse	☐ Yes	☐ No
other safety or welfare concerns	☐ Yes	☐ No

If you answered Yes to any of the above, **you must complete form C1A** (Supplemental information form) **and file it with this C100 form.**

Additional information required

Are you asking for permission to make this application, where that is required?	☐ Yes	☐ No	If Yes, complete section 3a
Is an urgent hearing or without notice hearing required?	☐ Yes	☐ No	If Yes, complete section 4a or 4b
Are there previous or ongoing proceedings for the child(ren)?	☐ Yes	☐ No	If Yes, complete section 5
Are you applying for an order to formalise an agreement (consent order)?	☐ Yes	☐ No	If Yes, **attach the draft order to this form**
Is this a case with an international element or factors affecting litigation capacity?	☐ Yes	☐ No	If Yes, complete section 6 or 7

C100 Application under the Children Act 1989 for a child arrangements, prohibited steps, specific issue section 8 order or to vary or discharge a section 8 order (11.14)

© Crown copyright 2014

1. The Child(ren)

Please also read the information notes and complete the checklist at the end of the form.
- Failure to complete every question or state if it does not apply, could delay the case, as the court will have to ask you to provide the additional information required.
- If there is not enough space please attach separate sheets clearly showing the details of the children, parties, question and page number they refer to.
- Cafcass/CAFCASS CYMRU will carry out checks as it considers necessary. See Section J of leaflet CB1 for more information about Cafcass and CAFCASS CYMRU.

Summary of children's details

Please list the name(s) of the child(ren) and the type(s) of order you are applying for, starting with the oldest. To understand which order to apply for read the booklet CB1 Section D.

Child 1 - Full name of child	Date of birth	Gender	Order(s) applied for
	D D / M M / Y Y Y Y	☐ Male	
	☐ Don't know	☐ Female	
Relationship to applicant(s)	**Relationship to respondent(s)**		

Child 2 - Full name of child	Date of birth	Gender	Order(s) applied for
	D D / M M / Y Y Y Y	☐ Male	
	☐ Don't know	☐ Female	
Relationship to applicant(s)	**Relationship to respondent(s)**		

Child 3 - Full name of child	Date of birth	Gender	Order(s) applied for
	D D / M M / Y Y Y Y	☐ Male	
	☐ Don't know	☐ Female	
Relationship to applicant(s)	**Relationship to respondent(s)**		

Child 4 - Full name of child	Date of birth	Gender	Order(s) applied for
	D D / M M / Y Y Y Y	☐ Male	
	☐ Don't know	☐ Female	
Relationship to applicant(s)	**Relationship to respondent(s)**		

2

1a. Are any of the children known to the local authority children's services?

☐ Yes ☐ No ☐ Don't know

If Yes please state which child and the name of the Local Authority and Social worker (if known)

1b. Are any of the children the subject of a child protection plan?

☐ Yes ☐ No ☐ Don't know

1c. Do all the children have the same parents?

☐ Yes ☐ No

If Yes, what are the names of the parents?

If No, please give details of each parent and their children involved in this application

Please state everyone who has parental responsibility for each child and how they have parental responsibility (e.g. 'child's mother', 'child's father and was married to the mother when the child was born' etc.)
(See Section E of leaflet CB1 for more information)

1d. Who do the children currently live with?

☐ Applicant(s) ☐ Respondent(s) ☐ Other

If other, please give the full address of the child, the names of any adults living with the children and their relationship to or involvement with the child.

If you do not wish this information to be made known to the Respondent, leave the details blank and complete Confidential contact details Form C8.

3

2. Requirement to attend a Mediation, Information and Assessment Meeting (MIAM)

Before making an application for a child arrangements order, prohibited steps order or specific issue order (a section 8 order) you must first attend a Mediation, Information and Assessment Meeting (MIAM). At the MIAM an authorised family mediator will consider with you (and the other party if present) whether family mediation, or another form of non-court dispute resolution, would be a more appropriate alternative to court. The mediator will also be able to sign post you to other help and support services.

You **must** have attended a MIAM before making this application **unless** the requirement to attend a MIAM does not apply because the section 8 order you are applying for:

- is for a consent order; **or**
- concerns a child who is the subject of separate ongoing emergency proceedings, care proceedings or supervision proceedings (or is already the subject of an emergency, care or supervision order); **or**
- you are exempt from the requirement to attend a MIAM. (Some exemptions you can claim yourself, others must be certified by an authorised family mediator).

All applicants must complete sections 1 to 12 and complete and sign section 15 of this form.

In addition, you must tick one of the boxes below and ensure that you, your legal adviser or a family mediator completes (and where indicated signs) the relevant section(s) of this form as shown.

2a. If you ticked 'Yes' to the question on page 1 about current or previous court cases, are/were any of those cases about an emergency protection, care or supervision order?	☐ Yes	☐ No	**If Yes, complete section 5** to provide additional details. **Do not complete sections 13 and 14** **If No**, please **answer question 2b.**
2b. Are you claiming exemption from the requirement to attend a MIAM?	☐ Yes	☐ No	**If Yes, complete section 13.** **If No**, please **answer question 2c.**
2c. Has a family mediator informed you that a mediator's exemption applies, and you do not need to attend a MIAM?	☐ Yes	☐ No	**If Yes**, you must ensure that the **family mediator completes and signs section 14a.** **If No**, please **answer question 2d.**
2d. Have you attended a MIAM?	☐ Yes	☐ No	**If Yes**, you must ensure that **the family mediator completes and signs section 14b.** **If No, you cannot make this application.**

4

3. Why are you making this application?

Have you applied to the court for permission to make this application? ☐ Yes ☐ No - permission not required ☐ No - permission now sought

3a. Reasons for permission if permission is required.

3b. Please give brief details:

- any previous agreements (formal or informal) or parenting plans, and how they have broken down
- your reasons for bringing this application to the court
- what you want the court to do
- reasons given by the respondent(s) for their actions in relation to this application.

Do not give a full statement, please provide a summary of any relevant reasons. You may be asked to provide a full statement later.

3c. Have you previously prepared a Parenting Plan? ☐ Yes ☐ No

If No, you can download a copy from the website www.cafcass.gov.uk/parentingplan

If Yes, please attach the plan to this application form

5

4. Urgent and without notice hearings

Complete this section if you have ticked the relevant box on the front of the form

4a. Urgent hearing

Set out the order(s)/directions sought

Set out the reasons for urgency

Proposed timetable

The application should be considered within [   ] hours/days

If consideration is sought within 48 hours, you must complete the section below

What efforts have you made to put each respondent on notice of the application?

6

Complete this section if you have ticked the relevant box on the front of the form

4b. Without notice hearing

Set out the reasons for the application to be considered without notice. (This information is a requirement, a without notice hearing will **not** be directed without reason)

Do you require a without notice hearing because it is not possible to give notice including abridged or informal notice?

☐ Yes   ☐ No

If Yes, please set out reasons below

Do you require a without notice hearing because notice to a respondent will frustrate the order that is being applied for?

☐ Yes   ☐ No

If Yes, please set out reasons below

7

5. Other court cases which concern the child(ren) listed in Section 1

Complete this section if you have ticked the relevant box on the front of this form.

Use this section to provide details of any other court cases now, or at any time in the past, which concern any of the child(ren) listed in section 1.

Additional details

Name of child(ren)

Name of the court where proceedings heard

Case no.

Date/year (if known)

Name and office (if known) of Cafcass/CAFCASS CYMRU officer

Type of proceedings if known - please tick all that apply

	Yes	No
Emergency Protection Order	☐ Yes	☐ No
Supervision Order	☐ Yes	☐ No
	☐ Yes	☐ No
Child abduction	☐ Yes	☐ No
Family Law Act 1996 Part 4 (proceedings for non-molestation order or occupation order)	☐ Yes	☐ No
A contact or residence order (Section 8 Children Act 1989) made within proceedings for a divorce or dissolution of a civil partnership	☐ Yes	☐ No
A contact or residence order (Section 8 Children Act 1989) made in connection with an Adoption Order	☐ Yes	☐ No
An order relating to child maintenance (Schedule 1 Children Act 1989)	☐ Yes	☐ No
A child arrangements order (Section 8 Children Act 1989)	☐ Yes	☐ No

Please tick if additional sheets are attached. ☐

Please attach a copy of any relevant order.

8

6. Cases with an international element

Complete this section if you have ticked the relevant box on the front of this form.

Do you have any reason to believe that any child, parent or potentially significant adult in the child's life may be habitually resident in another state?

☐ Yes ☐ No

If Yes, please give details

Do you have any reason to believe that there may be an issue as to jurisdiction in this case (for example under Brussels 2 revised)?

☐ Yes ☐ No

If Yes, please give details

Has a request been made or should a request be made to a Central Authority or other competent authority in a foreign state or a consular authority in England and Wales?

☐ Yes ☐ No

If Yes, please give details

7. Factors affecting ability to participate in proceedings

Complete this section if you have ticked the relevant box on the front of this form.

Please give details of any factors affecting litigation capacity

Provide details of any referral to or assessment by the Adult Learning Disability team, and/or any adult health service, where known, together with the outcome

Are you aware of any other factors which may affect the ability of the person concerned to take part in the proceedings?

9

8. Attending the court

Section N of the booklet **'CB1 - Making an application - Children and the Family Courts'** and the leaflet 'CB7 - Guide for separated parents: children and the family courts' provide information about attending court.

If you require an interpreter, you must tell the court now so that one can be arranged.

8a. Do you or any of the parties need an interpreter or other assistance (e.g. sign language signer) at court?

☐ Yes   ☐ No

If Yes, please specify the language and dialect:

[ ]

8b. Are you aware of whether an intermediary will be required?

☐ Yes   ☐ No

If Yes, please give details

[ ]

8c. If attending the court, do you or any of the parties involved have a disability for which you require special assistance or special facilities?

☐ Yes   ☐ No

If Yes, please say what the needs are

[ ]

Please say whether the court needs to make any special arrangements for you to attend court (e.g. providing you with a separate waiting room from the respondent or other security provisions).

[ ]

Court staff may get in touch with you about the requirements

10

9. About you (the applicant(s))

	Applicant 1 (You)	**Applicant 2 (if applicable)**
Full names		
Previous names (if any)		
Gender	☐ Male ☐ Female	☐ Male ☐ Female
Date of birth (If under 18 read section R of leaflet CB1)	☐☐/☐☐/☐☐☐☐	☐☐/☐☐/☐☐☐☐
Place of birth (town/county/country)		

If you do not wish your address to be made known to the respondent, leave the details below blank and complete Confidential contact details Form C8.

	Applicant 1	Applicant 2
Address	Postcode ☐☐☐☐ ☐☐☐☐	Postcode ☐☐☐☐ ☐☐☐☐
Home telephone number		
Mobile telephone number		
Email address		
Have you lived at this address for more than 5 years?	☐ Yes ☐ No	☐ Yes ☐ No

If No, please provide details of all previous addresses you have lived at for the last 5 years.

If you do not wish your contact details to be made known to the Respondent, leave the details blank and complete Confidential contact details Form C8		

11

10. The respondent(s)

Sections G and H of the booklet **'CB1 - Making an application - Children and the Family Courts'** explain who a respondent is.

If there are more than 2 respondents please continue on a separate sheet.

	Respondent 1	**Respondent 2**
Full names		
Previous names (if known)		
Gender	☐ Male ☐ Female	☐ Male ☐ Female
Date of birth (If party under 18 read section R of leaflet CB1)	D D / M M / Y Y Y Y ☐ Don't know	D D / M M / Y Y Y Y ☐ Don't know
Place of birth (town/county/country)		
Address (to which documents relating to this application should be sent)	Postcode ☐ Don't know	Postcode ☐ Don't know
Home telephone number		
Mobile telephone number		
	☐ Don't know	☐ Don't know
Email address		
	☐ Don't know	☐ Don't know
Have they lived at this address for more than 5 years?	☐ Yes ☐ No ☐ Don't know	☐ Yes ☐ No ☐ Don't know

If No, please provide details of all previous addresses for the last 5 years below (if known, including the dates and starting with the most recent)

12

11. Others who should be given notice

There may be other people who should be notified of your application, for example, someone who cares for the child but is not a parent. Sections G and I of the booklet **'CB1 - Making an application - Children and the Family Courts'** explain who others are.

	Person1	**Person 2**
Full names		
Previous names (if known)		
Gender	☐ Male ☐ Female	☐ Male ☐ Female
Date of birth	☐☐/☐☐/☐☐☐☐ ☐ Don't know	☐☐/☐☐/☐☐☐☐ ☐ Don't know
Address	Postcode ☐☐☐☐ ☐☐☐☐ ☐ Don't know	Postcode ☐☐☐☐ ☐☐☐☐ ☐ Don't know
Please state their relationship to the children listed on page 1. If their relationship is not the same to each child please state their relationship to each child.		

13

12. Solicitor's details

Do you have a solicitor acting for you?

☐ Yes   ☐ No   If No, see section Q of leaflet CB1 for more information

If Yes, please give the following details

Your solicitor's name

Name of firm

Address

Postcode ☐☐☐☐ ☐☐☐☐

Telephone number

Fax number

DX number

Solicitor's Reference

Fee account no.

Email address

14

13. Applicant claims exemption(s) from attendance at a Mediation, Information and Assessment Meeting (MIAM)

(To be completed by the person intending to make a court application or their solicitor)

The applicant has not attended a MIAM because the following MIAM exemption(s) applies:

☐ Domestic violence (you must complete **section 13a**)

☐ Child protection concerns (you must complete **section 13b**)

☐ Urgency (you must complete **section 13c**)

☐ Previous MIAM attendance or previous MIAM exemption (you must complete **section 13d**)

☐ Other (you must complete **section 13e**)

Now complete the relevant section 13a, b, c, d or e by ticking the appropriate box(s)

Further details of MIAM exemption(s) claimed by the applicant

If you have claimed a MIAM exemption in above you must also tick the relevant box(s), as shown below to confirm that you have the necessary evidence to support your ground(s) for exemption. Where you are asked to provide additional details you must do so.

Section 13a - Domestic violence evidence

The applicant confirms that there is evidence of domestic violence, as specified below:

☐ a relevant unspent conviction for a domestic violence offence;

☐ a relevant police caution for a domestic violence offence given within the twenty four month period immediately preceding the date of the application;

☐ evidence of relevant criminal proceedings for a domestic violence offence which have not concluded;

☐ a relevant protective injunction which is in force or which was granted within the twenty four month period immediately preceding the date of the application;

☐ an undertaking given in England and Wales under section 46 or 63E of the Family Law Act 1996 Act (or given in Scotland or Northern Ireland in place of a protection injunction)—

    (i)   by any prospective party in relation to another prospective party; and

    (ii) within the twenty four month period immediately preceding the date of the application;

☐ evidence that a prospective party is on relevant police bail for a domestic violence offence;

☐ a letter from any person who is a member of a multi-agency risk assessment conference confirming that—

    (i)   any prospective party was referred to the conference as a victim of domestic violence; and

    (ii) the conference has, within the twenty four month period immediately preceding the date of the application put in place a plan to protect that party from a risk of harm by another prospective party;

15

Section 13a - Domestic violence
evidence - **continued**

☐ a copy of a finding of fact, made in proceedings in the United Kingdom within the twenty four month period immediately preceding the date of the application, that there has been domestic violence giving rise to a risk of harm by one prospective party to another prospective party;

☐ a letter or report from a health professional who has access to the medical records of a prospective party confirming that that professional, or another health professional—

    (i)   has examined any prospective party in person within the twenty four month period immediately preceding the date of the application; and

    (ii) was satisfied following that examination that that party had injuries or a condition consistent with those of a victim of domestic violence;

☐ a letter from a social services department in England or Wales (or its equivalent in Scotland or Northern Ireland) confirming that, within the twenty four month period immediately preceding the date of the application, any prospective party was assessed as being, or at risk of being, a victim of domestic violence;

☐ a letter or report from a domestic violence support organisation in the United Kingdom affirming—

    (i)   that any prospective party was, within the twenty four month period immediately preceding the date of the application (and, where relevant, that period commences with the date on which that prospective party left the refuge), admitted to a refuge established for the purpose of providing accommodation for victims of, or those at risk of, domestic violence;

    (ii) the dates on which that prospective party was admitted to and, if applicable, left the refuge; and

    (iii) that that party was admitted to the refuge because of allegations by that party of domestic violence;

☐ a letter or report from a domestic violence support organisation in the United Kingdom confirming—

    (i)   that a prospective party was, within the twenty four month period immediately preceding the date of the application, refused admission to a refuge established for the purpose of providing accommodation for victims of, or those at risk of, domestic violence, on account of there being insufficient accommodation available in the refuge; and

    (ii) the date on which that prospective party was refused admission to the refuge;

☐ a letter or report from—

    (i)   the person to whom the referral described below was made;

    (ii) the health professional who made the referral described below; or

    (iii) a health professional who has access to the medical records of a prospective party,

confirming that there was, within the twenty four month period immediately preceding the date of the application, a referral by a health professional of a prospective party to a person who provides specialist support or assistance for victims of, or those at risk of, domestic violence;

☐ a relevant domestic violence protection notice issued under section 24 of the Crime and Security Act 2010, or a relevant domestic violence protection order made under section 28 of that Act, against a prospective party within the twenty four month period immediately preceding the date of the application; or

16

Section 13a - Domestic violence evidence - continued

☐ evidence of a relevant court order binding over a prospective party in connection with a domestic violence offence, which is in force or which was granted within the twenty four month period immediately preceding the date of the application.

Section 13b – Child protection concerns

The applicant confirms that a child would be the subject of the application and that child or another child of the family who is living with that child is currently—

☐ the subject of enquiries by a local authority under section 47 of the Children Act 1989 Act; or

☐ the subject of a child protection plan put in place by a local authority.

Section 13c – Urgency

The applicant confirms that the application must be made urgently because:

☐ there is risk to the life, liberty or physical safety of the prospective applicant or his or her family or his or her home; or

☐ any delay caused by attending a MIAM would cause—

 ☐ a risk of harm to a child; or

 ☐ a risk of unlawful removal of a child from the United Kingdom, or a risk of unlawful retention of a child who is currently outside England and Wales; or

 ☐ a significant risk of a miscarriage of justice; or

 ☐ unreasonable hardship to the prospective applicant; or

 ☐ irretrievable problems in dealing with the dispute (including the irretrievable loss of significant evidence); or

☐ there is a significant risk that in the period necessary to schedule and attend a MIAM, proceedings relating to the dispute will be brought in another state in which a valid claim to jurisdiction may exist, such that a court in that other State would be seised of the dispute before a court in England and Wales.

Section 13d – Previous MIAM attendance or MIAM exemption

The applicant confirms that one of the following applies:

☐ in the 4 months prior to making the application, the person attended a MIAM or participated in another form of non-court dispute resolution relating to the same or substantially the same dispute; or

☐ at the time of making the application, the person is participating in another form of non-court dispute resolution relating to the same or substantially the same dispute; or

☐ in the 4 months prior to making the application, the person filed a relevant family application confirming that a MIAM exemption applied and that application related to the same or substantially the same dispute; or

☐ the application would be made in existing proceedings which are continuing and the prospective applicant attended a MIAM before initiating those proceedings; or

☐ the application would be made in existing proceedings which are continuing and a MIAM exemption applied to the application for those proceedings.

17

Section 13e – Other exemptions

The applicant confirms that one of the following other grounds for exemption applies:

☐ the prospective applicant does not have sufficient contact details for any of the prospective respondents to enable a family mediator to contact any of the prospective respondents for the purpose of scheduling the MIAM.

☐ the application would be made without notice (Paragraph 5.1 of Practice Direction 18A sets out the circumstances in which applications may be made without notice.)

☐ (i) the prospective applicant is or all of the prospective respondents are subject to a disability or other inability that would prevent attendance at a MIAM unless appropriate facilities can be offered by an authorised mediator; (ii) the prospective applicant has contacted as many authorised family mediators as have an office within fifteen miles of his or her home (or three of them if there are three or more), and all have stated that they are unable to provide such facilities; and (iii) the names, postal addresses and telephone numbers or e-mail addresses for such authorised family mediators, and the dates of contact, can be provided to the court if requested.

☐ the prospective applicant or all of the prospective respondents cannot attend a MIAM because he or she is, or they are, as the case may be (i) in prison or any other institution in which he or she is or they are required to be detained; (ii) subject to conditions of bail that prevent contact with the other person; or (iii) subject to a licence with a prohibited contact requirement in relation to the other person.

☐ the prospective applicant or all of the prospective respondents are not habitually resident in England and Wales.

☐ a child is one of the prospective parties by virtue of Rule 12.3(1).

☐ (i) the prospective applicant has contacted as many authorised family mediators as have an office within fifteen miles of his or her home (or three of them if there are three or more), and all of them have stated that they are not available to conduct a MIAM within fifteen business days of the date of contact; and (ii) the names, postal addresses and telephone numbers or e-mail addresses for such authorised family mediators, and the dates of contact, can be provided to the court if requested.

☐ there is no authorised family mediator with an office within fifteen miles of the prospective applicant's home.

Now complete Section 15.

18

14. Mediator certifies that the prospective applicant is exempt from attendance at Mediation Information and Assessment Meeting (MIAM) or confirms MIAM attendance

(To be completed and signed by the authorised family mediator)
(tick the boxes that apply)

14a.   **The following MIAM exemption(s) applies:**

☐ An authorised family mediator confirms that he or she is satisfied that -

   ☐ (a) mediation is not suitable as a means of resolving the dispute because none of the respondents is willing to attend a MIAM; or

   ☐ (b) mediation is not suitable as a means of resolving the dispute because all of the respondents failed without good reason to attend a MIAM appointment; or

   ☐ (c) mediation is otherwise not suitable as a means of resolving the dispute.

14b.   **The prospective applicant attended a MIAM:**

☐ The prospective applicant only attended a MIAM.

☐ The prospective applicant and respondent party(s) also attended the MIAM together.

☐ The prospective and respondent(s) have each attended separate MIAM.

☐ The prospective respondent party(s) has/have made or is/are making arrangements to attend a separate MIAM.

Mediation or other form of Dispute Resolution is not proceeding because:

☐ The applicant has attended a MIAM alone and
   • the applicant does not wish to start or continue mediation; or
   • the mediator has determined that mediation is unsuitable

☐ Both the applicant and respondent have attended a MIAM (separately or together) and
   • the applicant does not wish to start or continue mediation; or
   • the respondent does not wish to start or continue mediation; or
   • the mediator has determined that mediation is unsuitable

☐ Mediation has started, but has:
   • broken down; or
   • concluded with some or all issues unresolved

Signed	

Authorised Family Mediator
(a family mediator who is authorised to undertake MIAMs)

Family Mediation Service name	
Sole trader name	
Address	

Dated ☐☐ / ☐☐ / ☐☐☐☐

19

15. Statement of truth

*delete as appropriate

*[I believe] [The applicant believes] that the facts stated in this application are true.

*I am duly authorised by the applicant to sign this statement.

Print full name

Name of applicant solicitors firm

Signed

(Applicant) (Applicant's solicitor)

Dated [ ][ ] / [ ][ ] / [ ][ ][ ][ ]

Position or office held
(If signing on behalf of firm or company)

Proceedings for contempt of court may be brought against a person who makes or causes to be made, a false statement in a document verified by a statement of truth.

20

Checklist for completing form C100

Relevant sections of this application will be provided to Cafcass/CAFCASS CYMRU upon issue of proceedings. The information contained in pages 1 to 14 of this form enables Cafcass/CAFCASS CYMRU to conduct enquiries prior to the first court hearing, without it they cannot conduct their initial safeguarding checks and enquiries.

Every question in pages 1 to 14 of this form should be completed, or stated that information is not available. This essential information is required by Cafcass/CAFCASS CYMRU and failure to provide this information could lead to unnecessary delays to proceedings:

Page 1

- ☐ Write in your full names
- ☐ Tick the type of order you are applying for
- ☐ Specify in the box the nature of the order you seek
- ☐ If you have any concerns about the risk of harm, tick the relevant box(s) and complete a separate Form C1A and give this to the court with your completed Form C100.
- ☐ Tick whether you are asking permission to make this application (and if so complete section 3a)
- ☐ Tick whether the application is urgent (and if so complete section 4a) or whether the application is to be made without notice to another party (and if so complete section 4b)
- ☐ Tick whether there are linked proceedings (and if so complete section 5)
- ☐ Tick whether your application is for an order to formalise an agreement (consent order) and if so attach the draft order to this form.
- ☐ Tick whether your case has an international element or whether there are any factors that affect the ability of any party to these proceedings to participate in proceedings.

Page 2

- ☐ The full name(s) of the child(ren)
- ☐ Their date(s) of birth
- ☐ Their gender
- ☐ The relationship of the child(ren) to the applicant
- ☐ The relationship of the children to the respondent(s)

Page 3

- ☐ Answer questions 1a to 1d about the children.

Page 4

- ☐ Answer questions 2a to 2d about whether there are parallel proceedings for an emergency protection, care or supervision order, whether a MIAM exemption applies or whether you have attended a MIAM.

Page 5

- ☐ Tick whether you have or are applying for permission to make this application (and if seeking permission complete section 3a).
- ☐ Complete section 3b to provide brief details about why you are making the application

- ☐ Complete section 3c about any previously prepared Parenting Plan.

Page 10

- ☐ Answer questions 8a to 8c by ticking the relevant boxes and provide details in the box of any special arrangements you need in order to be able to attend court.

Page 11

- ☐ Your (applicant's) full name
- ☐ Any previous names
- ☐ Your (applicant's) gender and date of birth
- ☐ Your (applicant's) address, including the Postcode

  Note: if you (the applicant) does not wish the address to be made known it should be included in an accompanying form C8 (confidential contact details).

- ☐ Your (the applicant's) telephone number and if applicable, mobile telephone

Page 12

- ☐ The respondent's full name
- ☐ Previous surnames (if known)
- ☐ The respondent's gender and date of birth
- ☐ The respondent's address, including the Postcode
- ☐ The respondent's telephone number and if applicable, mobile telephone
- ☐ Whether the respondent has lived at their address for more than 5 years

Page 13

- ☐ Full details for other parties who should be given notice of the application

Page 14

- ☐ Your solicitor's details (if applicable), including a telephone number.

Page 15 to 18

- ☐ If you answered question 2b on page 4 with "yes" you must tick one of the first five boxes box in section 13 to indicate the category of MIAM exemption that you are claiming. You must then complete section 13a, b, c, d or e as shown.

Page 19

☐ If a family mediator needs to certify that a mediator's exemption applies you must ask them to complete section 14a of this form and sign where shown.

☐ If you have attended a MIAM you must ask the family mediator who conducted it to complete section 14b of the form and sign where shown.

Page 20

☐ Check that you (or your solicitor if relevant) have completed and signed the statement of truth.

What you do next
You should normally make your application to the Designated Family Centre for your area. You can find this, and a full list of courts and what type of work they do online at courttribunalfinder.service.gov.uk

Fees
You may need to pay a fee with your application. You should read leaflet **EX50 Civil and family court fees** to find out what fee, if any, you need to pay. This leaflet is available from your local court or online at hmctsformfinder.justice.gov.uk

---

General information for completing this form

1. You need to complete this form if you want to ask the court to make an (or change an existing) order about a child(ren) and your application is for:

   • a child arrangements order (where a child should live, who a child should spend time with or both); or

   • a specific issue order (for example, if you are asking the court to decide whether a child's surname should be changed); or

   • a prohibited steps order (for example, if you are asking the court to prevent a person from removing a child from a school).

2. These orders are known as "Section 8 orders" and are orders made by the court under section 8 of the Children Act 1989 to decide issues in relation to a child. You must tick the relevant box on page 1 to indicate which type of order(s) you are applying for. (If you wish to ask the court to enforce a previous Section 8 order you need to complete a different court form – the C79).

3. Pages 1 to 14 set out the core information you need to provide if you wish to make an application to the court (Sections 1 to 12). You need to answer as many questions as possible at pages 1 to 14. You or your solicitor must also sign and date the Statement of Truth in Section 15 of this form.

4. If your application is urgent, or if you are making your application without notice to another party - the respondent(s) - you must tick the relevant boxes on page 1 of this form. You must then provide details in the relevant Section, as indicated on page 1.

5. If you are aware of any previous or current court cases concerning the child(ren) who would be the subject of the Section 8 order you are seeking then you must tick the box on page 1 to indicate this and provide as much information as you can in the relevant Section, as indicated in page 1.

6. If you are applying for an order by consent you should tick the box on page 1 to make this clear and attach the draft order with this C100 form.

Requirement to attend a Mediation, Information and Assessment Meeting

7. It is now a legal requirement that, unless an exemption applies, a person who wishes to apply to court for one or more of the orders listed at paragraph 1 of these notes must first attend a Mediation, Information and Assessment Meeting (a MIAM). At the stage before proceedings the other party (the respondent) is expected to attend either the same MIAM or a separate MIAM.

8. At the MIAM, a trained family mediator will give you (the applicant) and the other person if present (the respondent) information about family mediation and other types of non-court dispute resolution. They will consider with you whether non-court dispute resolution would be an appropriate way to resolve the dispute. It is then for the applicant and respondent to decide whether or not to do so.

9. The requirement for the applicant to attend a MIAM does not apply if a Section 8 order is being applied for and:

   • the other person is in agreement about what you are asking the court to order (the order is a "consent order"); or

   • there is an ongoing case about the child(ren) who would be the subject of the Section 8 application and that case concerns an emergency protection order, a supervision order or a care order, or if one of those orders has previously been made.

10. You must tick the relevant box in Section 2 of this form so that the court knows whether the MIAM requirement applies, whether an exemption applies (and why) or whether you have attended a MIAM.

MIAM exemptions and MIAM attendance

11. As the applicant you are expected to have contacted an authorised family mediator in order to make arrangements to attend a MIAM unless :

   • the MIAM requirement does not apply for one of the reasons explained at paragraph 9 of these notes, or

   • you are claiming a MIAM exemption, or a family mediator certifies that a mediator's exemption applies.

12. You can find an authorised family mediator by using the 'Find your local mediator' search facility available at: www.familymediationcouncil.org.uk

13. You should give the mediator the contact details of the other person so that the family mediator can contact them to check their willingness to attend a MIAM. If the other persons (or none of the other persons if there is more than one respondent) is or are unwilling to attend a MIAM this is a ground for the family mediator to exempt you from attending a MIAM.

14. If you or your solicitor believe that you have grounds for claiming exemption from MIAM attendance you or your solicitor must tick the relevant box in Section 2 of this form and complete Section 13.

15. If a family mediator wishes to certify that a mediator's exemption applies, so that you do not need to attend a MIAM, you must ask the family mediator to complete Section 14a of this form and sign it where shown.

16. If you have attended a MIAM you must ask the family mediator who conducted the MIAM to complete Section 14b of this form and sign it where shown.

17. If you claim a MIAM exemption and make an application to the court, the court will inquire into the grounds for exemption. The court may ask you to produce written evidence (see Section 13 of this form for details against each exemption shown).

18. If the court determines that the exemption was not validly claimed it may direct you, or you and the other party, to attend a MIAM and, if the case has already progressed to the first hearing, may adjourn the case to enable to make arrangements to attend a MIAM.

19. The detailed procedure relating to the MIAM requirement and MIAM exemptions and attendance is set out in Part 3 of the Family Procedure Rules and in supporting Practice Direction 3A (judicial guidance). These are available online at: www.justice.gov.uk/courts/procedure-rules/family/practice_directions/pd_part_03a

Paying for MIAM attendance or for family mediation

20. Legal aid is available for MIAMs and for family mediation. If you are eligible for legal aid you could receive both the MIAM and mediation sessions free of charge, as well as some advice from a solicitor to support you in the mediation process.

21. If you, or the prospective respondent, is eligible for Legal Aid then the total cost of MIAM attendance can be met by the Legal Aid Agency, whether you and the prospective respondent attend the same MIAM or separate MIAMs.

22. If neither you nor the respective respondent is eligible for Legal Aid then the mediator will agree with you how the cost of MIAM attendance is to be met.

23. See paragraph 32 below on how to find out whether you are eligible for Legal Aid.

Safety and MIAM attendance

24. Please note: the family mediator will discuss with you and with the other person whether you wish to attend the MIAM separately or together. Family mediators have a responsibility to ensure the safety and security of all concerned and will always check with each of you that attending together is your individual choice and is safe.

Information about mediation

25. If suitable, mediation can be a better way of resolving issues about arrangements for children when you and your partner separate or divorce. Mediation can be less expensive than going to court and much less stressful for all the family. It can also help you as parents to focus on your child(ren)'s needs in making decisions about them.

26. Family Mediation is an impartial process that involves an independent third person who assists both parties involved in a family dispute to reach a resolution. Family mediation can be used to settle any or all of the following issues:

   • Arrangements for children

   • Financial arrangements and dividing up property

   • Any combination of these

   • Any other disputes to do with separation and divorce.

27. Family Mediation is not just for divorcing or separating couples – it is a means for resolving a range of family disputes, whether they arise from divorce or the separation of cohabiting parents. Family Mediation could also help resolve issues with wider family members such as grandparents.

28. The family mediator helps the process of negotiation between the parties to agree their own arrangements by way of a Memorandum of Understanding. You can ask a solicitor, if you have one, to check the Memorandum of Understanding.

29. If both parties agree, you can ask the court to endorse what you have agreed by issuing a consent order. The mediator will help you to decide whether your case is complicated and does in fact need the court to consider your situation and make an order. The mediator should also tell you about other local services and options for resolving your dispute.

Further information and sources of help

30. General information about family mediation is available from the Family Mediation Council website at: www.familymediationcouncil.org.uk

31. The family mediator who undertakes the MIAM for you must be a member of a national mediation organisation which adheres to the Family Mediation Council's Code of Conduct and the mediator must be authorised to conduct MIAMs. The service finder will help you find such a local mediator.

32. You can find out more about legal aid for family matters, including whether you may eligible for legal aid, on the Legal Aid Information Service on the Gov.UK site at: www.gov.uk/check-legal-aid or you can telephone the Civil Legal Advice direct helpline 0345 345 4345.

33. For general advice on separation services and options for resolving disputes: www.sortingoutseparation.org.uk

34. For general advice about sorting out arrangements for children, the use of post-separation mediation, and/or going to court: www.advicenow.org.uk; www.advicenow.org.uk/advicenow-guides/family/sorting-out-arrangements-for-your-children/

35. For general advice about sorting out arrangements for children: www.theparentconnection.org.uk/

36. For advice about Contact Centres, which are neutral places where children of separated families can enjoy contact with their non-resident parents and sometimes other family members, in a comfortable and safe environment; and information about where they are: www.naccc.org.uk

37. For help with taking a case to court without a solicitor, the Personal Support Unit: www.thepsu.org/

38. For guidance on representing yourself at court, including a list of commonly used terms that you may come across: www.barcouncil.org.uk/instructing-a-barrister/representing-yourself-in-court/

39. For advice about finding and using a family law solicitor see: Law Society www.lawsociety.org.uk, and Resolution (family law solicitors): www.resolution.org.uk

40. For advice about finding using a family law barrister: see www.barcouncil.org.uk/about-the-bar/find-a-barrister/ and for arrangements for using a barrister directly see www.barcouncil.org.uk/instructing-a-barrister/public-access/

41. Judicial guidance that sets out the approach of the courts to deciding child arrangements is available online at: www.justice.gov.uk/courts/procedure-rules/family/practice_directions/pd_part_12b

Online videos

42. There are several videos explain more about the mediation process, making your application, what will happen in court and will help you prepare for the hearing. To watch the videos visit www.bit.ly/guides_for_separating_parents

28 CHILD ABDUCTION

28.1 INTRODUCTION

This chapter will:

- examine the phenomenon of parental child abduction;
- examine the national and international law assisting parents seeking the return of a child;
- examine the law and procedure relevant to preventing child abduction.

'Child abduction' is an emotive term conjuring images of children being removed by strangers and disappearing and the involvement of police and the criminal law. In the context of family, child abduction refers to the removal of children by a parent to another country without the permission of the other parent or the permission of the court. This chapter covers the law and procedure of recovering a child removed from the jurisdiction as well as considering what steps can be taken to prevent a child being removed in the first place. This chapter covers a highly specialist area of law and does so as an introduction only. The Law Society's Family Law Protocol recommends that all lawyers should know the steps and procedures to be taken if a child is threatened with abduction or is actually abducted. However, this area of work is highly complex and should only be undertaken by specialist lawyers.

28.2 THE PROBLEM

online
resource
centre

On the Online Resource Centre, you will find links to organizations dealing with child abduction and also the Ministry of Justice and the Foreign Office. There are three main categories of parental child abduction dealt with by the Foreign Office:

- wrongful removal abduction—the removal of a child from the jurisdiction without the other parent's consent;
- wrongful retention—where a child has been wrongfully retained during an overseas trip;
- threat of abduction—a risk that a child may be taken out of the jurisdiction.

Reunite, a charity specializing in advice and information on parental child abduction, reports a 158% increase in the number of abduction cases reported to it between 1995 and 2007. It reports that one child per day is abducted by a parent. Clearly the 'left behind' parent will wish to see the child and satisfy themselves that the child is safe and well. From a legal point of view, the parent has disobeyed the law and taken the child from the jurisdiction, irrespective of whether it is in the best interests of the child.

28.2.1 JURISDICTION

When a child is removed from 'the jurisdiction', this means from England and Wales. Removal of a child to Scotland and Northern Ireland will be considered a removal from the jurisdiction as much as a removal to the USA would be. Where the child has been removed to or wrongfully retained in has an impact on which rules will apply (see **28.5**).

28.2.2 IN WHICH CIRCUMSTANCES IS REMOVAL LAWFUL?

There are some circumstances when the removal of a child from the jurisdiction is lawful, e.g. if there are no Children Act 1989 (CA 1989) orders preventing the parent from removing the child from the jurisdiction (see **28.4**) and all parents and people with parental responsibility (PR) or guardians agree to the child being removed. This would be the case where the child goes on a foreign holiday with the consent of every parent and person with PR.

Where a child arrangements order (CAO) with provisions for whom the child shall live is in force (see **Chapter 26**) under s13(2) CA 1989, a child may be taken out of the jurisdiction for a period of less than one month by the person in whose favour the order is made.

28.2.3 CHILD ABDUCTION ACT 1984

Section 1(1) Child Abduction Act 1984 (CAA 1984) makes it a criminal offence for a person 'connected' with a child under 16 to take or send the child out of the UK without the appropriate consent. When advising a client about taking a child out of the jurisdiction, their attention should be drawn to this offence, as many clients are not aware of it.

A person is connected with a child if:

- he is a parent of the child; or
- in the case of a child whose parents were not married to each other at the time of his birth, there are reasonable grounds for believing that he is the father of the child; or
- he is a guardian of the child; or
- he is a person named in a child arrangements order as a person with whom the child is to live is in force with respect to the child; or
- he has custody of the child.

'Appropriate consent', in relation to a child, means the consent of the child's mother or father (if he has PR), any guardian of the child, any person in whose favour a child arrangements order as a person with whom the child is to live is in force, any person who has custody of the child, or the leave of the court granted under or by virtue of any provision of Part **II** of the CA 1989.

As stated at **28.2.2**, a person named in a CAO as a person with whom the child is to live can remove the child for a period of less than one month.

The law does provide a limited defence to this offence. A person does not commit an offence under this section by doing anything without the consent of another person whose consent is required if he does it in the belief that the other person has consented; or would consent if he was aware of all the relevant circumstances; or he has taken all reasonable steps to communicate with the other person but has been unable to communicate with him; or the other person has unreasonably refused to consent.

As with all criminal offences, it is a deterrent to such actions but not a preventative measure in its own right. There are other measures that a parent fearing unlawful removal can take.

28.3 PREVENTATIVE MEASURES AND THE CRIMINAL LAW

There are some preventative measures that can be taken by a parent concerned by the risk of abduction by the other parent.

28.3.1 SELF-HELP

 Practical Considerations

Reunite is a charity specializing in advice and support to parents involved in child abduction cases. Reunite produces an extremely useful guide to preventing abduction, which can be accessed by parents who wish to take any preventative measures they can.

Further details can be found on the Online Resource Centre.

 online resource centre

A parent can compile a file of documents relating to the child including photographs, birth certificate, any CA 1989 orders, and a set of fingerprints. For a potential abductor, a recent photograph should be kept and as much information as possible about them, including details of any family abroad or possible contacts.

28.3.2 PASSPORTS

A passport is obtainable for the child by either parent unless an objection has been lodged at a passport office of the United Kingdom Identity and Passport Service. A father will require the consent of the mother if he does not have PR. An objector can ask the Passport Service not to issue a child with a passport if a UK court has made one of the following orders:

- a prohibited steps order under s8 CA 1989;
- a residence order if the objector has the residence order made in favour of the objector;
- an order that the removal of the child from the jurisdiction is against the court's wishes (e.g. s36 Family Law Act 1986);
- an order awarding the objector care and control or custody of the child;
- an order specifying that the objector's consent is necessary to the removal of the child;
- an order requiring surrender of the passport and forbidding the issue of a further passport.

A mother can lodge an objection where the father does not have PR. If the child has their own passport, it should be recovered, if necessary by court order.

28.3.3 PORT ALERT

If the client is fearful of their child being removed by the other parent within the next 48 hours, the police should be contacted and the system of 'port alert' commenced. Details of port alert can be found in Practice Direction [1986] 1 All ER 983. This system is operated by the police in conjunction with immigration officers who attempt to prevent the removal of the child.

In order to issue a port alert, the police must be satisfied that:

- there is a real and imminent danger of the child being removed. 'Imminent' means within the next 24–48 hours and 'real' means that the port alert is necessary and must not be used as an insurance measure;
- the child is under 16 or a ward or there is a residence order in force or an order of the court preventing removal.

The client or their solicitor should attend a police station and be prepared to give detailed information concerning the child, the potential abductor's flights or travel plans, and the person applying. If there is a court order in existence, this should be produced to the police or, if one is being applied for, the details should be telephoned or faxed to the police as soon as possible.

If the police are satisfied that there is a real and imminent danger of the child being abducted, the child's name and details are circulated on a 'stop list' to airports and ferry ports. The child's name remains on the stop list for four weeks and immigration officers will attempt to prevent the child from being removed. Realistically, a port alert has a much better chance of success if the travel details (e.g. flight numbers) can be given in as much detail as possible or the port from which the child may be taken is known.

28.4 COURT APPLICATIONS

Child abduction cases involve great urgency and great expertise in a complex area of national and international law. The Family Law Protocol cautions that international child abduction law is a rapidly developing, highly specialist area of law and that specialist advice is essential for parents.

The Solicitors Regulatory Code of Conduct also states that a solicitor should not act for a client where they have insufficient resources or lack the competence to deal with the matter.

Unless a solicitor has experience in dealing with international child abduction, the case must be passed urgently to a firm that has the necessary experience.

There are a variety of applications that can be taken before the courts and each will depend upon whether abduction is threatened and where the child has been removed to.

 Practical Considerations

When a client walks through the door, an adviser should act urgently and do the following:

- take full details of the child—the parents, people with PR, their foreign connections, any recent travel or travel plans, the whereabouts of the child's passport (if they have one), and the current whereabouts of the child;

- take full details of the events leading up to the abduction or any threats of abductions;

- take full details of any existing CA 1989 orders or any proceedings already in existence in this jurisdiction or any other jurisdiction;

- consider involving the police for a port alert—find out as much as possible about the potential routes of travel;

- take the names and addresses of anyone who may have information concerning the child's whereabouts or may be hiding the child and abducting parent;

- if the child has been removed consider which law will apply—the European Convention or the Hague Convention.

As stated earlier, do not take on a case unless the firm has sufficient experience of acting in such cases. Reunite's website contains a list of firms that undertake this type of work should a referral be required. This can be found on the Online Resource Centre.

online resource centre

28.4.1 DISCLOSURE OF CHILD'S WHEREABOUTS

Section 33 Family Law Act 1986 allows the court to order a person to disclose information concerning a child if the court has reason to believe they may have relevant information. A person is not excused by reason that giving the information may incriminate them, although any admission or statement made in compliance with an order under s33 Family Law Act 1986 will not be admissible in evidence against them except in proceedings for any offence other than perjury.

An order can be ordered against a person who is not a party to the proceedings, e.g. a legal adviser, relatives, or friends. Where a mother has taken a child to a domestic violence refuge, the police should be directed not to disclose the address (*Chief Constable of West Yorkshire Police v S* [1998] 2 FLR 973).

 Example

There are often people with information about a child's whereabouts, including family members, travel agents, or work colleagues. A solicitor should use their skills of deduction and interview skills in order to build up a picture of the abducting parent's life and who may have information concerning the child.

28.4.2 ENFORCING CHILD ARRANGEMENT ORDERS

As stated at **28.2.2**, under s13(2) CA 1989, when a person is named in a CAO as a person with whom the child is to live, they can remove the child for a period of less than one month.

A CAO can also be enforced using s34 Family Law Act 1986, which allows a court to order that a child be delivered up to the care of the person in accordance with the CAO. The court can make an order authorizing a police officer or an officer of the court to take charge of the child and deliver them to the person concerned.

For a consideration of seeking leave to remove a child, see **Chapter 26**.

28.4.3 PROHIBITED STEPS ORDER

The prohibited steps order is a useful tool for the prevention of removal of a child from the jurisdiction and further details of this order can be found in **Chapter 26**.

In the context of parental child abduction, the removal of a child from the jurisdiction is a step that can be taken in the exercise of PR. As such, a prohibited steps order can be obtained preventing the removal of the child from the jurisdiction.

28.4.4 REGISTRATION OF ORDERS IN OTHER PARTS OF THE UK

Sections 27–31 Family Law Act 1986, as amended by the CA 1989, establish a procedure for a 'Part 1 order' (e.g. a s8 CA 1989 order) made in one part of the UK in relation to a child aged under 16 to be registered in another part of the UK and recognized as if it had been made in that part of the UK. Once registered, the order can be enforced as if it were one of the court's own orders. This is relevant for children living in England and Wales being removed to Scotland or Northern Ireland.

 Example

Hannah lives with her mother in the north east of England. There are great problems surrounding contact and domestic abuse between her mother, Elizabeth, and her father, Henry. A CAO concerning with whom the child shall have contact is made in Newcastle county court. After further problems, Elizabeth moves, without telling Henry, to Glasgow and refuses to allow contact.

Henry uses the Family Law Act 1986 to register his CAO in Glasgow and enforce contact with Hannah through the Scottish courts.

A specialist practitioner text should be consulted for the procedure of such an application.

28.5 **RECOVERING A CHILD REMOVED ABROAD**

If a child has been removed abroad, the next step will be to secure their recovery. The law in this area is extremely complex and should not be undertaken by a non-specialist lawyer. This part of the chapter gives an overview of the law. For a more detailed consideration of the law, reference should be made to a specialist practitioner text.

28.5.1 **APPLICABLE LAW**

There are two main pieces of legislation:

- the Hague Convention on the Civil Aspects of International Child Abduction;
- Council Regulation (EC) No. 2201/2003 of 27 November 2003.

Both pieces of legislation are discussed here in outline.

28.5.1.1 The Hague Convention

The Hague Convention on the Civil Aspects of International Child Abduction (the Hague Convention) is an international treaty with over 50 signatories, which was brought into being as a response to concern about the harm that parental child abduction causes children. The list of signatories can be found on the Online Resource Centre as the list does change from time to time.

The principle at the heart of the Hague Convention is that disputes over children should be resolved in the country where the child is habitually resident.

Any person, institution, or other body claiming that a child has been removed or retained in breach of custody rights can invoke the Hague Convention. It applies to any child under 16 who is habitually resident in one contracting state but has been wrongfully removed or retained in another contracting state.

'Habitual residence' is where the child lives normally and is settled. Children normally take the habitual residence of their parents and, if parents separate, the child's habitual residence follows that of their primary carer. A wrongful removal does not change the child's habitual residence. To change a habitual residence requires an intention to settle in the new country.

28.5.1.2 'Right of custody'

A removal or retention is wrongful if the act is contrary to the rights of custody under the law of the contracting state in which the child is habitually resident. Clearly, if there were a court order or a general law against removal this would be wrongful but in *Re V-B (Abduction: Custody Rights)* [1999] 2 FLR 192 the Court of Appeal stated that a right to be consulted but not to veto the removal did not amount to a custody right.

Under the Hague Convention, if an application is brought within 12 months of the removal or retention, the court must order the return of the child unless one of the defences available under the Hague Convention applies.

The defences available in the Hague Convention are:

- if the person bringing the application consented or acquiesced in the removal or retention. The evidence of purported consent must be unequivocal but, once given, consent cannot be withdrawn. Acquiescence depends upon the state of mind of the person said to have acquiesced and whether or not the other parent believed them to have acquiesced. Delay can be evidence of acquiescence;
- a court may refuse to return a child if there is a grave risk that his or her return would expose the child to physical or psychological harm or otherwise place the child in an intolerable situation. Risk of violence to a mother may also fall within this defence. There must be clear and compelling evidence of grave and serious harm. This defence was considered fully by the Supreme Court in *Re E (Children)* [2011] UKSC 27 where the abducting

mother made serious allegations of abuse against the children's father. The Supreme Court found that the exceptions to the obligation to return are by their nature restricted in scope and should be applied without extra interpretation or gloss. Violence and abuse between parents may constitute a grave risk to the children. But where there are disputed allegations which can neither be tried nor objectively verified, the focus of the inquiry is bound to be on the sufficiency of any protective measures which can be put in place to reduce the risk. The clearer the need for protection, the more effective the measures will have to be. In this case, the trial judge was satisfied that medical treatment would be available for the mother and that there were legal remedies to protect the children should they be needed;

- if the child objects to being returned and has attained an age and degree of maturity at which it is appropriate to take account of their views. The child's wishes will never finally determine the issue; the court takes into account the surrounding policies of the Hague Convention including the welfare of the child;

- if a child was in England and Wales, a court could refuse to return a child if it were contrary to respect for human rights and fundamental freedoms. This is rarely relied upon;

- the court also has a residual discretion to refuse to return a child.

28.5.1.3 The Council Regulation

Council Regulation (EC) No. 2201/2003 of 27 November 2003 (the Council Regulation) is relevant as Art. 60(e) provides that in relations between member states of the European Union the Regulations take precedence over the Hague Convention. The regulation is commonly known as 'Brussels II Regulation' (BIIR) and revises an earlier regulation. BIIR binds all EU member states except for Denmark.

The impact on the Hague Convention is that BIIR preserves the pre-eminence of the Hague Convention for dealing with applications for the return of abducted children but gives direction as to how the Hague Convention should be applied between member states.

Article 11 BIIR regulates how the courts should operate return applications under the Hague Convention.

This may, of course, change once the UK leaves the European Union.

28.5.1.4 Children abducted to a non-Hague Convention country

If a child is wrongfully removed or retained in a country that is not a signatory to the Hague Convention or BIIR, the parent left behind will face grave difficulties in retrieving the child. There are only two alternatives: one is to take proceedings in the country where the child is (if they can be found); the other is to seek extradition of the removing parent for an offence under the CAA 1984. This is only an option if there is an extradition treaty in force between the UK and that country.

If the child has been removed to a non-Hague Convention country, the court can make use of wardship and the court's inherent jurisdiction. Wardship is where the court takes control of a child's person and property; it is not often used following the passing of the CA 1989. Once a child is a ward no important step can be taken without the court's consent and the court will make an assessment of what is in the child's best interests. There is a presumption that it is in the best interests of the child for the child's future to be decided by the courts of the country from which the child has been abducted. The inherent jurisdiction is the court's power to make orders concerning a child living or connected with the UK.

The UK has reached consensus with a limited number of countries regarding the approach that courts shall take where a child is abducted to a non-Hague Convention country, e.g. the Protocol (Child Abduction Cases Between the UK and Pakistan) [2003] Fam Law 199 or the Cairo Declaration (resulting from Anglo-Egyptian Meetings on Judicial Co-operation in International Child Abduction Matters between Egypt and the UK) 17 January 2005. These agreements do not have the force of an international agreement but are a useful starting point for the conduct of proceedings in these countries.

SUMMARY POINTS

- Parental child abduction is a significant problem.

- Abduction can refer to the removal of a child from the jurisdiction or the retention of a child following contact outside of the jurisdiction.

- The removal of a child without the appropriate permission is a criminal offence.

- If there is a real and imminent danger of removal, the police can institute a port alert in order to prevent a child being removed from the jurisdiction.

- Applications can be made under the CA 1989 for a prohibited steps order, under ss33 and 34 Family Law Act 1986 for an order for disclosure of the child's whereabouts and their recovery, or to enforce a residence order.

- The Family Law Act 1986 allows the registration of a CA 1989 order in the courts of other jurisdictions within the UK.

- If the child has been abducted to a country within the European Union (save for Denmark), the Council Regulation will apply to proceedings to recover the child. If the child is outside of the European Union, the Hague Convention will apply.

- The court will look at the habitual residence of the child before the abduction and will return the child to that country unless a defence applies.

SELF-TEST QUESTIONS

1. Your client, Ali, has two children with his ex-wife Samantha. The couple cannot agree where their children shall live. Ali receives a telephone call from Samantha threatening to take the children to live with her in Edinburgh. Advise Ali which court orders he can seek to prevent Samantha from taking the children.

2. Would your answer differ if Samantha had threatened to take the children to Spain?

3. Samantha manages to remove the children to Spain. Advise Ali on the steps that can be taken to recover the children.

4. Would your answer differ if Samantha had removed the children to India? (You may need to use your IT skills to look on the internet for signatories to the Hague Convention!)

online resource centre

Answers to the questions above can be found on the Online Resource Centre: **www.oxfordtextbooks.co.uk/orc/sendall17/.**

29 CHILDREN IN LOCAL AUTHORITY CARE

29.1 INTRODUCTION

This chapter will:

- discuss the nature of public children law proceedings;
- discuss the 'threshold criteria' under the Children Act 1989;
- discuss the role of the local authority in public children law;
- discuss the orders available under the Children Act 1989 in public children law proceedings.

When children and their families need assistance or intervention from their local authority, this kind of law is referred to as public children law. This is an area of law that trainee solicitors may encounter during a family law seat but one in which they will have limited involvement. Most public law children work is done by specialist solicitors who are members of the specialist children law panel. However, trainee solicitors are often involved in assisting in such cases; trainees often attend hearings to assist advocates, prepare documents, and assist clients at case protection conferences.

Children at risk of harm and the protection offered by local authorities are often the subject of news headlines. On the Online Resource Centre there are details of high-profile cases, for example in 2008, the death of Baby P at the hands of his carers, following the death in the same local authority of Victoria Climbie in 2000. These cases brought publicity due to the reported failures of the local authorities to protect them. In 2003, Lord Laming reported, following a public inquiry into the death of Victoria Climbie, and his recommendations are still being implemented by local authorities and will influence practice in this area for some time to come. The Online Resource Centre contains more background information.

Public children law can be an extremely emotive and challenging area of law. Clients are in the position of having their children removed from their care and are obviously upset and worried about proceedings. Many clients have mental health difficulties, drug and alcohol addictions, or a combination of many problems and this can make giving legal advice complicated; such clients require skilful handling.

This chapter will look at the role of local authorities in protecting the child from harm and the orders available under the Children Act 1989 (CA 1989) which are used in cases of alleged harm to children. The 'threshold criteria' is the standard which the court uses to decide whether an order should be made. This is an important concept and will be applied in many of the subsequent chapters dealing with public children law. The following chapters also describe how children are protected in emergency situations and the procedures followed for orders involving local authority care of children.

The Family Justice Review (discussed throughout this text) has taken particular interest in public children law proceedings and the Children and Families Act 2014 (CFA 2014) has implemented a number of changes. The main changes concern the time proceedings take and other procedural issues. These will be addressed fully in **Chapter 30**. Further details are available on the Online Resource Centre.

online resource centre

29.2 **THRESHOLD CRITERIA**

Making a care order or supervision order is a serious step and the CA 1989 has rigorous criteria under s31(2) CA 1989. This states that the court must be satisfied:

(a) that the child concerned is suffering, or is likely to suffer, significant harm; and

(b) that the harm, or likelihood of harm, is attributable to:

(i) the care given to the child, or likely to be given to him if the order were not made, not being what it would be reasonable to expect a parent to give to him; or

(ii) the child's being beyond parental control.

This is referred to as the 'threshold criteria' as these criteria must be met before the court can make a care, supervision, or emergency protection order. The grounds in s31(2)(a) and (b) are cumulative and both must be satisfied before the court can make a care or supervision order. In s31(2)(b) CA 1989, either part may be satisfied.

In addition to s31(2) CA 1989, the court must also take into account s1 CA 1989, including:

- the child's welfare is the paramount consideration under s1(1) CA 1989;

- the court must apply the welfare/statutory checklist under s1(3) CA 1989;

- the principle that any delay in proceedings is likely to prejudice the welfare of the child under s1(2) CA 1989;

- the principle that the court should not make an order unless it considers that making it would be better for the child than making no order at all under s1(5) CA 1989.

In s31(2) CA 1989, the following terms are defined:

- 'harm' means ill-treatment or the impairment of health or development;

- 'development' means physical, intellectual, emotional, social, or behavioural development;

- 'health' means physical or mental health; and

- 'ill-treatment' includes sexual abuse and forms of ill-treatment that are not physical.

29.2.1 **WHAT IS 'SIGNIFICANT'?**

'Significant' is not defined in the CA 1989 but s31(10) CA 1989 states that where the question of whether harm suffered by a child is significant turns on the child's health or development, his health or development shall be compared with that which could reasonably be expected of a similar child. The term 'significant' turns on the health and development of an individual child and s31(10) CA 1989 allows the court to firstly take a subjective view of the individual child in question. The court then takes an objective view of whether the standard of her health and development is a standard that could reasonably be expected of a child with similar characteristics.

Practical Considerations

How the court interprets this objective standard is well illustrated by the case of *Re L (Care: Threshold Criteria)* [2007] 1 FLR 2050. In this case Hedley J held that it would not be wise for the courts to attempt an all-embracing definition of significant harm. The parents in this case had learning disabilities and were in many ways inadequate as parents, although not malicious. The judge found that society must be tolerant of the diverse standards of parenting that exist. Some children are disadvantaged from their experience of parenting while others will flourish and the state cannot protect children from all of the consequences of flawed parenting. It is important that the CA 1989 should operate in this context. It is not possible to have an all-embracing definition of significant harm. It is dependent on the facts of each case and needs to be sufficiently broad to encompass human fallibility. It must involve something more than commonplace human inadequacy.

'Care' is similarly not defined in the CA 1989 but encompasses mental and emotional care as well as providing for a child's physical needs.

29.2.2 STANDARD AND BURDEN OF PROOF

29.2.2.1 'Is suffering/is likely to suffer'

Section 31(2)(a) CA 1989 refers to the child 'suffering or likely to suffer' significant harm. The date at which this is measured is the date on which the local authority initiates procedures for protection of the child (*Re M (A Minor)(Care Order: Threshold Criteria)* [1994] 3 All ER 298).

 Example

A local authority takes steps to protect a child on 1 March 2009. A care order is subsequently made nine months later. The court will look to see if on 1 March 2009 the child was suffering significant harm.

The Public Law Outline (see **Chapter 31**) 'frontloads' applications for orders by a local authority, and the local authority should have undertaken a core assessment and a number of investigatory steps before an application is made. The local authority's investigations do not have to be complete at the time of the initiation of protection and the local authority will continue to gather evidence; this evidence can be taken into account by the court. On the issue of 'likely harm', the court can hear evidence that has been gathered after the relevant date (*Re G (Care Proceedings: Threshold Conditions)* [2001] 2 FLR 1111). The court will have to evaluate on the balance of probabilities whether the events alleged occurred and whether harm is likely to occur in the future.

29.2.2.2 Cause of harm

Section 31(2) CA 1989 requires the court to attribute the harm and to find the cause of the harm:

(b) that the harm, or likelihood of harm, is attributable to:

   (i) the care given to the child, or likely to be given to him if the order were not made, not being what it would be reasonable to expect a parent to give to him; or

   (ii) the child's being beyond parental control.

'Attributable' implies a causal connection between the harm and the care given to the child or the child being beyond parental control. The causal connection can be direct, e.g. where a parent physically injures their child, or indirect, e.g. where a parent does not sufficiently check the credentials of a person and leaves the child in that person's care and the child is injured or abused in some way. The harm suffered by the child can be considered to be attributed to the inadequate care of the parent as well as the third party (*Lancashire County Council v B* [2000] 1 FLR 583).

There may be doubt about who has caused the harm where the care of the child is shared between the parents and other carers. In the case of *Lancashire County Council v B*, the child was looked after by a number of carers including a child minder. The child suffered a serious intentional assault, which caused significant harm. The local authority applied for a care order but it was difficult to pinpoint blame on one individual on the evidence available to the court. The House of Lords held that s31(2)(b) CA 1989 and 'care of the child' refers primarily to the care given to the child by the parent(s) or other primary carers. Where the care is shared and the court is unable to distinguish between the care given by the parent(s) or primary carers and the care given by other carers then the court will approach the matter differently. Where the care given by one or other of the carers is proved to have been inadequate with the child suffering harm as a consequence, but the court is unable to identify which one carer was responsible for the inadequate care, then the care given to the child embraces not just the care given by the parents or primary carer but any of the carers. This leads to the possibility of a parent losing their child even if they are wholly innocent; the court still has discretion to grant a supervision or care order.

29.2.2.3 Case-law on burden and standard of proof

The legal burden rests on the applicant to establish that the threshold criteria have been met. The standard of proof is the balance of probabilities, the usual civil standard of proof.

In the case of *Re H and R (Child Sexual Abuse)* [1996] 1 FLR 80, the House of Lords held that the burden of proof is upon the applicant to establish on the balance of probabilities that the alleged events occurred and in all cases the standard of proof is the ordinary civil standard. However (as per Lord Nicholls) stronger evidence is required for a court to be satisfied that an event that is inherently improbable actually occurred than where an event is more likely to have occurred. When the court is satisfied that the alleged event has occurred according to the requisite standard of proof, it may then (on the strength of that finding) decide that there is a real risk of significant harm occurring in the future. It is not necessary for the court to be satisfied that the future significant harm is more likely than not.

However, this test has been questioned in the case of *Re B* [2008] UKHL 35. Both Lord Hoffmann and Baroness Hale made clear there is only one standard of proof and that is proof that the fact in issue more probably occurred than it did not.

Baroness Hale made clear that the s31(2) CA 1989 threshold is there to protect both the children and their parents from unjustified intervention in their lives from local authorities and that it would provide no protection if the threshold could be established on the basis of unsubstantiated suspicions or allegations.

Lord Hoffmann held that the often quoted formula of Lord Nicholls in *Re H and R* (discussed earlier) is not a rule of law, but rather, an application of common sense to whatever is required by the particular case. It would be absurd that the tribunal must in all cases assume serious conduct is unlikely to have occurred. So if, for example, it is clear that a child was sexually assaulted, it would make no sense to start one's reasoning by saying sexually assaulting children is a serious matter and therefore neither of the carers is likely to have done it.

Baroness Hale went further by announcing 'loud and clear' that the standard of proof in care cases is the simple balance of probabilities, 'neither more nor less'. When determining the fact and considering the standard of proof, the court should ignore the seriousness of the allegations and the seriousness of the consequences. Baroness Hale gave the example of a parent causing multiple fractures as being unlikely, but once the evidence establishes that to have occurred, it ceases to be improbable. Someone looking after the child at the relevant time must have done it, however improbable the event is. Proof of likelihood depends on the facts and circumstances of a particular case.

There were some proceedings, though civil in form, whose nature was such that it was appropriate to apply a higher standard of proof. But care proceedings were not of that nature. They were not there to punish or deter anyone but were there to protect a child from harm. The consequences for the child of getting them wrong were equally serious either way.

In *Re B (A Child)* [2013] UKSC 22 the Supreme Court held that in relation to threshold, the nature of the significant harm should be clearly identified and a common-sense approach should be taken to 'significant harm'; there is no mental element or intention required—the causation required is only as between the care and the harm.

29.3 LOCAL AUTHORITY DUTIES, CHILDREN IN NEED, AND VOLUNTARY ACCOMMODATION

A local authority is under an obligation (s17 CA 1989) to provide services for children in need, their families and others, and to:

- safeguard and promote the welfare of children within their area who are in need; and

- so far as is consistent with that duty, to promote the upbringing of such children by their families.

Section 17 CA 1989 requires the local authority to provide a range and level of services appropriate to that child's needs. The CA 1989 imposes a duty to *promote* a child's upbringing by their parents. The CA 1989 requires a local authority to assist parents to undertake this responsibility by providing services to parents. All local authorities have children's services and/or a social services department to provide services. A local authority may offer services to parents that try to improve parenting skills and abilities.

The duty of the local authority applies to children within their area, although the level of services varies enormously from authority to authority. A child, for these purposes, is a person under 18 years old. 'Within their area' refers to a physical presence within the area (*R v Wandsworth London Borough Council, Hammersmith & Fulham London Borough Council and Lambeth London Borough Council, ex p Stewart* [2002] EWHC 709 (Admin)). There may be more than one local authority involved with a child if the child of the family moves from one authority to another. In *R v London Borough of Barking & Dagenham, ex p Bilkisu Mohammed* [2002] EWHC 2663 (Admin), Crane J stated that as there are no formal guidelines to assist local authorities, it is vital that the needs of the children are considered primarily and that arguments about who considers and meets those needs do not hold up the provision of services to those children. These needs must be met first and redistribution of resources should take place afterwards.

A 'child in need' is defined by s17(10) CA 1989 if:

(a) he is unlikely to achieve or maintain, or have the opportunity of achieving or maintaining, a reasonable standard of health or development without the provision for him of services by a local authority;

(b) his health or development is likely to be significantly impaired, or further impaired, without the provision for him of such services; or

(c) he is disabled.

'Development' means physical, intellectual, emotional, social, or behavioural development and health means both physical and mental health (s17(11) CA 1989).

 Example

Simone is eight years old and has cerebral palsy. Simone's parents care for her very well but Simone requires a great deal of care. She requires special equipment in order for her to be bathed and adaptations for the family car are required. Simone can communicate using a special computer, which she can use with help from her school. Simone's local authority provides Simone's parents with some of the specialist equipment and a regular carer as she is a child in need.

29.3.1 **VOLUNTARY ACCOMMODATION**

Every local authority has a duty to provide accommodation under s20(1) CA 1989 for any child in need within their area who appears to them to require accommodation as a result of:

- there being no person who has parental responsibility (PR) for them;
- there being no special guardian of the child;
- his being lost or having been abandoned;
- the person who has been caring for them being prevented (whether or not permanently and for whatever reason) from providing him with suitable accommodation or care.

When a child is accommodated by the local authority, they are described as being 'looked after'. If a child is accommodated by the local authority other than through a care order (see **29.6**), the child can be removed by the person with PR at any time (except where a person has a child arrangements order (CAO) or is a special guardian). If there is more than one person with PR, then everyone with PR must agree to the accommodation of the child, or if a child is 16 or older they can consent.

Only a care order can grant the local authority PR for the child (see **29.6** and **Chapter 30** for emergency protection).

Section 20(6) CA 1989 directs the local authority, as far as is reasonably practicable and consistent with the child's welfare, to ascertain the child's wishes and feelings regarding the provision of accommodation and give due consideration (having regard to his age and understanding) to such wishes and feelings of the child as they have been able to ascertain. When a child is over 16, the CA 1989 allows the child autonomy in that she can consent to being provided with local authority care even if those with PR object or if those with PR can provide the child with accommodation (s20(4) CA 1989).

 Example

Andy cares for his children, Ben (aged two) and Molly (aged three), as their mother is in prison for drug offences. Andy uses Class A drugs regularly and the local authority has become involved with the family as they are concerned about Andy's drug use. The local authority was contacted by a concerned neighbour who had witnessed Andy's drug use. Andy is offered a place in a drug rehabilitation scheme to address his drug use. Andy agrees to the children being accommodated with the local authority on a voluntary basis whilst he is undergoing drug rehabilitation.

When a child is looked after by a local authority, s22(3) CA 1989 imposes some general duties on the local authority. The local authority has a duty to safeguard and promote the welfare of the child as well as making such use of services available for children cared for by their own parents as appears reasonable to the authority. Section 3A CA 1989 further imposes a particular duty to promote the child's educational achievement. Before a local authority can make a decision about a child, s22(4) CA 1989 requires the local authority to ascertain the wishes and feelings of:

- the child;
- the child's parents;
- any person with PR;
- any other person whose wishes and feelings the local authority believes to be relevant.

When actually making the decision, the local authority is required to give consideration to the wishes and feelings of those listed above and also to have regard to the child's religious persuasion, racial origin, and cultural and linguistic background.

29.3.2 ACCOMMODATION AND CONTACT

Under s23(1) and (2) CA 1989, when a local authority is looking after a child, it has a duty to provide him with accommodation and maintain him. The local authority must make arrangements for the child to live with a parent, a person who is not a parent but has PR, a person who had a CAO immediately before a care order was made, or a relative, friend, or person connected with him unless this would not be reasonably practicable or consistent with her welfare (s23(6) CA 1989).

When a child is being looked after by the local authority, it must, as far as practicable and consistent with a child's welfare, promote contact between the child and his parents, a person who is not a parent but has parental responsibility, and any other person connected with him.

29.3.3 REVIEWS OF CARE

When a child is being looked after or accommodated by the local authority, the local authority is under a duty to regularly review the progress of the child. This is required by the Review of Children's Cases Regulations 1991.

Section 118 Adoption and Children Act 2002 introduced the new role of an independent reviewing officer (IRO) to review the progress of children being accommodated. The IRO must review the care plan and undertake revision of it if necessary. The IRO can refer the case to CAFCASS if required and detailed provisions can be found in the Review of Children's Cases (Amendment) (England) Regulations 2004.

CAFCASS Legal can require that the case is brought to court to seek an order against the local authority requiring it to correct any failing in its care plan (see **29.4**).

29.4 LOCAL AUTHORITY INVESTIGATIONS

When the local authority becomes aware of a child potentially requiring an intervention due to the care that the child is receiving, the local authority has a duty to investigate whether the child is likely to suffer harm or is suffering harm. These investigations will be undertaken by the social services department within the local authority. **Chapter 31** has details of the investigations that a local authority should undertake.

 Practical Considerations

A common question from students concerns how a local authority becomes aware of a family requiring assistance or investigation. There are a number of ways in which a local authority can become aware:

- reports from professionals involved with the family, e.g. GP, health visitor, teacher, or probation officer;
- concerned neighbours or friends contacting the local authority anonymously or otherwise;
- the police if the parents are investigated for criminal offences;
- during court proceedings for private children matters.

This is not an exhaustive list.

29.4.1 **LOCAL AUTHORITY'S DUTY TO INVESTIGATE**

Section 47 CA 1989 places a duty on a local authority to investigate where it suspects that a child may be at risk of significant harm or is suffering significant harm. Section 47(1) CA 1989 states that where a local authority is informed that a child who lives, or is found, in their area:

- is the subject of an emergency protection order; or

- is in police protection; or

it has reasonable cause to suspect that a child who lives, or is found, in its area is suffering, or is likely to suffer, significant harm, the authority shall make, or cause to be made, such enquiries as it considers necessary to enable it to decide whether it should take any action to safeguard or promote the child's welfare. For a discussion of significant harm, see **29.2**.

Where a local authority has obtained an emergency protection order with respect to a child, it shall make, or cause to be made, such enquiries as it considers necessary to enable it to decide what action it should take to safeguard or promote the child's welfare (see **Chapter 30** for further details on emergency protection orders).

Section 47(3) CA 1989 states that the enquiries shall, in particular, be directed towards establishing whether the authority should make any application to the court, or exercise any of its other powers, with respect to the child.

 Example

Andy's children have been turning up to their nursery looking unwashed and smelly in dirty clothes and appear to be hungry, according to nursery staff. A visit from a social worker to Andy's home confirms that Andy is not looking after them properly. The local authority decides to investigate the children's home and care.

Where a local authority is undertaking investigations with respect to a particular child, the local authority shall (with a view to enabling it to determine what action, if any, to take with respect to him) take such steps as are reasonably practicable, to obtain access to him or to ensure that access to him is obtained, on its behalf, by a person authorized by it for the purpose, unless it is satisfied that it already has sufficient information with respect to him.

Where, in the course of enquiries made under this section, any officer of the local authority concerned or any person authorized by the authority to act on its behalf in connection with those enquiries is refused access to the child concerned or is denied information as to his whereabouts, the authority shall apply for either an emergency protection order, a child assessment order, a care order, or a supervision order with respect to the child unless it is satisfied that his welfare can be satisfactorily safeguarded without its doing so (s47(6) CA 1989).

The local authority may decide that it is not necessary to apply for an emergency protection order, a child assessment order, a care order, or a supervision order. If these orders are not necessary the local authority shall consider whether it would be appropriate to review the case at a later date and, if it decides that it would be, determine the date on which that review is to begin. If under s47(8) CA 1989 the local authority concludes that it should take action to safeguard or promote the child's welfare, it shall take that action (so far as it is both within its power and reasonably practicable for it to do so).

29.4.2 **CHILD ASSESSMENT ORDER**

If a local authority believes that a child is at risk but does not require emergency intervention (see **Chapter 30**) and the parents refuse to cooperate to make an assessment, then the court may make a child assessment order under s43 CA 1989.

A child assessment order allows the local authority to complete an assessment in order to decide whether or not to take any further action.

A local authority may apply for an order and the court may make the order if, but only if, it is satisfied that:

- the applicant has reasonable cause to suspect that the child is suffering, or is likely to suffer, significant harm;

- an assessment of the state of the child's health or development, or of the way in which he has been treated, is required to enable the applicant to determine whether or not the child is suffering, or is likely to suffer, significant harm; and

- it is unlikely that such an assessment will be made, or be satisfactory, in the absence of an order under this section.

For a discussion of significant harm, see **29.2**. Where the application is made, under s43(11) CA 1989 the applicant shall ensure that they take such steps as are reasonably practicable to ensure that notice of the application is given to:

- the child's parents;

- any person who is not a parent of the child but who has PR for him;

- any other person caring for the child;

- any person in whose favour a contact order is in force with respect to the child;

- any person who is allowed to have contact with the child by virtue of an order under s34; and

- the child;

before the hearing of the application. A court will not make a child assessment order if it is satisfied that there are grounds for making an emergency protection order with respect to the child and that it ought to make such an order rather than a child assessment order. Under s43(3) CA 1989 a court may treat an application as an application for an emergency protection order if the court believes that it is necessary.

If the court makes a child assessment order, the order will specify the date by which the assessment is to begin and have effect for such period, not exceeding seven days beginning with that date, as may be specified in the order. Section 43(6) CA 1989 makes it the duty of any person who is in a position to produce the child to produce him to such person as may be named in the order and to comply with such directions relating to the assessment of the child as the court thinks fit to specify in the order.

The effect of a child assessment order is to authorize any person carrying out the assessment, or any part of the assessment, to do so in accordance with the terms of the order (s43(7) CA 1989) although under s43(8) CA 1989, regardless of this, if the child is of sufficient understanding to make an informed decision he may refuse to submit to a medical or psychiatric examination or other assessment.

 Example

Andy has not allowed any of the social workers or health professionals into the house and has not taken the children to appointments arranged by the local authority. The children have stopped attending their nursery and their allocated social worker is concerned that the children's health and well-being may be suffering. The local authority applies for a child assessment order in order to ensure that Andy brings the children to the local health centre for a medical assessment.

A child may only be kept away from home when a child assessment order is in force in accordance with directions specified in the order, if it is necessary for the purposes of the assessment and for such period or periods as may be specified in the order (s43(9) CA 1989). Where the child is kept away from home the court may order directions for contact with their parents and other family members.

29.4.3 POWER OF THE COURT TO ORDER INVESTIGATIONS

Section 37 CA 1989 allows the court of its own motion to direct a local authority to investigate the circumstances of a child with a view to taking action with respect to the child in terms of making a care or supervision order or providing assistance for the child and her family.

Section 37(1) CA 1989 states that where, in any family proceedings in which a question arises with respect to the welfare of any child, it appears to the court that it may be appropriate for a care or supervision order to be made with respect to him, the court may direct the appropriate authority to undertake an investigation of the child's circumstances. The local authority concerned shall, when undertaking the investigation, consider whether they should:

- apply for a care order or for a supervision order with respect to the child;
- provide services or assistance for the child or his family; or
- take any other action with respect to the child.

Where a local authority undertakes an investigation under s37(1) CA 1989 and decides not to apply for a care order or supervision order with respect to the child concerned, it shall inform the court of its reasons for its decision and any service or assistance that it has provided, or intends to provide, for the child and his family and any other action that it has taken, or proposes to take, with respect to the child under s37(3) CA 1989. There is a requirement that this information shall be given to the court before the end of the period of eight weeks beginning with the date of the direction, unless the court otherwise directs.

29.5 INTERIM ORDERS

It is very unlikely that a court will have all the evidence that it requires to make a final order straightaway. Investigations will have to be carried out and time is needed for all parties to prepare their cases. The court can make an interim order where proceedings are adjourned on an application for a care or supervision order.

Interim orders can be granted by the court under s38 CA 1989, if the grounds in s38(2) CA 1989 are met. These are that a court shall not make an interim care order or interim supervision order under this section unless it is satisfied that there are reasonable grounds for believing that the circumstances with respect to the child are as mentioned in s31(2) CA 1989. This means that the court only has to have reasonable grounds for believing that the threshold criteria have been met. Further guidance was given in *Hampshire County Council v S* [1993] 1 FLR 559, where it was held that an interim order is no more than a holding position and an early hearing of substantive issues is essential.

An interim order will last until the disposal of the case (s38 (4) CA 1989 as amended by s14 CFA 2014). As discussed in **Chapter 31**, the court must draw up a timetable in order to ensure the early resolution of the case.

The effect of an interim order is the same as a full order. Orders for contact can be given at the time of the interim order. An exclusion order can be made under s38A CA 1989 in the same terms as discussed in **Chapter 30**.

29.6 CARE ORDERS

Orders under the CA 1989 are the only way of a child being taken into the care or supervision of a local authority. A care order allows the local authority to gain PR for the child and allows the local authority to remove the child from their parents if this is necessary.

29.6.1 **WHO CAN APPLY FOR AN ORDER?**

A local authority or 'authorised person' can apply for a care or supervision order under s31(1) CA 1989. The only authorized person under the CA 1989 to date is the NSPCC (see the **Glossary**). The court cannot order or instigate proceedings and the most a court can order is an investigation under s37(1) CA 1989 (see **29.4.3**).

The respondents to an application are found at r4.7 FPR 1991 and r7 of the Family Proceedings Court (Children Act 1989) Rules 1991 and are as follows:

- every person whom the applicant believes to have parental responsibility for the child;
- where the child is the subject of a care order, every person whom the applicant believes to have parental responsibility immediately prior to the making of the care order;
- in the case of an application to extend, vary, or discharge an order, the parties to the proceedings leading to the order that it is sought to have extended, varied, or discharged;
- the child.

Anyone can make a written request to become a party to proceedings or to cease to be a party (r4.7(2) FPR 1991). If a person with PR seeks to become a party, the court must grant the request. If the natural father of the child does not have PR, he will generally be allowed to do so unless there are justifiable reasons for not doing so (*Re B (Care Proceedings: Notification of Father without Parental Responsibility)* [1999] 2 FLR 408). For persons seeking to be parties, the court can grant permission without a hearing, or the court can fix a date for a hearing to consider the request, or the existing parties can make written representations.

29.6.2 **WHERE CAN AN ORDER BE MADE?**

Since 22 April 2014, there is a Single Family Court.

All applications made in public children proceedings will be issued by Her Majesty's Courts and Tribunal Service (HMCTS) and then placed before 'gatekeepers'. Gatekeepers will be appointed by the Designated Family Judge (DFG), who is a senior judge who provides leadership within a geographical area. The President's Guidance on Allocation and Gatekeeping for Care, Supervision and other proceedings under Part IV Children Act 1989 (Public Law) which were issued under Part 21 of the Family Court (Composition and Distribution of Business) Rules 2014 includes in the gatekeeping team, the DFG (or nominated person) and equal number of justices' clerks and district judges. The gatekeeping team will allocate the case to the most appropriate judge at the most appropriate court. The gatekeepers will consider principles including the most effective and efficient use of judicial resources, delay, the location of the parties and the child, and the complexity of the case.

29.6.3 **EFFECT OF A CARE ORDER**

Where a care order is made with respect to a child it shall be the duty of the local authority designated by the order to receive the child into its care and to keep him in its care while the order remains in force. Section 33(3) CA 1989 states that while a care order is in force with respect to a child, the local authority designated by the order shall:

- have parental responsibility for the child; and
- have the power to determine the extent to which a parent or guardian of the child may meet his parental responsibility for him.

However, under s33(4) CA 1989 the authority may not exercise its power and responsibilities attached to PR unless it is satisfied that it is necessary to do so in order to safeguard or promote the child's welfare.

Example

An interim care order is made in respect of Andy's children, Ben and Molly, as he continues to use Class A drugs and the children have been found to be hungry, dirty, and living in a house that is littered with used needles and frequented by drug users. The local authority decides that Andy is not looking after the children and has failed to deal with his drug habit. The children are taken to live with foster parents as the local authority believes this is necessary to safeguard the children's welfare.

There are some limits to the local authority's exercise of parental responsibility. Section 33(6) CA 1989 states that while a care order is in force with respect to a child, the local authority designated by the order shall not:

- cause the child to be brought up in any religious persuasion other than that in which he would have been brought up if the order had not been made; or
- have the right to consent or refuse to consent to the making of an application with respect to the child under s18 of the Adoption Act 1976;
- have the right to agree or refuse to agree to the making of an adoption order, or an order under s55 of the 1976 Act, with respect to the child; or
- appoint a guardian for the child.

Similarly under s33(7) CA 1989, while a care order is in force with respect to a child, no person may:

- cause the child to be known by a new surname; or
- remove him from the UK;

without either the written consent of every person who has PR for the child or the leave of the court. This does not, however, prevent the removal of such a child, for a period of less than one month, by the authority in whose care he is, nor does it apply to arrangements for such a child to live outside England and Wales. Under s22(4) and (5) CA 1989, the child could choose to practise a different religion if he was of sufficient age and understanding as the child is entitled to be consulted about such matters.

A care order has the effect of discharging all existing s8 CA 1989 orders.

29.6.4 CARE PLANS AND TWIN-TRACK PLANNING

Section 121 Adoption and Children Act 2002 (ACA 2002) amends the CA 1989 to introduce s31A CA 1989. Section 15 CFA 2014 has subsequently amended s31(A) to introduce a new s31(3A) CA 1989.

Where an application is made on which a care order might be made with respect to a child, the appropriate local authority must, within such time as the court may direct, prepare a plan (a s31A plan) for the future care of the child. This plan outlines what steps the local authority intends to take if a care order is made.

While the application is pending, the authority must keep any care plan prepared by it under review and, if it is of the opinion some change is required, revise the plan, or make a new plan, accordingly. This does not apply if the local authority has an interim care order.

There is guidance on the form and content of the s31A plan in 'Care Plans and Care Proceedings under the Children Act 1989' (Local Authority Circular of 12 August 1999 (LAC (99)129)) and this requires:

- reasons for the placement or course of action proposed by the local authority;
- achievable timescales leading up to specific outcomes for overall implementation.

However, s31(3A) CA 1989 now provides that the court should only consider the permanence provisions and is not required to consider the rest of the plan (subject to s34 CA 1989).

The local authority should keep parents properly involved in the planning process when care proceedings are initiated (*Re S (Minors) (Care Order: Implementation of Care Plan); Re W (Minors) (Care Order: Adequacy of Care Plan)* [2002] 1 FLR 815).

 Practical Considerations

Problems can arise when the local authority recognizes that steps should be taken in order to try to rehabilitate the family and return the child to the care of the family if possible but also recognizes that, should this fail, it will be necessary to plan for the child to be adopted. If the plans for adoption are not considered until a late stage in the proceedings, the court can face difficulties when making a care order and trying to approve a care plan. If an adoption is not planned for early in the proceedings, there will be a considerable delay in placing the child with a suitable family.

In order to plan for both rehabilitation within the family (often within quite strict timetables) or adoption without incurring delay, which may be detrimental to the child, 'twin-track' or 'parallel' planning can be employed by the local authority. Twin-track planning allows the local authority to plan for both options outlined earlier, although parents of the child should be informed as early as possible that both options are being considered. This will help to reduce delay at the end of the proceedings (see *Re D and K (Care Plan: Twin Track Planning)* [1999] 2 FLR 872).

Alternatively 'concurrent planning' allows a local authority to choose foster parents who are trained and willing to foster children with a view to working with the family and rehabilitation.

29.6.5 **PARENTAL CONTACT WITH CHILDREN IN CARE**

Section 34(1) CA 1989 states that where a child is in the care of a local authority, the authority shall (subject to the provisions of this section) allow the child reasonable contact with:

- his parents;
- any guardian of his;
- where there was a residence order in force with respect to the child immediately before the care order was made, the person in whose favour the order was made; and
- where, immediately before the care order was made, a person had care of the child by virtue of an order made in the exercise of the High Court's inherent jurisdiction with respect to children, that person.

When an application is made for contact, the court may make such order as it considers appropriate with respect to the contact that is to be allowed between the child and any named person. If a person not listed above wishes to make an application for contact, they must have permission of the court.

29.6.5.1 Refusal of contact

As well as making an order for contact between a child and another person, the court has the power under s34(4) CA 1989 to make an order authorizing the authority to refuse to allow contact between the child and any person who is named in the order.

Section 34(5) CA 1989 states that when making a care order with respect to a child, or in any family proceedings in connection with a child who is in the care of a local authority, the court may make an order under this section, even though no application for such an order has been made with respect to the child, if it considers that the order should be made. Alternatively under s34(6) CA 1989, a local authority may refuse to allow the contact that would otherwise be required by virtue of s34(1) CA 1989 under this section if it is satisfied that it is necessary to do so in order to safeguard or promote the child's welfare and the refusal is decided upon as a matter of urgency and does not last for more than seven days. The court may impose such conditions as the court considers appropriate in order to safeguard the children's welfare.

If the local authority wishes to refuse contact for more than the seven days in s34(6) CA 1989, it must obtain an order for the contact to be refused for a longer period. Section 34(4) CA 1989 allows the court a complete discretion to authorize the refusal of contact for as long as it considers it to be for the child's welfare (*West Glamorgan County Council v P (No. 1)* [1992] 2 FLR 369). This is not an order that should be made lightly. In *Re K* [2008] EWHC 540 (Fam), Munby J stated that the circumstances for granting such an order should be 'extraordinarily compelling'. He also pointed out that such an order:

> only 'authorises' the local authority to refuse to allow contact. It does not forbid such contact and a local authority, even if clothed with authority under section 34(4), is, of course, under a continuing duty to keep matters under review and to allow contact to resume as soon as it is safe and appropriate to do so.

Section 8 CFA 2014 amends the CA 1989 to clear up a small inconsistency. Section 34(6A) CA 1989 removes the requirement for a local authority to promote contact where it has been authorized to refuse to allow contact.

 Example

Andy's children are still with foster carers. The children had not seen Andy for some time and so he (through his solicitors) applies for contact. The court is concerned that Andy is not under the influence of drugs when he attends for contact and so contact remains supervised by the foster carers with the condition that contact will be refused if Andy is suspected to have taken drugs.

The court must start with the presumption that contact between parents and the child should continue. When an application is made under s34(4) CA 1989, the court must weigh up the benefits of contact against the disadvantages of disrupting the local authority's long-term plans (should these be inconsistent with continuing contact). *In Re E (A Minor) (Care Order: Contact)* [1994] 1 FLR 146 the Court of Appeal found that even when the threshold criteria under s31 CA 1989 are met, the court must consider that the long-term welfare of the child may require contact. Contact may allow a child to avoid a damaging sense of loss and provide a sense of security. Even if the child is to be adopted, contact may help to allow a child a necessary sense of family and personal identity. However, there will be cases in which the cessation of contact is necessary (e.g. *Re S (Care: Parental Contact)* [2005] 1 FLR 469).

If an order is made ending contact, it is possible to apply for a discharge of such an order, but the court stated in *Re T (Termination of Contact: Discharge of Order)* [1997] 1 FLR 517 that there must have been a change in circumstances between the making of the order and the application to discharge it.

29.6.6 REQUIREMENT OF AN ORDER BEFORE REMOVAL OF A CHILD

There must be a care order in place before a child is removed from the family, although under s20 CA 1989, a child can be removed from a family with consent. The case of *R v Nottingham City Council* [2008] EWHC 152 (Admin) received a high level of media attention. The applicant mother (M) applied for an order that she should be reunited with her newborn baby (X). M had a history of substance abuse and had self-harmed and had been in the care of the respondent local authority. As such, she was entitled to look to the local authority for continuing support at the time of the birth. Prior to M giving birth, it was recommended that the local authority should apply for an interim care order following X's birth and organize a foster placement following a case conference. The birth plan given to the hospital stated that X was to be removed from M's care at birth but made no reference to obtaining an emergency protection order or interim care order. Approximately two hours after M gave birth, X was removed from her mother and placed in a different room in the hospital. M submitted that separating her from X was unlawful as it had been done without legal authority.

The court held that local authorities and social workers had no power to remove children from their parents unless they had first obtained judicial sanction for what they were proposing to do. Only a court could make a care order. Only if a court had authorized that step, whether by making a care order or an interim care order or in some other way, could a local authority or social worker remove a child from a parent.

29.6.7 DISCHARGE OF A CARE ORDER

Under s91(12) CA 1989, a care order will remain in force until a child reaches 18 years unless it is discharged in one of the following ways:

- the court makes a residence order in respect of the child, so the care order is automatically discharged (s91(1) CA 1989);
- the court makes an adoption order (s46(2) ACA 2002);
- a successful application is made under s39 CA 1989 for a discharge of the order by a person with PR, the child, or the relevant local authority.

During an application to discharge a care order, the court can consider whether to make a supervision order (s39(4) CA 1989).

29.7 SUPERVISION ORDERS

A supervision order differs from a care order in that the local authority does not acquire PR for the child and, under s35(1) CA 1989, a supervision order allows the person supervising the child:

(a) to advise, assist, and befriend the supervised child;

(b) to take such steps as are reasonably necessary to give effect to the order; and

(c) where—

　(i) the order is not wholly complied with; or

　(ii) the supervisor considers that the order may no longer be necessary, to consider whether or not to apply to the court for its variation or discharge.

A supervision order lasts for one year but this may be extended to up to three years in total from the date it was first made following an application by the local authority (Sch 3, para 6 CA 1989). If the local authority wishes to apply for another supervision order, it will have to be proved that the threshold criteria still exist.

Further details can be found in Sch 3 to CA 1989 concerning the types of directions that the supervisor can give:

(a) to live at a place or places specified in the directions for a period or periods so specified;

(b) to present himself to a person or persons specified in the directions at a place or places and on a day or days so specified and to participate in activities specified in the directions.

A supervision order may include a requirement that he take all reasonable steps to ensure that the supervised child complies with any direction or requirement given by the supervisor and that he comply with any directions given by the supervisor requiring him to attend at a place specified in the directions for the purpose of taking part in activities so specified.

As well as undertaking particular activities, under para 4(1), Sch 3 CA 1989, a supervision order may require the supervised child to submit to:

(a) a medical or psychological examination; or

(b) any such examination from time to time as directed by the supervisor.

Should a psychological examination be required, the court must be satisfied, on the evidence of a registered medical practitioner, that the child may be suffering from a physical or mental condition that requires, and may be susceptible to, treatment and a period as a resident patient is necessary if the examination is to be carried out properly. **Table 29.1** provides a comparison of a care order and a supervision order.

29.8 **COMPARISON OF A CARE ORDER AND A SUPERVISION ORDER**

TABLE 29.1 COMPARISON OF A CARE ORDER AND A SUPERVISION ORDER

Care order	Supervision order
Threshold criteria must be met.	Threshold criteria must be met.
Local authority gains PR and makes most of the decisions concerning the child.	Parents retain PR and the local authority does not obtain it.
Section 34 CA 1989 allows the local authority to control contact in connection with the child.	The local authority cannot control contact.
Section 22 CA 1989 imposes a duty for the local authority to safeguard the welfare of the child.	The parent with PR retains the duty to safeguard the welfare of the child.
A care order allows the local authority to intervene to enforce its requirements and can remove a child from its parents.	A supervision order allows the supervisor to advise and assist the supervised child, not the parent.
A care order gives a local authority a greater ability to enforce its requirements as the local authority can remove a child if it feels the child is no longer safe.	A supervision order can require that information and access to a child is given by the carer and this can be enforced by warrant.

SUMMARY POINTS

- Where children are at risk of suffering harm or are in need, the local authority has a duty to investigate such allegations and safeguard the welfare of the children in its area.

- A child can be voluntarily accommodated by the local authority at the request of the parents or if there is no one to care for the child. Contact should be facilitated by the local authority and the child's welfare should be safeguarded.

- The local authority has a duty to investigate any child that it has reasonable cause to believe is suffering or is likely to suffer significant harm and to make enquiries into the child's health and development and whether there is a need to apply for a care or supervision order.

- A child assessment order can be used if a local authority's investigations are being obstructed by the child's parents or carers.

- A court can also direct that a local authority undertakes an investigation if the court believes that an investigation is necessary to establish whether a care or supervision order should be applied for.

- A care order has the effect of giving the local authority PR for the child with the ability to make the decisions in a child's life including whether the child shall live with their family. A local authority cannot change a child's surname or the child's religion.

- During the proceedings, a local authority may have a twin-track plan where rehabilitation is attempted with the child's family and an adoptive placement. Alternatively, concurrent planning may be appropriate where a potential adoptive family works with the child and family to attempt rehabilitation and adopts the child if the rehabilitation does not work.

- A parent can apply for contact if their child is taken into care. The court starts with a presumption that contact will continue although contact can be stopped in limited circumstances.

- A supervision order does not grant PR to a local authority. A supervision order permits a supervisor to befriend and advise the child.

- A court may only grant a care or supervision order if the 'threshold criteria' under s31(2) CA 1989 have been met. The threshold criteria examine whether a child is suffering or is likely to suffer significant harm attributable to the care from their parents or the child being beyond parental control.

- Harm relates to physical and mental harm and a child shall be compared to a child with similar characteristics.

- The burden of proof is on the applicant and the standard of proof is on the balance of probabilities.

- Interim orders are available where the court finds there is reasonable cause to believe that the threshold criteria have been met.

SELF-TEST QUESTIONS

1. Explain the standard of proof that the court must apply in care and supervision order applications.

2. The court finds that a child has suffered very serious physical harm at the hands of her parents. Which order should the court make and what is the effect of that order? In this case, the court asks whether twin-track planning is appropriate. What is twin-track planning?

3. List three differences between a care order and a supervision order.

Case Study Two

Helena has allowed her new partner to move into the house with her and Richard. Helena's new partner is a 42-year-old bailiff called Sean, whom she met through an online dating website. Everything works very well for the first month or so, although David is not very happy that Richard has a stepfather.

Helena comes into the office unexpectedly. Your supervisor takes instructions and these can be found in the case study on the Online Resource Centre. Your supervisor asks you to consider what advice to give Helena on:

(a) what investigations the local authority may undertake; and

(b) what order(s) the local authority may apply for.

The Online Resource Centre contains a full attendance note for you to compare your advice.

---

online
resource
centre

Answers to the questions above can be found on the Online Resource Centre:
www.oxfordtextbooks.co.uk/orc/sendall17/.

30.1 INTRODUCTION

This chapter will:

- discuss the use of emergency protection orders in public children law;
- examine the powers of the police to protect children.

As we have seen in **Chapter 29**, local authorities can become involved in a child's life if there appear to be serious concerns about their health, development, or safety. This is not a decision that is taken lightly and without the supervision of the court. There can be circumstances when a local authority must take urgent steps to secure a child's safety and to prevent a situation becoming very dangerous for the child. Such emergency steps are draconian measures and there are strict guidelines for emergency protection of children. This chapter will look at the orders available to the court and the factors a court will consider when being asked to make an emergency order. This chapter will also look at the powers available to the police when faced with a child in need of protection. This order is used in urgent situations. If the situation involving the child does not warrant the use of an emergency protection order, the local authority will apply for a care order in the usual way.

30.2 EMERGENCY PROTECTION ORDERS

When a child is in imminent need of protection, the order used to protect the child is an emergency protection order (EPO) under s44 Children Act 1989 (CA 1989). At the time of passing the CA 1989, the guidance given for EPO was as follows:

> the purpose of the new order, as its name suggests, is to enable the child in a *genuine emergency* to be removed from where he is or be kept where he is, if and only if this is what is necessary to provide immediate short-term protection. (Emphasis added.)

30.2.1 WHO CAN APPLY AND TO WHICH COURT?

Under s44(1) CA 1989, any person can apply, including a local authority or an authorized person such as the NSPCC or a designated police officer.

Applications are now made to the Single Family Court but the allocation of cases (see **Chapter 29**) will be considered urgently.

The application can be free-standing or made within existing proceedings or on application for a child assessment order (see **29.4.2**).

30.2.2 **GROUNDS FOR APPLICATION**

Under s44(1) CA 1989 where any person applies to the court for an order to be made under this section with respect to a child, the court may make the order if, but only if, it is satisfied that there is reasonable cause to believe that the child is likely to suffer significant harm if:

- he is not removed to accommodation provided by or on behalf of the applicant; or
- he does not remain in the place in which he is then being accommodated.

In the case of an application made by a local authority, the court may make an order if enquiries are being made with respect to the child under s47(1)(b) CA 1989 and those enquiries are being frustrated by access to the child being unreasonably refused to a person authorized to seek access and the applicant has reasonable cause to believe that access to the child is required as a matter of urgency.

In the case of an application made by an authorized person, the court may make the order if:

- the applicant has reasonable cause to suspect that a child is suffering, or is likely to suffer, significant harm;
- the applicant is making enquiries with respect to the child's welfare; and
- those enquiries are being frustrated by access to the child being unreasonably refused to a person authorized to seek access and the applicant has reasonable cause to believe that access to the child is required as a matter of urgency.

For a discussion of 'significant harm', see **Chapter 29**.

 Example

Erin is brought to the hospital by her mother, Anji. The medical staff are concerned that the explanations given for Erin's injuries are not consistent with the injuries. A check of Erin's medical records reveals that Erin has attended A&E 12 times within the past nine months for injuries that are similar to the injuries that are presented on this occasion. When the paediatrician tries to talk to Anji about the injuries, a nurse chats to Erin. Erin tells the nurse that mummy has been nasty to her and that she does not want to go home. Anji tells the paediatrician that she is taking Erin home. The paediatrician contacts the local authority as he is concerned that Erin will suffer continuing harm at home.

In *X Council v B (Emergency Protection Orders)* [2004] EWHC 2015 (Fam), Munby J undertook a review of the law and practice relating to EPOs and gave a set of key points that all courts should consider when deciding whether to make an EPO:

- An EPO, summarily removing a child from his parents, is a 'draconian' and 'extremely harsh' measure, requiring 'exceptional justification' and 'extraordinarily compelling reasons'. Such an order should not be made unless the family proceedings court (FPC) is satisfied that it is both necessary and proportionate and that no other less radical form of order will achieve the essential end of promoting the welfare of the child. Separation is only to be contemplated if immediate separation is essential to secure the child's safety: 'imminent danger' must be 'actually established'.
- Both the local authority that seeks an EPO and the FPC that makes an EPO assume a heavy burden of responsibility. It is important that both the local authority and the FPC approach every application for an EPO with an anxious awareness of the extreme gravity of the relief being sought and a scrupulous regard for the European Convention rights of both the child and the parents.
- Any order must provide for the least interventionist solution consistent with the preservation of the child's immediate safety.

- If the real purpose of the local authority's application is to enable it to have the child assessed, then consideration should be given to whether that objective cannot equally effectively, and more proportionately, be achieved by an application for, or by the making of, a child assessment order under s43 of the CA 1989.

- No EPO should be made for any longer than is absolutely necessary to protect the child. Where the EPO is made on a without notice application very careful consideration should be given to the need to ensure that the initial order is made for the shortest possible period commensurate with the preservation of the child's immediate safety.

- The evidence in support of the application for an EPO must be full, detailed, precise, and compelling. The sources of hearsay evidence must be identified. Expressions of opinion must be supported by detailed evidence and properly articulated reasoning.

- Save in wholly exceptional cases, parents must be given adequate prior notice of the date, time, and place of any application by a local authority for an EPO. They must also be given proper notice of the evidence the local authority is relying upon.

- Where the application for an EPO is made without notice the local authority must make out a compelling case for applying without first giving the parents notice. A without notice application will normally be appropriate only if the case is genuinely one of emergency or other great urgency—and even then it should normally be possible to give some kind of albeit informal notice to the parents—or if there are compelling reasons to believe that the child's welfare will be compromised if the parents are alerted in advance to what is going on.

- The evidential burden on the local authority is even heavier if the application is made ex parte. Those who seek relief ex parte are under a duty to make the fullest and most candid and frank disclosure of all the relevant circumstances known to them. This duty is not confined to the material facts: it extends to all relevant matters, whether of fact or of law.

- The FPC must 'keep a note of the substance of the oral evidence' and must also record in writing not merely its reasons but also any findings of fact. Parents against whom an EPO is made ex parte are entitled to be given, if they ask, proper information as to what happened at the hearing and to be told exactly what documents, bundles, or other evidential materials were lodged with the FPC either before or during the course of the hearing. The local authority's legal representatives should respond forthwith to any reasonable request from the parents or their legal representatives either for copies of the materials read by the FPC or for information about what took place at the hearing.

- The local authority's positive obligation under Art. 8 to take appropriate action to reunite parent and child imposes on the local authority a continuing duty to keep the case under review day by day so as to ensure that parent and child are separated for no longer than is necessary to secure the child's safety. In this, the local authority is under a duty to exercise exceptional diligence.

- Section 44(13) of the CA 1989 requires the local authority (subject to s46 CA 1989) to obey any direction given by the FPC under s44(6) to allow a child who is subject to an EPO 'reasonable contact' with his parents. Arrangements for contact must be driven by the needs of the family and not stunted by lack of resources.

In *Re X (Emergency Protection Orders)* [2006] EWHC 510 (Fam), McFarlane J added that the hearing ought to be tape recorded. Further, unless there is very good reason to the contrary, the parents should always be given a full account of the material submitted to the court, the evidence given at the hearing, the submissions made to support the application, and the judge's reasons for the decision, whether they ask for this information or not. McFarlane J also added that the key points made by Munby J in *X Council v B* earlier should be copied and made available to the justices hearing an EPO on each and every occasion such an application is made.

30.2.3 **EFFECT OF AN EPO**

While an EPO is in force, s44 CA 1989 operates as a direction to any person who is in a position to do so to comply with any request to produce the child to the applicant, authorizing:

- the removal of the child at any time to accommodation provided by or on behalf of the applicant and his being kept there; or
- the prevention of the child's removal from any hospital, or other place, in which he was being accommodated immediately before the making of the order.

It also gives the applicant PR for the child.

The effect of the EPO is to allow the applicant to bring the child to a safe place or to prevent their removal from a place, e.g. a hospital.

Under s44(5) CA 1989 where an EPO is in force with respect to a child, the applicant:

- shall only exercise the power given by virtue of sub-s (4)(b) in order to safeguard the welfare of the child;
- shall take, and shall only take, such action in meeting his parental responsibility for the child as is reasonably required to safeguard or promote the welfare of the child (having regard in particular to the duration of the order).

Where the court makes an EPO, it may give such directions (if any) as it considers appropriate under s44(6) CA 1989 with respect to:

- the contact which is, or is not, to be allowed between the child and any named person (see **30.2.5**);
- the medical or psychiatric examination or other assessment of the child. Where any direction is given under sub-s (6)(b), the child may, if he is of sufficient understanding to make an informed decision, refuse to submit to the examination or other assessment.

The ability to conduct a medical or psychiatric examination fits in with the idea that the child is at risk of harm in a genuine emergency and that it is necessary to find out the extent of the risk or harm that has occurred.

However, where an EPO is in force with respect to a child and the applicant has exercised the power to remove the child but it appears to him that it is safe for the child to be returned, or the applicant has exercised the power given to prevent a removal of a child but it appears to him that it is safe for the child to be allowed to be removed from the place in question, he shall return the child or (as the case may be) allow him to be removed under s44(10) CA 1989.

30.2.4 **EXCLUSION REQUIREMENT IN EMERGENCY PROTECTION**

The court may include an exclusion requirement in an EPO or an interim care order under s44A CA 1989 (as amended by the Family Law Act 1996).

This allows a perpetrator to be removed from the home instead of having to remove the child. The court must be satisfied that there is reasonable cause to believe that if the person is excluded from the home in which the child lives:

- the child will cease to suffer, or cease to be likely to suffer, significant harm; or
- that enquires will cease to be frustrated; and
- another person living in the home is able, and willing, to give the child the care that it would be reasonable to expect a parent to give; and
- that person consents to the exclusion requirement.

Example

A child may be at risk from a particular person living in their home and an exclusion order may be a short-term method of removing that person and allowing the child to return home. An exclusion order will allow the person to be removed if there is another carer willing to care for the child.

An exclusion requirement is one or more of the following:

- a provision requiring the relevant person to leave a dwelling house in which he is living with the child;
- a provision prohibiting the relevant person from entering a dwelling house in which the child lives;
- a provision excluding the relevant person from a defined area in which the child lives or is situated.

A power of arrest may be attached to the order under s44A(5) CA 1989. Both the exclusion order and power of arrest can be for a shorter period than the EPO, although the period of duration of the power of arrest can be varied.

Section 44B CA 1989 allows the court to accept undertakings in any case where the court has a power to make an exclusion requirement.

See **Chapter 36** for a discussion of an undertaking. An undertaking is a promise to the court to do or not to do something and in this case would be a promise not to return to a certain place. An undertaking is enforced using the court's powers of contempt of court. However, a power of arrest cannot be attached to an undertaking.

If an exclusion requirement or undertaking is made, either will be discharged by the applicant removing the child from the dwelling house from which the relevant person is excluded to other accommodation for a continuous period of more than 24 hours (ss44A(10) and 44B(3) CA 1989).

30.2.5 CONTACT WHEN AN EPO IS IN FORCE

As an EPO is a major upheaval for a child, the CA 1989 makes provision for contact. Section 44(13) CA 1989 allows that where an EPO has been made with respect to a child, the applicant shall, subject to any exclusion requirement, allow the child reasonable contact with:

- his parents;
- any person who is not a parent of his but who has PR for him;
- any person with whom he was living immediately before the making of the order;
- any person in whose favour a contact order is in force with respect to him;
- any person who is allowed to have contact with the child by virtue of an order under s34; and
- any person acting on behalf of any of those persons.

30.2.6 DURATION AND DISCHARGE OF AN EPO

Section 45(1) CA 1989 states that an EPO shall have effect for such period, not exceeding eight days, as may be specified in the order.

Where an EPO is made on an application under s46(7), the period of eight days mentioned in sub-s (1) shall begin with the first day on which the child was taken into police protection under s44(3) CA 1989. See **30.3** for a discussion of police protection of children.

An application for an EPO to be extended may be made by any person who has parental responsibility for a child as the result of an EPO and is entitled to apply for a care order with respect to the child under s44(4) CA 1989. The court may extend the period during which the order is to have effect by such period, not exceeding seven days, as it thinks fit, but may do so only if it has reasonable cause to believe that the child concerned is likely to suffer significant harm if the order is not extended (s44(5) CA 1989). An EPO may only be extended once.

If a party applies for an extension, a court hearing an application for, or with respect to, an EPO may take account of any statement contained in any report made to the court in the course of, or in connection with, the hearing, or any evidence given during the hearing which is, in the opinion of the court, relevant to the application.

Any of the following may apply to the court for an EPO to be discharged under s44(8) CA 1989:

- the child;
- a parent of his;
- any person who is not a parent of his but who has PR for him; or
- any person with whom he was living immediately before the making of the order.

However, under s44(9) CA 1989 no application for the discharge of an EPO shall be heard by the court before the expiry of the period of 72 hours beginning with the making of the order.

30.2.7 PROCEDURE FOR APPLICATION

An application for an EPO is made on a Form C110A and Supplement C11 with copies for each respondent. There is a fee of £180 payable unless the fee is remitted.

The respondents will be every person whom the applicant believes has PR (including the situation of the family prior to a care order, if one is in force). Notice of the application should additionally be given in Form C6A to a local authority if they are providing care to the child, persons caring for the child at the commencement of proceedings, and every person whom the applicant believes is a parent.

A copy of the application, together with a Form C6, is to be served on the respondents at least one day before the date of the hearing or directions appointment (Practice Direction 12C, 2.1 FPR 2010). The Form C6A is to be served on additional persons at the same time the other parties are served.

30.2.7.1 Without notice application

An application can be made by telephone and a Form C110 and Supplement C11 must be filed within 24 hours of the application.

30.3 POLICE POWERS AND VULNERABLE CHILDREN

When the police find a child in need of protection the CA 1989 places a duty on the police to safeguard the child's welfare under s46 CA 1989. The police may find that a child needs protection as their parents have been arrested and taken into custody and the child has no one to care for them. Alternatively the child may be discovered to be in need of protection during unrelated police enquiries into their parents' activities.

Section 46 CA 1989 allows a constable who has reasonable cause to believe that a child would otherwise be likely to suffer significant harm to:

- remove the child to suitable accommodation and keep him there; or
- take such steps as are reasonable to ensure that the child's removal from any hospital, or other place, in which he is then being accommodated is prevented.

A child with respect to whom a constable has exercised his powers under this section is referred to as having been taken into police protection.

According to s46(3) CA 1989, as soon as is reasonably practicable after taking a child into police protection, the constable concerned shall inform the local authority within whose area the child was found of the steps that have been, and are proposed to be, taken with respect to the child under this section and the reasons for taking them, and inform the child (if she has sufficient understanding) about the steps already taken and those to be taken, and try to discover the wishes and feelings of the child. If the child has been removed to accommodation not provided by the local authority or a refuge, the police should move the child to accommodation provided by either the local authority or a refuge.

As soon as is reasonably practicable after taking a child into police protection, under s46(4) CA 1989 the constable concerned shall take such steps as are reasonably practicable to inform the child's parents, and every person who is not a parent of his but who has PR for him, and any other person with whom the child was living of the steps that he has taken under this section with respect to the child, the reasons for taking them, and the further steps that may be taken with respect to him under this section.

On completing any inquiry by an officer under s46(3) CA 1989, the officer conducting it shall release the child from police protection unless he considers that there is still reasonable cause for believing that the child would be likely to suffer significant harm if released.

No child may be kept in police protection for more than 72 hours. Under s44(7) CA 1989, while a child is being kept in police protection, the designated officer may apply on behalf of the appropriate authority for an EPO to be made under s44 with respect to the child.

While a child is being kept in police protection, under s44(9) CA 1989, the police do not assume PR for the child, but shall do what is reasonable in all the circumstances of the case for the purpose of safeguarding or promoting the child's welfare (having regard in particular to the length of the period during which the child will be so protected). Under s44(10) CA 1989, the police shall allow contact with the child with the same persons listed in s44(13) CA 1989 (see **30.2.5**), if it is reasonable or in the child's best interests.

SUMMARY POINTS

- If a child is in need of protection from harm in a genuine emergency, the court may grant an EPO.

- The ground for granting such an order is if the child is likely to suffer significant harm if they are not removed to accommodation or prevented from being removed from the place where they are being accommodated.

- An EPO is an extremely draconian order and the courts have given strict guidelines concerning when it should be granted and the information that should be given to parents regarding the application and hearing.

- An EPO permits the applicant to remove the child from their current accommodation or prevent their removal from current accommodation. An EPO also permits the medical or psychiatric examination of the child.

- In certain circumstances an exclusion order can be made, allowing an alleged perpetrator to be removed from the child's home and prevents them from returning to the home or a defined area.

- During the course of an EPO, provision is made for contact between the child and their parents.

- The police have a duty to protect children if they believe that they will suffer significant harm.

SELF-TEST QUESTIONS

1. You work as a solicitor at Longtown City Council and you have received a telephone message from a paediatrician working at Longtown Royal Hospital concerning a child with non-accidental injuries whose mother wishes to remove the child from the hospital. The injuries are quite serious

and include a deep cut to the head and a broken arm. The paediatrician is concerned that the child is being seen on an increasingly regular basis with ever more serious injuries and the child is afraid of her mother and is showing disturbed behaviour.

(a) Do you think that the grounds for an EPO are met?

(b) If an EPO is applied for, what steps will be taken?

(c) Do you think that you should apply for an EPO without notice? Justify your decision with reference to *X Council v B (Emergency Protection Orders)*.

Case Study Two

Look at the documents on the Online Resource Centre. Richard is in hospital. Helena wishes to take him home. Does the local authority have sufficient grounds to apply for an EPO?

online resource centre

Answers to the questions above can be found on the Online Resource Centre: **www.oxfordtextbooks.co.uk/orc/sendall17/.**

31 PUBLIC CHILDREN PROCEDURE

31.1 INTRODUCTION

This chapter will:

- discuss the procedure undertaken to obtain orders in public children proceedings;
- discuss how a child's voice is heard in public children law.

As seen from the previous chapters discussing public children law, any proceedings involving children potentially being taken into the care of the local authority must be very carefully and sensitively handled. Proceedings must strike the balance between thoroughly and carefully examining all the relevant evidence and ensuring that a decision is reached without delay and which is in the child's best interests. A study in 2009 found that 70% of cases were completed in 40 weeks and 84% within 50 weeks; however, Barnardo's found that children in care cases often waited 65 weeks for a decision in their case. The issue of delay was central to the current set of reforms which have culminated in a new Public Law Outline (PLO) for proceedings as well as a 26-week limit in s14 Children and Families Act 2014.

This chapter will look at the procedural issues involved in public children law proceedings. The procedure is technical and complex and this chapter will give an overview of the procedural steps taken in public children law proceedings in order to allow a trainee new to practice to understand the procedure.

31.2 PUBLIC LAW OUTLINE

Major changes to procedure were made in 2003 when the Protocol for Judicial Case Management in Public Law Children Act Cases (the Protocol) came into operation. The Protocol distilled existing practice and promoted a new approach of active case management. The Protocol was designed to reduce delay, which was a feature of the system prior to the Protocol.

However, the Protocol did not solve all the outstanding problems present in the system. Causes of delay were identified as insufficient pre-proceedings work being done before the issue of a case, and lack of judicial case management leading to the failure to identify the major issues early in a case and also to resolve those issues early. Parents were not sufficiently involved in both pre-proceeding work and in the case itself and children may have suffered as a result.

As a result of these continuing problems, the Practice Direction: Guide to Case Management in Public Law Proceedings (2008) was revised again in 2010.

A new PLO has been issued and is incorporated into the FPR in PD 12A and is designed to bring cases to disposal within a 26-week timeframe.

The PLO applies to care and supervision proceedings and, as far as practicable, to all other public law proceedings.

31.2.1 **OVERRIDING OBJECTIVE**

As seen with proceedings for financial orders in **Chapter 14**, the PLO must have regard to FPR 1 and the overriding objective which applies to the courts and all parties in the case.

The overriding objective of the PLO is to enable the court to deal with cases justly, having regard to the welfare issues involved. Dealing with a case justly includes, so far as is practicable:

- ensuring that it is dealt with expeditiously and fairly;
- dealing with the case in ways that are proportionate to the nature, importance, and complexity of the issues;
- ensuring that the parties are on an equal footing;
- saving expense; and
- allotting to it an appropriate share of the court's resources, while taking into account the need to allot resources to other cases.

The court must seek to give effect to the overriding objective when it:

- exercises the case management powers referred to in the Practice Direction; or
- interprets any provision of the Practice Direction.

The parties are required to help the court further the overriding objective.

31.2.2 **CASE MANAGEMENT**

The court has flexible powers of case management. This might mean that the court gives directions without a hearing, takes steps in the procedure out of the ordinary order of proceedings or to cancel or repeat a hearing. This is complemented by Part 4 FPR 2010 which covers the court's general management power.

Active case management includes encouraging the parties to cooperate with each other in the conduct of the proceedings, identifying all facts and matters that are in issue at the earliest stage in the proceedings and at each hearing, deciding promptly which issues need full investigation and hearing and which do not, and considering whether the likely benefits of taking a particular step justify any delay that will result and the cost of taking it. The court should also direct discussion between advocates and Litigants in Person before the case management conference (CMC) and issues resolution hearing (IRH). There should be control of the nature and extent of the documents that are to be disclosed to the parties and presented to the court, whether and, if so, in what manner the documents disclosed are to be presented to the court, and the progress of the case. The parties should be encouraged to reach agreement in relation to the whole or part of the case. The court should not waste court time and should deal with as many aspects of the case as it can on the same occasion and give directions to ensure that the case proceeds quickly and efficiently.

The parties can assist the court in good case management. The applicant should prepare the case before proceedings are issued. In care and supervision proceedings the local authority should use the pre-proceedings checklist and the parties must use the case management documentation. The parties and their representatives should cooperate with the court in case management, including the fixing of timetables to avoid unacceptable delay, and in the crystallization and resolution of the issues on which the case turns.

The parties or their legal representatives should also monitor compliance with the court's directions and tell the court or court officer about any failure to comply with a direction of the court or any other delay in the proceedings.

31.2.2.1 Timetable

At para 5.1 PD 12A FPR 2010, the new provisions on timetables are set out. They are:

(1) The court will draw up a timetable for the proceedings with a view to disposing of the application—

    (a) without delay; and

    (b) in any event within 26 weeks beginning with the day on which the application was issued in accordance with section 32(1)(a)(ii) of the Children Act 1989.

(2) The court, when drawing up or revising a timetable under paragraph (1), will in particular have regard to—

    (a) the impact which the timetable or any revised timetable would have on the welfare of the child to whom the application relates; and

    (b) the impact which the timetable or any revised timetable would have on the duration and conduct of the proceedings.

The impact which the timetable for the proceedings, any revision or extension of that timetable would have on the welfare of the child to whom the application relates are matters to which the court is to have particular regard. The court will use the Timetable for the Child to assess the impact of these matters on the welfare of the child and to draw up and revise the timetable for the proceedings.

This is the first time that a specific timeframe has been set and is enshrined in legislation in s14 CFA 2014. Clearly, some cases involving very complex issues of evidence and law may take longer. At para 5.8 PD 12A FPR 2010, the example is given of a case which has parallel criminal and civil proceedings, which will inevitably lead to delay. The time limit of resolving the proceedings within 26 weeks applies unless a longer timetable has been set by the court in order to resolve the proceedings justly in accordance with s32(1)(a)(ii) and (5) CA 1989. Early disclosure and listing of hearings is necessary in proceedings in a linked care and criminal case.

Paragraph 6.2 PD 12A FPR 2010 deals with extensions to the timetable generally. This provides that, having regard to the circumstances of the particular case, the court may consider that it is necessary to extend the time by which the proceedings are to be resolved beyond 26 weeks to enable the court to resolve the proceedings justly (s32(5) CA 1989). When making this decision, the court is to take account of the guidance that extensions are not to be granted routinely and are to be seen as requiring specific justification (s32(7) of the CA 1989). The decision and reason(s) for extending a case should be recorded in writing (in the case management order) and orally stated in court, so that all parties are aware of the reasons for delay in the case. The case management order must contain a record of this information, as well as the impact of the court's decision on the welfare of the child. Applications for extension can be granted for up to eight weeks at a time.

Timetabling also takes into account any milestones in a child's life or in the proceedings in para 5.5 PD 12A FPR 2010 including:

(1) any formal review by the Local Authority of the case of a looked after child (within the meaning of section 22(1) of the 1989 Act);

(2) any significant educational steps, including the child taking up a place at a new school and, where applicable, any review by the Local Authority of a statement of the child's special educational needs;

(3) any health care steps, including assessment by a paediatrician or other specialist;

(4) any review of Local Authority plans for the child, including any plans for permanence through adoption, Special Guardianship or placement with parents or relatives;

(5) any change or proposed change of the child's placement;

(6) any significant change in the child's social or family circumstances; or

(7) any timetable for the determination of an issue in a case with an international element.

31.3 REPRESENTATION OF THE CHILD

The child is a party to the proceedings for a care or supervision order. Section 41(6) CA 1989 lists the proceedings in which a representative should be appointed for the child in order to safeguard their welfare. Only if the court is satisfied that it is not necessary to appoint a representative will one not be appointed. The proceedings covered by s41(6) CA 1989 include:

- an application for a care or supervision order;
- where the court has been given a discretion under s37(1) CA 1989 and has made or is considering whether to make an interim order.

Further details can be found in Part 16 FPR 2010, which now deals with the issue of representation of children in one single chapter of the FPR. A children's guardian (previously known as a 'guardian ad litem') provides the court with an independent view of the child's needs and wishes. A children's guardian (often simply referred to as a 'guardian') is an experienced social worker who has expertise in working with children and families. The children's guardian will review all of the files, visit the children, and will speak to all of the parties in order to write reports for the court, giving their views and those of the child (if of sufficient age and understanding to give a view). The children's guardian will appoint a solicitor to represent the child. The solicitor appointed by the children's guardian will present the child's case to the court with the children's guardian giving the solicitor instructions on the child's case. If the child is old enough to give independent instructions, the solicitor will present the views of the child whilst telling the court how these views differ from those of the children's guardian.

31.4 STEPS TO BE TAKEN BEFORE PROCEEDINGS

There is a pre-proceedings checklist that parties should refer to before commencing proceedings. The rule 'frontloads' proceedings so that the court has a wide range of documents with details of the investigations undertaken by the local authority.

The checklist documents
The documents to be disclosed from the local authority's files are:

- any relevant evidential and decision-making materials:
  - initial and core assessments;
  - s7 and s37 reports;
  - previous court orders;
  - relatives' and friends' materials (e.g. a genogram);
  - single, joint, or inter-agency materials (e.g. health and education/Home Office and Immigration documents);
  - records of discussions with the family;
  - key local authority minutes and records for the child (including strategy discussion record);
- pre-existing care plans (e.g. child in need plan, looked after child plan, and child protection plan);
- social work chronology;
- letters before proceedings.

Annex documents
Annex documents are the documents specified in the annex to the application form (C110A), which are to be attached and filed with the court:

- social work chronology;
- social work statement and genogram;

- care plan;
- index of checklist documents.

Practical Consideration

A core assessment is an in-depth study of the child and their family undertaken by social workers in order to understand the family better.

The applicant, which in care and supervision proceedings will ordinarily be the local authority, must apply on the Form C110A.

The documents that the court will expect to see attached to the application form for a care or supervision order are set out in the pre-proceedings checklist. The pre-proceedings checklist should be used at the earliest opportunity as a guide to what documents the court will expect to see at the start of the proceedings and should be filed with the application form. The pre-proceedings checklist will promote good case preparation.

Practical Consideration

It is recognized that in some cases the circumstances are such that the safety and welfare of the child may be jeopardized if the start of proceedings is delayed until all of the documents appropriate to the case and referred to in the pre-proceedings checklist are available. The court recognizes that the preparation may need to be varied to suit the circumstances of the case. The court is likely to make directions relating to the preparation of any missing documentation at the start of the proceedings and at the first appointment. The court also recognizes that some documents on the pre-proceedings checklist may not exist and may never exist, e.g. the s37 report, and that in urgent proceedings no letter before proceedings may have been sent.

31.5 ISSUE AND ALLOCATION

Day 1 is the date of issue of proceedings and 'day' means a business day (the interpretation rules at para 7 PD 12A).

ON DAY 1:

- the local authority files:
  - application form C110A;
  - annex documents.
- court officer issues application. The local authority should notify the court if there is a need for an urgent preliminary case management hearing (CMH) or an urgent contested hearing or interim care order (ICO) hearing when this is known or expected.

ON DAY 2 (WITHIN A DAY OF ISSUE):

- court considers jurisdiction in a case with an international element;
- court considers allocation to a specified level of judge (see **Chapter 29**), in accordance with the Allocation Rules and any President's Guidance on the distribution of business;
- local authority serves the application, annex documents, and evidential checklist documents;

- court gives standard directions on issue including:
  - pre-proceedings checklist compliance including service of any missing annex documents;
  - appointing children's guardian;
  - appointing solicitor for the child, if necessary;
  - filing and service of a case analysis by the children's guardian;
  - inviting official solicitor to act for protected persons (non-subject children and incapacitated adults);
  - considering any request for an urgent hearing;
  - listing the CMH.

The court will consider giving directions appropriate to the case and in care and supervision proceedings, relating to the preparation and filing of documents on the pre-proceedings checklist that are not yet available. The court will appoint a children's guardian in specified proceedings (in relation to care and supervision proceedings the court will expect that CAFCASS will have received notice from the local authority that proceedings were going to be started) and appoint a solicitor for the child under s41(3) CA 1989 where appropriate and request the children's guardian to prepare a case analysis and recommendations for the CMH and to make arrangements for a contested hearing, if necessary.

There will be an advocates' meeting no later than two business days before the CMH. At the advocates' meeting, the idea is to narrow the issues in the proceedings by considering the information on the application form and annex documents, the local authority case summary, and the case analysis. In the advocates' meeting, the advocates should:

- identify the parties' positions to be recited in the draft case management order;
- identify the parties' positions about jurisdiction, in particular arising out of any international element;
- if necessary, identify proposed experts and draft questions in accordance with Part 25 FPR 2010 and the Experts Practice Directions;
- identify any disclosure that in the advocates' views is necessary;
- immediately notify the court of the need for a contested ICO hearing and any issue about allocation;
- local authority advocate to file a draft case management order in prescribed form with court by 11am on the business day before the CMH.

31.6 CASE MANAGEMENT HEARING

Not before Day 12 and no later than Day 18 of the proceedings, the court will give detailed case management directions. The following box details the steps to be taken by the court.

- identifying additional parties, intervenors, and representation (including confirming that CAFCASS have allocated a children's guardian and that a litigation friend is appointed for any protected party or non-subject child);
- confirming allocation;
- drawing up a timetable for the child and the timetable for proceedings;
  - giving directions for the determination of any disputed issue about litigation capacity;
  - identifying the key issues;

- identifying the evidence necessary to enable the court to resolve the key issues;
- deciding whether there is a real issue about threshold to be resolved;
- determining any application made under Part 25 FPR 2010 and otherwise ensuring compliance with Part 25 FPR 2010 where it is necessary for expert(s) to be instructed;
- identifying any necessary disclosure and if appropriate giving directions;
- giving directions for any concurrent or proposed placement order proceedings;
- ensuring compliance with the court's directions;
- directing filing of any threshold agreement, final evidence, and care plan and responses to those documents for the issues resolution hearing (IRH);
- directing a case analysis for the IRH;
- directing an advocates' meeting for the IRH;
- listing IRH, final hearing (including early final hearing);
- giving directions for special measures and/or interpreters and intermediaries;
- issuing the case management order.

The CMH is the first hearing in the proceedings, unless an urgent hearing has been necessary. The main objectives of the CMH are to confirm allocation and to give initial case management directions.

The court will confirm the timetable for the child and make arrangements for any contested interim hearing such as an application for an interim care order. The court will confirm the allocation of the case and transfer the case, if necessary. The court will request the children's guardian and scrutinize the care plan. If necessary, the court will consider giving directions relating to those matters in the proceedings that remain to be considered and the joining of a person who would not otherwise be a respondent under the Rules as a party to the proceedings.

31.6.1 EXPERTS

An expert is a person who assists the court to understand issues through their knowledge of a particular subject.

 Example

In public children law, experts commonly called to provide reports or evidence to the court include psychologists and paediatricians. The court's permission is required to instruct an expert.

In January 2013, r25 FPR 2010 was amended to read: 'Expert evidence will be restricted to that which in the opinion of the court is *necessary* to assist the court to resolve the proceedings' (emphasis added). Section 13(6) CFA 2014 alters this provision subtly by stating that 'The court may give permission ... only if the court is of the opinion that expert evidence is necessary to resolve the proceedings justly'. The addition of the word 'justly' greatly refines the definition in a way which may be helpful to parents and helps to allay fears of justice denied in a sensitive area of law.

Section 13(8) CFA 2014 further states that social workers (or anyone who is a member of staff at the local authority bringing proceedings) or a CAFCASS officer are not to be treated as expert witnesses in proceedings under Part IV CA 1989.

In the Court of Appeal in *Re H-L (A Child)* [2013] EWCA Civ 655, the court's language and tone indicated a much more restrictive approach to permission for expert evidence.

A party who wishes to instruct an expert should comply with PD 25A FPR 2010, which incorporates and supersedes the Experts in Family Proceedings Relating to Children Practice Direction of 1 April 2008. The court should be provided with early information to decide whether an expert or expert evidence will assist the court to identify, narrow, and (where possible) to agree the issues between the parties, provide an opinion about a question that is not within the skill and experience of the court, as well as the identification of the questions that require assistance from an expert, and to encourage full and frank disclosure between the parties, court, and any expert instructed.

An expert's overriding duty is to the court, which takes precedence over any obligation to the person from whom the expert has received instructions or by whom the expert is paid.

Practice Direction 25A FPR 2010 gives full details of the process of instruction and should be consulted before instructing an expert. Where the parties are agreed on any matter relating to experts or expert evidence, the draft agreement must be submitted for the court's approval as early as possible in the proceedings.

At the advocates' meeting or discussion before the CMH, the advocates should also try to agree the questions to be put to any proposed expert (whether jointly instructed or not) if not previously agreed. Under the Practice Direction, the questions on which the proposed expert is to give an opinion are a crucial component of the expert directions that the court is required to consider.

 Practical Considerations

When preparing for the CMH, a solicitor should:

- consider all the other parties' case summaries and case analysis and recommendations;
- identify proposed experts and draft questions in accordance with the Experts Practice Direction;
- draft the case management order;
- notify the court of the need for a contested hearing;
- file the draft case management order with the case manager/case management judge by 11am one working day before the CMH.

31.7 ISSUES RESOLUTION HEARING (IRH)

The objectives of this IRH are to resolve and narrow issues and to identify key remaining issues requiring resolution by the court. The IRH is likely to be the hearing before the final hearing. Final case management directions and other preparations for the final hearing will be made at this hearing.

There should be another advocates' meeting at least seven days before the IRH and the following box shows the matters that the advocates should discuss.

- review evidence and the positions of the parties;
- identify the advocates' views of—
  - the remaining key issues and how the issues may be resolved or narrowed at the IRH including by the making of final orders;
  - the further evidence which is required to be heard to enable the key issues to be resolved or narrowed at the IRH;
  - the evidence that is relevant and the witnesses that are required at the final hearing;
  - the need for a contested hearing and/or time for oral evidence to be given at the IRH.
- local authority advocate to—
  - notify the court immediately of the outcome of the discussion at the meeting;
  - file a draft case management order with the court by 11am on the business day before the IRH.

The following box indicates the steps a court will take during the IRH.

- court identifies the key issue(s) (if any) to be determined and the extent to which those issues can be resolved or narrowed at the IRH;
- court considers whether the IRH can be used as a final hearing;
- court resolves or narrows the issues by hearing evidence;
- court identifies the evidence to be heard on the issues which remain to be resolved at the final hearing;
- court gives final case management directions including:
  - any extension of the timetable for the proceedings which is necessary;
  - filing of the threshold agreement or a statement of facts/issues remaining to be determined;
  - filing of—
    - final evidence and care plan;
    - case analysis for final hearing (if required);
    - witness templates;
    - skeleton arguments;
  - judicial reading list/reading time, including time estimate and an estimate for judgment writing time;
  - ensuring Compliance with PD 27A FPR 2014 (the Bundles Practice Direction);
  - listing the Final Hearing.
- court issues case management order.

The purpose of an IRH is to identify key issues that are not agreed, examine if those key issues can be agreed, and where those issues cannot be agreed, examine the most proportionate method of resolving those issues. The expectation is that the method of resolving the key issues that cannot be agreed will be at a hearing (ordinarily the final hearing) where there is an opportunity for the relevant oral evidence to be heard and challenged.

An advocate who has conduct of the final hearing should ordinarily attend the CMH and the IRH. Where the attendance of this advocate is not possible, then an advocate who is familiar with the issues in the proceedings should attend.

The court may give directions without a hearing, including setting a date for the final hearing or a period within which the final hearing will take place. The steps, which the court will ordinarily take at the various stages of the proceedings provided for, may be taken by the court at another stage in the proceedings if the circumstances of the case merit this approach.

31.8 **THE FINAL HEARING**

The final hearing is used to resolve any remaining issues, but will ultimately be concerned with the courts deciding whether the threshold criteria have been met and whether an order should be made. In preparation for the final hearing, all parties file and serve updated case management documents and bundles for the court's reading.

The court will hear evidence from the parents, experts, social workers, and anyone else necessary to resolve the case. These witnesses can be cross-examined. The judge will give a judgment with reasons and an order will be drafted.

FIGURE 31.1 THE STAGES OF THE PUBLIC LAW OUTLINE

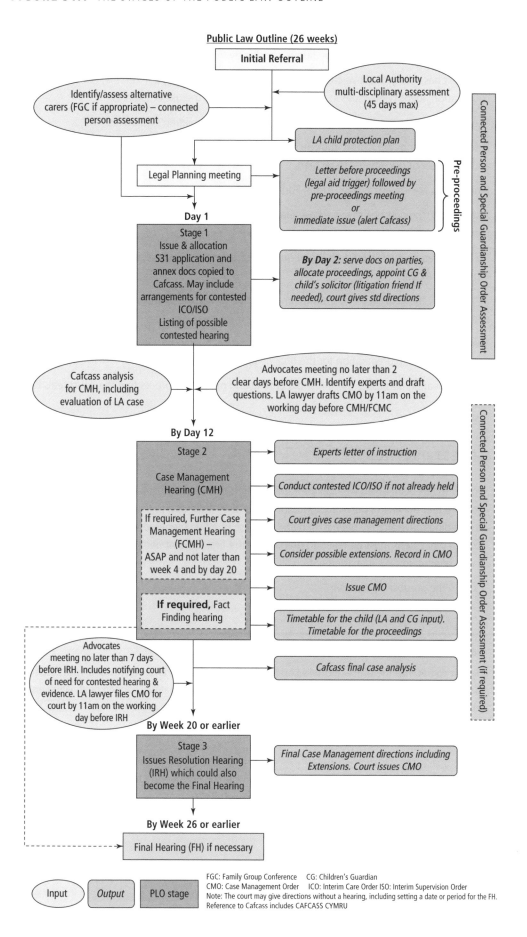

SUMMARY POINTS

- Practice Direction 12 A FPR 2010 applies to care and supervision proceedings and its overriding objective is to deal with cases expeditiously and fairly.

- The court has a duty of active case management, including setting a timetable, encouraging cooperation, identifying issues in the case, and controlling the use of experts.

- The child is a party to proceedings and is represented by a children's guardian.

- Before proceedings are issued, the courts will expect a number of investigations to be completed and a number of documents to be filed.

- Proceedings are issued on Day 1 using Forms C110A.

- At the CMH, the court gives initial case management decisions including a timetable of proceedings.

- An expert can be instructed with the permission of the court if expert opinion is required on an aspect of the case.

- At the CMH, the court will confirm the timetable, scrutinize the care plan, make any further directions, and set a date for an IRH.

- The IRH resolves and narrows issues and identifies any remaining issues between the parties, and makes directions in preparation for the final hearing.

- The final hearing addresses the threshold criteria and makes any orders that the court feels is necessary.

SELF-TEST QUESTIONS

1. Your firm has been asked by a children's guardian to act in care proceedings. The local authority believes that the child's parents cannot look after their child due to their heroin addiction. Proceedings have already been issued and the case must be prepared for the first appointment. Explain what steps must be taken to prepare for the first appointment and what duties the court has in relation to case management.

2. Explain the purpose of the CMH.

Case Study Two

Helena comes into the office and tells you that care proceedings have been issued with respect to Richard. Helena brings in a number of documents and asks you what will happen next. Write a short letter advising Helena what will happen in care proceedings.

Answers to the questions above can be found on the Online Resource Centre: **www.oxfordtextbooks.co.uk/orc/sendall17/.**

FORM 31.1 C110A: APPLICATION FOR A CARE OR SUPERVISION ORDER AND OTHER ORDERS UNDER PART 4 OF THE CHILDREN ACT 1989 OR AN EMERGENCY PROTECTION ORDER UNDER SECTION 44 OF THE CHILDREN ACT 1989

C110A

Application for a care or supervision order and other orders under Part 4 of the Children Act 1989 or an Emergency Protection Order under section 44 of the Children Act 1989

To be completed by the court	
The family court sitting at	
Case number	Date issued
Child(ren)'s name(s)	
Fee charged	

Name of applicant

Full name of respondent(s)

Nature of application

What order(s) are you applying for? *(tick all which apply)*

☐ **Care and supervision or other Part 4**

    ☐ Care

    ☐ Supervision

    ☐ Interim care order

    ☐ Interim supervision order

    ☐ Other *(please specify)*

Is the Local Authority considering adoption?

    ☐ Yes   ☐ No

    If Yes, please complete Section 7b

☐ **Emergency Protection Order**

    ☐ information on the whereabouts of the child[ren] (Section 48(1) Children Act 1989).

    ☐ authorisation for entry of premises (Section 48(3) Children Act 1989).

    ☐ authorisation to search for another child on the premises (Section 48(4) Children Act 1989).

    ☐ Other *(please specify)*

Additional information required

Is an urgent hearing required?	☐ Yes	☐ No	If Yes, complete Section 1
Is a without notice hearing required?	☐ Yes	☐ No	If Yes, complete Section 2
Are there previous or ongoing proceedings for the child(ren)?	☐ Yes	☐ No	If Yes, complete Section 3
Are there factors affecting litigation capacity?	☐ Yes	☐ No	If Yes, complete Section 4
Is this a case with an international element?	☐ Yes	☐ No	If Yes, complete Section 5

Summary of children's details

Child 1 - Full name of child	Date of birth	Order(s) applied for (including interim orders)
	D / M / Y Y Y Y	
	Is the child accommodated? ☐ Yes ☐ No	
	If Yes, from what date? D / M / Y Y Y Y	

Name of mother	Name of father	Parental Responsibility
		☐ Yes ☐ No

Child 2 - Full name of child	Date of birth	Order(s) applied for (including interim orders)
	D / M / Y Y Y Y	
	Is the child accommodated? ☐ Yes ☐ No	
	If Yes, from what date? / /	

Name of mother	Name of father	Parental Responsibility
		☐ Yes ☐ No

Child 3 - Full name of child	Date of birth	Order(s) applied for (including interim orders)
	/ /	
	Is the child accommodated? ☐ Yes ☐ No	
	If Yes, from what date? / /	

Name of mother	Name of father	Parental Responsibility
		☐ Yes ☐ No

Child 4 - Full name of child	Date of birth	Order(s) applied for (including interim orders)
	D / M / Y Y Y	
	Is the child accommodated? ☐ Yes ☐ No	
	If Yes, from what date? / /	

Name of mother	Name of father	Parental Responsibility
		☐ Yes ☐ No

2

1. Is the application for urgent consideration?

Complete this section if you have ticked the relevant box on the front of the form

Is the urgent hearing for:
(tick as required)

☐ Contested ICO

☐ EPO

☐ urgent preliminary Case Management Hearing

Part A - All applications

Set out the order(s)/directions sought

Set out the reasons for urgency

Proposed timetable

The application should be considered within [ ] hours/days

If consideration is sought within 48 hours, you must complete the section below

What efforts have been made to put each respondent on notice of the application?

3

If the application is for an Emergency Protection Order only, please complete B, C and D as appropriate

B – The grounds are

Any applicant

☐ that there is reasonable cause to believe that [this] [these] child[ren] [is] [are] likely to suffer significant harm if

or ☐ the child[ren] [is] [are] not removed to accommodation provided by or on behalf of this applicant

or ☐ the child[ren] [does] [do] not remain in the place where [the child] [they] [is] [are] currently being accommodated.

Local authority applicants

☐ that enquiries are being made about the welfare of the child[ren] under Section 47(1)(b) of Children Act 1989 **and** those enquiries are being frustrated by access to the child[ren] being unreasonably refused to someone who is authorised to seek access **and** there is reasonable cause to believe that access to the child[ren] is required as a matter of urgency.

Authorised person applicants

☐ that there is reasonable cause to suspect that the child[ren] [is] [are] suffering, or [is] [are] likely to suffer, significant harm **and** enquiries are being made with respect to the welfare of the child[ren] **and** those enquiries are being frustrated by access to the child[ren] being unreasonably refused to someone who is authorised to seek access **and** there is reasonable cause to believe that access to the child[ren] is required as a matter of urgency.

C – The additional order(s) applied for

☐ information on the whereabouts of the child[ren] (Section 48(1) Children Act 1989).

☐ authorisation for entry of premises (Section 48(3) Children Act 1989).

☐ authorisation to search for another child on the premises (Section 48(4) Children Act 1989).

D – The direction(s) sought

☐ contact with any named person (Section 44(6)(a) Children Act 1989).

☐ a medical or psychiatric examination or other assessment of the child[ren] (Section 44(6)(b) Children Act 1989).

☐ to be accompanied by a registered medical practitioner, registered nurse or registered midwife (Section 45(12) Children Act 1989).

☐ an exclusion requirement (Section 44A(1) Children Act 1989).

2. Is the application for a without notice hearing?

Complete this section if you have ticked the relevant box on the front of the form

Set out the order/directions sought

Set out the reasons for the application to be considered without notice. (This information is a requirement, a without notice hearing will **not** be directed without reason)

Do you require a without notice hearing because it is not possible to give notice including abridged or informal notice?

☐ Yes   ☐ No

If Yes, please set out reasons below

Do you require a without notice hearing because notice to a respondent will frustrate the order that is being applied for?

☐ Yes   ☐ No

If Yes, please set out reasons below

Other *(please specify)*

5

3. Previous or ongoing proceedings

Complete this section if you have ticked the relevant box on the front of this form.

Please give details (include name of child(ren), case no., date(s) of application, dates proceedings concluded, order made)

Please also provide the name of any children's guardian who has been involved in any previous or ongoing proceedings involving a child of one or both respondents

Is continuity of the children's guardian required?

☐ Yes ☐ No

If No, why not?

6

4. Factors affecting ability to participate in proceedings

Complete this section if you have ticked the relevant box on the front of this form.

Please give details of any factors affecting litigation capacity

Provide details of any referral to or assessment by the Adult Learning Disability team, and/or any adult health service, where known, together with the outcome

Are you aware of any other factors which may affect the ability of the person concerned to take part in the proceedings?

7

5. Cases with an international element

Complete this section if you have ticked the relevant box on the front of this form.

Do you have any reason to believe that any child, parent or potentially significant adult in the child's life may be habitually resident in another state?

☐ Yes   ☐ No

If Yes, please give details

Do you have any reason to believe that there may be an issue as to jurisdiction in this case (for example under Brussels 2 revised)?

☐ Yes   ☐ No

If Yes, please give details

Has a request been made or should a request be made to a Central Authority or other competent authority in a foreign state or a consular authority in England and Wales?

☐ Yes   ☐ No

If Yes, please give details

6. Grounds for the application

The grounds for the application are that the child(ren) is suffering or is likely to suffer, significant harm and the harm or likelihood of harm is because the child is:

☐ not receiving care that would be reasonably expected from a parent

☐ beyond parental control

Set out in not more than the two following pages the threshold criteria relied upon

Continued from overleaf – Set out
the threshold criteria relied upon

10

7. Plans for the child(ren)

7a. Please give a brief summary of the plans for the child(ren).

The summary must include any contact arrangements that are in place or are proposed.

What is the local authority's proposal including placement and support services and are there any requirements which the local authority wish the court to impose under Part 1 of Schedule 3 Children Act 1989?

It is not sufficient just to refer to or repeat the Care Plan.

7b. Having regard to s. 22 Adoption and Children Act 2002 is the local authority considering adoption?

☐ Yes ☐ No

Does the application for a placement order(s) accompany this application?

☐ Yes ☐ No

If not, why not and when will it be submitted?

Have you notified the relevant Central Authority or the competent authority in the foreign state in cases to which section 5 of this form applies?

☐ Yes ☐ No

11

8. Timetable for the child(ren)

The timetable for the child will be set by the court to take account of dates of the significant steps in the child's life that are likely to take place during the proceedings. Those steps include not only legal steps, but also social, care, health, education and developmental steps and any timetable for a case with an international element.

Please give any relevant dates/events in relation to the child(ren)
  • it may be necessary to give different dates for each child.

Are you aware of any significant event in the timetable, before which the case should be concluded?

☐ Yes   ☐ No

If Yes, please give a date

☐☐ / ☐☐ / ☐☐☐☐

and give your reasons

By what date should the child(ren) be placed on a permanent basis?

Name of child

☐☐ / ☐☐ / ☐☐☐☐

Name of child

☐☐ / ☐☐ / ☐☐☐☐

Name of child

☐☐ / ☐☐ / ☐☐☐☐

Name of child

☐☐ / ☐☐ / ☐☐☐☐

Please give your reasons

12

9. Attending the court

Are you aware of whether an interpreter will be required?

If an interpreter will be required, you must tell the court now so that one can be arranged.

☐ Yes   ☐ No

If Yes, please specify the language and dialect:

| |
| |

Are you aware of whether an intermediary will be required?

☐ Yes   ☐ No

If Yes, please give details

| |
| |
| |
| |

If attending the court, do any of the parties involved have a disability for which special assistance or special facilities would be required?

☐ Yes   ☐ No

If Yes, please specify what the needs are:

| |
| |
| |
| |
| |

Please state whether the court needs to make any special arrangements for the parties attending court (e.g. providing a separate waiting room or other security requirements).

| |
| |
| |
| |

Court staff may get in contact with you about the requirements

13

10. Allocation proposal

Part 1 (To be completed by the applicant Local Authority on issue)

Judicial continuity
Please give the following details of other proceedings:

Case number

Name of Judge

Date of last relevant order

Are proceedings finished or outstanding?

☐ Finished   ☐ Outstanding

Applicant's allocation proposal

☐ Lay justices

☐ District Judge level

☐ Circuit Judge level

☐ DFJ/Section 9 sitting as a Judge of the High Court

☐ High Court Judge level

Set out the applicable paragraphs of the schedule to the President's Guidance on the distribution of business

Part 2 (To be completed by the Court)

Allocation decision in accordance with the Allocation Rules and the President's Guidance on the distribution of business

☐ Lay justices

☐ District Judge level

☐ Circuit Judge level

☐ High Court Judge level

Listed for Case Management Hearing

Time [ ]   Date [ ][ ]/[ ][ ]/[ ][ ][ ][ ]

14

	Location of court	
	or	
	Name of Judge	
Allocated by	District Judge	
	Legal Adviser	
	Date	☐☐ / ☐☐ / ☐☐☐☐

11. Signature

Print full name

Your role/position held

The facts in this application are true to the best of my knowledge and belief and the opinions set out are my own.

Signed

Applicant

Date ☐☐ / ☐☐ / ☐☐☐☐

15

Details of parties – please complete this section in full

The applicant

Name of applicant
(local authority or authorised person)

Name of contact

Job title

Address

Postcode

Contact telephone number

Mobile telephone number

Fax number

Email

DX number

Solicitor's details

Solicitor's name

Address

Postcode

Telephone number

Mobile telephone number

Fax number

Email

DX number

Solicitor's Reference

16

If there are more than two respondents please continue on a separate sheet.

The respondents

Respondent 1

Respondent's full name

Date of birth [ ] / [ ] / [ ]   Gender [ ] Male [ ] Female

Place of birth
(town/county/country, if known)

Current address

Postcode [ ][ ][ ][ ] [ ][ ][ ][ ]

Telephone number

Relationship to the child(ren)

Name of child(ren)	Relationship	Parental Responsibility	
		[ ] Yes	[ ] No
		[ ] Yes	[ ] No
		[ ] Yes	[ ] No
		[ ] Yes	[ ] No

Respondent 2

Respondent's full name

Date of birth [ ] / [ ] / [ ]   Gender [ ] Male [ ] Female

Place of birth
(town/county/country, if known)

Current address

Postcode [ ][ ][ ][ ] [ ][ ][ ][ ]

Telephone number

Relationship to the child(ren)

Name of child(ren)	Relationship	Parental Responsibility	
		[ ] Yes	[ ] No
		[ ] Yes	[ ] No
		[ ] Yes	[ ] No
		[ ] Yes	[ ] No

17

The child(ren)

Please give details of the child(ren) and the order(s) you are applying for.
If there are more than four children please continue on a separate sheet.

Child 1

Child's full name

Date of birth ☐☐ / ☐☐ / ☐☐☐☐   Gender ☐ Male   ☐ Female

Name of social worker and telephone number

If the child is not accommodated, who does the child live with?

At which address does the child live?

Postcode ☐☐☐☐ ☐☐☐☐

Child 2

Child's full name

Date of birth D D / M M / Y Y Y Y   Gender ☐ Male   ☐ Female

Name of social worker and telephone number

If the child is not accommodated, who does the child live with?

At which address does the child live?

Postcode ☐☐☐☐ ☐☐☐☐

18

Child 3

Child's full name

Date of birth [ ] / [ ] / [   ]   Gender [ ] Male [ ] Female

Name of social worker and telephone number

If the child is not accommodated, who does the child live with?

At which address does the child live?

Postcode [   ] [   ]

Child 4

Child's full name

Date of birth [ ] / [ ] / [   ]   Gender [ ] Male [ ] Female

Name of social worker and telephone number

If the child is not accommodated, who does the child live with?

At which address does the child live?

Postcode [   ] [   ]

If more than four children, continue on a separate sheet.

19

Others who should be given notice

Person 1

Person's full name

Date of birth [ ] [ ] / [ ] [ ] / [ ] [ ] [ ] [ ]   Gender [ ] Male [ ] Female

Address

Postcode [ ] [ ] [ ] [ ] [ ] [ ] [ ] [ ]

Relationship to the child(ren)

Name of child	Relationship	Parental Responsibility
		[ ] Yes [ ] No
		[ ] Yes [ ] No
		[ ] Yes [ ] No
		[ ] Yes [ ] No

Relationship to the respondents

Name of respondent	Relationship

Person 2

Person's full name

Date of birth [ ] [ ] / [ ] [ ] / [ ] [ ] [ ] [ ]   Gender [ ] Male [ ] Female

Address

Postcode [ ] [ ] [ ] [ ] [ ] [ ] [ ] [ ]

Relationship to the child(ren)

Name of child	Relationship	Parental Responsibility
		[ ] Yes [ ] No
		[ ] Yes [ ] No
		[ ] Yes [ ] No
		[ ] Yes [ ] No

Relationship to the respondents

Name of respondent	Relationship

Annex Documents

This annex must be completed by the applicant with any application for a care, supervision or other Part 4 order.

The documents specified in this annex must be filed with the application if available.

If any relevant document is not filed with the application, the reason and any expected date of filing must be stated.

All documents filed with the application must be clearly marked with their title and numbered consecutively.

1. Social Work Chronology
(A succinct summary)

☐ attached   ☐ to follow

If **to follow** please give reasons why not included and the date when the document will be sent to the court.

2. Social Work Statement and genogram

☐ attached   ☐ to follow

If **to follow** please give reasons why not included and the date when the document will be sent to the court.

3. The current assessment relating to the child and/or the family and friends of the child to which the Social Work Statement refers and on which the local authority relies

☐ attached   ☐ to follow

If **to follow** please give reasons why not included and the date when the document will be sent to the court.

4. Care plan

☐ attached   ☐ to follow

If **to follow** please give reasons why not included and the date when the document will be sent to the court.

5. Index of checklist documents

☐ attached   ☐ to follow

If **to follow** please give reasons why not included and the date when the document will be sent to the court.

21

What to do once you have completed this form

Ensure that you have:

☐ attached copies of any **annex** documents.

☐ **signed** the form at Section 11.

☐ provided a **copy** of the application and attached documents for each of the respondents, and for Cafcass or CAFCASS CYMRU.

☐ given details of the additional children if there are more than four.

☐ given details of the additional respondents if there are more than two.

☐ the correct fee.

It is good practice to inform Cafcass or CAFCASS CYMRU that you are making this application. The court will expect the local authority to have informed Cafcass or CAFCASS CYMRU that proceedings are being issued.

Have you notified Cafcass - Children and Family Court Advisory and Support Service (for England)
or
CAFCASS CYMRU - Children and Family Court Advisory and Support Service Wales.

☐ Yes ☐ No

If Yes, please give the date of notification

☐☐ / ☐☐ / ☐☐☐☐

Now take or send your application with the correct fee and four copies to the court.

Please refer to the Family Proceedings Fees Order for the correct fee in respect of your application.

32.1 INTRODUCTION

This chapter will:

- discuss the role of Child Protection Conferences in public children law;
- discuss the role of the solicitor in such meetings.

As part of a local authority's investigation into a child's health and development under s47 Children Act 1989 (CA 1989), a Child Protection Conference (CPC) will be held so that information about the child can be shared by those who are involved with the child and family. CPCs are key to all agencies involved with the child by communicating and sharing information with each other. Following an inquiry into the death of Victoria Climbie (see the Online Resource Centre), Lord Laming's report identified themes that led to the child being left at risk, including poor coordination and a failure to share information. Clients frequently ask their solicitors to attend the CPC and it is a job often undertaken by trainees. This chapter is a brief introduction to the function of a CPC and the role of a solicitor.

online
resource
centre

32.2 CHILD PROTECTION CONFERENCES

There are a number of meetings which can be held with families before action starts under the CA 1989. A Family Group Conference may be held. This brings together the child's family with an independent coordinator to help them to prepare to discuss the welfare of the child with a variety of professionals involved in the child's life. Guidance from the Department of Education states that its purpose is to:

- have an independent coordinator to facilitate the involvement of the child, family network, and professionals in the family group conference process;
- allow the family private time at the family group conference to produce their plans for the child or young person; and
- agree and resource the family's plan unless it places the child at risk of significant harm.

The use of family group conferences ensures that wider family members understand at an early stage the seriousness of the situation and have the opportunity to make contingency plans for alternative care within the family if the parents do not satisfactorily resolve their problems within the child's timescale. There can also be a CPC, which brings together a wider set of participants and this will be the focus of this chapter. The purpose of a CPC has been defined by Government Guidance as:

> To bring together and analyse, in an inter-agency setting, all relevant information and plan how best to safeguard and promote the welfare of the child. It is the responsibility of the conference to make recommendations on how agencies work together to safeguard the child in future.

Conference tasks include:

- appointing a lead statutory body (either local authority children's social care or NSPCC) and a lead social worker, who should be a qualified, experienced social worker and an employee of the lead statutory body;
- identifying membership of the core group of professionals and family members who will develop and implement the child protection plan;
- establishing timescales for meetings of the core group, for production of a child protection plan, and for child protection review meetings; and
- agreeing an outline child protection plan, with clear actions and timescales, including a clear sense of how much improvement is needed, by when, so that success can be judged clearly.

32.3 **WHO ATTENDS THE CHILD PROTECTION CONFERENCE?**

The CPC encompasses the child, the parents, and all the professionals most closely involved with the child and family following s47 CA 1989 enquiries (see **Chapter 29**).

Professionals and others involved with children include:

- GPs, practice nurses, and other community-based health professionals;
- midwives;
- health visitors;
- hospital doctors and nurses;
- school or nursery teachers and the school nurse;
- youth workers or services;
- social workers;
- police;
- foster carers;
- NSPCC or other voluntary organizations;
- housing associations or council housing departments;
- drugs and alcohol counsellors.

Those attending the CPC should be able to make a significant contribution, either through their knowledge of the child and/or their professional expertise. There should be sufficient expertise if information is required in a specialist area, e.g. a medical professional who can present and explain medical evidence. The CPC should have sufficient information and expertise to make decisions, but the CPC should not be too full and intimidate the child and family members.

As well as the professionals listed earlier, the child (or their representative) and family members may attend. The child would attend if they are of a sufficient age and understanding, and the operation of the CPC will be explained to the child. If a child does not attend the CPC, the social care professional working most closely with the child should ascertain their wishes and feelings and make these known to the conference. Family members should normally be invited to attend and helped to participate. There may be times when it is not appropriate for a family member to be present.

 Example

A child may allege violence or sexual abuse on the part of their parent, step-parent, or carer. It may not be appropriate for the alleged perpetrator to be party to some of the discussions regarding the child.

32.4 **WHEN WILL A CHILD PROTECTION CONFERENCE BE HELD?**

The CPC will be held within 15 working days of the strategy discussion. The urgency of the case and the length of time that is required to gather relevant information may affect this timing. In order for a conference to reach a well-informed decision, it is essential for the conference to have an adequate assessment of the child's needs and circumstances.

The first child protection review conference should be held within three months of the initial CPC, and further reviews should be held at intervals of not more than six months for as long as the child remains the subject of a child protection plan.

This is to ensure that momentum is maintained in the process of safeguarding and promoting the welfare of the child. Where necessary, reviews should be brought forward to address changes in the child's circumstances. Attendees should include those most involved with the child and family in the same way as at an initial CPC.

 Practical Considerations

A parent or carer of a child may be shocked at the involvement of social services or, equally, they could be hostile, distressed, or uncooperative. If you are attending a CPC with a client, you must ensure that they understand what will happen at the CPC, how much they will be allowed to say, and the decisions that will be made. It is also important for the client to understand the effect that an angry outburst or inappropriate behaviour will have on their case.

32.5 **PURPOSE OF A CHILD PROTECTION CONFERENCE**

A meeting may be held in order to:

- review the safety, health, and development of the child against planned outcomes set out in the child protection plan;
- ensure that the child continues to be safeguarded from harm; and
- consider whether the child protection plan should continue in place or should be changed.

The reviewing of the child's progress and the effectiveness of interventions are critical to achieving the best possible outcomes for the child. The child's wishes and feelings should be sought and taken into account during the reviewing process.

32.6 **ROLE OF A LEGAL ADVISER AT A CHILD PROTECTION CONFERENCE**

The Law Society's Family Law Committee issued guidance for solicitors attending CPCs and a link to this can be found on the Online Resource Centre. More recent guidance can be

 online resource centre

found from the Department of Education, which adopts the Family Rights Group's stated aims for legal advisors. A legal adviser should help their client to:

- understand their rights and options and how child protection planning and decision-making works;

- reflect on why social workers are worried about their child;

- make safe plans for their child (which may include alternative care within the family) within the child's timescale; and

- have their voice heard by professionals.

The CA 1989 places strong emphasis on the need for all to work in partnership in all stages of planning and decision making affecting children. Solicitors are involved in the decision-making process, either working for local authorities, representing the parents or the child, or other parties. The chair of the CPC should clarify the role of the solicitor within the conference, and local practice may vary.

Representatives of the parents should not make legal representations, but should assist their client to express their views. Ideally, permission should be sought from the chair to speak. Anyone attending meetings with a parent should be knowledgeable in child protection law and procedures and fully informed of the circumstances of the case. Parents should be encouraged to attend and advised on what may happen during the CPC. Consideration should be given to advising the parents on what information they give to the CPC, especially if court proceedings may follow with the cross-examination of the client.

The Law Society has also issued a practice note for solicitors representing the local authority should they also attend a meeting. As public funding is restricted, many parents may attend pre-action meetings without a solicitor. The guidance covers the application of Outcome 11.01 and Indicative Behaviour 11.4 in the Solicitors Regulation Authority Code of Conduct 2011. A local authority solicitor attending a pre-action meeting may risk breaching the rules if they were to listen to the discussion at a meeting in which parents are participating but are not legally represented and then were to use the knowledge of that discussion to advantage in the cross-examination of a parent in any subsequent court proceedings. The practice note states that:

> A local authority solicitor attending a local authority Children Act meeting may fall foul of these regulatory provisions if they were to listen to the discussion at a meeting in which parents are participating but are not legally represented and then were to use the knowledge of that discussion to advantage in the cross-examination of a parent in any subsequent court proceedings.

online
resource
centre

The practice note can be found in the Online Resource Centre.

32.7 CONFIDENTIALITY AND THE CHILD PROTECTION CONFERENCE

Parents can be excluded from the CPC if this is considered necessary and a point may arise about the confidentiality of information given in the absence of parents and their advisers. In *Re X (Emergency Protection Orders)* [2006] EWHC 510 (Fam), the court gave some guidance on confidential information and held that, in line with the guidance, and in accordance with fairness, good practice, and, if proceedings take place, the need for the court to have an accurate record of what is said in all parts of a CPC, the following are basic requirements:

- if the circumstances are sufficient to justify the exclusion of the parents from part of a CPC (such circumstances are described in the paragraphs of the guidance referred to above), or the parents are otherwise absent, a full minute should nevertheless be taken of everything that is said during the CPC;

- if it is considered necessary to treat part of what is minuted as confidential from the parents, that part of the minutes should be disclosed for approval to the professionals who attended the conference, but that part of the draft/approved minutes should be maintained separately from the body of the minutes that are sent to the parents;

- the non-confidential section of the minutes should expressly record at the appropriate stage that confidential information was disclosed or discussed;

- the need for continued confidentiality with respect to confidential sections of the minutes should be kept under review by the conference chair, with confidentiality only being maintained if it continues to be necessary.

SUMMARY POINTS

- Child Protection Conferences (CPCs) are a meeting of professionals and agencies involved with the child and family and are an opportunity for information to be shared.

- Decisions about the child and future plans to safeguard the child's welfare will be made at the CPC.

- Parents can attend the CPC and often take their legal representatives to the CPC.

- The role of the legal adviser at the CPC varies according to local practice, but the legal adviser should assist their client in taking their part in the CPC.

- Whether or not the legal representative can speak or raise points on behalf of their client depends upon the discretion of the chair of the CPC.

- If a client is excluded from part of the CPC, any confidential minutes should be kept separately from the non-confidential minutes and the need for confidentiality should be kept under review.

SELF-TEST QUESTIONS

1. Your client has been asked to come to a CPC regarding their child. Explain the purpose of a CPC, who will be there, and when it will be held.

2. Your client wishes you to question members of the CPC. Is this your role?

online
resource
centre
Answers to the questions above can be found on the Online Resource Centre:
www.oxfordtextbooks.co.uk/orc/sendall17/.

Part 6

DOMESTIC ABUSE

33 PROTECTION UNDER THE FAMILY LAW ACT 1996: NON-MOLESTATION ORDERS

33.1 INTRODUCTION

This chapter will:

- discuss the law regarding domestic abuse;
- consider practical issues arising from acting for clients facing domestic abuse;
- consider the availability of remedies under the Family Law Act 1996;
- consider funding for orders under the Family Law Act 1996;
- consider the concept of 'associated persons';
- consider non-molestation orders under the Family Law Act 1996;
- consider remedies for clients escaping a forced marriage.

Clients seeking advice because of domestic violence will form a part of all family lawyers' caseloads. Most commonly referred to as domestic *violence,* the Law Society's Family Law Protocol chooses the term domestic *abuse*, as it covers a wider set of behaviour than domestic violence suggests. This text will use the term domestic violence, as it is most commonly used in practice.

There are many definitions of domestic violence. In 2013 the Home Office published its definition to be used across government and the public sector:

Any incident of or pattern of incidents of controlling, coercive or threatening behaviour, violence or abuse between those aged 16 or over who are or have been intimate partners or family members regardless of gender or sexuality. This can encompass, but is not limited to, the following types of abuse:

- psychological
- physical
- sexual
- financial
- emotional.

Controlling behaviour is: a range of acts designed to make a person subordinate and/or dependent by isolating them from sources of support, exploiting their resources and capacities for personal gain, depriving them of the means needed for independence, resistance and escape and regulating their everyday behaviour.

Coercive behaviour is: an act or pattern of acts of assault, threats, humiliation and intimidation or other abuse that is used to harm, punish or frighten the victim.

 Practical Considerations

Domestic violence can include but is not limited to:

- physical abuse (pushing, slapping, punching, or intimidation);
- sexual abuse (including female genital mutilation);
- psychological abuse (harassment, pestering, shouting) and controlling behaviour (financial control and social isolation);
- forced marriage;
- causing a child to witness abuse.

Domestic violence may be a series of acts forming a pattern of behaviour or a single act.

Clients need clear advice on protection available from the courts but will also require practical advice too. Clients will need advice on:

- housing;
- welfare benefits;
- help from the police and social services;
- debt and financial problems;
- immigration status;
- support services, e.g. local refuges.

While many incidents of domestic violence are criminal acts, the following chapters cover the orders available under Part IV of the Family Law Act 1996 (FLA 1996). Part IV of the FLA 1996 came into force on 1 October 1997, with the exception of s60. The orders available are non-molestation orders and occupation orders. This chapter (see **33.5**) and **Chapter 34** will explore the essential characteristics of each order as well as considering if the parties are associated persons. Choosing the correct occupation order is essential and this will be explored in depth later in this chapter. Whether to apply with or without notice will be considered in **Chapter 35**, as will court procedure and the enforcement of orders, which is essential to ensuring that the client is protected. The Domestic Violence, Crime and Victims Act 2004 (DVCVA 2004) made important changes to the FLA 1996 and will be considered fully.

33.2 **PRACTICAL ISSUES**

 online resource centre

The suggested reading on the Online Resource Centre will assist you to understand the main issues regarding domestic violence. Your clients may not fall into the expected categories and you must be careful not to fall into stereotyping.

 Practical Considerations

The clients seen by solicitors seeking advice about domestic violence tend to be women in a heterosexual relationship, although this is not always the case.

Many other categories of people suffer domestic violence including:

- gay men and women;
- men;
- parents, suffering violence from adult children;

- adult children being forced into marriage;
- separated or divorced spouses;
- parents of the same child.

Not all clients seeking protection from domestic violence will take court proceedings. There are many reasons for this: some clients do not wish to involve others in what they regard as a private matter, some clients are too afraid to bring court proceedings, and some clients return many times to see their solicitor before having the courage to leave the abuser. The interplay between the civil and criminal law is discussed at **33.8**.

Practitioners should be aware of all agencies and organizations in their area working in domestic violence. There may be refuges (see the **Glossary**) that provide a secure place for those fleeing domestic violence, but they can be overcrowded as budget cuts have hit such services very hard. There will often be a domestic violence forum in your local area. This is an umbrella body for agencies working with those affected by domestic violence including local authority social services departments, education, police, voluntary agencies, and local courts. These forums are a useful source of contacts and solicitors are frequently involved with them. Some clients may also require specialist advice, e.g. regarding immigration or housing in cases of homelessness, and so you should be aware of where a client can seek advice.

Clearly, clients seeking advice on domestic violence issues may also require advice on many other aspects of family law. For example, failure to protect a child from domestic violence or witnessing domestic violence may amount to significant harm and involvement by the local authority social services department.

 Practical Considerations

A client seeks advice on domestic violence. What other family law issues could flow from this? What other legal issues could arise?

- a client may seek a divorce or dissolution of civil partnership;
- a client may require assistance with a child arrangements order if there has been a separation;
- social services may be investigating the welfare of the child under s47 CA 1989 to see if the child has suffered significant harm;
- the client may need assistance with housing or immigration issues.

In domestic abuse proceedings, the party applying for the order is an applicant and the person against whom the order is sought is the respondent.

33.3 **FUNDING**

The funding types appropriate for domestic violence cases are legal help for initial advice and then legal representation for the court hearing. A certificate may be restricted to a certain limit of costs or a step in proceedings (e.g. directions for trial). Although public funding was cut severely in April 2013, this area of work will continue to be within the scope of funding. The evidence required to apply for funding for other areas of work includes a protective injunction, and so an application for an order under the FLA 1996 may be a step taken by those trying to obtain public funding. In **Chapter 2**, the domestic violence gateway is discussed and this will be relevant to clients facing domestic abuse. However, there is some evidence that many clients find it very difficult to access the evidence required and so many will be unable to access public funding. The Online Resource Centre has more details.

online
resource
centre

The statutory charge may also apply. Mediation is a requirement of applying for legal representation but an exemption may apply because of the domestic violence alleged by the client.

The Legal Advice Agency requires that consideration is given to sending a warning letter to the alleged perpetrator and/or reporting the matter to police before applying for public funding. As discussed earlier, there are reasons why the police are not called. A warning letter must also be very carefully considered and it is very important that a client's safety is not put at risk by the sending of a warning letter. Warning letters can be successful in some cases.

33.4 **THE FAMILY LAW ACT 1996**

Part IV of the FLA 1996 provides remedies for domestic violence. Prior to the FLA 1996, there was a patchwork of statutes offering protection to a limited category of people. The FLA 1996 has brought a much wider range of applicants into the courts and offers a coherent set of orders.

33.4.1 **JURISDICTION**

The FLA 1996 unifies the jurisdiction between the High Court, county courts, and family proceedings courts for all orders; in practice, most applications are commenced in the county court. Since 22 April 2014, there is now a Single Family Court and a discussion about this can be found in **Chapter 4**. This will be considered in further detail in **Chapter 36**.

33.4.2 **WHO CAN APPLY?**

Before the FLA 1996, only a limited number of people could apply to the court for protection. The FLA 1996 introduced the concept of associated persons, defined in s62. It is a long list that encompasses most family situations that a practitioner will encounter. It is essential that the status of the parties as associated persons is established as a first step when considering whether to apply for an order.

Persons are 'associated' under ss62–63 FLA 1996 if:

(a)   they are or have been married to each other;

(aa) they are or have been civil partners;

(b)   they are cohabitants or former cohabitants;

(c)   they live in the same household other than by reason of one of them being the other's employee, tenant, lodger or boarder;

(d)   they are relatives;

(e)   they have agreed to marry one another (whether or not that agreement has been terminated);

(eza) they have entered into a civil partnership agreement (as defined by section 73 of the Civil Partnership Act 2004) (whether or not that agreement has been terminated);

(ea) they have or have had an intimate personal relationship with each other which is or was of significant duration;

(f)   in relation to a child, they are a parent of that child or have or had parental responsibility for the child;

(g)   they are parties to the same family proceedings.

Some categories require greater scrutiny.

33.4.2.1 Cohabitants
Section 62(1)(a) FLA 1996 defines cohabitants as two persons who are neither married to each other nor civil partners of each other but are living together as man and wife or, if of the same sex, an equivalent relationship. *G v F (Non-Molestation Order; Jurisdiction)* [2000]

2 FCR 638 stated that the concept of cohabitation should be generously interpreted in order not to exclude borderline cases.

33.4.2.2 Relative

Relatives are defined by s63 FLA 1996 to include the following:

- father; mother; stepfather; stepmother; son; daughter; stepson; stepdaughter; grandmother; grandfather; grandson; granddaughter of a person, or of that person's spouse or former spouse or civil partner or former civil partner; or

- brother; sister; uncle; aunt; niece; nephew; first cousin (whether of the first blood or of the half blood or by affinity) of a person, or of that person's spouse or former spouse, civil partner or former civil partner.

The above applies also to people who are cohabiting or were cohabiting and will include same-sex couples. Clearly, the definition of a relative is extremely wide.

 Example

Vera asks for advice. She is a 55-year-old woman living in a two-bedroom house in your local area. She is married to Eric and works in a local hospital as a medical secretary. Eric works as a caretaker in a local sports centre. She is not eligible for community legal service (CLS) funding.

Vera has been suffering intimidation and physical assault by Jimmy. Jimmy lives with Vera and Eric as he is a drug addict and his own mother finds him difficult to cope with. Jimmy is 22 and unemployed. He does not have a criminal record but Vera suspects that he is involved in petty crime. Jimmy regularly steals from Vera and becomes enraged when Vera refuses to give him money. Jimmy is Eric's sister's son.

Vera and Jimmy will be associated persons as they are relatives as Jimmy is a nephew of Eric who in turn is Vera's spouse.

Vera would be able to apply for orders under the FLA 1996.

33.4.2.3 Relevant child

Section 62(2) FLA 1996 defines a relevant child as:

- any child who is living with either party to the proceedings;
- any child who might reasonably be expected to live with either party to the proceedings;
- any child in relation to whom an order under the Adoption Act 1967 or Adoption and Children Act 2002 is in question in the proceedings;
- any child in relation to whom an order under the Children Act 1989 is in question in the proceedings;
- any other child whose interests the court considers relevant.

This is a wide-ranging definition that will cover children relevant to most families.

33.4.2.4 Agreement to marry/enter a civil partnership

This is the only category of associated persons where a time limit applies. Section 44 FLA 1996 defines an agreement to marry as one that is evidenced in writing or by a gift of a ring in contemplation of marriage/civil partnership or by a ceremony entered into by the parties in the presence of one or more witnesses assembled for the purposes of marriage/civil partnership. The agreement itself need not be in writing but there should be some form of written evidence, e.g. a press announcement or wedding/party invitations.

33.4.2.5 Intimate personal relationships

This category was added by the DVCVA 2004 and came into force on 1 July 2007. It addresses a category of people who have 'dated' for a period of time but have not lived together. Before this amendment, people in this category had to use the Protection from Harassment Act 1997 (see **Chapter 37**) as they were not associated persons. The terms 'intimate personal relationship' and 'significant duration' are untested by the higher courts but are generally unproblematic in practice.

33.4.2.6 Body corporate

Corporate bodies are exempt. The most practical application of this rule would be a local authority which acquires parental responsibility for a child when a care order is granted.

33.4.3 FAMILY PROCEEDINGS

These are defined in s63 FLA 1996 as any proceedings under:

(a) the inherent jurisdiction of the High Court in relation to children;

(b) Part IV and 4A of the FLA 1996;

(c) the Matrimonial Causes Act 1973;

(d) the Adoption Act 1976;

(e) the Domestic Proceedings and Magistrates' Courts Act 1978;

(f) Part III of the Matrimonial and Proceedings Act 1984;

(g) Parts I, II, and III of the Children Act 1989;

(h) s30 of the Human Fertilisation and Embryology Act 1990;

(i) the Adoption and Children Act 2002;

(j) Schs 5–7 Civil Partnership Act 2004.

33.5 NON-MOLESTATION ORDER

The applicant and respondent must be associated persons or the child to be protected a relevant child.

Non-molestation order means an order containing either or both of the following provisions:

(a) a provision prohibiting the respondent from molesting another person who is associated with the respondent;

(b) a provision prohibiting the respondent from molesting a relevant child (s42(1)).

33.5.1 MOLESTATION

'Molestation' is not defined in the Act and so case-law has produced guidelines. Molestation embraces a wide range of behaviour, from violence and threats of violence to nuisance phone calls. The courts describe a situation where someone is at least pestering another (*Vaughan v Vaughan* [1973] 3 All ER 449). There must be a degree of harassment involved sufficient to justify intervention by the court (*Horner v Horner* (1982) Fam 90). Subject to the former, the behaviour covered is as wide as the ability of people to annoy, pester, and molest each other.

C v C (Non-Molestation Order: Jurisdiction) [1998] 1 FLR 554 indicates clearly that a non-molestation order should be made only if there was some deliberate conduct by the respondent that harassed the applicant and this affected the applicant to the extent that the intervention of the court was required. Non-molestation orders were not appropriate in a dispute about family property, which should be resolved by the civil courts; or in a case where the privacy of an applicant was at risk from publication of details of a marriage between the applicant and his former wife.

33.5.2 TEST FOR A NON-MOLESTATION ORDER

Section 42(5) FLA 1996 sets out the test for a non-molestation order:

In deciding whether to exercise its powers under this section and, if so, in what manner, the court shall have regard to all the circumstances including the need to secure the health, safety and well-being—

(a) of the applicant or, in a case falling within subsection (2)(b), the person for whose benefit the order would be made; and

(b) of any relevant child.

'Health' as defined in s63 FLA 1996 includes both physical and mental health. This clearly encompasses a greater scope of behaviour than violence. As stated earlier, there is no definition of molestation and courts are guided by decided case-law and common sense. There is a very wide range of behaviour that this will cover and one should be careful of thinking too narrowly:

- pestering at home or place of work;
- persistent and/or abusive text messages or telephone calls;
- shouting or verbal abuse during contact visits;
- threatening language or physical intimidation;
- damaging property in the home, e.g. punching walls or doors;
- violence including pushing, shoving, slapping, punching, or kicking;

will all be covered by s42(5) FLA 1996.

In *Davies v Johnson* [1979] AC 264 Viscount Dilhorne stated:

Violence is a form of molestation, but molestation may take many forms without a threat or use of violence and still be serious and inimical to mental or physical health.

 Example

Vera is distressed and wants advice on protection from Jimmy.

Vera tells you that Jimmy sends her abusive texts, up to 50 a day, asking for money. These texts contain foul language and threats of violence. Almost every evening, he returns to the house clearly under the influence of drink or drugs and shouts abusive comments at Vera and Eric until they seek refuge in their bedroom. Vera says that she has asked Jimmy to leave, but he says that if she makes him leave or calls the police, he will send his friends to the house 'to sort Eric out'.

Last night Eric was out. After an argument, Jimmy held Vera by the throat until she agreed to give him money. Vera suffered bruising to her throat and is now fearful of being in the house on her own. She cannot stop crying during the client interview. You advise her that a non-molestation order would offer her protection from further molestation from Jimmy.

Would she be successful? Applying s42(5) FLA 1996 to her situation, Vera would probably be successful as she has suffered physical injury and her health (both physical and mental), safety, and well-being are at risk from Jimmy's behaviour.

33.5.3 EVIDENCE

In order to support an application for a non-molestation order, evidence must be produced to the court. This will be discussed further when considering procedure in **Chapter 36**.

33.5.4 APPLICATIONS BY CHILDREN

Children under 16, if of sufficient understanding, can apply for a non-molestation order with leave: s43(1) FLA 1996. The application is made to the court with a litigation friend and is highly unusual in practice.

33.6 **DURATION OF ORDER**

The order may be for a specified period or until further order (which gives the court a great deal of flexibility). This was confirmed by the Court of Appeal in *Re B-J (A Child) (Non-molestation Order: Power of Arrest)* (2000) 1 FLR 107.

33.7 **FORCED MARRIAGE**

The Forced Marriage (Civil Protection) Act 2007 amends the FLA 1996 to introduce a new order, the forced marriage protection order under s63A FLA 1996.

This order protects:

- a person from being forced into a marriage or from any attempt to be forced into a marriage; or
- a person who has been forced into a marriage.

In deciding whether to grant an order, the court must have regard to all the circumstances, including the need to secure the health, safety, and well-being of the person to be protected. In ascertaining that person's well-being, the court must, in particular, have such regard to the person's wishes and feelings (so far as they are reasonably ascertainable) as the court considers appropriate in the light of the person's age and understanding. It is not uncommon for those being forced into marriage to be teenagers or young adults and for others to take proceedings on their behalf. 'Force' includes coercion by threats or other psychological means.

Under s63B FLA 1996, the terms of any order may, in particular, relate to conduct outside England and Wales as well as (or instead of) conduct within England and Wales. The Online Resource Centre contains details of an order made concerning behaviour abroad. The forced marriage protection order can be made against respondents who force or attempt to force, or may force or attempt to force, a person to enter into a marriage and other persons who are, or may become, involved in other respects as well as respondents of any kind. This encompasses a wide variety of people, some of whom may not be family members. The FLA 1996 has recently been amended to include a new provision making the breach of a forced marriage protection order a criminal offence. Section 63CA FLA 1996 provides that a person must know about the order to be convicted. Section 121 of the Anti-social Behaviour, Crime and Policing Act 2014 provides that:

(1) A person commits an offence under the law of England and Wales if he or she—

    (a) uses violence, threats or any other form of coercion for the purpose of causing another person to enter into a marriage, and

    (b) believes, or ought reasonably to believe, that the conduct may cause the other person to enter into the marriage without free and full consent.

Further details of the criminal law offence may be found in a specialist criminal law text. The Online Resource Centre contains more information concerning forced marriage.

33.8 **CRIMINAL LAW REMEDIES**

The criminal law provides a remedy for those who have suffered physical assault, coercive control (see s76 Serious Crime Act 2015), or harassment (see the Protection from Harassment Act 1997). The DVCVA 2004 makes the offence of common assault an arrestable one and so the police can remove an abuser from the scene of a potential crime more easily than in the past. Police forces have specialist domestic violence teams that deal specifically with this work and officers are highly experienced. Some clients will have involved the police but some will not due to fear of what the abusive person will do should the police become involved.

If a person is charged with an offence, bail conditions may be imposed that prevent an offender from contacting or visiting the victim of crime. Bail conditions can be problematic as the victim of crime is rarely at court and is often unaware of a change in bail conditions. These bail conditions end either at conviction or if the criminal charge is dropped, even though the domestic violence may continue. Criminal charges may be dropped as the victim of crime is too afraid to give evidence or does not wish to criminalize the perpetrator; however, the CPS can continue the case against the wishes of the victim of crime.

A Domestic Violence Protection Notice (DVPN) can be issued by police if the police reasonably believe that a person has used or threatened violence and the victim needs protection. A DVPN places certain conditions on the person which may include stopping him/her from entering, and being within a certain distance of the victim's home, stopping him/her from making them leave or excluding them from their home or requiring him/her to leave the home. If the person subject to the DVPN does not comply with it, the police can apply to a magistrates' court for a Domestic Violence Protection Order (DVPO) in much the same terms as a DVPN. If a DVPO is breached, the magistrates can fine or imprison the offender. The legislation is found in the Crime and Security Act 2010.

The Serious Crime Act 2015 creates an offence of controlling or coercive behaviour in intimate or familial relationships with a maximum sentence of five years, a fine, or both. The Online Resource Centre contains the statutory guidance for this new offence, which is very useful. online resource centre

SUMMARY POINTS

- Domestic abuse describes a wide variety of behaviour including threats, violence, harassment, coercive control, and sexual and psychological abuse.

- Clients frequently come for advice on domestic abuse and require advice on the law as well as practical matters.

- There are two main orders under the FLA 1996. These are non-molestation orders and occupation orders.

- The DVCVA 2004 has introduced amendments to the FLA 1996.

- Non-molestation orders offer protection from many forms of behaviour constituting domestic violence.

- To apply for an order, an applicant must be an associated person, as defined in ss62–63 of the FLA 1996.

- The definition of associated person is wide-ranging and encompasses a huge variety of possible relationships.

- There is no definition of 'molestation' in the FLA 1996 and the test for a non-molestation order considers the 'health, safety and well-being' of an applicant under s42(5) of the Act.

- A forced marriage protection order can assist those being forced into marriage or those trying to escape a forced marriage.

- Practitioners should also be aware that the criminal law is increasingly involved in the prevention of domestic abuse as well as the prosecution of offences.

SELF-TEST QUESTIONS

1. Alice and Julie are a same-sex couple who are not in a civil partnership. They have been going out for a year, regularly spend the night at each other's houses, but do not cohabit. Alice has become abusive to Julie. Will Julie be able to apply for a non-molestation order?

2. Your client was engaged to an alleged abuser two years ago. Can she apply for a non-molestation order? What evidence could you produce to the court?

3. Fela is applying for parental responsibility for his child and has suffered constant threats from the child's mother. Is he an associated person?

4. Explain the test that a court must consider when deciding whether to grant a non-molestation order.

Case Study Two

Helena comes into the office at the same time as the care proceedings are ongoing concerning Richard. She tells you that Sean, her new partner, has been violent towards her and Richard. Your supervisor takes instructions and asks you to write a letter to advise Helena. Compare your letter to the case study on the Online Resource Centre.

---

online
resource
centre

Answers to the questions above can be found on the Online Resource Centre:
www.oxfordtextbooks.co.uk/orc/sendall17/.

34.1 INTRODUCTION

This chapter will:

- examine the availability of occupation orders under the Family Law Act 1996;
- consider any ancillary orders under the Family Law Act 1996 when applying for occupation orders.

As we have seen in **Chapter 33**, the Family Law Act 1996 (FLA 1996) offers orders to protect those suffering domestic abuse. A non-molestation order offers protection against pestering, harassment, and molestation, but does not deal with the issue of people who share a home and the exclusion of one party from the home. In addition to non-molestation orders, the FLA 1996 also allows a court to make occupation orders to regulate the occupation of the family home. These orders are extremely serious as they can exclude someone from the home in which they are entitled to live. For this reason, the FLA 1996 has strict tests for the different orders available. This chapter will discuss the effect of occupation orders, the tests for each order, and which order to choose for the client.

34.2 THE EFFECT OF AN OCCUPATION ORDER

Although the level of protection offered varies according to the order made by the court, the general aim of an occupation order is to regulate the occupation of the family home. The common perception is that an occupation order simply excludes someone from the family home. However, an occupation order can also:

- enforce the applicant's entitlement to remain in occupation as against the other person;
- require the respondent to permit the applicant to enter and remain in the dwelling house or part of the dwelling house;
- regulate the occupation of the dwelling house by either or both parties;
- prohibit, suspend, or restrict the exercise by him of his right to occupy the dwelling house;
- require the respondent to leave the dwelling house or part of the dwelling house;
- exclude the respondent from a defined area in which the dwelling house is included.

 Practical Considerations

When applying for an occupation order it is important to consider what the occupation order should achieve. If the applicant has fled the home, the order should be drafted to allow the applicant to enter the property, for the respondent to leave and not to return. Alternatively, the respondent can be required to leave the home and not to return, to allow the applicant to remain there without the respondent.

It is possible for a court to make an order that restricts a respondent from entering distinct parts of the house, e.g. a bedroom. This brings with it some practical difficulties but could be a solution where the parties live in a large house and a part of the house could be used by one person.

Alternatively, a person can be excluded from the property and an area around the property. This can be by reference to an area around the property defined by distance, e.g. 500 metres around the home. This could be problematic if this inadvertently includes a major road, bus route, or the respondent's work or close family. This may have a disproportionately disruptive effect beyond what was intended by the order. Using a map and highlighting the excluded area is more effective and proportionate.

The exact availability of all of the above will be looked at with individual orders in the following paragraphs.

34.3 **OCCUPATION ORDERS**

Sections 33–41 FLA 1996 deal with occupation orders. There are five different sections of the FLA 1996 and the sections differ according to the property rights of the applicant. The different sections, each with different, self-contained tests for eligibility, apply to different situations and so the correct section must be chosen.

34.3.1 **OCCUPATION ORDER WHERE THE APPLICANT HAS AN ESTATE OR INTEREST OR HAS HOME RIGHTS**

Section 33 FLA 1996 applies to those applicants who have a legal or contractual right to occupy the dwelling house, and is much wider in scope than the other sections applying to occupation orders. There are three requirements that must be met before an applicant can apply under s33 FLA 1996. The first is that they have a legal or contractual benefit in the property or a right to occupy the property.

Section 33(1) FLA 1996 states that if the applicant is entitled to occupy a dwelling house by virtue of a beneficial estate or interest or contract or by virtue of any enactment giving him the right to remain in occupation, or has home rights (s30 FLA 1996) in relation to a dwelling house, the applicant qualifies to apply.

 Example

The applicant can qualify to apply under s33 FLA 1996 in a number of ways:

- being a legal owner (solely or jointly);
- establishing a beneficial interest in the property;
- being a legal tenant (solely or jointly);
- having home rights.

The second requirement is that the dwelling house (so called in s33(1)(b) FLA 1996) is or at any time has been the home of the person entitled and of another person with whom he is associated or was at any time intended by the person entitled and any such other person to be their home.

 Practical Considerations

This requirement has three separate possibilities for the client:

- the dwelling house *is* the home of the applicant and of another person with whom s/he is associated;

- the dwelling house *has been* the home of the applicant and of another person with whom s/he is associated;

- the dwelling house was at any time *intended* to be the home of the applicant and of another person with whom s/he is associated.

This means that a second or holiday home will probably not qualify for an order under this section, nor a property bought by one of the parties with no intention of the parties living in it.

The third requirement is that the parties must be associated as s33(1)(b)(i) FLA 1996 refers to 'another person with whom he is associated'. For a discussion of associated persons, see **Chapter 33**.

 Example

Martin and Andrea become engaged and discuss whether to move in together. Eventually they decide to rent a flat jointly for a while rather than move into Martin's flat, as both wish to start a new home together. Things go very well for the first six months, but Martin starts to question Andrea about where she has been and becomes possessive and jealous. Andrea hopes that this will change but becomes alarmed when Martin begins to push her around and shouts and screams in extremely abusive terms when she comes home a little late. Martin starts to drink heavily and one night attacks Andrea, causing her to be hospitalized.

Andrea can apply under s33 FLA 1996. She has a contractual right to occupy the property as she is a joint tenant of the property. The dwelling house is their home, whereas Martin's flat would not be, as they have never intended to live there. Martin and Andrea are associated as they have agreed to marry.

Section 33(4) FLA 1996 allows a county court to declare that the applicant is entitled to occupy the dwelling house by declaring a beneficial estate or interest in a contract or has matrimonial home rights.

34.3.2 THE TEST FOR AN ORDER UNDER S33 FLA 1996

34.3.2.1 The 'balance of harm' test

Section 33(7) FLA 1996 is often described as the 'balance of harm' test. This is because the court balances up the harm which will be suffered by the applicant or relevant child if the order is not made against the harm that will be suffered by the respondent or relevant child if the order is made. If the applicant will suffer significant harm if the order is not made, the court must make an order unless the harm suffered by the respondent or any relevant child is as great as or greater than that of the applicant if the order is made. The wording of s33(7) FLA 1996 makes the order mandatory if the balance of harm test is made out.

 Example

Andrea suffered serious injuries when Martin attacked her. She has nowhere to live if she cannot return to the house. She does not have a highly paid job and so may struggle to find housing. She is at risk of serious injury if she returns to the flat.

Martin has a flat in which he can go to live and has enough money to live on if he is ordered to leave the home. He is at no risk of injury from Andrea.

Andrea is likely to suffer significant harm if an order is not made and the potential harm to be suffered by Martin if an order is made does not outweigh this. The court must make an occupation order as the court finds that the balance of harm is made out.

'Harm' is defined in s63 FLA 1996 as ill-treatment or impairment of health (or health and development if a relevant child under 18). Ill-treatment can include treatment that is not purely physical and health includes physical and mental health.

If the applicant is not successful on the balance of harm test, the court still has discretion to make the order under s33(6). The courts have been active in elaborating on the balance of harm test in s33(7) and how it works along with the discretionary test in s33(6). In *Chalmers v Johns* [1999] 1 FLR 392 there was a history of domestic abuse between both husband and wife. The court ordered an occupation order in favour of the wife, who had left the property with her daughter. This order was set aside by the Court of Appeal who found that a court should first apply s33(7) FLA 1996 to consider that if an order were not made, the applicant would suffer significant harm greater than the respondent if an order were made. If the answer was no, then the court still had a discretion to make an occupation order under s33(6) FLA 1996. The court found in this case that no significant harm would occur to the husband if the order were not made and so the case was one for the exercise of the court's discretion.

In *G v G (Occupation Order: Conduct)* [2000] 2 FLR 36 the court emphasized that an occupation order that overrides proprietary rights should only be made in exceptional circumstances. In this case, the court re-emphasized the need to consider s33(7) FLA 1996 to see if an order must be made and then to move on to s33(6) FLA 1996 to see if the court should exercise its discretion to make an order.

Further, under s33(7) FLA 1996, significant harm must be attributable to the respondent's conduct, but it does not have to be intentional conduct. Thorpe LJ also reiterated that occupation orders are draconian and only to be made in exceptional circumstances.

34.3.2.2 Section 33(6) test

Section 33(6) FLA 1996 provides that in deciding whether to exercise its powers under s33(3) the court shall have regard to all the circumstances including:

(a) the housing needs and housing resources of each of the parties and of any relevant child;

(b) the financial resources of each of the parties;

(c) the likely effect of any order, or of any decision by the court not to exercise its powers under subsection (3), on the health, safety, or well-being of the parties and of any relevant child; and

(d) the conduct of the parties in relation to each other and otherwise.

In *Grubb v Grubb* [2009] EWCA Civ 976 a husband's application for permission to appeal an occupation order that he should vacate the matrimonial home was refused.

The husband and wife lived on an estate where the husband's family had lived for over a century although there were other homes on the estate. There were five children of the family and it was accepted that the wife should remain in the family home. The husband ran businesses from the family home and was perceived to be fearful of the situation after financial proceedings, although the wife did not wish to remain in the family home after the final settlement.

As the marriage broke down, the husband, among other acts, refused the wife keys to the house and threatened to lock her out if she did not return home in time from an evening out. The wife made the application for the occupation order under s33(6) FLA 1996 so that there was no requirement to establish the prospect of significant harm (in contrast to an application under s33(7) FLA 1996). At first instance the wife succeeded with her application.

The husband appealed on the basis that the trial judge had failed to recognize the seriousness of the order and that the likely duration of the order given the existing divorce proceedings, may be too long. The Court of Appeal rejected these arguments, as the seriousness of the order was 'greatest' when there was no alternative accommodation available.

The Court of Appeal held that an occupation order was always serious, and no doubt could sometimes be particularly serious when it related to a spouse's removal from (in this particular case) his 'ancestral home'. The Court of Appeal held that in this case the husband had access to alternative accommodation and in light of the husband's refusal to make proposals for alternative accommodation for the wife, it was the only way to achieve a necessary outcome of separate accommodation for the wife. The husband had plentiful resources with which to fund accommodation elsewhere.

The Court of Appeal was critical of the drafting of the order in terms of restraining the husband from threatening or using violence when (on the facts before the court) no violence had been alleged or proved.

The Court of Appeal approved the use of s33(6) FLA 1996 and that the wife did not seek the occupation order by reference to s33(7) FLA 1996 and did not argue that the wife or any of the children were likely to suffer 'significant harm' attributable to the husband's conduct were an occupation order not made. The Court accepted that the case was founded on s33(6) FLA 1996; and agreed that the facility to make an occupation order by reference to s33(6) FLA 1996, as an alternative to s33(7) FLA 1996, indicated that Parliament did not require the establishment of likely 'significant harm' before such an order could be made.

34.3.3 DURATION OF THE ORDER

Orders made under s33 FLA 1996 can be made for a specified period, until the occurrence of a specific event or until further order (s33(10) FLA 1996). In practice, orders tend to be for fairly short periods as a way of allowing the parties to find new housing arrangements.

34.3.4 WHAT THE COURT CAN ORDER UNDER S33 FLA 1996

Under s33(3) FLA 1996 an order may:

(a) enforce the applicant's entitlement to remain in occupation as against the other person;

(b) require the respondent to permit the applicant to enter and remain in the dwelling-house or part of the dwelling-house;

(c) regulate the occupation of the dwelling-house by either or both parties;

(d) if the respondent is entitled to occupy, prohibit, suspend, or restrict the exercise by him of his right to occupy the dwelling-house;

(e) if the respondent has matrimonial home rights in relation to the dwelling-house and the applicant is the other spouse, restrict or terminate those rights;

(f) require the respondent to leave the dwelling-house or part of the dwelling-house; or

(g) exclude the respondent from a defined area in which the dwelling-house is included.

34.3.5 SECTION 35 ORDERS

Section 35 FLA 1996 applies where one former spouse or former civil partner is entitled to occupy a dwelling house by virtue of a beneficial estate or interest or contract, or by virtue of any enactment giving him the right to remain in occupation where the other former spouse is not so entitled. The former spouse not so entitled may apply to the court for an order under this section against the other former spouse. This is not a commonly used provision in practice.

The dwelling house must have been their matrimonial home or was at any time intended by them to be their matrimonial home or, in the case of former civil partners, their partnership home.

Under s35(3) FLA 1996, if the applicant is in occupation, an order under this section must contain provisions giving the applicant the right not to be evicted or excluded from the dwelling house or any part of it by the respondent for the period specified in the order and prohibiting the respondent from evicting or excluding the applicant during that period. If the applicant is not in occupation, an order under this section must contain provisions giving the applicant the right to enter into and occupy the dwelling house for the period specified in the order and requiring the respondent to permit the exercise of that right.

34.3.5.1 The test for an order under s35 FLA 1996

Under s35(6) FLA 1996, in deciding whether to make an order under this section declaring that the applicant has rights to occupy the dwelling house, the court shall have regard to all the circumstances including:

(a) the housing needs and housing resources of each of the parties and of any relevant child;

(b) the financial resources of each of the parties;

(c) the likely effect of any order, or of any decision by the court not to exercise its powers under subsection (3) or (4), on the health, safety, or well-being of the parties and of any relevant child;

(d) the conduct of the parties in relation to each other and otherwise;

(e) the length of time that has elapsed since the parties ceased to live together;

(f) the length of time that has elapsed since the marriage was dissolved or annulled; and

(g) the existence of any pending proceedings between the parties—

    (i) for an order under sections 23A or 24 of the Matrimonial Causes Act 1973 (property adjustment orders in connection with divorce proceedings);

    (ia) for a property adjustment order under Part 2 of Schedule 5 to the Civil Partnership Act 2004;

    (ii) for an order under paragraph 1(2)(d) or (e) of Schedule 1 to the Children Act 1989 (orders for financial relief against parents); or

    (iii) relating to the legal or beneficial ownership of the dwelling-house.

This is similar to the test in s33(6) FLA 1996, although it can be seen that the court will look at the past history of the parties, including any prior legal proceedings and whether they have lived together recently. As well as this provision, under s35(8) FLA 1996 if the court decides to make a declaratory order under this section and it appears to it that, if the order does not include a s35(5) FLA 1996 regulatory provision, the applicant or any relevant child is likely to suffer significant harm attributable to conduct of the respondent, the court shall include the s35(5) FLA 1996 provision in the order unless it appears to the court that:

(a) the respondent or any relevant child is likely to suffer significant harm if the provision is included in the order; and

(b) the harm likely to be suffered by the respondent or child in that event is as great as or greater than the harm attributable to conduct of the respondent which is likely to be suffered by the applicant or child if the provision is not included.

This is a similar test to the 'balance of harm' test but only applies when the court is considering whether to make an order under s35(5) FLA 1996. The provisions of s35(5) FLA 1996 are that an order under this section may:

(a) regulate the occupation of the dwelling-house by either or both of the parties;

(b) prohibit, suspend, or restrict the exercise by the respondent of his right to occupy the dwelling-house;

(c) require the respondent to leave the dwelling-house or part of the dwelling-house; or

(d) exclude the respondent from a defined area in which the dwelling-house is included.

34.3.5.2 Duration of an order

Orders under s35 FLA 1996 can only be for a specified period not exceeding six months but can be extended on one or more occasions for a maximum of six months each (s35(10) FLA 1996).

34.3.6 **SECTION 36 ORDERS**

Orders made under s36 FLA 1996 are much more common in practice than under s34 FLA 1996 (or, indeed, ss37 and 38 FLA 1996). Section 36(1) FLA 1996 applies where one cohabitant or former cohabitant with no existing right to occupy applies against a cohabitant or former cohabitant with a right to occupy the property or dwelling house. There is the customary requirement that the dwelling house is the home in which they live together or a home in which they at any time cohabited or intended so to cohabit.

34.3.6.1 Test for a s36 FLA 1996 order

Under s36(6) FLA 1996, in deciding whether to make an order under this section, the court shall have regard to all the circumstances including—

    (a) the housing needs and housing resources of each of the parties and of any relevant child;

    (b) the financial resources of each of the parties;

    (c) the likely effect of any order, or of any decision by the court not to exercise its powers on the health, safety, or well-being of the parties and of any relevant child;

    (d) the conduct of the parties in relation to each other and otherwise;

    (e) the nature of the parties' relationship and in particular the level of commitment involved in it;

    (f) the length of time during which they have cohabited;

    (g) whether there are or have been any children who are children of both parties or for whom both parties have or have had parental responsibility;

    (h) the length of time that has elapsed since the parties ceased to live together; and

    (i) the existence of any pending proceedings between the parties—

        (i) for an order under paragraph 1(2)(d) or (e) of Schedule 1 to the Children Act 1989 (orders for financial relief against parents); or

        (ii) relating to the legal or beneficial ownership of the dwelling-house.

There is a 'balance of harm' test similar to s33(7) FLA 1996 but the questions that it asks the court to consider do not impose a duty on the court. The court must simply consider the questions:

- whether the applicant or any relevant child is likely to suffer significant harm attributable to conduct of the respondent if the sub-s (5) provision is not included in the order; and

- whether the harm likely to be suffered by the respondent or child if the provision is included is as great as or greater than the harm attributable to conduct of the respondent that is likely to be suffered by the applicant or child if the provision is not included.

Therefore under s36 FLA 1996, the court has only discretion whether to make an order and is under no duty to do so.

34.3.6.2 Protection offered by a s36 FLA 1996 order

Under s36(3) FLA 1996 if the applicant is in occupation, an order under this section must contain provision giving the applicant the right not to be evicted or excluded from the dwelling house or any part of it by the respondent for the period specified in the order; and prohibiting the respondent from evicting or excluding the applicant during that period.

Similarly, s36(4) FLA 1996 states that if the applicant is not in occupation, an order under this section must contain provision giving the applicant the right to enter into and occupy the dwelling house for the period specified in the order and requiring the respondent to permit the exercise of that right.

Section 36(5) FLA 1996 further allows an order under this section to:

    (a) regulate the occupation of the dwelling-house by either or both of the parties;

    (b) prohibit, suspend, or restrict the exercise by the respondent of his right to occupy the dwelling-house;

    (c) require the respondent to leave the dwelling-house or part of the dwelling-house; or

    (d) exclude the respondent from a defined area in which the dwelling-house is included.

34.3.6.3 Duration of an order

Orders under s36 FLA 1996 can only be for a specified period not exceeding six months but can be extended on one occasion for a maximum of six months (s36(10) FLA 1996).

34.3.7 SECTION 37 ORDERS

Orders under s37 FLA 1996 are very rare in practice and will be considered here in outline only. This section applies where neither spouse nor civil partner or former spouse or civil partner is entitled to occupy a dwelling house that is or was the matrimonial or partnership home. The court is obliged to apply the 'balance of harm' test found at s33(7) FLA 1996 (s37(4) FLA 1996) in order to decide whether to make an order.

Either of the parties may apply to the court for an order against the other under this section.

An order under s37 FLA 1996 may:

    (a) require the respondent to permit the applicant to enter and remain in the dwelling house or part of the dwelling house;

    (b) regulate the occupation of the dwelling house by either or both of the spouses;

    (c) require the respondent to leave the dwelling house or part of the dwelling house; or

    (d) exclude the respondent from a defined area in which the dwelling house is included.

34.3.7.1 Duration of an order

Section 37(5) FLA 1996 states that an order under this section must be limited so as to have effect for a specified period not exceeding six months, but may be extended on one or more occasions for a further specified period not exceeding six months.

34.3.8 SECTION 38 ORDERS

Section 38 orders are also extremely rare (the author has never used this section in practice) and so this section is explained only in outline. Section 38 FLA 1996 applies where neither cohabitant nor former cohabitant are entitled to occupy a dwelling house that they cohabit or cohabited. Either of the parties may apply to the court for an order against the other under this section.

34.3.8.1 Test for an order under s38 FLA 1996

Under s38(4) FLA 1996 in deciding whether to exercise its powers, the court shall have regard to all the circumstances including those set out in **Figure 34.1:**

    (a) the housing needs and housing resources of each of the parties and of any relevant child;

    (b) the financial resources of each of the parties;

FIGURE 34.1 FLOWCHART ILLUSTRATING OCCUPATION ORDERS

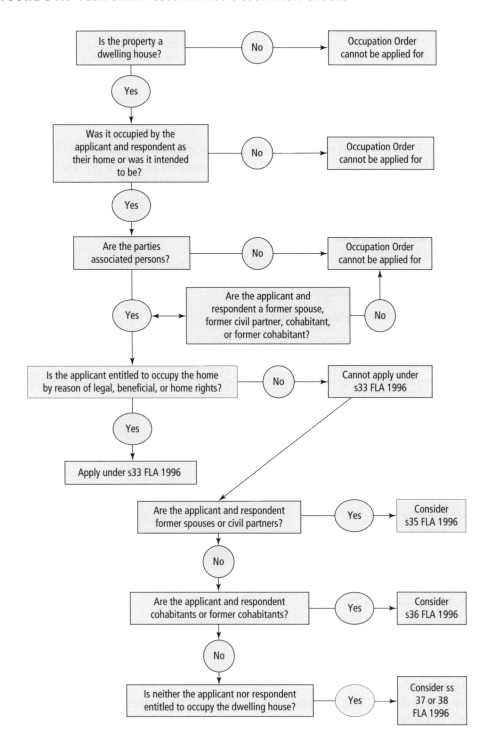

(c) the likely effect of any order, or of any decision by the court not to exercise its powers under subsection (3), on the health, safety, or well-being of the parties and of any relevant child;

(d) the conduct of the parties in relation to each other and otherwise; and

(e) the questions mentioned in s38(5) FLA 1996.

The questions are:

(a) whether the applicant or any relevant child is likely to suffer significant harm attributable to conduct of the respondent if the subsection (3) provision is not included in the order; and

(b) whether the harm likely to be suffered by the respondent or child if the provision is included is as great as or greater than the harm attributable to conduct of the respondent which is likely to be suffered by the applicant or child if the provision is not included.

Section 38(3) FLA 1996 states that an order under this section may:

(a) require the respondent to permit the applicant to enter and remain in the dwelling-house or part of the dwelling-house;

(b) regulate the occupation of the dwelling-house by either or both of the parties;

(c) require the respondent to leave the dwelling-house or part of the dwelling-house; or

(d) exclude the respondent from a defined area in which the dwelling-house is included.

34.3.8.2 Duration of the order

Under s38(6) FLA 1996 an order under this section shall be limited so as to have effect for a specified period not exceeding six months, but may be extended on one occasion for a further specified period not exceeding six months.

34.4 ANCILLARY ORDERS

If the court makes an occupation order, s40(1) FLA 1996 allows the court to impose additional orders to the occupation order including to:

(a) impose on either party obligations as to:

   (i) the repair and maintenance of the dwelling-house; or

   (ii) the discharge of rent, mortgage payments, or other outgoings affecting the dwelling-house;

(b) order a party occupying the dwelling-house or any part of it (including a party who is entitled to do so by virtue of a beneficial estate or interest or contract or by virtue of any enactment giving him the right to remain in occupation) to make periodical payments to the other party in respect of the accommodation, if the other party would (but for the order) be entitled to occupy the dwelling-house by virtue of a beneficial estate or interest or contract or by virtue of any such enactment;

(c) grant either party possession or use of furniture or other contents of the dwelling-house;

(d) order either party to take reasonable care of any furniture or other contents of the dwelling-house;

(e) order either party to take reasonable steps to keep the dwelling-house and any furniture or other contents secure.

In deciding whether and, if so, how to exercise its powers under this section, under s40(2) FLA 1996, the court shall have regard to all the circumstances of the case including:

(a) the financial needs and financial resources of the parties; and

(b) the financial obligations that they have, or are likely to have in the foreseeable future, including financial obligations to each other and to any relevant child.

An order under this section ceases to have effect when the occupation order to which it relates ceases to have effect.

Unfortunately, s40 FLA 1996 has been held to be unenforceable. In *Nwogbe v Nwogbe* [2000] 2 FLR 744, Butler-Sloss P held that:

> it was clear that orders under s40...were unenforceable and of no value to the spouse or cohabitee remaining in occupation. That was a serious omission which required urgent alteration.

The order may have some value if the respondent is likely to comply without the need for compliance proceedings.

34.4.1 TRANSFER OF TENANCIES

Schedule 7 FLA 1996 allows the court to transfer a range of tenancies (including statutory tenancies) held by one or both spouses, civil partners, former spouses or civil partners, or cohabitants. The court has to consider the parties' suitability as tenants and whether to award compensation payable by the transferee. These orders are beyond the scope of this text and a specialist practitioner text should be consulted.

SUMMARY POINTS

- Occupation orders under the FLA 1996 regulate the occupation of the home, including ordering someone to leave a property or allowing a person to return.

- The parties must be associated persons, the home must be or intended to be the home of the applicant and respondent, and must be a dwelling house.

- There are a number of different sections of the FLA 1996 under which an application can be made. Choosing the correct section is essential.

- Section 33 FLA 1996 should be used where the applicant has a legal, beneficial right to remain in the home or has 'home' rights.

- When deciding whether to make an order under s33 FLA 1996, the court considers the 'balance of harm' test as well as a series of factors under s33(6) FLA 1996 including housing and financial resources, the likely effect of not making an order on the health, safety, and well-being of the parties, and the conduct of the parties.

- The balance of harm test is found in s33(7) FLA 1996 and asks the court to balance the risk of significant harm to the applicant if the order is not made with the risk of significant harm to the respondent if the order is made.

- If the applicant has no right to occupy the home but is a former spouse or cohabitant of the respondent who is entitled to occupy the home, s35 FLA 1996 will apply.

- If the applicant and respondent are cohabitants or former cohabitants and the respondent is entitled to occupy the home, s36 FLA 1996 may apply.

- If neither party is entitled to occupy the property, then ss37 or 38 FLA 1996 may apply.

- Sections 35, 36, 37, and 38 FLA 1996 have varying qualifying tests for entitlement and reference should be made to the individual section for the criteria.

- The duration of an occupation order depends on the section under which the order is granted.

- The court can make ancillary orders concerning the care and upkeep of the home, although there are some doubts about their enforceability.

SELF-TEST QUESTIONS

1. Louise and Imran are married and live at 25 Acacia Avenue with Amy, Louise's daughter from her first marriage. Louise has a very poorly paid part-time job and is Amy's full-time mum. Imran works as a highly paid accountant and owns a number of rental properties. It is a very large house and Louise and Imran own it jointly. In order to help to pay the mortgage, they take in lodgers and Martin moves into one room. Martin invites his girlfriend, Susi, to live with him but Louise and Imran do not realize this and think that she just comes to see Martin a great deal.

   Imran and Louise begin to experience difficulties in their marriage and Imran assaults Louise seriously on a number of occasions and also threatens to assault Amy.

   (a) Louise wishes to apply for an occupation order. Advise Louise which section she should use to apply and whether she is likely to be successful.

   (b) If Louise is successful, how long can any order last?

   (c) Would your answer be any different if Louise and Imran were not married?

   (d) If Imran owned the property in his sole name and Louise and Amy had moved in with him six months ago, would your advice be any different?

   (e) Susi is also experiencing violence and threats from Martin. Would she be entitled to apply for an occupation order?

Case Study Two

Helena owns her own home. Sean is refusing to leave the home and your supervisor has asked you to advise on:

(a) under which section of the FLA 1996 should Helena apply for an occupation order?

(b) will Helena be successful? Apply s33(6) and (7) FLA 1996 to the case.

online
resource
centre

Answers to the questions above can be found on the Online Resource Centre: **www.oxfordtextbooks.co.uk/orc/sendall17/.**

PROTECTION UNDER THE FAMILY LAW ACT 1996: EMERGENCY PROTECTION AND ENFORCEMENT

35.1 **Introduction**

35.2 **Orders made without notice**

35.3 **Enforcing an order**

35.1 INTRODUCTION

This chapter will:

- examine in which circumstances an order under the Family Law Act 1996 will be made without notice to the other party to proceedings;
- determine the availability and methods of enforcement of orders made under the Family Law Act 1996.

Clients come to see a solicitor if they have suffered domestic abuse from a violent partner and require urgent protection and, as a result, a solicitor must be prepared to re-arrange their day and to take urgent steps. Once an order has been obtained, it must be properly enforced if the respondent does not obey the terms of the order. An order is essentially only a piece of paper from a court. It is really important to explain to a client that the order must be enforced properly and it is the responsibility of the client to contact their solicitor or the police to enforce the order.

This chapter covers the law on applications made without notice and the enforcement of orders.

35.2 ORDERS MADE WITHOUT NOTICE

An order may be made without notice to the respondent. The old terminology for a without notice hearing was 'ex parte' and sometimes it is still referred to in that way. If a client is at risk of serious harm, giving the respondent notice can exacerbate an already dangerous situation for the client. A without notice application is used when a client cannot move away to a refuge or another safe place whilst the respondent has notice of the hearing. This occurs fairly often in practice and often is very disruptive to a solicitor's day. However, if a client is in need of urgent protection, then a without notice application should be made.

The grounds for making an application are listed in s45 of the Family Law Act 1996 (FLA 1996) and the court may, in any case where it considers that it is *just and convenient* to do so, make an occupation order or a non-molestation order even though the respondent has not been given such notice of the proceedings as would otherwise be required by rules of court.

In determining whether to exercise its powers under s45(1) FLA 1996, the court shall have regard to all the circumstances including the factors listed in s45(2) FLA 1996:

(a) any risk of significant harm to the applicant or a relevant child, attributable to conduct of the respondent, if the order is not made immediately;

(b) whether it is likely that the applicant will be deterred or prevented from pursuing the application if an order is not made immediately; and

(c) whether there is reason to believe that the respondent is aware of the proceedings but is deliberately evading service and that the applicant or a relevant child will be seriously prejudiced by the
delay involved:

(i) where the court is a magistrates' court, in effecting service of proceedings; or

(ii) in any other case, in effecting substituted service.

 Example

Nosizwe lives with Josh. Josh has always been controlling of Nosizwe and has restricted her contact with
friends and family since they moved in together. Josh has been increasingly abusive over the past few
months and in the last couple of weeks has started to push, slap, and punch Nosizwe when he has had
a few drinks. The assaults have grown increasingly serious over the last couple of weeks and Nosizwe
has become increasingly afraid. Last night Nosizwe packed a bag and tried to leave. Unfortunately, Josh
came home just as Nosizwe was on the point of leaving. Josh assaulted Nosizwe very seriously causing
her bruising, a split lip, black eyes, and (she suspects) fractured ribs. Nosizwe managed to leave the house
when Josh went to work and has come for advice. Josh has sent her text messages saying that she has to
come home or he will come and find her at her family and friends and that he will not stop looking for her.

Nosizwe is terrified that Josh will find her and assault her more seriously. She says that there is nowhere that is safe for her to go. She states that if she cannot get an order straightaway she will not
make an application as she will be worse off.

Nosizwe should apply for an order without notice as she is at risk of significant harm and will be
deterred if an application is not made immediately.

If the court makes an order by virtue of s45(1) FLA 1996, under s45(3) FLA 1996 it must afford the respondent an opportunity to make representations relating to the order as soon as
just and convenient at a full hearing, called a 'return date'.

 Example

Nosizwe obtains a non-molestation order without notice. The judge orders that a hearing is held in
three days' time with Josh present. This is the 'return date'.

The court may accept that if an applicant has suffered violence they require the protection
of a non-molestation order and may order a respondent to refrain from acts that are not
lawful in any event. However, an occupation order deprives a respondent of their home and
proprietary rights. Case-law prior to the FLA 1996 suggests that occupation orders should
seldom be granted without notice and will apply to exceptional cases only (*G v G (Ouster: Ex
parte application)* [1990] 1 FLR 395 and *Masich v Masich* [1977] Fam Law 245) and, in practice,
occupation orders are very rarely made without notice.

35.2.1 **GOOD PRACTICE**

Applications for orders made without notice are often fraught with potential difficulties for
the courts and practitioners. An order can be made which can have serious consequences for
the respondent. In *R v R (Family Court: Procedural Fairness)* [2014] EWFC 48, Peter Jackson J
set out a number of points for the courts when considering whether to make an order without notice:

• The default position of a judge faced with a without notice application should always be
'Why?', not 'Why not?' Without notice orders can only be made in exceptional circumstances and with proper consideration for the rights of the absent party.

• The court should use its sweeping powers under the Family Law Act 1996 with caution,
particularly at a one-sided hearing. Where an order is made, it is the responsibility of the

court (and, where applicable, the lawyers) to ensure that it is accurately drafted. This consideration applies with special force when a breach of the order will amount to a criminal offence.

- Extra injunctive provisions such as exclusion areas and orders prohibiting any direct communication between parties should not be routinely included in non-molestation orders. They are serious infringements of a person's freedom of action and require specific evidence to justify them.

- The court should be on guard against the potential for unfairness arising from the Legal Aid, Sentencing and Punishment of Offenders Act 2012, whereby the applicant is entitled to legal representation as a result of unproven allegations, while the respondent is not. In this case, the fact that one party had no legal advice at any stage was critical to the outcome.

 Practical Considerations

Peter Jackson J explicitly stated that solicitors have a duty to ensure that the court makes an order which the court has the jurisdiction and power to make. In the case, the judge stated that he would not make an occupation order but the draft order excluded the respondent from the street he lived in. Although the judge arguably should have spotted this, it was also the duty of the solicitor to point out this anomaly.

35.2.2 DURATION OF A WITHOUT NOTICE ORDER

There was a practice in some courts (although never in the author's experience) of making orders with an unlimited duration. In *Practice Guidance: Family Court – Duration of Ex Parte (Without Notice) Orders* issued by the President, several principles were laid down when the court makes a without notice order:

(i) An ex parte (without notice) injunctive order must never be made without limit of time. There must be a fixed end date.

(ii) It is not sufficient merely to specify a return day. The order must specify on its face and in clear terms precisely when it expires (e.g. 4.30pm on 19 November 2015).

(iii) The duration of the order should not normally exceed 14 days.

(iv) The order must also specify the date, time, and place of the hearing on the return day. It is usually convenient for this date to coincide with the expiry date of the order (e.g. list the return day for 10.30am on 19 November 2015 and specify that the order expires at 4.30pm on 19 November 2015).

(v) The order must spell out that the respondent is entitled, without waiting for the return day, to apply on notice (the details of which and the need for which must be set out on the face of the order) to set aside or vary the order.

(vi) If the respondent does apply to set aside or vary the order the court must list the application as a matter of urgency, within a matter of days at most.

It is usual that a return date is listed by the court to be within seven to 14 days.

35.3 ENFORCING AN ORDER

The system of enforcing orders under the FLA 1996 differs for non-molestation orders and occupation orders. The Domestic Violence, Crime and Victims Act 2004 (DVCVA 2004) introduced a criminal sanction for the breach of a non-molestation order. This came into force in July 2007.

35.3.1 **NON-MOLESTATION ORDERS**

The DVCVA 2004 amended s42 FLA 1996 to make the breach of a non-molestation order a criminal offence. Section 42A(1) FLA 1996 states that a person who without reasonable excuse does anything that he is prohibited from doing by a non-molestation order is guilty of an offence. However, s42A(2) FLA 1996 ensures that a person cannot be convicted if they are unaware of the existence of the order. This makes it extremely important to serve an order promptly and to have good evidence of service (see **Chapter 9**). A person guilty of an offence under this section is liable on conviction on indictment to imprisonment for a term not exceeding five years, or a fine, or both and on summary conviction to imprisonment for a term not exceeding 12 months, or a fine not exceeding the statutory maximum, or both. For further details of the criminal charge, please refer to a specialist criminal law text.

 Example

At the return date, the court makes a non-molestation order and Josh is served with the order the following day. A week later, Nosizwe starts to receive abusive text messages from Josh. Later the same day, Josh comes to where Nosizwe works and shouts abusive comments at her as she leaves work. Nosizwe calls the police and they arrest Josh and charge him with the criminal offence of breaching a non-molestation order.

The police can arrest someone they suspect of committing this offence and the prosecution will be dealt with by the CPS. This has the advantage of removing the responsibility for enforcement from the applicant. The potential disadvantages of this system are that the applicant may not wish to criminalize their partner and an applicant may be left unprotected if bail conditions are changed without notice to them. There are details of an initial appraisal of these provisions on the Online Resource Centre.

It is possible for an applicant to enforce a non-molestation order by applying for a warrant of arrest under s47(8) FLA 1996 for the respondent to be brought to the court. The court will hear the allegations of the breach and decide whether the order has been breached. The punishment for breach is contempt of court and this is dealt with further at **35.3.3**. It is unlikely that a client will gain public funding to pursue a warrant.

The FLA 1996 avoids the potential pitfall of 'double jeopardy'; the respondent being convicted of a criminal offence and then being brought to a civil court in contempt proceedings. Section 42A(3) and (4) FLA 1996 provide that where a person is convicted of an offence under this section in respect of any conduct, that conduct is not punishable as a contempt of court. Similarly, a person cannot be convicted of an offence under this section in respect of any conduct that has been punished as a contempt of court.

35.3.2 **OCCUPATION ORDERS**

Section 47(2) FLA 1996 states that if:

(a) the court makes an occupation order; and

(b) it appears to the court that the respondent has used or threatened violence against the applicant or a relevant child,

it shall attach a power of arrest to one or more provisions of the order unless satisfied that in all the circumstances of the case the applicant or child will be adequately protected without such a power of arrest.

A power of arrest is a warning to the respondent that if the terms of the order are breached then s/he can be arrested and taken back to the court where the order was made. As discussed in **Chapter 36**, an order with a power of arrest must be delivered to a local police station. Should such an order be breached by the respondent, the police will arrest the respondent and then bring the respondent to the court that made the order.

Where an order is made without notice, the court may attach a power of arrest to one or more provisions of the order if it appears to it that:

(a) the respondent has used or threatened violence against the applicant or a relevant child; and

(b) there is a risk of significant harm to the applicant or child, attributable to conduct of the respondent, if the power of arrest is not attached to those provisions immediately under s47(3) FLA 1996.

Under s47(4) FLA 1996 if the court attaches a power of arrest to any provisions of a relevant order, it may provide that the power of arrest is to have effect for a shorter period than the other provisions of the order.

If a power of arrest is attached to certain provisions of an order, a constable may arrest without warrant a person whom he has reasonable cause for suspecting to be in breach of any such provision. He must be brought before the relevant judicial authority within the period of 24 hours beginning at the time of his arrest and if the matter is not then disposed of forthwith, the relevant judicial authority before whom he is brought may remand him. In reckoning for the purposes of this provision any period of 24 hours, no account is to be taken of Christmas Day, Good Friday, or any Sunday.

For the procedure for enforcement, see **Chapter 36**.

35.3.3 POWERS OF THE COURT TO ENFORCE AN OCCUPATION ORDER

When a breach of an order is proved, the court must consider the punishment of the respondent. The sentencing powers of the court arise as any breach of an order is contempt of court and the court can order a fine or up to two years' imprisonment. The Court of Appeal in *Neil v Ryan* [1998] EWCA Civ 1277 held that a serious breach of an order would indicate an immediate custodial sentence. In *Hale v Tanner* [2000] 2 FLR 879 the Court of Appeal established some guidelines on sentencing, although this was in the context of the law concerning a breach of a non-molestation order prior to the amendment to s42 FLA 1996 by the DVCVA 2004. The guidance was given in the judgment by Hale LJ. She stated that she would not wish to suggest that there should be any general principle that the statutory provisions related to sentencing in ordinary criminal cases should be applied to sentencing for contempt. The circumstances surrounding contempt cases are much more various and the objectives underlying the court's actions are also much more various. The guidance included:

- the full range of criminal sentencing options is not available;

- custody is not automatic;

- there is a power to fine, and a power to suspend a custodial sentence, which should nevertheless not affect the length of the sentence; i.e. you do not make the sentence longer because you are going to suspend it;

- the length of the sentence depends on the court's objectives, which will always include marking the court's disapproval of the disobedience of its order and securing compliance with it in the future;

- the length of the committal has to bear some relationship to the maximum statutory sentence of two years;

- the court has to bear in mind the context, which may be aggravating or mitigating in terms of the seriousness of the breach.

Hale LJ also said that it was rare to find reported cases of sentences of six months' imprisonment in the context of much more serious breaches than took place in the case then before the court, which mainly concerned serious, persistent, and threatening telephone calls.

Practical Considerations

In terms of sentencing, it is the experience of the author that the courts tend to balance the need to punish the breach with ensuring compliance with the order. The use of a suspended sentence is common. A suspended sentence is one where the court imposes a custodial sentence but suspends its implementation for a set period of time, e.g. three months. The respondent will not go to prison immediately but if there are any further breaches of the order, the custodial sentence will be implemented plus any further sentence for the further breach.

SUMMARY POINTS

- A client often requires protection urgently and this is dealt with by applying for an order without notice.

- 'Without notice' means that the respondent will not be given notice of the hearing for an order under the FLA 1996 and the court will not hear any evidence from the respondent.

- The court can only make an order without notice if there is risk of significant harm to the applicant or the applicant will be deterred from pursuing the application or the respondent is avoiding service.

- After the hearing of a without notice application, the court must order a hearing for all parties to attend, which is called a return date.

- A non-molestation order is enforced through the criminal law; breach of a non-molestation order is a criminal offence. Alternatively, the client may rely upon a warrant of arrest to enforce a non-molestation order.

- Occupation orders can still have a power of arrest attached to them allowing the police to arrest for a breach of the order. The enforcement proceedings are heard in the civil court in which the original order was made.

- A breach of an occupation order is a contempt of court that is punishable by a fine or imprisonment.

SELF-TEST QUESTIONS

1. See the example involving Nosizwe and Josh (starting at **35.2**). On the return date the court makes both an occupation order and a non-molestation order in favour of Nosizwe. The court attaches a power of arrest to the occupation order. Explain the effect of a power of arrest to Josh.

2. The terms of the occupation order are for Josh not to enter the family home. Nosizwe comes home on Friday evening after a night out to find Josh in the house. He calmly states that he is collecting some clothes and leaves immediately. Advise Josh on what enforcement action Nosizwe can take and the procedural steps required.

Case Study Two

Helena is extremely afraid of Sean. Helena is reluctant to admit that she and Richard have been suffering violence but states that if she does not get some form of protection they will both continue to suffer violence. What would you advise Helena to do?

Helena is granted a non-molestation order. She receives abusive texts from Sean and last night, at about 2am, Helena is woken up by a stone breaking her window. Her neighbours (who are returning from a night out) tell her that they saw Sean running away from the house. What would you advise Helena to do?

online
resource
centre

Answers to the questions above can be found on the Online Resource Centre:
www.oxfordtextbooks.co.uk/orc/sendall17/.

36 PROTECTION UNDER THE FAMILY LAW ACT 1996: PROCEDURE

36.1 INTRODUCTION

This chapter will:

* examine the procedure for obtaining and enforcing orders under the Family Law Act 1996.

The procedure to obtain an order under the Family Law Act 1996 (FLA 1996) is reasonably straightforward but often has to be undertaken in a hurry if a client instructs you at the last minute or requires an order without notice. This chapter will outline the procedure involved in applying for orders under the FLA 1996 without notice, on notice, and when enforcing orders.

36.2 COURTS AND RULES

An application for an order under the FLA 1996 is made to the Single Family Court. In practice, the vast majority of orders are heard in the county court.

36.2.1 RULES

In all courts, the relevant rules are the Family Procedure Rules 2010 (FPR 2010).

This chapter will describe the procedure in the county court as this is where the majority of applications are heard but will also highlight any differences in procedure between the courts. In practice, applications for orders are made mainly to the county court.

36.2.2 WHICH COURT?

This is guided by the Family Law Act 1996 (Part IV) (Allocation of Proceedings) Order 1997, SI 1997 No. 1896. There are some cases that have particular considerations:

* any case requiring the court to resolve a disputed question concerning any party's entitlement to occupy a property cannot be heard in a magistrates' court unless it is unnecessary to resolve the question in order to hear the application or make the order;

* the magistrates' court cannot hear applications for the transfer of tenancies on divorce or separation of cohabitants;

* applications from an applicant aged under 18 and applications under s43 FLA 1996 where the applicant requires permission to proceed as they are aged under 16 years and proceedings under this section must be commenced in the High Court.

36.3 **FUNDING**

Clients can fund proceedings privately or through Legal Aid Agency (LAA) funding, if eligible. As discussed in **Chapters 1** and **2**, a privately paying client will have to have the costs of the case discussed clearly and be given regular updates.

36.3.1 **LAA FUNDING**

Chapter 2 contains details of the types of funding available in domestic abuse proceedings. Despite severe cuts in family law, cases involving applications under the FLA 1996 are still within the scope of public funding. Currently, there are some particular considerations for clients seeking funding for domestic abuse orders. For an application for legal representation, the usual requirement is that the parties attend a mediation appointment. This, for obvious reasons, may be totally unsuitable for a client at risk of further violence and will be sufficient for a client not to attend such an appointment. Emergency funding may be necessary (see **Chapter 2**).

online
resource
centre

The Funding Code deals with several aspects of domestic abuse cases and funding and can be found on the LAA's website (and on the Online Resource Centre).

Funding is not limited just to persons who have suffered actual physical violence.

Note that emergency cover should only be granted to take injunction proceedings where the applicant or relevant child is in imminent danger of significant harm. Significant harm is imminent if there is a real risk that it will occur before a substantive application can be processed and the matter brought before the court.

Legal representation will be refused if the prospects of obtaining the order sought in the proceedings are poor. Funding can therefore only be granted where the prospects of success are at least borderline or above. In relation to non-molestation orders the issue is whether the court is likely to be satisfied that the respondent has molested the other party or a relevant child and that an order is considered necessary by the court for the protection of that party or child having regard to all the circumstances, including the need to secure the health, safety, and well-being of the applicant, or of another party to the proceedings or of any relevant child.

 Practical Considerations

As an example, the prospects of obtaining an order are likely to be poor if:

- the incidents complained of are of a trivial nature. However, where there has been a history of incidents, the cumulative effect of those incidents may be taken into account; or

- the conduct complained of is not likely to be repeated. If the conduct complained of took place more than three weeks prior to the application it will be necessary to set out in the application why it is considered that repetition is likely, e.g. if there has been a history of violent conduct.

The Funding Code states that an application may be refused to cover court proceedings if no warning letter has first been sent to the respondent. However, this is not an absolute rule. Practitioners should demonstrate that consideration has been given to whether a warning letter might endanger the client. A warning letter may be inappropriate, e.g. if the applicant and respondent are still living under the same roof or if the threat to the applicant is serious and imminent or if receipt of a warning letter by the respondent may trigger further violence to the applicant or any relevant child before a protective order can be obtained. However, in most other cases a warning letter, which can be issued under the legal help scheme, will be the appropriate first step.

The LAA may also require an explanation if the applicant has not involved the police. The LAA Funding Code states that where the incidents complained of constitute an assault or other crime against the applicant the police should normally be notified and given an opportunity to deal with the respondent. The LAA recognizes that there may be good reason not to pursue criminal proceedings, e.g. where this might jeopardize the long-term financial or other interests of the family. If so, or if there is reason to believe that the police will not be able to assist or if they are contacted but have failed to respond or to provide adequate assistance to protect the applicant and any relevant children, then a grant of legal representation may be appropriate.

For occupation orders, legal representation will only be granted where there are at least borderline prospects of obtaining an order. This involves considering whether the parties and property qualify to be covered by an order and whether an order is likely to be considered necessary by the court having regard to all the circumstances of the case including the 'balance of harm' test. Legal representation is most likely to be granted where the applicant is in a refuge or other temporary accommodation, having recently been excluded from a property, or where there is otherwise a significant likelihood of risk in remaining in or returning to the property without the protection of an order. Legal representation is likely to be refused if the respondent has already left voluntarily and does not appear likely to return.

Respondents are likely to be granted funding when defending committal proceedings as there is the potential for the respondent to be imprisoned and so the interests of justice will usually require that the respondent is represented.

36.4 PROCEDURE FOR OBTAINING AN ORDER

36.4.1 THE APPLICATION FORM

An application for a non-molestation or occupation order in a free-standing application is made on a Form FL401 (which is reproduced at the end of this chapter). If a client wishes to keep their address confidential they must complete Confidential Address Form C8. A witness statement must be attached as well as a draft of the order (r10.2 FPR 2010). The witness statement will contain a statement of truth.

There is no fee for this application.

 Practical Considerations

The witness statement to accompany the Form FL401 must contain a statement of truth. The drafting of the statement must be carefully considered and the following points should be considered:

- the statement should start with an indication of what the statement concerns;
- the statement should be clear about how the parties are associated or how the party is entitled to live in the property;
- there should be a chronology of the parties' lives together, including dates of marriage/civil partnership/cohabitation, dates of birth of any children, and any other important dates;
- the statement should set out the incidents relied upon in chronological order and give full details of the incidents including any injuries, whether the police were called, and whether medical help was sought;
- the statement should address the statutory tests for the order sought under the FLA 1996, e.g. for a non-molestation order, and should cover how the health, safety, and well-being of the applicant or relevant child is affected;
- the statement should refer to all parts of the FLA 1996 that apply to the applicant's case; e.g. if applying without notice for an order, ensure the court understands that the client has the requisite grounds or state why a power of arrest should be attached to the order;
- if drafting a statement for a respondent who is replying to allegations made by the applicant, avoid the situation of flat denials or further attacks on the applicant. Give a full account of the respondent's actions, including an expression of remorse where appropriate;

- if drafting a statement for a respondent illustrate (in an application for an occupation order) the impact of an order and whether they will suffer significant harm;
- ask the court to make the orders applied for.

If an application is made to vary, extend, or discharge an order, a Form FL403 should be used. For the procedure to be adopted for an application by a child under 18, reference should be made to a practitioner text.

36.4.1.1 Application without notice

A Form FL401 is completed for a without notice application and the witness statement should address the reasons for applying without notice.

36.4.2 SERVICE

36.4.2.1 Respondent

The respondent should be served with the Form FL401 and the witness statement in support together with notice of proceedings on FL402 (r10.3(1) FPR 2010). Service must be personal service not less than two days before the application is to be heard. It is usual for a process server to be engaged to effect service. A process server is someone who, amongst other things, specializes in serving court proceedings and has a great deal of experience in finding recalcitrant respondents and serving individuals who can be volatile. To assist the process server, full details of the respondent, including a photograph, should be given and as much detail as possible about their home, work, and where and when is a suitable time for service.

Service will not be required if the application is made without notice. Once service has been completed, the applicant should file a statement in Form FL415 as proof of service (r10.3(4) FPR 2010).

36.4.2.2 Third parties

Where the applicant makes an application for an occupation order under ss33, 35, or 36 FLA 1996 a copy of the application must be served by first class post on the mortgage lender or the landlord of a rented house in Form FL 416. This form informs them of the right to make representations in writing or at any hearing (r10.3(3) FPR 2010).

36.4.3 THE HEARING

The rules in r10.5 FPR 2010 give little direction on the form of the hearing except that the application is dealt with in chambers unless the court otherwise directs. The court must make a note of the hearing in Form FL405.

When the hearing is in a without notice case, the court will consider the witness statement and may ask the applicant some questions. The applicant should be told about the layout of the court, the personnel they are likely to encounter and the possibility of having to answer questions. The court must set a date for the matter to be heard with both parties present; this is referred to as the 'return date'. This is generally set to be fairly close to the initial hearing, as a potentially draconian order may be made without giving the respondent an opportunity to put their case.

When the hearing is on notice or the return date, the court may either make the order or make a date for a further hearing. If a final hearing is necessary the court can make directions for statements from the respondent, any witnesses, or any medical or other expert evidence. At a final hearing, the court will hear oral evidence from any witnesses relevant to the case.

 Practical Considerations

It is tempting to use the suggested guidelines in the FL401 as a basis for drafting and to produce generic orders. As the breach of a non-molestation order is a criminal offence (s42A FLA 1996), it may be worth considering a more specific form of drafting and to consider the ongoing contact between the parties if there are children in common.

For example, if a particular feature of a case is the persistent use of text messages to harass and threaten the applicant, an order could be drafted specifically to prevent the respondent texting the applicant. Any breach of the non-molestation order by sending a text would be far easier to prove in criminal proceedings.

36.4.3.1 Serving the order

Any order made after a hearing must be served on the respondent personally (r10.6(1) FPR 2010). In an application for an occupation order under ss33, 35, or 36 FLA 1996, a copy of the order must be served by first class post on the mortgage lender or the landlord of a rented house (r10.6(3) FPR 2010). Please note that a respondent cannot be prosecuted under s42A FLA 1996 unless the respondent has notice of the order. An order cannot be served on the respondent within the precincts of the court.

36.4.4 NOTIFICATION OF THE POLICE

If the court makes an occupation order with a power of arrest or a non-molestation order (r10.10(2) FPR 2010), the following documents must be delivered to the officer in charge of the police station local to the applicant's address (or other station as the court orders):

- a copy of the Form FL404a and/or Form FL404; and
- a statement showing the respondent has been served with the order or informed of its terms (whether by being present when the order was made or by telephone or otherwise).

The applicant must deliver these documents unless the court is responsible for service (if the applicant is acting in person). If any order or part of the order is discharged or varied, the court must inform the officer and deliver a copy of the order to that officer (r10.10(6) FPR 2010).

36.4.5 DIFFERENCES IN PROCEDURE AT THE FAMILY PROCEEDINGS COURT

The FPR 2010 have largely unified the procedures in all courts. The main exception is the position where a person is arrested pursuant either to a power of arrest or a warrant of arrest. The procedure in this situation (highly unusually) is found in s144 Magistrates' Courts Act 1980. This is beyond the scope of this text and a practitioner's text should be consulted.

36.5 ENFORCEMENT PROCEDURE

36.5.1 RULES

The rules are found in r10.11 FPR 2010. Each order made by the court contains a 'penal notice' warning the respondent of the consequences of a breach of an order and the wording of the non-molestation order encompasses the breach as a criminal offence.

If a non-molestation order is breached, the client should contact the police using 999 (if an urgent situation) or the local police contact number.

36.5.2 OCCUPATION ORDER WITH A POWER OF ARREST

The provisions of an occupation order that have a power of arrest attached should be re-corded on Form FL406. If the order is breached, the applicant should telephone the police in order to report it. Section 47(7) FLA 1996 allows the police to arrest the respondent if there appear to be sufficient grounds for arrest. The arrested person should be brought before the family court within 24 hours beginning at the time of arrest.

The President's Practice Direction of 9 December 1999: Family Law Act 1996—Attendance of Arresting Officer [2000] 1 FLR 270 states that when an arrested person is brought before the relevant judicial authority, the attendance of the arresting officer is not necessary unless the arrest itself is in issue. The officer may have to attend if they were a witness to the events leading up to the arrest or the breach of the order.

Once the respondent has been arrested, the court may:

- conduct a full hearing in open court to determine whether the facts, and the circumstances which led to the arrest, amounted to disobedience of the order;

- adjourn the proceedings and, where such an order is made, the arrested person may be released.

The proceedings must be listed for hearing within 14 days of the date upon which the respondent was arrested, and the respondent should be given two business days' notice of the adjourned hearing. An application for bail can be made and applies where the respondent is kept in custody following arrest. For further details, a practitioner text should be consulted.

36.5.3 WARRANT OF ARREST

Where an occupation order contains no power of arrest or the applicant does not wish to use criminal proceedings to enforce a non-molestation order, a warrant of arrest can be used. Section 47(8) FLA 1996 can be used in order to apply to the court for a warrant of arrest to arrest the respondent. The application is made on Form FL407 and the warrant issued on Form FL408. The applicant must give evidence on oath to satisfy the court that a breach of the order has occurred. The warrant authorizes the court bailiff or police to arrest the respondent. Once arrested, the procedure is as described at **36.5.2**.

36.5.4 COMMITTAL PROCEEDINGS

Committal proceedings are used where there has been a breach of an undertaking, breach of a term of an occupation order where there is no power of arrest, or a non-molestation order where there are no criminal proceedings. The application for the issue of a committal order, which is a notice to show good reason, is on Form N78 and must:

- specify the provisions of the order or undertaking that has been disobeyed;

- set out the ways in which it is alleged that the order has been disobeyed or broken;

- be supported by a statement by the applicant setting out the grounds for the application. These documents must be served personally on the respondent.

A fee of £60 is payable. Committal proceedings try the allegation that the respondent has committed a contempt of court and if the court finds that there is contempt, it has the power to imprison the respondent. The President's Direction of 16 March (Committal Applications and Procedure in which a Committal Order can be made) [2000] 1 FLR 949 gives guidance on the procedure to be followed.

36.5.5 ENFORCEMENT OF A NON-MOLESTATION ORDER UNDER S42A FLA 1996

When a respondent breaches a non-molestation order, the police may arrest the respondent as breach is a criminal offence. As a result, the usual criminal procedure will apply and the Crown Prosecution Service will be responsible for the conduct of the case.

SUMMARY POINTS

- Proceedings are commenced using a Form FL401 and a statement in support.

- Proceedings can be commenced in either the county court or family proceedings court (or occasionally in the High Court).

- Funding is available for those eligible for LAA funding. Consideration must be given to sending a warning letter or contacting the police before applying for funding.

- A statement in support of the application should be carefully drafted to ensure that the court has all the necessary information, including information required by the FLA 1996.

- The respondent should be personally served with the FL401 and the statement in support unless the application is to be made without notice.

- The application will be heard by the court and either an order will be made, directions given for a further hearing, or the application will be withdrawn.

- If an order is made, it is extremely important that the order is served. If applicable, the police should be notified of the order.

- If a non-molestation order is breached, the police should be contacted. Alternatively, the applicant may apply for a warrant of arrest, although it is unlikely that funding will be granted.

- If an occupation order has a power of arrest attached to it, the police should be contacted. If there is no power of arrest, a warrant of arrest should be sought.

- Committal proceedings can be used where there is an alleged breach of an undertaking or an order under FLA 1996 where there is no power of arrest.

SELF-TEST QUESTIONS

1. You represent Pamina who has been severely assaulted by her husband. She is extremely concerned that if her husband has notice of the proceedings, she will be assaulted again. You advise that she has the grounds to apply for a non-molestation and occupation order without notice. Describe the procedure required to obtain an order without notice.

Case Study Two

Your supervisor asks you to look at the statement in support of Helena's application. This can be found on the Online Resource Centre. Suggest which, if any, change you would make.

---

online
resource
centre

Answers to the questions above can be found on the Online Resource Centre:
www.oxfordtextbooks.co.uk/orc/sendall17/.

FORM 36.1 APPLICATION FOR: A NON-MOLESTATION ORDER AN OCCUPATION ORDER

.Application for: a non-molestation order an occupation order *Family Law Act 1996 (Part IV)* **The court**	**To be completed by the court** Date issued Case number

---

Please read the accompanying notes as you complete this form.

1 About you (the applicant)

State your title (Mr, Mrs etc), full name, address, telephone number and date of birth (if under 18):

Helena Wilson
31 Roseberry Avenue
Longtown
LG3 8GH

State your solicitor's name, address, reference, telephone, FAX and DX numbers:

Burrell, Young and Hepple
23 High Street
Longtown
LG1 9HN
Tel: 01336722777

2 About the respondent

State the respondent's name, address and date of birth (if known):

Sean Brown
31 Roseberry Avenue
Longtown
LG3 8GH

3 The Order(s) for which you are applying

This application is for:

☑ a non-molestation order

☑ an occupation order

☑ Tick this box if you wish the court to hear your application without notice being given to the respondent. The reasons relied on for an application being heard without notice must be stated in the statement in support.

1

4 Your relationship to the respondent (the person to be served with this application)

Your relationship to the respondent is:

(Please tick only one of the following)

1 ☐ Married

2 ☐ Civil Partners

3 ☐ Were married

4 ☐ Former civil partners

5 ☑ Cohabiting

6 ☐ Were cohabiting

7 ☐ Both of you live or have lived in the same household

8 ☐ Relative
State how related:

9 ☐ Agreed to marry.
Give the date the agreement was made.
If the agreement has ended, state when.

10 ☐ Agreed to form a civil partnership.
Give the date the agreement was made.
If the agreement has ended, state when.

11 ☐ Both of you are parents of, or have parental responsibility for, a child

12 ☐ One of you is a parent of a child and the other has parental responsibility for that child

13 ☐ One of you is the natural parent or
grandparent of a child adopted, placed or freed
for adoption, and the other is:

    (i)   the adoptive parent

  or (ii) a person who has applied for an
adoption order for the child

  or (iii) a person with whom the child has
been placed for adoption

  or (iv) the child who has been adopted,
placed or freed for adoption.

State whether (i), (ii), (iii) or (iv):

14 ☐ Both of you are the parties to the same family
proceedings (see also Section 11 below).

5 Application for a non-molestation order

If you wish to apply for a non-molestation order,
state briefly in this section the order you want.

That Sean Brown do not harass, pester, threaten or
molest Helena Wilson

Give full details in support of your application in
your supporting evidence.

6 Application for an occupation order

*If you do not wish to apply for an occupation order,
please go to section 9 of this form.*

(A) State the address of the dwelling-house to which
your application relates:

31 Roseberry Avenue
Longtown
LG3 8GH

(B) State whether it is occupied by you or the respondent
now or in the past, or whether it was intended to be
occupied by you or the respondent:

I occupy the property with the respondent

(C) State whether you are entitled to occupy the
dwelling-house: ☑ Yes   ☐ No

If yes, explain why:

(D) State whether the respondent is entitled to occupy
the dwelling-house: ☑ Yes ☐ No

If yes, explain why:

**On the basis of your answers to (C) and (D) above,
tick one of the boxes 1 to 6 below to show the category
into which you fit**

1 ☑ a spouse or civil partner who has home rights
in the dwelling-house, or a person who is
entitled to occupy it by virtue of a beneficial
estate or interest or contract or by virtue of
any enactment giving him or her the right to
remain in occupation.

If you tick box 1, state whether there is a
dispute or pending proceedings between you
and the respondent about your right to occupy
the dwelling-house.

2 ☐ a former spouse or former civil partner with no
existing right to occupy, where the respondent
spouse or civil partner is so entitled.

3 ☐ a cohabitant or former cohabitant with no
existing right to occupy, where the respondent
cohabitant or former cohabitant is so entitled.

4 ☐ a spouse or former spouse who is not entitled
to occupy, where the respondent spouse or
former spouse is also not entitled.

5 ☐ a civil partner or former civil partner who is not
entitled to occupy, where the respondent civil
partner or former civil partner is also not entitled.

6 ☐ a cohabitant or former cohabitant who is
not entitled to occupy, where the respondent
cohabitant or former cohabitant is also not
entitled.

Home Rights

If you do have home rights please:

State whether the title to the land is registered or unregistered (if known):

Registered

If registered, state the Land Registry title number (if known):

48372621

If you wish to apply for an occupation order, state briefly here the order you want. Give full details in support of your application in your supporting evidence:

That Sean Brown leave the property and not return and not come within 100 metres of the property

7 Application for additional order(s) about the dwelling-house

If you want to apply for any of the orders listed in the notes to this section, state what order you would like the court to make:

8 Mortgage and rent

Is the dwelling-house subject to a mortgage?

☑ Yes ☐ No

If yes, please provide the name and address of the mortgagee:

Haliwide Building Society
33 High Street
Longtown
LG1 8TF

Is the dwelling-house rented?

☐ Yes ☑ No

If yes, please provide the name and address of the landlord:

9 At the court

Will you need an interpreter at court?

☐ Yes   ☑ No

If yes, specify the language:

If you require an interpreter, you must notify the court immediately so that one can be arranged.

If you have a disability for which you require special assistance or special facilities, please state what your needs are. The court staff will get in touch with you about your requirements.

10 Other information

State the name and date of birth of any child living with or staying with, or likely to live with or stay with, you or the respondent:

Richard Wilson
DOB: 23.2.2008

State the name of any other person living in the same household as you and the respondent, and say why they live there:

11 Other Proceedings and Orders

If there are any other current family proceedings or orders in force involving you and the respondent, state the type of proceedings or orders, the court and the case number. This includes any application for an occupation order or non-molestation order against you by the respondent.

There are care proceedings issued in Longtown County Court, case number 4/CA1989

This application is to be served upon the respondent

Signed: Date:

FORM 36.2 APPLICATION FOR NON-MOLESTATION ORDER OR OCCUPATION ORDER: NOTES FOR GUIDANCE

Application for non-molestation order or occupation order
Notes for guidance

Section 1

If you do not wish your address to be made known to the respondent, leave the space on the form blank and complete Confidential Address Form C8. The court can give you this form.

If you are under 18, someone over 18 must help you make this application. That person, who might be one of your parents, is called a 'next friend'.

If you are under 16, you need permission to make this application. You must apply to the High Court for permission, using this form. If the High Court gives you permission to make this application, it will then either hear the application itself or transfer it to a county court.

Section 3

An urgent order made by the court before the notice of the application is served on the respondent is called an ex-parte order. In deciding whether to make an ex-parte order the court will consider all the circumstances of the case, including:

- any risk of significant harm to the applicant or a relevant child, attributable to conduct of the respondent, if the order is not made immediately

- whether it is likely that the applicant will be deterred or prevented from pursuing the application if an order is not made immediately

- whether there is reason to believe that the respondent is aware of the proceedings but is deliberately evading service and that the applicant or a relevant child will be seriously prejudiced by the delay involved.

If the court makes an ex-parte order, it must give the respondent an opportunity to make representations about the order as soon as just and convenient at a full hearing.

'Harm' in relation to a person who has reached the age of 18 means ill-treatment or the impairment of health, and in relation to a child means ill-treatment or the impairment of health and development.

'Ill-treatment' includes forms of ill-treatment which are not physical and, in relation to a child, includes sexual abuse. The court will require evidence of any harm which you allege in support of your application.

Section 4

For you to be able to apply for an order you must be related to the respondent in one of the ways listed in this section of the form. If you are not related in one of these ways you should seek legal advice.

Cohabitants are two persons who, although not married to each other, nor civil partners of each other, are living together as husband and wife or civil partners. People who have cohabited, but have then married or formed a civil partnership will not fall within this category but will fall within the category of married people or people who are civil partners of each other.

Those who live or have lived in the same household do not include people who share the same household because one of them is the other's employee, tenant, lodger or boarder.

You will only be able to apply as a relative of the respondent if you are:
(A) the father, mother, stepfather, stepmother, son, daughter, stepson, stepdaughter, grandmother, grandfather, grandson, granddaughter of the respondent or of the respondent's spouse, former spouse, civil partner or former civil partner.

(B) the brother, sister, uncle, aunt, niece, nephew or first cousin (whether of the full blood or of the half blood or by marriage or by civil partnership) of the respondent or of the respondent's spouse, former spouse, civil partner or former civil partner.

This includes, in relation to a person who is living or has lived with another person as husband and wife or as civil partners, any person who would fall within (A) or (B) if the parties were married to, or civil partners of, each other (for example, your cohabitee's father or brother).

Agreements to marry: You will fall within this category only if you make this application within three years of the termination of the agreement. The court will require the following evidence of the agreement:

> evidence in writing

or the gift of an engagement ring in contemplation of marriage

or evidence that a ceremony has been entered into in the presence of one or more other persons assembled for the purpose of witnessing it.

Agreements to form a civil partnership: You will fall within this category only if you make this application within three years of the termination of the agreement. The court will require the following evidence of the agreement:

> evidence in writing

or a gift from one party to the agreement to the other as a token of the agreement

or evidence that a ceremony has been entered into in the presence of one or more other persons assembled for the purpose of witnessing it.

Parents and parental responsibility:
You will fall within this category if

> both you and the respondent are either the parents of the child or have parental responsibility for that child

or if one of you is the parent and the other has parental responsibility.

1

Section 4 continued

Under the Children Act 1989, parental responsibility is held automatically by a child's mother, and by the child's father if he and the mother were married to each other at the time of the child's birth or have married subsequently. Where a child's father and mother are not married to each other at the time of the child's birth, the father may also acquire parental responsibility for that child, if he registers the birth after 1st December 2003, in accordance with section 4(1)(a) of the Children Act 1989. Where neither of these circumstances apply, the father, in accordance with the provisions of the Children Act 1989, can acquire parental responsibility.

From 30 December 2005, where a person who is not the child's parent ("the step-parent") is married to, or a civil partner of, a parent who has parental responsibility for that child, he or she may also acquire parental responsibility for the child in accordance with the provisions of the Children Act 1989.

From 1st September 2009, specific provision has been made in relation to parental responsibility in certain cases involving assisted reproduction. Parental responsibility is held automatically by a woman if—

- she and the child's mother were in a civil partnership with each other at the time of treatment unless that woman did not consent to the treatment; or

- she is a parent of the child by virtue of section 43 of the Human Fertilisation and Embryology Act 2008 and subsequently enters into a civil partnership with the mother.

A woman who is a parent of the child by virtue of section 43 of the 2008 Act but who does not subsequently enter into a civil partnership with the mother may acquire parental responsibility in accordance with the provisions of section 4ZA of the Children Act 1989.

Section 5

A non-molestation order can forbid the respondent from molesting you or a relevant child. Molestation can include, for example, violence, threats, pestering and other forms of harassment. The court can forbid particular acts of the respondent, molestation in general, or both.

Section 6

If you wish to apply for an occupation order but you are uncertain about your answer to any question in this part of the application form, you should seek legal advice.

(A) A dwelling-house includes any building or part of a building which is occupied as a dwelling; any caravan, houseboat or structure which is occupied as a dwelling; and any yard, garden, garage or outhouse belonging to it and occupied with it.

(C) & (D) The following questions give examples to help you to decide if you or the respondent, or both of you, are entitled to occupy the dwelling-house:

(a) Are you the sole legal owner of the dwelling-house?

(b) Are you and the respondent joint legal owners of the dwelling-house?

(c) Is the respondent the sole legal owner of the dwelling-house?

(d) Do you rent the dwelling-house as a sole tenant?

(e) Do you and the respondent rent the dwelling-house as joint tenants?

(f) Does the respondent rent the dwelling-house as a sole tenant?

If you answer

- **Yes** to (a), (b), (d) or (e) you are likely to be entitled to occupy the dwelling-house

- **Yes** to (c) or (f) you may not be entitled (unless, for example, you are a spouse or civil partner and have home rights – see notes under 'Home Rights' below)

- **Yes** to (b), (c), (e) or (f), the respondent is likely to be entitled to occupy the dwelling-house

- **Yes** to (a) or (d) the respondent may not be entitled (unless, for example, he or she is a spouse or civil partner and has home rights).

Box 1 For example, if you are sole owner, joint owner or if you rent the property. If you are not a spouse, former spouse, civil partner, former civil partner, cohabitant or former cohabitant of the respondent, you will only be able to apply for an occupation order if you fall within this category.

If you answer yes to this question, it will not be possible for a magistrates' court to deal with the application, unless the court decides that it is unnecessary for it to decide this question in order to deal with the application or make the order. If the court decides that it cannot deal with the application, it will transfer the application to a county court.

Box 2 For example, if the respondent is or was married to you, or if you and the respondent are or were civil partners, and he or she is sole owner or rents the property.

Box 3 For example, if the respondent is or was cohabiting with you and is sole owner or rents the property.

Home Rights
Where one spouse or civil partner "**(A)**" is entitled to occupy the dwelling-house by virtue of a beneficial estate or interest or contract or by virtue of any enactment giving him or her the right to remain in occupation, and the other spouse or civil partner "**(B)**" is not so entitled, then **B** (who is not entitled) has home rights.

The rights are

(a) if **B** is in occupation, not to be evicted or excluded from the dwelling-house except with the leave of the court; and

(b) if **B** is not in occupation, the right, with the leave of the court, to enter into and occupy the dwelling-house.

Section 6 (continued)

Note: Home Rights do not exist if the dwelling-house has never been, and was never intended to be, the matrimonial or civil partnership home of the two spouses or civil partners. If the marriage or civil partnership has come to an end, home rights will also have ceased, unless a court order has been made during the marriage or civil partnership for the rights to continue after the end of that relationship.

Occupation Orders

The possible orders are:

If you have ticked box 1 above, an order under section 33 of the Act may:

- enforce the applicant's entitlement to remain in occupation as against the respondent
- require the respondent to permit the applicant to enter and remain in the dwelling-house or part of it
- regulate the occupation of the dwelling-house by either or both parties
- if the respondent is also entitled to occupy, the order may prohibit, suspend or restrict the exercise by him, of that right
- restrict or terminate any home rights of the respondent
- require the respondent to leave the dwelling-house or part of it
- exclude the respondent from a defined area around the dwelling-house
- declare that the applicant is entitled to occupy the dwelling-house or has home rights in it
- provide that the home rights of the applicant are not brought to an end by the death of the other spouse or civil partner or termination of the marriage or civil partnership.

If you have ticked box 2 or box 3 above, an order under section 35 or 36 of the Act may:

- give the applicant the right not to be evicted or excluded from the dwelling-house or any part of it by the respondent for a specified period
- prohibit the respondent from evicting or excluding the applicant during that period
- give the applicant the right to enter and occupy the dwelling-house for a specified period
- require the respondent to permit the exercise of that right
- regulate the occupation of the dwelling-house by either or both of the parties
- prohibit, suspend or restrict the exercise by the respondent of his right to occupy
- require the respondent to leave the dwelling-house or part of it
- exclude the respondent from a defined area around the dwelling-house.

If you have ticked box 4 or box 5 above, an order under section 37 or 38 of the Act may:

- require the respondent to permit the applicant to enter and remain in the dwelling-house or part of it
- regulate the occupation of the dwelling-house by either or both of the parties
- require the respondent to leave the dwelling-house or part of it
- exclude the respondent from a defined area around the dwelling-house.

You should provide any evidence which you have on the following matters in your evidence in support of this application. If necessary, further statements may be submitted after the application has been issued.

If you have ticked box 1, box 4 or box 5 above, the court will need any available evidence of the following:

- the housing needs and resources of you, the respondent and any relevant child
- the financial needs of you and the respondent
- the likely effect of any order, or any decision not to make an order, on the health, safety and well-being of you, the respondent and any relevant child
- the conduct of you and the respondent in relation to each other and otherwise.

If you have ticked box 2 above, the court will need any available evidence of:

- the housing needs and resources of you, the respondent and any relevant child
- the financial resources of you and the respondent
- the likely effect of any order, or of any decision not to make an order on the health, safety and well-being of you, the respondent and any relevant child
- the conduct of you and the respondent in relation to each other and otherwise
- the length of time that has elapsed since you and the respondent ceased to live together
- where you and the respondent were married, the length of time that has elapsed since the marriage was dissolved or annulled
- where you and the respondent were civil partners, the length of time that has elapsed since the dissolution or annulment of the civil partnership

Section 6 (continued)

- the existence of any pending proceedings between you and the respondent:

  under section 23A of the Matrimonial Causes Act 1973 (property adjustment orders in connection with divorce proceedings etc.)

  or under Part 2 of Schedule 5 to the Civil Partnership Act 2004 (property adjustment on or after dissolution, nullity or separation)

  or under Schedule 1 para 1(2)(d) or (e) of the Children Act 1989 (orders for financial relief against parents)

  or relating to the legal or beneficial ownership of the dwelling-house.

If you have ticked box 3 above, the court will need any available evidence of:

- the housing needs and resources of you, the respondent and any relevant child

- the financial resources of you and the respondent

- the likely effect of any order, or of any decision not to make an order, on the health, safety and well-being of you, the respondent and any relevant child

- the conduct of you and the respondent in relation to each other and otherwise

- the nature of your and the respondent's relationship

- the length of time during which you have lived together as husband and wife or civil partners

- whether you and the respondent have had any children, or have both had parental responsibility for any children

- the length of time that has elapsed since you and the respondent ceased to live together

- the existence of any pending proceedings between you and the respondent under Schedule 1 para 1(2)(d) or (e) of the Children Act 1989 or relating to the legal or beneficial ownership of the dwelling-house.

Section 7

Under section 40 of the Act the court may make the following additional orders when making an occupation order:

- impose on either party obligations as to the repair and maintenance of the dwelling-house

- impose on either party obligations as to the payment of rent, mortgage or other outgoings affecting it

- order a party occupying the dwelling-house to make periodical payments to the other party in respect of the accommodation, if the other party would (but for the order) be entitled to occupy it

- grant either party possession or use of furniture or other contents

- order either party to take reasonable care of any furniture or other contents

- order either party to take reasonable steps to keep the dwelling-house and any furniture or other contents secure.

Section 8

If the dwelling-house is rented or subject to a mortgage, the landlord or mortgagee must be served with notice of the proceedings in Form FL416. He or she will then be able to make representations to the court regarding the rent or mortgage.

Section 10

A person living in the same household may, for example, be a member of the family or a tenant or employee of you or the respondent.

37 PROTECTION FROM HARASSMENT

37.1 INTRODUCTION

This chapter will:

- examine the law on harassment;
- examine the remedies available to clients not protected by the Family Law Act 1996.

In **Chapter 34** the protection offered by the Family Law Act 1996 (FLA 1996) was discussed, including the group of associated persons who can apply for non-molestation or occupation orders. However, there will be those who are not protected as an associated person. Family lawyers may be consulted by those who are being harassed or stalked by someone who is not an associated person. Until the passage of the Protection from Harassment Act 1997 (PfHA 1997), a victim of stalking or harassment had few remedies. This chapter will look at both the civil and criminal remedies available to a client and is intended as an introduction only. Reference should be made to a practitioner's text for further detail.

37.2 RELEVANCE TO FAMILY LAW

The definition of 'associated persons' under s62(1)(b) FLA 1996 is very wide and will encompass most family relationships, especially in light of the amendment made to encompass people who have had an intimate relationship which is or was of significant duration (s62(3)(ea) FLA 1996). However, this provision is not yet tested by the courts and may not cover a situation where the parties have 'dated' just once or twice. The FLA 1996 does not protect those who are work colleagues, neighbours, or those who have met socially but have not dated or had any form of relationship. In the case of *Tuppen v Microsoft Corporation Ltd* (2000) *Times*, 15 November, it was held, after referring to Hansard, that the PfHA 1997 was directed at the prevention of stalking, anti-social behaviour by neighbours, and racial harassment. Those not protected by the FLA 1996 can report harassment to the police or can bring civil proceedings for an injunction or damages.

 Example

Emir works as an IT manager at a large department store. He works across the shop floor and the administration offices and looks after IT for the company. He is married to Anji and has two children. He often chats casually to shop assistants when repairing computers. He often chats to Katrina, a shop assistant working in the ladies clothing department. He notices that she has her lunch hour at the same time as his and they often chat in the shop canteen.

Emir begins to get up to 50 emails a day from Katrina, which he finds intrusive. He asks her to stop and makes a point of avoiding her. Katrina finds out his mobile phone number and sends him hundreds of texts, which are often sexually explicit. Katrina starts to follow Emir home and hangs around at his gate. He finds that he cannot leave the house without Katrina being there. Katrina tells everyone at work they are engaged and asks him to buy her a ring. Emir becomes very angry at this point and tells Katrina to leave him alone. Emir is then horrified to find that Katrina has rung his wife and his parents and told them that Katrina is having an affair with Emir. He finds that Katrina has been hanging around at his children's school telling the parents collecting the children that she is pregnant with Emir's child. The last straw for Emir is when Katrina breaks into the house and steals some of Emir's clothing. Katrina leaves a note for Emir's wife stating that Katrina is Emir's real wife.

Emir uses the PfHA 1997 in order to obtain an injunction to prevent Katrina from any further harassment.

Of course, if a person is assaulted by another, the criminal law can be used.

37.3 **PROHIBITION OF HARASSMENT**

Section 1(1) PfHA 1997 states that a person must not pursue a course of conduct:

(a) which amounts to harassment of another, and

(b) which he knows or ought to know amounts to harassment of the other.

Section 2 PfHA 1997 explains that the person whose course of conduct is in question ought to know that it amounts to harassment of another if a reasonable person in possession of the same information would think the course of conduct amounted to harassment of the other.

There are some circumstances where the PfHA 1997 will not apply to a course of conduct, e.g. if a person can show that:

- it was pursued for the purpose of preventing or detecting crime;
- it was pursued under any enactment or rule of law or to comply with any condition or requirement imposed by any person under any enactment; or
- in the particular circumstances the pursuit of the course of conduct was reasonable.

Conduct includes speech (s7(4) PfHA 1997). 'Harassment' includes, but is not restricted to, 'alarming the person' and 'causing the person distress' under s7(2) PfHA 1997. According to Lord Donaldson in *Johnson v Walton* [1990] 1 FLR 350, 'harassment … includes within it an element of intent, intent to cause distress or harm'.

 Example

Katrina's actions in telling Emir's wife and parents lies about their relationship and breaking into the house clearly demonstrate intent to cause alarm or distress.

Alternatively, s1A PfHA 1997 states that a person must not pursue a course of conduct which involves the harassment of two or more persons and which he knows or ought to know involves harassment to those persons and by which he intends to persuade any person (whether or not one of those mentioned earlier) not to do something that he is entitled or required to do or to do something that he is not under any obligation to do. The person whose course of conduct is in question ought to know that it amounts to harassment of another if a reasonable person in possession of the same information would think the course of conduct amounted to harassment of the other.

37.4 CIVIL REMEDY FOR HARASSMENT

Under s3 PfHA 1997, an actual or apprehended breach of s1 PfHA 1997 may be the subject of a claim in civil proceedings by the person who is or may be the victim of the course of conduct in question. If such a claim is successful, damages can be awarded for (amongst other things) anxiety caused by the harassment and any financial loss resulting from the harassment. Of more practical use is the ability of the court to grant an injunction in free-standing proceedings in the county court or High Court and the terms of this injunction can be enforced by a warrant for the arrest of the defendant under s3(3) PfHA 1997.

Where the court has granted an injunction and without reasonable excuse the defendant does anything that he is prohibited from doing by the injunction, he is guilty of an offence under s3(6) PfHA 1997. Such an offence is punished by contempt of court or by criminal proceedings, but not both. A person found guilty of such an offence is liable for a fine or up to six months' imprisonment.

37.5 CRIMINAL LIABILITY FOR HARASSMENT

If a person pursues a course of conduct in breach of s1(1) or 1A PfHA 1997 he is guilty of an offence under s2 PfHA 1997. It is a summary offence, which means that it can only be tried in the magistrates' court. If convicted the defendant would be liable for a fine or up to six months' imprisonment. The PfHA 1997 also contains offences of stalking (under s2A) and stalking involving fear of violence and serious alarm or distress (s4A).

37.5.1 RESTRAINING ORDERS

Section 5 PfHA 1997 allows a court sentencing or otherwise dealing with a defendant convicted of an offence, as well as sentencing him or dealing with him in any other way, to make an order under this section.

The order may be made for the purpose of protecting the victim of the offence, or any other person mentioned in the order, from further conduct that:

- amounts to harassment; or
- will cause a fear of violence,

or to prohibit the defendant from doing anything described in the order.

The order may have effect for a specified period or until further order. In 2006, there were 194 restraining orders issued.

Section 5A PfHA 1997 (introduced into the PfHA 1997 by the Domestic Violence, Crime and Victims Act 2004) allows a court to make a restraining order even if the defendant is acquitted of an offence, if it considers it necessary to do so to protect a person from harassment by the defendant.

37.6 PROTECTION FROM HARASSMENT ACT 1997 AND FAMILY PRACTICE

The PfHA 1997 offers protection for those clients who are not within the scope of associated persons under the FLA 1996. Those advising clients in such a situation must weigh up whether the client should seek protection from the criminal law, which has the advantage for the client of not requiring funding of any kind, and for which the court has wide-ranging powers. There may be occasions where a client does not wish to involve the criminal law and will use the civil courts to pursue an injunction.

SUMMARY POINTS

- The PfHA 1997 was enacted to assist those who were suffering harassment through stalking, anti-social behaviour, or racial harassment.

- The provisions of the PfHA 1997 are useful protection for those clients who are not associated persons under the FLA 1996.

- The PfHA 1997 prohibits a course of conduct that amounts to the harassment of a person and conduct includes speech.

- 'Harassment' is where a person is alarmed or distressed.

- A client may pursue a civil remedy of damages or an injunction to prevent further harassment.

- Alternatively, a client can involve the criminal law, as harassment is a criminal offence and the courts have extensive powers, e.g. the grant of a restraining order, even when the defendant is acquitted.

SELF-TEST QUESTIONS

1. Can you think of any categories of people who may suffer harassment but not be an associated person under the FLA 1996?

2. Bill drinks regularly at a pub in his town. He gets to know Shellie, who works as a barmaid. They have one date and she tells him that she doesn't want to see him anymore. Bill continues to text, telephone, and email Shellie. Shellie finds that Bill has begun to follow her and sits outside her house in his car. Shellie finds that Bill turns up to any social event that she is at and threatens any man who tries to talk to her. Advise Shellie.

online
resource
centre

Answers to the questions above can be found on the Online Resource Centre: **www.oxfordtextbooks.co.uk/orc/sendall17/.**

INDEX